Maker Innovations Series

T0185392

Jump start your path to discovery with the Apress Maker Innovations series! From the basics of electricity and components through to the most advanced options in robotics and Machine Learning, you'll forge a path to building ingenious hardware and controlling it with cutting-edge software. All while gaining new skills and experience with common toolsets you can take to new projects or even into a whole new career.

The Apress Maker Innovations series offers projects-based learning, while keeping theory and best processes front and center. So you get hands-on experience while also learning the terms of the trade and how entrepreneurs, inventors, and engineers think through creating and executing hardware projects. You can learn to design circuits, program AI, create IoT systems for your home or even city, and so much more!

Whether you're a beginning hobbyist or a seasoned entrepreneur working out of your basement or garage, you'll scale up your skillset to become a hardware design and engineering pro. And often using low-cost and open-source software such as the Raspberry Pi, Arduino, PIC microcontroller, and Robot Operating System (ROS). Programmers and software engineers have great opportunities to learn, too, as many projects and control environments are based in popular languages and operating systems, such as Python and Linux.

If you want to build a robot, set up a smart home, tackle assembling a weather-ready meteorology system, or create a brand-new circuit using breadboards and circuit design software, this series has all that and more! Written by creative and seasoned Makers, every book in the series tackles both tested and leading-edge approaches and technologies for bringing your visions and projects to life.

More information about this series at https://link.springer.com/bookseries/17311

Introductory Programs with the 32-bit PIC Microcontroller

A Line-by-Line Code Analysis and Reference Guide for Embedded Programming in C

Hubert Ward

Apress®

Introductory Programs with the 32-bit PIC Microcontroller: A Line-by-Line Code Analysis and Reference Guide for Embedded Programming in C

Hubert Ward
Leigh, UK

ISBN-13 (pbk): 978-1-4842-9050-7   ISBN-13 (electronic): 978-1-4842-9051-4
https://doi.org/10.1007/978-1-4842-9051-4

Managing Director, Apress Media LLC: Welmoed Spahr
Acquisitions Editor: Susan McDermott
Development Editor: James Markham
Coordinating Editor: Jessica Vakili

Distributed to the book trade worldwide by Springer Science+Business Media New York, 1 New York Plaza, New York, NY 10004. Phone 1-800-SPRINGER, fax (201) 348-4505, e-mail orders-ny@springer-sbm.com, or visit www.springeronline.com. Apress Media, LLC is a California LLC and the sole member (owner) is Springer Science + Business Media Finance Inc (SSBM Finance Inc). SSBM Finance Inc is a **Delaware** corporation.

For information on translations, please e-mail booktranslations@springernature.com; for reprint, paperback, or audio rights, please e-mail bookpermissions@springernature.com.

Apress titles may be purchased in bulk for academic, corporate, or promotional use. eBook versions and licenses are also available for most titles. For more information, reference our Print and eBook Bulk Sales web page at http://www.apress.com/bulk-sales.

Any source code or other supplementary material referenced by the author in this book is available to readers on the Github repository: https://github.com/Apress/Introductory-Programs-with-the-32bit-PIC-Microcontroller. For more detailed information, please visit http://www.apress.com/source-code.

Printed on acid-free paper

Dedicated to my wife Ann.

You have been so supportive and patient while I typed away, forever, on my laptop.

Love always.

Pinch Pinch Pinch

Table of Contents

About the Author

Hubert Ward has nearly 25 years of experience as a college lecturer delivering the BTEC, and now Pearson's, Higher National Certificate and Higher Diploma in Electrical and Electronic Engineering. Hubert has a 2.1 Honors Bachelor's Degree in Electrical and Electronic Engineering. Hubert has also worked as a consultant in embedded programming. His work has established his expertise in the assembler and C programming languages, within the MPLAB X IDE from Microchip, as well as designing electronic circuits and PCBs using ECAD software. Hubert was also the UK technical expert in Mechatronics for three years, training the UK team and taking them to enter in the Skills Olympics in Seoul 2001, resulting in one of the best outcomes to date for the UK in Mechatronics.

About the Technical Reviewer

Mike McRoberts is the author of *Beginning Arduino* by Apress. He is the winner of Pi Wars 2018 and a member of Medway Makers. He is an Arduino and Raspberry Pi enthusiast.

The Aims and Objectives of the Book

My main aim in writing this book is to introduce you to the 32-bit micro and help you understand how to program them in the C programming language. I also want to show you that you can program them and that you can make a career as an embedded programmer. I hope that after reading this book, you will have developed your understanding of C and that you will have the confidence to go and develop your own programs.

The Objectives of the Book

After reading this book, you should be able to do some or all of the following:

- Create a project using MPLAB X

- Configure the 32-bit PIC

- Write local and global header files

- Write programs using timers to create a delay

- Understand a range of C instructions

- Create one-dimensional and two-dimensional arrays in C

- Write C programs to control and use the following displays:

  - Seven-segment displays

  - 8 by 8 dot matrix displays

  - Liquid Crystal Display, LCD

- Create a real-time clock

- Use analog inputs

- Create square waves and PWM

- Control RGB LEDs using the PWM

- Write programs that use interrupts

- Understand and use a range of logic operations

- Understand and use binary and hexadecimal number systems

Introduction

This book will introduce you to the exciting world of embedded programming. It will teach you how the main functions of C programming work and how you can use them to control a 32-bit PIC microcontroller. You might think that a 32-bit PIC is too far advanced to start with and that you should try a simpler PIC first. Well, really, that's not the case. You can start with all the simple programs, such as simply turning on and off an LED, using a simple delay, controlling a seven-segment display, and writing a simple message to an LCD, with this 32-bit PIC. However, you can progress to the more advanced programs that are out of reach with most of the 8-bit PICs.

It really comes down to cost. I use the explorer 16 development board with a plugin board for the 32-bit PIC. The development board, shown in Figure 2, comes in at around £100, and the plugin 32-bit PIC, shown in Figure 1, comes in at around £30. On top of that, you will need a programming tool to download your programs to the PIC. I use the ICD3 can or the PICKIT3 tool. The ICD3 can costs around £70. However, this is no longer available, and the ICD4 can is very expensive. They do have the PICKIT4 which I believe programs 32-bit PICs, and that costs around £70. So, you could possibly be looking at spending around £200 or more. But you should see it as an investment in your career as an embedded programmer. Working as an embedded programmer, one can earn around £40 to £100 an hour if not more.

If you went down the 8-bit PIC route first, you would spend less, but your programming experience could be greatly reduced.

The original version of this book was revised. A correction to this book is available at https://doi.org/10.1007/978-1-4842-9051-4_15

Prerequisites

As to any prerequisites you need before reading this book, there are none. I will assume you are a complete novice, and I will explain every step as you progress through the book. Every instruction will be analyzed to explain how the C instruction works and how it achieves what we want from the instructions. The only things you will definitely need to use this book are as follows.

MPLAB X

This is the IDE, integrated development environment, from Microchip. I will be using versions 5.25 and 5.40, but any version from 2.2 will be fine as there will be only some minor differences. Also, as I know Microchip is constantly updating its IDE, I am confident that the changes will only be minor. This means the procedures for the IDE that you will learn from this book will still stand you in good stead for any later versions of the IDE.

Compiler Software

You will need a 32-bit compiler software to compile your programs within MPLAB X. I use v2.41, although for a lot of my programs, I use the older version 1.32, as the newer versions have some of the libraries missing.

MPLAB X and the compiler software are freely available from the Microchip website. You may have to search the archive section for some of the older compiler versions. You could upgrade to the paid version of the compiler software, but I have not done that for any of my programs. If you were to make a career in embedded programming, then the paid version of the compiler may have some advantages, such as more efficient code that uses less memory.

Simulation Software

MPLAB X does come with a simulation option for its PICs. This does mean that you can try some of the programs without spending any money on equipment. However, the simulation capabilities are not very extensive, and they are used more for debugging your programs. I will take you through using the simulation option within MPLAB X for some of the programs in the book, but most will be carried out on the explorer 16 development board. However, simulating the programs will give you a chance to see if you can enjoy programming these PICs. It is not just about making money, as you will earn more if you enjoy what you do.

There are some ECAD (electronic computer-aided design) software that you can use to simulate the programs. PROTEUS is one that I have used for 8-bit PICs. Multisim is another one, but you must make sure that it can support the PICs you want to use, and they are not free.

MPLAB Harmony

Microchip has invested a lot of time and money in creating its programming environment named MPLAB Harmony. It is aimed at saving a lot of time in developing PIC programs. If you just want to get something working and are not really interested in learning how it works, then this environment can be useful. However, be aware that once you go down that route, you can become dependent upon the environment, as you are not really learning how the programs work. That's great for Microchip but not for you. I believe this approach is counterproductive, as it does far too much for you and doesn't explain how it works. If you really want to become a versatile and productive programmer, then you need to really understand how every bit of your program works. Only then can you really say you wrote it and not just cobbled together bits of code that you don't understand. My main aim in writing this book is to show that it is not too difficult to learn how to program these PICs yourself. If you learn how PICs work and how we can write C instructions to make them do what we want, then you will become that versatile and experienced programmer that will find an exciting and useful career as an embedded programmer.

Why am I writing this book and not working as that embedded programmer? Well, really, I ventured into programming PICs a bit too late in my life. I have been in education, teaching electrical and electronic engineering at HND level, for over 25 years. So now I am ready to retire and concentrate on trying to pass my knowledge and experience onto you younger guys. I hope that in reading this book, you will learn enough to become that versatile and productive embedded programmer.

Why the 32-Bit PIC

I have been working with PIC microcontrollers since 1996, using them to teach the micros unit in the BTEC Higher National Certificate and Higher National Diploma course. In those early days, I used the 8-bit PICs starting off with the 16F88 and the 16F884, writing programs in assembly language. I actually started teaching the micros unit with the "Emma" boards that used the 6502 microprocessor. That did give me a great foundation in micros, but the PICs were much more versatile and relevant. My favorite 8-bit PIC is the 18F4525. I have written three textbooks on that PIC, but now it is time to start writing about an amazing 32-bit PIC that I have used, the 32MX360F512L. A picture of this PIC is shown in Figure 1.

Figure 1. *The PIC32MX360F512L Microcontroller*

The name of the PIC is quite a mouthful, but then that is Microchip for you. Microchip does make an extensive range of PICs.

There is one big drawback with this PIC, compared to the PIC18F4525, and that is, it is a surface mount device, whereas the PIC18F4525 comes in a 40-pin dual in-line package. This does make the 32-bit PIC much more difficult to use if you want to make simple circuit boards, on say some veroboard. It is a 100-pin device, and it can be bought from Microchip on a small self-contained board, as shown in Figure 1, that you could mount on some veroboard, but you would have to create a 100-pin housing for the PIC. The cost of this self-contained board with the PIC is around £30.

A simple way of using this type of PIC is to use the explorer 16 development board that I use. A picture of this is shown in Figure 2. When I bought it, some eight years ago, it came with a 24-bit PIC already included with it, so I had to buy the 32-bit PIC separately.

Figure 2. *The Explorer 16 Development Board from Microchip*

This is a very useful board that has the following peripheral devices:

- An LCD, Liquid Crystal Display

- A variable resistor to provide an analog input

- Four switches connected to four inputs

- Eight LEDs connected to PORTA

- A 25LC256 256k serial EEPROM

- A TC1074A temperature sensor

These are just a few of the devices that are available to you on the explorer board. All these make the board a very useful addition to your embedded programming equipment. This can easily justify the cost of around £100.

You will need a programming tool to download your programs from MPLAB X to your PIC. There are a couple of tools that you can use, such as

- ICD3 can that I use but Microchip has now stopped supplying this. Instead, they supply the ICD4 can. However, this is quite expensive at around £210.

- The PICKIT3 is a much cheaper device at around £30; however, Microchip has now moved on to the PICKIT4 programmer which they sell for around £70.

- You can buy plugin boards to help expand the explorer board. One such plugin board is shown in Figure 3. You will see that I use this extensively in my book.

Figure 3. *A Plugin Extension Board*

You could be spending around £250 plus, but you should find it a useful investment as you can earn a high rate of pay as an embedded programmer. There are cheaper tools you can use, but I can only write about the ones I have used.

There are many other programming environments, but I know these that I have shown you work and work well. Indeed, I have used my explorer boards, with the plugin expansion slot, to control a sophisticated industrial control system.

Some Important Aspects of C Programming

Before we move deep into the book, I think it would be useful to mention some aspects of C programming that we will come across in the analysis of the program listings.

The Main Loop

All C programs work in loops, usually more than one. However, all C programs must have the "main" loop. It is to this main loop that the PIC will go to find the very first instruction of the C program. All the other loops are within this main loop or are called, as subroutines, from the main loop.

Curly Brackets

C programming uses brackets to define the confines of these loops. These are what I call "curly brackets," that is, the opening curly bracket "{" and the closing curly bracket "}". These are used to group a series of instructions together. For example:

```
void main ()
{
    instructions go here
}
```

Normal Brackets

The C programming also uses what I call "normal brackets," that is, the opening normal bracket "(" and the closing normal bracket ")". These are used in conjunction with subroutines and subroutine calls.

We will look at these brackets as we analyze the programs in the book.

Subroutines or Functions or Methods

Subroutines are sections of instructions that lie outside the main loop of the program. They are used, primarily, to save memory, as if you want the PIC to carry out a section of instructions in exactly the same way more than once, then you should write them as a subroutine. Some programmers may call these "functions" or "methods," as they normally carry out a function of some sort. I am an old hat at programming, and so I call them subroutines.

Subroutines may or may not want values to be passed up to them and send data back to the main loop of the program. To create a subroutine, we use the general format as shown here:

keyword **name of subroutine** (request type of possible value to be sent up)

The keyword is used to indicate what type of data the subroutine will send back to the main program. If the subroutine will not send any data back, which is the most common type of subroutine, then the keyword would be "void." However, if the subroutine will be sending data back to the main program, then the keyword would indicate what data type the data would be, for example:

unsigned char

int

For example: void delay250 (unsigned char t)

Note the use of the "normal brackets."

This will create a subroutine that will not be sending data back to the main program, that is, the keyword "void." It will be expecting the main program to pass up a value of the data type "unsigned char." The subroutine will copy that value into the local variable "t."

When the main loop calls these subroutines, it is done using the general format:

subroutine name (send any variables that the subroutine may require)

For example: `delay250(4);`

This will call the subroutine called "delay250" and send the value "4" to be copied into the subroutine's local variable "t."

Local and Global Variables

As I have mentioned the term local variable, I thought I should explain what they are. C programming uses variables, which are newly created memory locations, whose number of bits depends upon the data type the variable will be, to store useful values that you will use in your program. You should give the variable a suitable name that helps explain what the variable is used for. However, we can use just simple letters if we wanted to. C has two main types of variables:

- **Local variables**: These are variables that are created when we create a subroutine, and they are only valid for use in the subroutine they were created in.

- **Global variables**: These are variables that we create when we construct the whole program. I usually list all the global variables at the beginning of the program listing. These global variables can be used anywhere within the program, that is, the main loop and any subroutines, etc.

We will look more closely at these aspects of C programming as we analyze the program listings.

Summary

In this introduction, we have looked at MPLAB X, the IDE from Microchip, and the possible development boards you may have to buy. I have tried to explain the aims of this book, and I have detailed some of my experiences in the hope of convincing you I do know enough about C programming for PIC micros.

In the first chapter, we will learn how to create a project in MPLAB X. We will look at creating a header file, within MPLAB X, and use it in our programs. This header file will look at how we use the configuration words to set the clocks of the PIC and some other important aspects of the PIC. I hope you will find this book useful and it will help you get started on your career as an embedded programmer.

CHAPTER 1

Creating Our First C Program

In this chapter, we will study the process of creating a project for the 32-bit PIC within Microchip's IDE, MPLAB X. We will study the important aspect of creating a clock for the PIC. Then we will create our first program that will look at the ports and learn how to set the direction of data through the ports. We will then write a simple program to light an LED and simulate it within MPLAB X.

After reading this chapter, you will have studied how to create a project in MPLAB X. You will also have a good understanding of the configuration words and how we can control the ports, so that we can write our first simple program.

You will also have used the simulation in MPLAB X to confirm our first program works correctly.

What Is MPLAB X

MPLAB X is Microchip's IDE, integrated development environment. It is a collection of programs designed to make the development of programs for the PIC microcontrollers an easy and enjoyable process. It uses a dedicated text editor that has coloring for keywords and uses an IntelliSense that works like predictive text on a mobile phone. It has a range of debugging

© Hubert Ward 2023

H. Ward, *Introductory Programs with the 32-bit PIC Microcontroller*,
Maker Innovations Series, https://doi.org/10.1007/978-1-4842-9051-4_1

tools that aid the debugging of your programs. It also has a simulation software that allows you to simulate most of your PIC programs. All this and the required compilers are freely available from the Microchip website.

Creating a Project in MPLAB X

Assuming you have downloaded the software and the compiler, you simply click the mouse on the following icon to start the program.

Once the software has started, the opening screen, shown in Figure 1-1, should appear.

Figure 1-1. *The Opening Screen of the IDE*

You should appreciate that when you create a project, a new folder will be created on your hard drive, where all the files and directories for the project will be stored.

To create a new project, simply click the word "File" in the main menu, and then select "New Project" from the fly-out menu that appears. An alternative approach would be to click the mouse on the small orange box with the green cross in it, which is the second item from the left on the second menu bar. The "Choose Project" window shown in Figure 1-2 should appear.

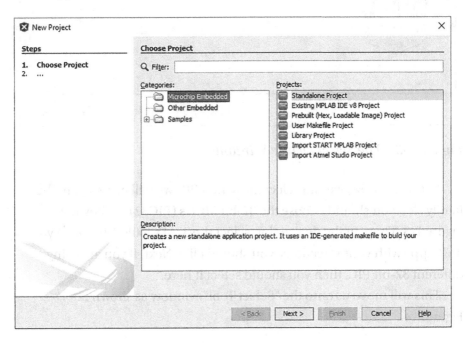

Figure 1-2. *The Choose Project Window*

Most of our projects will be stand-alone Microchip embedded, which means we can simply click Next here to move on to the next window, as those options should be highlighted. If the options, shown in Figure 1-2, are not already highlighted, you should select them now, then click Next. The next window is the "Select Device" window as shown in Figure 1-3.

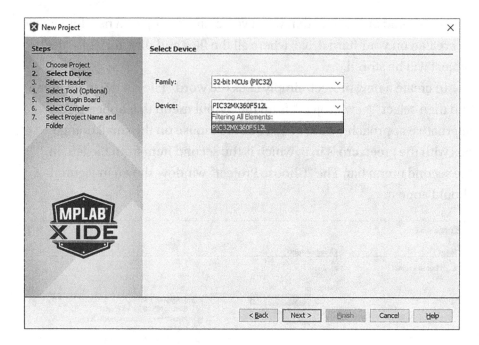

Figure 1-3. *The Select Device Window*

In this window, we can select the actual PIC we will be using. In the family slot, you should choose the 32-bit MCUs (PIC32) as shown in Figure 1-3. Then, in the device slot, select the 32MX360F512L. Once you are happy with your selections, you should click Next. If you are using a different 32-bit PIC, then you should select it here.

This will move us onto the "Select Tool" window as shown in Figure 1-4.

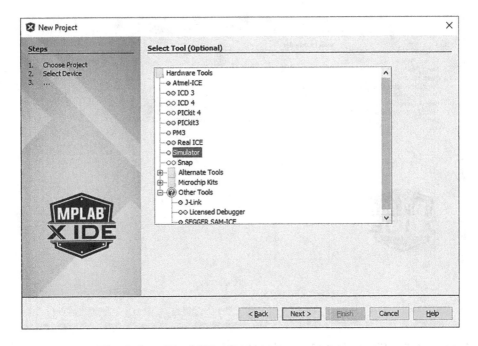

Figure 1-4. *The Select Tool Window*

Here, you can select the actual tool you are using to download the program from MPLAB X to the PIC. In this case, we will simply use the simulator option of MPLAB X. With this option, we don't need an actual PIC, as we will be using the PIC simulator from within MPLAB X.

Once you have selected your chosen tool, you should click Next to move on to the "Select Compiler" window as shown in Figure 1-5.

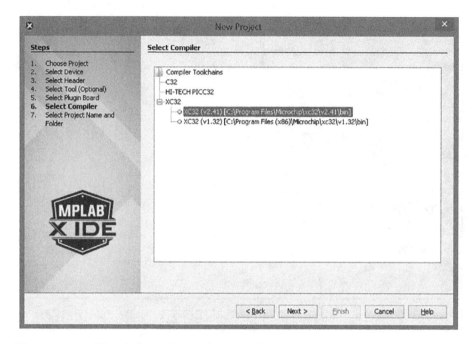

Figure 1-5. *The Select Compiler Window*

I am assuming you have downloaded the appropriate compiler software. I have selected the up-to-date version 2.41. However, I also have the earlier version v1.32 as shown here. As I said earlier, we will need this older version; you will have to look in the archive section of the Microchip website to find it. Indeed, it is when we look at using interrupts that we will use this older version of the compiler software.

Once you have selected your compiler, simply click Next to move on to the "Select Project Name and Folder" window as shown in Figure 1-6.

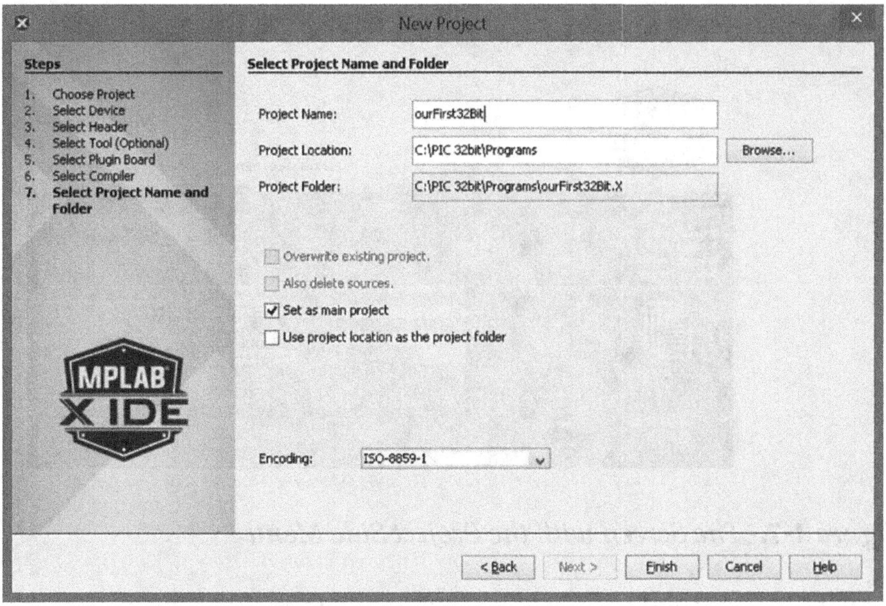

Figure 1-6. *The Select Project Name and Folder*

With this window, you can give the project a name and decide where to save the project. I have named the project "ourFirst32Bit," and I am using what is termed "Camel Font." This is where we combine multiple words to make one long word. The first letter of the first word is in lowercase, and the first letter of all subsequent words is in uppercase. In this way, the separate words of the newly created long word are still discernible.

I tend to save the projects on my root directory, but you must save it where you want.

Once you are happy with your selection, you should click Finish, and your project will be created.

The screen will now change to the main editing window as shown in Figure 1-7.

Figure 1-7.   *The Screen with the Project Side Menu*

Before we finish this chapter, we will create the program file for this first project. We will call it "ourFirst32BitProg." To create the file, we will need to expand the project tree that is shown on the left-side plane in Figure 1-7. This is simply done by clicking the mouse on the small box with the + sign in it, at the side of the "ourFirst32Bit" name in the project tree, as shown in Figure 1-7. If the project tree is not shown, you can click the mouse on the word "Window" on the main menu bar. You should then simply click the first choice, which depicts the orange box and word project. The project tree should then appear. You may have to move the box with the project tree in it around the screen. This can be done by clicking and dragging the mouse with the box selected. It will take some time to master the moving of the different boxes around the screen, so I will just leave it for you to practice.

Once the project tree is opened, you should right-click the mouse on the phrase Source Files. Then click the mouse on the option "New" from the fly-out menu. Then click the option "main_c" that appears. This is shown in Figure 1-8.

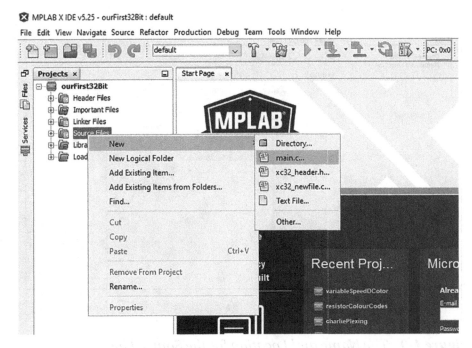

Figure 1-8. *The New Main_C Source File*

Once you do that, you will be presented with the "Name and Location" for the source file as shown in Figure 1-9.

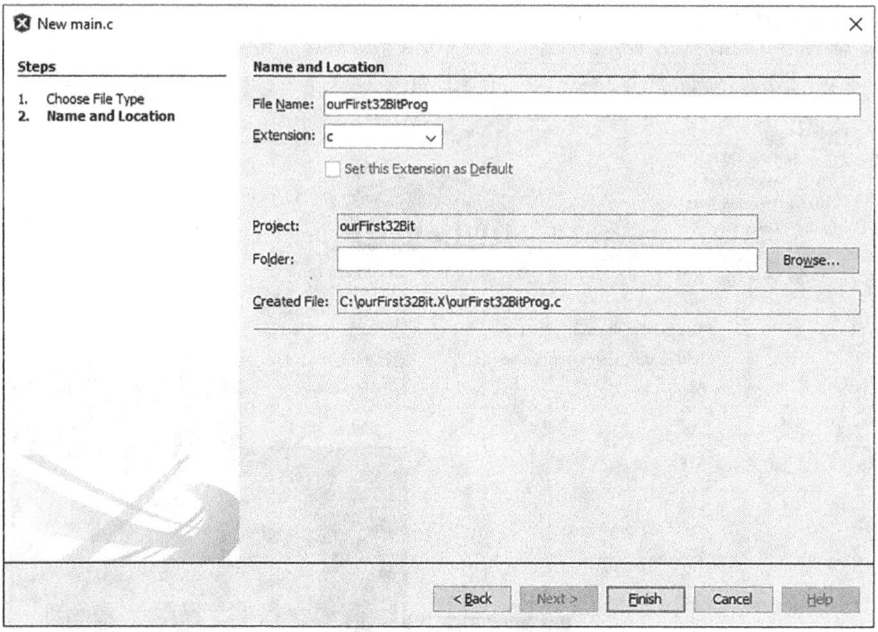

Figure 1-9. *The Name and Location for the Source File*

Here, you can give your c file a suitable name. I have given it the name "ourFirst32BitProg." The extension for the file is c, as shown in the small extension window. Once you are happy with the name, you should click Finish to create the file.

When you do this, you will create a new file that will appear in the main editing window. However, Microchip does insert a lot of text that you will not need at this starting level, if ever. Therefore, to make sure we all have the same window, I would ask you to delete all the text that is inserted in the file. After deleting that material, you should now have a screen that looks like that shown in Figure 1-10.

Figure 1-10. *The Empty Source File*

We have now created our first project within MPLAB X. I suggest you go through this process for every project you make. The more times you go through this process, the easier it becomes.

The Initial Comments

You should always lay claim to your program, you have written it, and you should be proud of what you have achieved. Therefore, the first thing you should write in the file is a paragraph of comments along the lines of what is suggested here:

```
/* A simple program to control an LED
Written by Mr. H. H. Ward for the PIC32
Dated 12/01/2020.*/
```

There are two types of comments:

- **Single-line comments**: This is anything written on the current line only after two forward slashes. For example, //the following are just comments, and the compiler will ignore them.

- **Multiple lines or a paragraph of comments**: This is anything written on one or more lines that are between the following symbols, for example, /* The next lines are comments*/.

As this is a paragraph of comments, we should enclose them between the following symbols: /* */.

My initial comments are shown in Figure 1-11.

Figure 1-11. *The Comments for the Program*

You will notice I have changed the font of the comments. This is to make them clearer in the book. If you want to do this, then you should select the word "Tools" on the main menu. Then select the word "Options" from the fly-out menu, and you should then be presented with the window shown in Figure 1-12. You will notice I have selected the term "Fonts & Colors" from the menu.

You should then be able to change the comments to what you want. Once you are happy with your changes, simply click OK to close the window and apply the changes.

Figure 1-12. *The Options Window*

The Speed of the Clock

The operation of all microcontrollers is synchronized to a clock signal. With all PICs, the programmer has total control over the frequency of this clock signal. It is therefore an important aspect of PIC programs and one that you should understand how we can control.

Like all PICs, the 32-bit PIC has a wide selection of possible sources for the oscillator that will form the basis of the clock. There are also different clocks for different aspects of the 32-bit PIC. Figure 1-13 depicts the block diagram of the system clock sources.

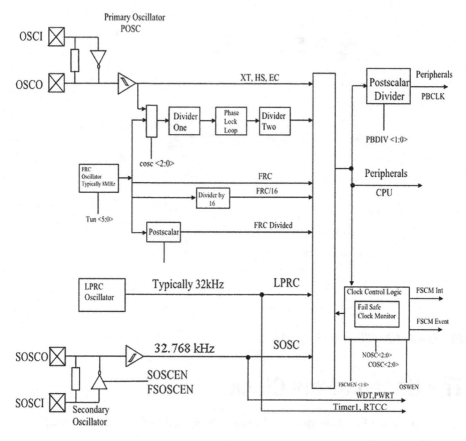

Figure 1-13. *Block Diagram of the 32-Bit PIC Clock System*

There are four sources of oscillators for the PIC. The two external sources are shown as the primary oscillator with terminals OSCI (oscillator in) and OSCO (oscillator out) and the secondary oscillator, shown as SOSCO and SOSCI. The other two oscillator sources are the FRC (fast resistor capacitor) and the LPRC (low-power resistor capacitor).

The primary oscillator and the FRC can be fed, unaltered, to produce the clock signal, or they can be passed through a divider circuit, divider one, then through a PLL (phase lock loop) circuit, where the frequency can be multiplied, then through a final divider circuit, divider two, before being used for the various clock signals.

The secondary oscillator and the LPRC sources are used to generate a relatively low frequency around 32kHz for the LPRC and an exact 32.768kHz from a crystal oscillator. Both of these can be used for the system clocks. The secondary oscillator can be used as an accurate source for timer1 and for the RTCC (Real-Time Clock Calendar). The LPRC can be used as the source for the WDT (the Watch Dog Timer) and the PWRT (Power Watch Reset Timer).

The FRC and LPRC are both internal oscillators, and the ability to use an internal oscillator is useful if you were short of I/O, as with the PIC18F4525. However, with this 32-bit PIC, I/O, the number of input and output pins, is not really a problem. Also, as the RC oscillators are not as accurate as crystal oscillators, I will use the external oscillator sources for my projects.

The primary oscillator on the explorer 16 development board is an 8MHz crystal. The board also has the 32.768kHz crystal as the secondary source, which can be used to run the RTCC (Real-Time Clock and Calendar). We have the option of increasing the frequency of the oscillator to produce a faster clock signal, and to do this, we must run the 8MHz crystal oscillator through the phase lock loop circuit. However, the phase lock loop circuit requires an input frequency of 4MHz. That is why we have the ability to run the oscillator through the divider one first. As we are using the 8MHz crystal, we must set the first divider to divide by 2.

Once in the phase lock loop, we have the ability to multiply the signal by a factor of 15 up to a factor of 24. At present time, the maximum clock frequency for the 32-bit PIC is 72MHz; therefore, we will multiply the 4MHz signal by 18. This means that the output of the phase lock loop will be a 72MHz clock signal. This means we don't need to divide the clock further, so set the divider two to divide by 1, that is, no change.

There is one final division we can make if we wanted to. This is to make the peripheral bus clock, the PBCLK, run at a lower frequency than the system clock, the CPU clock. We will choose to run the PBCLK at 36MHz. This means we need to divide the CPU clock by 2 before applying it to the PBCLK.

All of these changes can be achieved by writing the correct data to the configuration words. As this is something you have to do in all your projects, then Microchip has made this process as simple as possible.

Writing the Configuration Words

To start the process, simply click the mouse on the word "Window" on the main menu bar. Then select "Target Memory Views" from the first fly-out menu. Then select "Configuration Bits" from the second fly-out menu. This is shown in Figure 1-14.

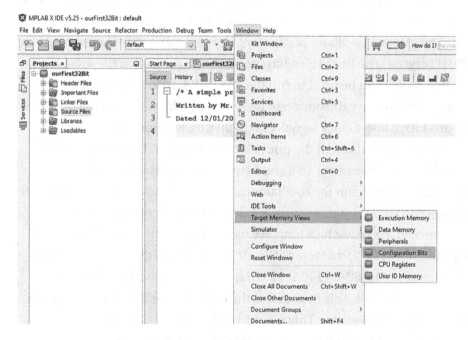

Figure 1-14. *Selecting the Configuration Bits*

The display will now show the configuration bits in the bottom half of the editing window. This is shown in Figure 1-15.

You can now make the changes that we need as follows:

- Change the second option FPLLIDIV, the input divider to the phase lock loop, to DIV_2.

- Change the third option FPLLMUL, the PLL multiplier, to MUL_18.

- Change the fourth option FPLLODIV, the PLL output divider, to DIV_1.

- Next, change the FNOSC option to PRIPLL, primary oscillator with phase lock loop. This tells the PIC that we will be passing the oscillator through the phase lock loop circuit.

- Next, change the FSOCEN, the secondary oscillator enable bit, to off to disable the secondary oscillator.

- Next, change the IESO to off to disable the two-speed startup.

- Next, set the POSCMOD, the primary oscillator mode, to XT. This is because the 8MHz external crystal is less than 10MHz which is within the XT range of frequencies.

- Next, set the FPBDIV, the frequency of the peripheral bus divider, to DIV_2. This is to reduce the frequency of the peripheral bus to 36MHz.

- Change the FWDTEN to off. The WDT is the Watch Dog Timer which will stop the program if nothing happens for a set period of time. This is really used in production lines, and we don't need this for our programs, so we must turn it off.

This is displayed in the editing window as shown in Figure 1-15. Note the changes will be highlighted in blue.

Figure 1-15. *The Changes to the Configuration Bits*

The changes are ready, but they will not take place until we have written the source code into the program. This can be done by clicking the mouse on the tab at the bottom of the window labeled "Generate Source Code to Output." When you do this, the source code for these changes will appear in the output window. This is shown in Figure 1-16.

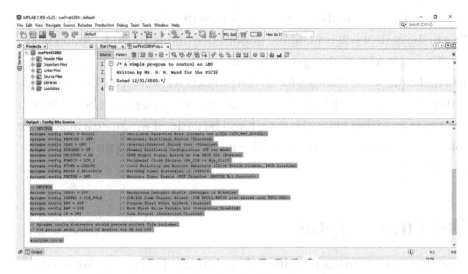

Figure 1-16. *The Source Code for the Changes to the Configuration Bits*

You then need to select all the text, including the "#include <xc.h>", in that window and copy it into your program in the editing window.

Your screen should now look something like that shown in Figure 1-17.

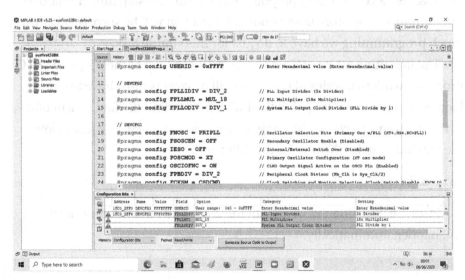

Figure 1-17. *The Code Pasted into the Editing Window*

Note, I have copied everything including the #include <xc.h>, the last line in the code. I will explain the importance of this #include option later.

There are a lot of changes we are making to the configuration bits. We will make the same changes for all the projects we will create in the book. This is because we will be using the explorer 16 development board for all our programs. That being the case, it will be easier if we create a header file for this. We will do this in Chapter 2, where we will discuss the importance of header files.

Our First Program

Now we are ready to start writing our first program in earnest. We need to know what it will do, so I will write the specification down now.

This program will wait until a momentary start switch is pressed. When that happens, it will turn on an LED. It will then wait for a momentary stop switch to be pressed at which point it will turn the LED off. It will then go back to waiting for the start button to be pressed and so repeat the process. Not a very exciting program, but for our first step into embedded programming, it is more than enough. I think you will be surprised by how much programming we have to do just for this simple task.

The first thing we must do is set up the main loop of the program. All C programs work in a series of loops, and all programs must have this main loop. It is to this main loop that the PIC will go to find the first instruction of the program. To create this loop, we must insert a new line just below the #include <xc.h>. Now write the following:

```
void main ()
```

Just type it in, don't worry about the color and emboldening, as this will happen automatically.

You should see that the word "void" is written in blue. This is because "void" is a keyword, and it is telling the compiler that this loop will not be sending any information back to the main loop, because it is the main loop.

You should also note that as you type the word "main" it writes it in bold text. As well as that, when you type in the first normal bracket "(" after the word main, the software will automatically insert the second closing normal bracket and place the cursor inside the two brackets.

These actions of coloring the keyword in blue, highlighting the name in bold, and adding the closing normal bracket are all done automatically by the IntelliSense of the MPLAB X software. This IntelliSense acts like predictive text on your phone, taking over, trying to help you. This is not just a simple text editor. We will not type anything inside these two normal brackets, so move the cursor outside the brackets. We will look at the syntax of this instruction and the keyword "void" as we analyze the program listings in the book.

Now press the enter key to move on to the next line. You should now enter the opening curly bracket "{", which is the upper part of the key to the right of "p" on your keyboard. When you do this, and press the enter key again, the IntelliSense will take over and insert a closing curly bracket and place the cursor between the two curly brackets, indenting the text at the same time.

Your screen should now look something like that shown in Figure 1-18.

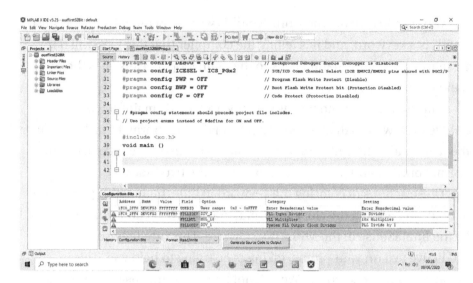

Figure 1-18. *The Main Loop Created*

You are now ready to write the instructions for your first program.

Setting the PORTS

As the program will require two inputs for the two switches and one output for the LED, we must set up the ports correctly. The ports are just like real ports in a country, in that real ports take goods into and out of the country. However, the ports on the PIC take data into and out of the PIC. In this PIC, the ports are a collection of 32 individual bits that make up a 32-bit register. However, only 16 bits actually work as input or output. As programmers, we can make these individual bits either input or output. This means that there has to be a way we can tell the PIC which way we want the bits to work. The way we do this is to write the correct data to a dedicated register that maps onto the bits in the ports. This register, which is one of a range of SFRs, Special Function Registers, is used to control which way the data goes through the ports. These registers are called TRIS registers, and there are TRISA, TRISB, TRISC, in fact a TRIS for each of the five ports on the PIC. As there are only two possible directions, input or output, then the binary data written to each bit of the TRIS can set the direction of data for each bit in its respective port. In this way, a logic '1' sets the bit as an input, whereas a logic '0' sets the bit as an output. As an example of this, if we set all the bits in TRISA to a logic '1', then we would be making all the bits in PORTA inputs. Also, if we made bits 0 to 7 of TRISA logic '0' and the rest to a logic '1', then we would be making the first 8 bits of PORTA outputs and the rest of the bits inputs. This concept gives us easy control of the direction of the data through the ports.

Exercise 1-1

What data would you have to write to what register to make bits 0 to 7 of PORTC inputs, then bits 8 to 10 outputs, then 11 to 15 as inputs?

The solution to this exercise will be given at the end of each chapter.

The Hexadecimal Number System

In the preceding exercise, you could be writing 32 binary bits; really, only the first 16 bits are important, but they are 32-bit registers. It's quite a task and one at which you could easily make a mistake. Even when dealing with 8 binary bits, it is quite easy to make a mistake. That is why programmers use the hexadecimal number system. Consider writing the binary number for the value of 225. This is

11100001

However, written in hexadecimal, it is

E1

There is much less of a chance of making a mistake with the hexadecimal format than with the binary format. In the appendix, there is a section that shows you how to convert decimal to binary and then to hexadecimal – a skill that you should take some time to learn. You can see that one digit in hexadecimal represents four binary digits. Therefore, we represent a 32-bit binary number by simply using eight hexadecimal numbers. For example, the 32-bit binary number

01011111000010101101100000100001

can be represented in hexadecimal as

5F0AD821

Using hexadecimal means there is less chance of making a mistake than if we use binary numbers. This is the only reason why we use the hexadecimal number system.

As the eight LEDs on the explorer 16 development board are connected to PORTA, then we will set PORTA as outputs. There are four switches on the explorer 16 development board, and the three switches we will use are allocated as follows:

- S3 is on RD6.

- S6 is on RD7.

- S5 is on RA7.

We will use the two switches connected to PORTD, that is, RD6 and RD7, so we will set them as inputs.

We will use bit 7 on PORTD for the start button and bit 6 of PORTD for the stop button. Note, we cannot use RA7 as we are setting the first 8 bits, bits 0 to bit 7, on PORTA as outputs. Therefore, we will simply make bits 7 and 6 on PORTD inputs and the others as outputs. To do this, we will simply set all bits in TRISD with the following instruction:

TRISD = 0X00C0 or 0b0000 0000 1100 0000

Note, the "0X" before the number tells the compiler the following number is hexadecimal. The "0b" tells the compiler the following number is in binary. If we don't place the "0X" or "0b" in front of a number, then the software will use the default radix, that is, the number system, which is decimal. For example, if we wrote PORTA = 255, the PIC would load the PORTA register with the decimal value of "255." In binary, this would be "0b11111111," and in hexadecimal, this would be "0X" FF.

Note, even though the TRISD is a 32-bit register, we only need to write to the first 16 bits. The register reads from right to left going from bit 0 on the right to bit 15 on the left.

Some points we need to be aware of about the format of the preceding instruction are as follows.

The word TRISD is written in uppercase. This is because we are using the label TRISD instead of the actual address of where the register TRISD is in the PIC's memory. TRISD is what is termed an SFR, Special Function Register, and there are quite a lot of them for the 32-bit PIC. They are stored in the PIC's memory in locations between 0XBF800000 and 0XBF8FFFFF. We should appreciate that the compiler software can't read English, and so it can't read TRISD. Indeed, all it really wants to know is the actual number of the address where it must load the data 0X00C0 to. We could write our instructions using these actual addresses if we could find out which address it is. However, if we did, it would make the reading of the programs very difficult. Therefore, instead of writing the actual address of the TRISD, we use the label TRISD. This would cause a problem, in that how then does the compiler know what the address of the label TRISD is? Well, this works because someone has been very helpful, in that they have written instructions that will tell the compiler the address of the labels of all the SFRs and the PORTS; PORTA, PORTB, etc., are SFRs that we can use in our programs. These instructions are written in a special header file called "xc.h". That is why we have to include this header file in all our programs. Also, because all the labels in that header file were written in capitals, we must write all the labels of the SFRs in capitals in our programs.

I know that is a wordy explanation about why we use labels, but it is important that you understand the importance of the header file "xc.h" that we included when we wrote the configuration words.

One last thing about the instruction is the semicolon ";". This denotes the end of the current instruction.

So, we have now set the direction of data through PORTD. The program will use an output for the LED. We will use bit 0 of PORTA. Therefore, we will make all 16 bits on PORTA outputs. To do this, we must set all the bits in TRISA to a logic 0. This can be done with the following instruction:

```
TRISA = 0;
```

Quite simple but there is a subtle format here. The number is a decimal number as we are using the default radix of decimal; note we don't need to indicate to the compiler this is a decimal number. We should appreciate that in 32-bit binary, 0 is

00000000000000000000000000000000

This means we are really setting all the bits in TRISA to logic 0 with this instruction. This, in turn, sets all the bits on PORTA as outputs.

Well, we have now set the direction of the data through the PORTS to what we want. So, we can write the rest of the program. Well, not really as there is one more aspect of the input that we need to consider. That is that we could have either analog inputs or digital inputs to the PIC. As the two inputs to our program are from switches, then they will be digital inputs. Note, an analog input would be a varying voltage from a sensor of some sort. However, the PIC doesn't know the inputs are switches; they are just inputs. We have to tell the PIC these are digital inputs, not analog.

Programmers can only use logic '1' or logic '0' to tell the PIC anything.

Well, thankfully, Microchip has given us access to SFRs that are control registers for any aspect of the PIC. It is the AD1PCFG SFR that we can use to control this aspect of the inputs. There are 16 possible inputs that can be used as analog or digital. It is the data in bits 0 to 15 of the AD1PCFG, ADC Port Configuration Register, that controls the use of the inputs. If the relevant bit in the AD1PCGF register is a logic '1', then the input will be digital. If the relevant bit is a logic '0', then it will be an analog input.

Therefore, as we are only using digital inputs, we can set all of the bits of this AD1PCFG register to a logic '1'. This is done by using the following instruction:

```
AD1PCFG = 0XFFFF;
```

As we are not using any analog inputs, then we might as well turn the ADC off, as this will save power. The ADC is a circuit inside the PIC, that is, an analog-to-digital converter circuit, that will convert the analog voltage at that input to a digital number. The control register that we can use to turn the ADC off is the AD1CON1, the ADC control register 1. It is bit 15 of this register that allows us to turn on or off the ADC. If this bit is a logic '1', then the ADC is turned on. If the bit is a logic '0', then the ADC is turned off. Therefore, we need only write 0 to the AD1CON1 register to turn off the ADC. This is done using the following instruction:

```
AD1CON1 = 0;
```

One last thing we should appreciate about the analog or digital inputs. This refers to the inputs on PORTB and none are on PORTA, so we could have missed this out. However, we should turn the ADC off, as we are not using it, and there will be times when we need to set the inputs on PORTB to either digital or analog.

Almost there, but we have to consider the JTAG terminal on the explorer 16 development board. This is used in some extensive debugging aspects of the PIC. It uses some of the bits on PORTA, and we should disable this function so that we can use all of the bits on PORTA as inputs. To do this, we need to write a logic '0' to bit 3 of the DDPCON, the control register that controls this function. The bits of all the control registers have cryptic names for all the bits that give some indication of what they control. Bit 3 is called JTAGEN, the JTAG Enable pin. Therefore, we need only set this bit to a logic '0' to disable this function. This can be done with the following instruction:

```
DDPCONbits.JTAGEN = 0;
```

This is setting the logic of just one particular bit in this DDPCON register, hence the precise syntax of the instruction.

The First Program Listing

There is quite a lot to consider before we can even start writing our program. However, I am not just giving you the instructions, I am also trying to explain their purpose and how they work. Also, once you have got the grasp of these initial instructions, it is quite easy to use them in other programs.

The complete listing for the first program is written in Listing 1-1.

Listing 1-1. Our First Simple Program

```
1  /* A simple program to control an LED
2  Written by Mr. H. H. Ward for the PIC32
3  Dated 12/01/2020.*/
4  // PIC32MX360F512L Configuration Bit Settings
5  // 'C' source line config statements
6  // DEVCFG3
7  #pragma config USERID = 0xFFFF          //
8  // DEVCFG2
9  #pragma config FPLLIDIV = DIV_2         // PLL Input
                                              Divider (2x
                                              Divider)
10 #pragma config FPLLMUL = MUL_18         // PLL Multiplier
                                              (18x Multiplier)
11 #pragma config FPLLODIV = DIV_1         //
12 // DEVCFG1
13 #pragma config FNOSC = PRIPLL           //
```

```
14  #pragma config FSOSCEN = OFF           // Secondary
                                              Oscillator
                                              Enable
                                              (Disabled)
15  #pragma config IESO = OFF              // Internal/
                                              External Switch
                                              Over (Disabled)
16  #pragma config POSCMOD = XT            //
17  #pragma config OSCIOFNC = ON           //
18  #pragma config FPBDIV = DIV_2          //
19  #pragma config FCKSM = CSDCMD          //
20  #pragma config WDTPS = PS1048576       //
21  #pragma config FWDTEN = OFF            /
22  // DEVCFG0
23  #pragma config DEBUG = OFF             //
24  #pragma config ICESEL = ICS_PGx2       //
25  #pragma config PWP = OFF               // Program Flash
                                              Write Protect
                                              (Disable)
26  #pragma config BWP = OFF               //
27  #pragma config CP = OFF                //
28  // #pragma config statements should precede project file
        includes.
29  // Use project enums instead of #define for ON and OFF.
30  #include <xc.h>
31  void main ()
32  {
33  TRISA = 0;
34  TRISD = 0X00C0;
35  AD1PCFG = 0XFFFF;
36  AD1CON1 = 0;
```

```
37  DDPCONbits.JTAGEN = 0;
38  while (1)
39  {
40  while (PORTDbits.RD7 == 0);
41  PORTAbits.RA0 = 1;
42  while (PORTDbits.RD6 == 0);
43  PORTAbits.RA0 = 0;
44  }
45  }
```

Analysis of Listing 1-1

I will analyze any new instructions in the program listings as they are initially used in the programs. In this way, I will explain how the instructions work and what they are doing.

Lines 1–3 are the basic comments used in all my programs. Lines 4–29 are the configuration settings we created for this program. We will create a header file with these settings so that we can use them in all our future projects that use the same settings. Most of the projects in this book will use them, as most of the projects are to be used on the explorer 16 development board that has an 8MHz crystal as the external clock source. If your board uses a different external crystal, then you would have to change some of the multiplier and divider settings to give a system clock and a peripheral clock of 76MHz and 36MHz, respectively. Note, you could use different frequency settings for these two clocks, but that would mean some changes in the timer settings. Therefore, to keep pace with the programs in the book, I suggest you ensure that your system clock is set to 76MHz and the peripheral clock is set to 36MHz.

Line 30 #include <xc.h>

This is a very important directive as it tells the compiler to include all the definitions in this header file when it compiles the program. This "xc.h" header file includes all the definitions for the labels we will use in our programs. The labels we will use in our programs are the names Microchip has given for the Special Function Registers, such as PORTA, TRISA, T0CON, etc. Really, all the compiler needs to know is the actual address of the SPF, Special Function Register. For example, the address of PORTA is 6010 in hexadecimal, and TRISA is 6000 in hexadecimal. We could write our program using these address numbers, but it would make it rather difficult to read and appreciate which registers we were working with. Therefore, to make the program more readable, we use these labels that have been created for us. However, to ensure that the compiler knows that when we use the labels it can replace them with the correct address, we have to include this header file in all our programs.

Line 31. void main ()

This is creating the only loop that *must* be in a C program. That is why it is called "main." The term void means the loop will not be sending any data back to the main loop as it can't; it is the main loop. The empty normal brackets "( )" mean it does not need any data to be sent up to it from the main program. I am making these statements as we will use other loops, which I call subroutines, that work outside the main program, and they may need data being sent up to them, and they may be sending data back to the main program. Note, some programmers may refer to these "subroutines" as "functions" or "methods"; however, I am old hat, and they are subroutines so I call them that. It is really down to personal preference.

There is no semicolon at the end of line 31, which is normally used to indicate the end of an instruction. This is because this is not the end of the instruction.

Line 32. {

This is the opening curly bracket of the main loop. These opening and closing curly brackets set out the confines of the instructions for the loop.

Line 33. TRISA = 0;

This loads all the bits in the SFR TRISA with logic 0. This then sets all the bits in PORTA as outputs.

Line 34. TRISD = 0X00C0;

This sets bits 7 and 6 of PORTD as inputs and the rest as outputs. Note, from now on when I write about 16 bits, I will call it a word, that is, the low word and the high word. This is because 16 bits can be referred to as a word.

Line 35. AD1PCFG = 0XFFFF;

This loads the low word of the 32-bit SFR AD1PCFG with all logic 1s. This sets all the inputs on PORTB as digital inputs instead of analog inputs.

Line 36. AD1CON1 = 0;

This loads the AD1CON1 control register with all logic 0s. Essentially, this turns the ADC off as we are not using it.

Line 37. DDPCONbits.JTAGEN = 0;

This is one method of referring to just one bit of a register that has more than one bit. Note the syntax has to be correct with the upper- and lowercase letters and the use of the full stop. This instruction simply sets the JTAGEN bit, which is bit 3 of the DDPCON control register, to a logic 0. This will disable the debugging capability of the JTAG terminal. This will free up the bits of PORTA for normal input/output operation.

Line 38. while (1)

We have now finished setting up the control registers of the PIC, and we will not need to do this again unless we need to alter any control; for example, we might need to turn on the ADC. So, assuming we don't need to make any changes, with this instruction, here on line 38, we are making sure the PIC never uses lines 33–37 again.

This while instruction uses the principle of

```
while (test is true)
{
Do what I tell you
to do here
}
```

This is a test type of instruction. However, in this case, the test, which is described between the set of normal brackets, is a very special test. To appreciate this test, you need to appreciate that the PIC will show that the result of the test is true by setting a "result bit" to a logic '1'. If the result of the test is untrue, then the "result bit" would go to a logic '0'. However, we don't have direct access to this "result bit." You should appreciate that the PIC does not understand C instructions. The PIC, like all microcontrollers, really only understands assembly instructions that are eventually written in binary. The process by which we can make a PIC understand C instructions is to use a C compiler. The C compiler will change all the C instructions we use into the assembler instructions that the PIC can understand. This process will involve the compiler adding relevant assembly instructions where needed. It is in this process that, for these test types of C instructions, the "result bit" is created. That is why it is there, but we can't see it.

This concept will hopefully make the forever loop easier to understand. The instruction setting up the forever loop is

```
while (1)
{
Do what I tell you
to do here
}
```

However, there is no real test described inside the normal brackets, as there is only the number "1." What this does is simply load the hidden "result bit" with the value "1." This means that the result of the test will always be true. This then means that the PIC must carry out the instructions written between the opening and closing curly brackets, in lines 39 and 44, forever, hence why it is referred to as the "forever loop." In this way, we make sure the PIC will never carry out the instructions on lines 33 to 37 again.

Line 39. {

This is the opening curly bracket of the forever while (1) loop.

Line 40 while (PORTDbits.RD7 == 0);

This uses the

```
while (test is true)
{
Do what I tell you
to do here
}
```

However, this while instruction is setting up the test, which is described inside the normal brackets, that asks, is the logic on bit 7 of PORTD a logic '0'? If it is a logic '0', then the test will be true. The instruction then states that, while the result of the test is true, the PIC must carry out the instructions that follow. Note the use of the double equal sign "==". My interpretation of what the double equal sign means is "has the logic become equal to what is stated?" This is opposed to the single "=" equal sign, which means "the logic will be forced to equal what is stated here." For example, PORTA = 0b00001111; will force the data in the PORTA register to take on the value 0b00001111.

RA0 == 1; is really asking the question: Has the logic on bit 0 of PORTA taken on the value of logic 1?

Therefore, the instruction on line 40 means that the result of the test will be true as long as the logic on bit 7 of PORTD has become equal to "0." This is assuming that the logic on the input at bit 7 of PORTD will be a logic '0', if no one has pressed the switch, and so the test will be true. If someone then pressed the switch on bit 7 of PORTD, the logic will go to a logic '1', and the result of the test will be untrue.

In this case, there are no instructions between the closing normal bracket and the semicolon. Note, the semicolon denotes the end of the current instruction. In this way, the instruction is making the PIC do nothing while the logic on bit 7 of PORTD is a logic '0'. The logic on bit "0" will go to a logic '1' when the start button is pressed. This assumes you have connected the switch to go high when pressed. Some circuits wire the switch to go low when pressed.

In this way, we are getting the PIC to do nothing until the logic on bit 0 of PORTD goes to a logic '1', that is, wait for the start button to be pressed.

Line 41. PORTAbits.RA0 = 1;

This is what the PIC must do when someone has pressed the start button, and the test on line 40 becomes untrue. The instruction sets bit 0 of PORTA to a logic '1'. This will put a 3.3V output on bit 0 of PORTA and so turn on whatever is connected to it, that is, we will turn on the LED connected to bit 0 of PORTA. Note, the single equal sign "=" will force the logic on bit 0 of PORTA to go to a logic '1'.

Line 42. while (PORTDbits.RD6 == 0);

This works in the same way as the instruction on line 40. The difference is that it is looking at bit 6 of PORTD. We could use an alternative method of identifying which bit we are using, and that would be to replace the instruction while (PORTDbits.RD6 == 0); with while (_RD6 == 0);. This would work in exactly the same way. Instead of writing "PORTDbits.", we can use the underscore "_". It's a much simpler syntax.

This instruction, on line 42, makes the PIC wait until the stop switch is pressed.

Line 43. PORTAbits.RA0 = 0;

This will put 0V onto bit 0 of PORTA and so turn off the LED.

Line 44. }

This is the closing curly bracket of the forever while loop set up on line 38.

Line 45. }

This is the closing curly bracket of the main loop set up on line 31.

You should appreciate that after carrying out the instruction on line 43, we are at the end of the confines of the while (1) loop. This means that the PIC will now loop back to the first instruction of the loop, that is, it will go back to line 40. Here, it will wait for the start button to be pressed and start the whole process again.

I hope this analysis helps you to understand how the instructions work. In future analysis of program listings, I will discuss any new instructions and refer back to those I have looked at before.

Simulating the Program in MPLAB X

The ability to simulate most of your programs inside MPLAB X is very useful, as you can try embedded programming at no cost. This process can be extended to include the debugging tools, so that you can monitor and debug real programs in a practical situation.

I will go through the process of simulating this first program now. It is a process that you should go through carefully, carrying out the steps in the right order to get the results you want.

However, before we do that, we should open up the input/output monitoring window and create a stimulus to simulate the operation of the start and stop switch.

To open up the stimulus window, click the mouse on the word "Window" from the main menu bar. Then select "Simulator" and then "Stimulus" from the fly-out menus. This is shown in Figure 1-19.

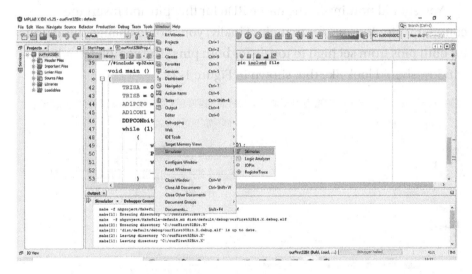

Figure 1-19. *Opening the Stimulus Window*

Once you click this option, the stimulus window should open, as shown in Figure 1-20.

Figure 1-20. *The Stimulus Window*

If you click the mouse on the small downward arrow in the box under the word pin, you should be able to scroll down and find the reference RD7. If you highlight this and then click the mouse, this pin will be inserted into the box. If you then move the mouse to the box under comments, you should be able to write the phrase "startButton" in there. Note you must hit the enter key on the keyboard to enter the comments into the box.

Now we need to create another row in the window to enter the PIN RD6. To create the new line, click the mouse on the icon indicated by the arrow in Figure 1-20.

You should now insert the name RD6 for that pin and insert the comment "stopButton" for that pin. Finally, you should change the action for both pins from set high to toggle for both pins. The completed stimulus window should look like that shown in Figure 1-21.

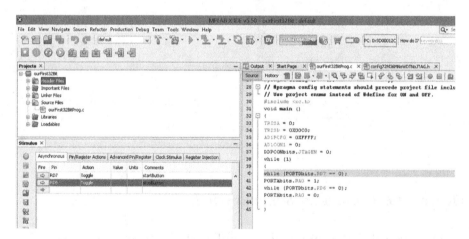

Figure 1-21. *The Completed Stimulus Window*

You might have to move the windows around the screen which can be done by clicking and dragging the mouse on the tab "Stimulus." You will have to practice this process to get it right.

Now we need to open up the input/output window, or I/O window. To do this, click the word "Window," then "Simulator," but now select the "IOPin" option as shown in Figure 1-22.

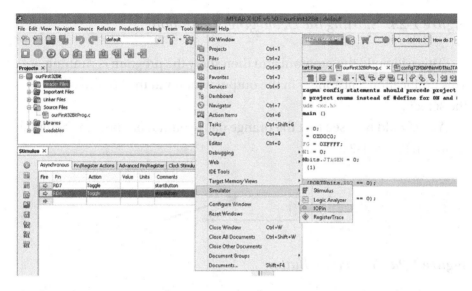

Figure 1-22. *Opening the IOPin Window*

The I/O Pins window should open, and you can insert the following three pins into it, in a similar fashion as with the stimulus, except that you don't need to insert extra rows:

- RA0

- RD7

- RD6

Now we are ready to simulate the program and start stepping through the program. However, this must be done in a precise and careful manner as follows.

To start with, we need to build the program. However, as we are debugging the program, we should select the Debug Project option by clicking the icon shown in Figure 1-23.

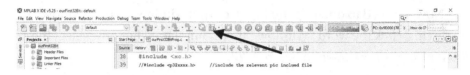

Figure 1-23. *Starting the Debugging Simulation*

This will build the program and then show the program is running. This notification will appear in the output window at the bottom of the screen.

You should now see that the orange pause button has become active as shown in Figure 1-24.

Figure 1-24. *The Pause Button*

You should click the mouse on the pause button. At this point, the blue reset button, with the two white arrows, should become active. If you now click the mouse on this reset button, the green highlight bar should move to the beginning of the main loop. We can now single-step through the instructions of the program and monitor what happens. First, move the stimulus and I/O windows around to give the best view. This is shown in Figure 1-25.

- Assuming the blue reset button has been pressed, after pausing the program, we can start single-stepping through the instructions of the program. The green cursor should be sitting under the phrase "void main ()".

CHAPTER 1   CREATING OUR FIRST C PROGRAM

- Now click the mouse on the orange step into button, or single step button, which is button 6, as indicated in Figure 1-26. The green highlight bar should then move onto the first line of the program, which is the instruction TRISA = 0;.

- Now click the single button arrow again, and the highlight will move onto TRISD = 0X00C0;. The reference to RA0 should change to RA0 DOUT.

- Click the single step button again, and the highlight moves to AD1PCFG = 0XFFFF;.

- When you click the single step button again now, MPLAB X will carry out that instruction, and the pins RD7 and RD6 will change to Din. This is because the instruction sets PORTD to digital, and the second instruction made them inputs. The highlight will now be on the instruction AD1CON1 = 0;.

- Click the single step button two more times, and the highlight will land on the first while instruction. Here, the program is waiting for the logic on bit 7 of PORTD to go high, that is, a logic 1. In the I/O Pins window, you should see that RD7 is gray, which means it is at a logic 0.

- If you now click the single step button, nothing will happen as RD7 is still at logic 0.

- Now fire the RD7 pin in the stimulus window by clicking the mouse once on the fire button. Be careful to only click the fire button once.

41

- Now click the mouse on the single step button. You should now see the highlight moves onto the next instruction, and the LED for RD7 goes green.

- Before you next click the mouse on the single step button, fire the RD7 stimulus by clicking the mouse on the fire button **once** more.

- Now click the single step button, and you should see the LED for RD7 go out and the LED for RA0 go green.

- The green highlight is now on the second while instruction. It is now waiting for the logic on RD6 to go high. At the moment, it is still low.

- If you now click the single step button, nothing will happen.

- So now fire the RD6 button and then click the single step button. The highlight should now move onto the next instruction.

- At the moment, both RA0 and RD6 should be green. If you now click the single step button, MPLAB X will carry out the instruction _RA0 = 0; and RA0 should go gray.

- Now fire the RD6 button **once** more.

- Now click the single step button, and the highlight will move from the closing curly bracket to the first while instruction in the loop. Also, the RD6 LED should go out.

You should now be able to repeat the process and see that the program works as we expected it to.

This should show you that you can simulate the program within MPLAB X. You do have to be very careful and click the buttons in a precise manner, but it is a useful process. We will try to simulate more programs as we go through them. However, to get the most out of this book, you may have to spend some money and buy some practical equipment, but if you like what you are doing, and you enjoy studying my book, then the investment could prove very productive.

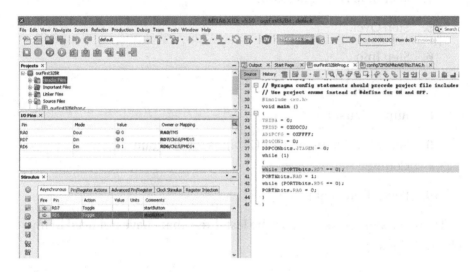

Figure 1-25. *The Debug Window*

Figure 1-26 details the buttons that you will use during the simulation or debugging of your program.

Figure 1-26. *The Control Buttons of the Debug Menu*

You may not see all the buttons as there may not be room on the menu, so you may have to expand the debug menu to see all the buttons.

There are ten buttons that have the following functions:

1. Finish Debug Session.

2. Pause Debug Session. This is grayed out as the session is paused.

3. Reset Debug Session.

4. Continue Debug Session.

5. Step Over.

6. Step Into.

7. Step Out.

8. Run to Cursor.

9. Set PC at Cursor where PC stands for Program Counter.

10. Focus Cursor at PC.

There are some keys, such as the last three, that I have not used in my debug sessions.

Solution to Exercise 1-1

You would have to use the following instruction to write the data shown here to the TRISC register:

TRISC = 0b1111100011111111; or TRISC = 0XF8FF;

Summary

In this chapter, we have learned how to create a project in MPLAB X. We have studied some of the configuration words and learned how to control the speed of the clocks within the PIC. We have studied how to set the direction of data through the PORTS. We have covered some useful C instructions and had our first glimpse of using the simulator from within MPLAB X.

We have covered quite a bit in this chapter, and I hope you have enjoyed reading it and have learned some useful aspects of PIC programming.

In the next chapter, we will look at creating a header file and learn why we use them. We will then learn how to control the timers of the PIC and create a variable time delay. We will then use that delay to create our first challenging project, that of a set of crossroads traffic lights, a typical first project for the would-be embedded programmers.

CHAPTER 2

Header Files and Delays

In this chapter, we will create our first header file, which will be concerned with the configuration words we write for our projects. Later, we will write other useful header files.

We will also look at an important aspect of PIC programs, that of slowing the PIC down. We will create two delays that we will use in our programs.

We will then look at writing a program to control a set of traffic lights.

After reading this chapter, you will know how to create a header file and a delay.

What Are Header Files and Why We Use Them?

Header files are simply files that contain a series of useful instructions. They are used when your programs use the same series of instructions, in exactly the same way, in all your projects and programs. The process of creating and using header files makes your program writing more efficient. There are many useful examples of when you should create a header file, and we will look at some of them in this book.

© Hubert Ward 2023
H. Ward, *Introductory Programs with the 32-bit PIC Microcontroller*,
Maker Innovations Series, https://doi.org/10.1007/978-1-4842-9051-4_2

Header files can be made available for all your projects, that is, be written as global header files, as opposed to local header files. Local header files are available only to the project they were created in, which is not all that useful.

You can also split the projects up, so that different programmers can write different sections of the programs and save them as header files to be used in all your projects by all the company's programmers.

Creating a Header File

Now that I have explained what header files are and why you would use them, it would be useful to create our first header file. The first header file will be for the configuration words we will use in all our projects. These configuration words must be written at the start of all our projects, as they configure how we will use the oscillator source to generate the two clock signals used in all our projects. As all our projects will use the 8MHz crystal, supplied on the explorer 16 development board, to generate a 72MHz CPU clock and a 36MHz peripheral clock, then we might as well create a header file that has all the configuration words to do this and a few bits more.

To speed things up, we will modify the current project we have opened already. This is the one and only time we will not create a new project. This is because we are going to use the existing configuration words to create the header file.

To start with, we will create a new header file. This is done by right-clicking the mouse on the word header files in the project tree in the main window. Then select New from the fly-out menu. Then select the xc32_header.h... option from the next fly-out menu. This is shown in Figure 2-1.

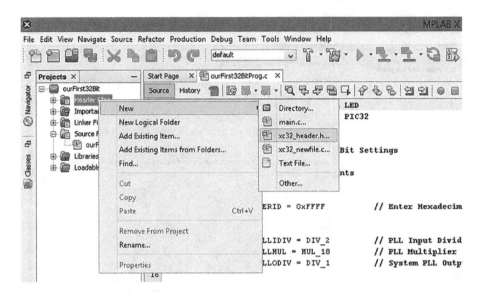

Figure 2-1. *Creating a New Header File Option*

You will be presented with the "Name and Location" window as shown in Figure 2-2.

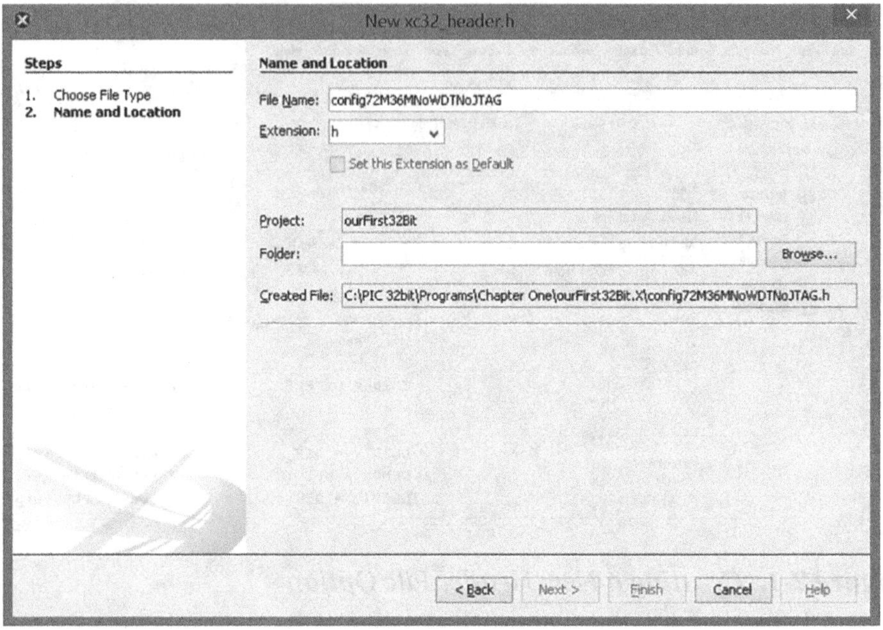

Figure 2-2. *Naming the New Header File*

You should give the file a name that describes what it is doing. I suggest that you should call it "config72M36MNoWDTNoJTAG" as this is what we are doing with it. Note the NoWDT and NOJTAG are in the name because we will be turning off the WDT and the JTAG option.

You should see the file created and displayed in the editing window. However, Microchip automatically inserts an awful lot of stuff that, at our starting level, we don't need. So, I would like you to delete all the text in that window, so that you have an empty file.

We will now copy all the configuration words in the program file and paste them into the empty header file.

You should start at line 4, in the program file, and copy all the lines up to and including line 29, that is, all the lines concerned with the configuration words. Note, you do not want to copy the #include <xc.h> line, as we will make sure we add this in the main program, so we don't need it in this header file. Once you have pasted these lines into your new header file, the file should look like that shown in Figure 2-3. You should now save the newly created header file.

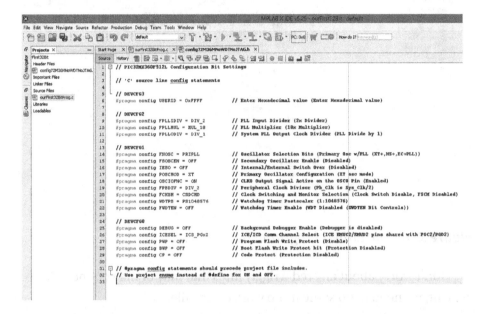

Figure 2-3. *The Newly Created Header File*

Now simply cut all the configuration words that you selected from the program file. Your program file should now look like that shown in Figure 2-4.

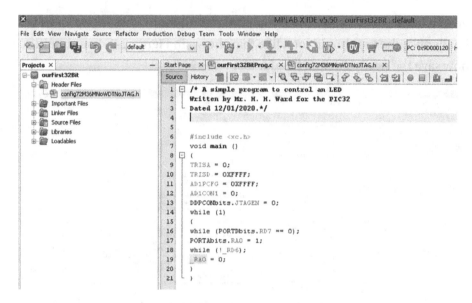

Figure 2-4. *The Edited Program File*

Don't worry about any red wriggly lines that may or may not be present, we need to do some more work on the file.

You should now add the #include <xc.h> line in, as shown, as this is needed for all the labels we will use. Remember we have not pasted it into the header file, but we do need this included in all our programs.

Using the Header File

Now we need to use the header file we have just created. We do this by including it in our projects. The file has been created within this project, which means it is local to this project. Therefore, to use it in this project, we need only insert the following line:

```
#include "config76M36MNoWDTNoJTAG".
```

Note you must use the quotation marks, and the name is the name of the header file we want to include.

When you type the "#" hash symbol, the IntelliSense should take over, or try to help us, as a window should appear with a selection of possible keywords in green. The one we want is at the bottom of this list. You could just click the mouse on the word "include" or simply type it in.

Now, when you press the spacebar, the IntelliSense will again take over and present us with a list of possible options we could use. Our file name should be among them. You can just click the mouse on the name of the file or type it in with the quotation marks. Once you have inserted the include keyword and header file, your screen should look like that shown in Figure 2-5.

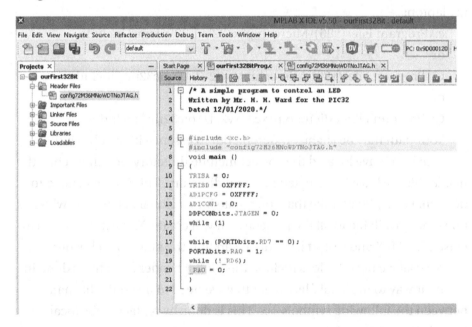

Figure 2-5. *The Program File with the Header File Included*

When we click the build option, which is the plane hammer symbol on the main menu bar, the program file should build correctly. Note, the compiler will look through the header file to compile the configuration words, as it has been told to include them in the listing.

This means we have created and used our first header file. However, this is what is termed a local file, in that it can only be used within this project. This is really not of much use, as we want to be able to use this header file in all our projects, as this would save us having to write the configuration words again. This means we must make it into a global header file.

To do this, we need to save a copy of this file in the include directory within the compiler directory that was created when we installed the compiler software. This means we need to find the path of where that directory is on your hard drive. The following is the path of where it is on my laptop:

c:\Program Files(x86)\Microchip\xc32\v1.32\picmx\include

or

C:\Program Files(x86)\Microchip\xc32\2.41\pic32mx\include

or

C:\Program Files\Microchip\xc32\v2.41\pic32mx\include

Your path may be slightly different, but in essence it must be similar.

Once you have located the correct include directory, you must copy the header file we have just created into that directory. This is all you need to do to make any header file that you create into a global header file, which is one that is available to all the projects you will create. You will now have to close MPLAB X and restart it so that it can find the new global header file.

Now all we need to do is include this global header file. This is done in a similar way to the local file, except that we need to insert the file name between the following symbols < >. This is done by replacing the local include line with the following:

```
#include <config76M36MNoWDTNoJTAG>
```

This is shown in Figure 2-6.

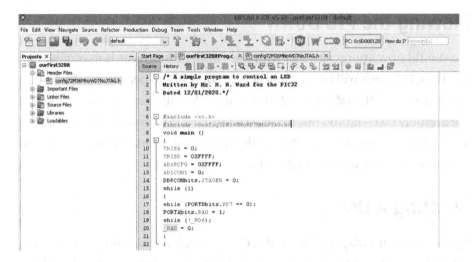

Figure 2-6. *Using the Global Header File*

Note the two quotation marks have been replaced by the following symbols: < >.

The IntelliSense will try to help as before; however, when you press the spacebar after inserting the include keyword, you should insert the first < symbol. When you do that, you should get a long list of options of files available to you. However, if you start to write the first characters of the header file name, that is, "conf," the IntelliSense should reduce the list. Once you have located the header file you want to include, simply click the mouse on the name, and you should see it insert between the two symbols "< >".

This means we have now created a header file and made it global, so that we can include it in all our projects. This means we won't have to go through the process of changing the configuration words again.

Note, in this listing, I have used the alternative method to identify the bits RD6 and also RA0. Also, the while (!_RD6); do nothing instruction uses this alternative method. Here, I am using the exclamation mark "!" which is the "C command" for NOT. This instruction states that while (NOT _RD6) do nothing. The NOT means that the logic on the bit is a logic '0'. Therefore, this instruction means that while the logic on RD6 is a logic '0', do nothing. This instruction works in the same way as while (PORTDbits.RD6 == 0); but it's more succinct.

Slowing the PIC Down

We should now appreciate that with our configuration words in our header file, the CPU clock will be running at 72MHz, and the peripheral clock will be running at 36MHz. At 72MHz, one cycle will take 13.9nsec, which is extremely fast – far too fast for us. We humans take around 20msec to absorb data. In 20msec, the PIC would have done 1.4 million operations in that time. This means we need to slow the PIC down.

Creating a Delay

If you remember playing hide and seek at school, you should know that the seeker had to count to 100. That was to delay the seeker and give the others time to hide. However, some seekers could count faster than others, so it wasn't consistent.

The principle shows what is involved in creating a delay; that is, we simply get the PIC to count up to a value. The length of the delay will depend on two things:

- The value the PIC must count up to

- How fast the PIC counts

Well, with a 16-bit PIC, we can store numbers that have a value from 0 to 65,535 – a very big number. However, with a CPU clock that runs at 72MHz, this would take around 0.91ms, assuming we can count at that rate. The other problem is that the CPU could be running at a slower rate. This means we need to cope with the fact that the PIC could be running at different speeds.

Well, all PICs have modules called timers. These simply increment, or count, at a controlled rate. There are five timers in this 32-bit PIC, that is, timer1, timer2, timer3, timer4, and timer5. These timers are peripheral devices, and so they will normally use the peripheral clock, that is, the PBCLK. We can control the rate at which these timers increment or count. We need this ability because the PIC can use a wide range of oscillator sources to form the basis of this frequency, at which these timers count. The easiest way to explain the process is to go through an example. We will use timer1 to create a variable delay.

We need to know how fast timer1 will be counting. This will depend upon a number of things, such as

- What oscillator source we will be using and the settings for the CPU clock and the PBCLK. As we will be using our header file for the configuration words, then the CPU will run at 72MHz and the PBCLK will run at 36MHz.

- What, if any, prescale has been applied.

These parameters and many others can be set by the programmer by writing the correct data to the T1CON, which is the timer1 control register. The contents of this control register are shown in Table 2-1.

Although this is a 32-bit register, only the lower 16 bits are used to control the different aspects of timer1.

Table 2-1. *The T1CON Register*

Bit Number	Bit Name	Application
15	ON	A logic '1' turns timer1 on A logic '0' turns timer1 off
14	FRZ Freeze in debug mode	A logic '1' freezes timer1 when the CPU is in debug mode A logic '0' doesn't freeze timer1 when the CPU is in debug mode
13	SIDL Stop in idle mode	A logic '1' stops timer1 when PIC enters idle mode A logic '0' doesn't stop timer1 when PIC enters idle mode

(*continued*)

Table 2-1. (*continued*)

Bit Number	Bit Name	Application
12	TMWDIS Asynchronous Write Disable bit	**When in asynchronous mode** A logic '1': Writes to timer1 are ignored until pending operation completes A logic '0': Back-to-back writes are enabled **When in synchronous timer mode** This bit has no effect
11	TWIP Asynchronous Timer Write In Progress bit	A logic '1': Asynchronous timer write is in progress A logic '0': Asynchronous timer write is complete This is really a signal to the programmer. Therefore, leave it at logic '0'
10	Not used; read as logic 0	
9	Not used; read as logic 0	
8	Not used; read as logic 0	
7	TGATE Gated Time Accumulation Enable bit	**When TCS = 1** This bit is ignored **When TCS = 0** A logic '1': Gated time accumulation is enabled A logic '0': Gated time accumulation is disabled
6	Not used; read as logic 0	

(*continued*)

Table 2-1. (*continued*)

Bit Number	Bit Name	Application		
5	TCKPS Input Clock Prescaler Select bits This works in conjunction with bit 4	Bit 5	Bit 4	Prescaler or divide rate
		1	1	Divide by 256
		1	0	Divide by 64
		0	1	Divide by 8
		0	0	Divide by 1
4	Used with bit 5			
3	Not used; read as logic 0			
2	TSYNC Timer External Clock Input Synchronization Select bit	When TCS = 1 A logic '1': External clock input is synchronized A logic '0': External clock input is not synchronized When TCS = 0 This bit is ignored		
1	TCS Timer Clock Source bit	A logic '1': External clock input from T1CK1 pin is used A logic '0': Internal peripheral clock is used		
0	Not used; read as logic 0			

The term asynchronous means that the device, in this case a timer, is not synchronized to any external source; it is free running. However, we will be using the timer in the synchronized mode. This is controlled by setting the TSYNC, bit 2, to a logic '0'.

All the timers will usually use the peripheral clock as their source if we set the TCS bit to a logic '0'. Setting this bit to a logic '0', as we will do, further enforces the timer to be synchronized, as the TSYNC bit is ignored. Doing this means that the timer counts at a rate of 36,000,000 ticks in one second. This is still far too fast, and so we will make use of the four different divide rates available to us with bits 5 and 4 of this control register. We will set both of these bits to a logic '1', which means we divide the 36MHz by 256, making timer1 count at a rate of 140.625kHz. This means each count will take 7.11µs. This is still very fast, and as the maximum number timer1 can count up to is 65,535, that is, 2^{16}, the delay will still only be 0.4660338 seconds. Note we start counting from 0. We will have to put this delay into a nested loop, which is simply a loop inside another loop. However, to make the nested loop simpler to appreciate, we will restrict the count value to 35,160. As each count takes 7.11µs, then a count of 35,160 will take 0.250s, approximately one quarter of a second. However, to be very accurate, we should try to account for the time required for the micro to carry out the actual instructions in the nested loop. When I programmed in assembler, it was possible to calculate the time taken to carry out the instructions; however, as C uses hidden instructions, the only way to be accurate is to try and time the operation. I will initially use a count value of 35,160, which will give us a delay of 0.2496s.

Before we can do anything, we will need to turn on timer1, which is done by setting bit 15 to a logic '1'. We will leave all the other bits that we haven't discussed at a logic '0'. Therefore, the 16-bit number we need to write to the T1CON register is 0b1000 0000 0011 0000 in binary going from bit 15 on the left down to bit 0 on the right, or 0X8030 in hexadecimal.

Bit 15, set to a logic '1', turns the timer on; bits 5 and 4, both set to a logic '1', set the divide rate to 256, the maximum divide rate available to us; and bit 1, set to a logic '0', sets the internal peripheral clock as the source for the timer. Note, bit 2 is also set to a logic '0', as timer1 will be synchronized to a clock, not free running.

Note, I have written the 16-bit number in lots of 4, as this makes it easy to convert to hexadecimal. See the appendix to learn about number systems.

The Variable Delay Subroutine

The nested loop to create the variable delay subroutine is shown in Listing 2-1.

Listing 2-1. The Variable Delay Subroutine

```
1  void delay250 (unsigned char t)
2  {
3  for (n = 0; n < t; n++)
      a {
            i  TMR1 = 0;
           ii  while (TMR1 < 35160) ;
      b }
4  }
```

The numbers and letters are there just for me to reference the instructions in my analysis.

What Is a Subroutine

The instructions in Listing 2-1 will be used as a subroutine. A subroutine is a small section of program instructions that are written outside the main program. The main program will have to "call" the subroutine every time it needs to use the subroutine. This is a good programming technique, as if you write a section of program instructions that have to be carried out, in exactly the same way, more than once in your program, then you should write them as a subroutine. This would save writing the same instructions again and again inside the main program. This saves memory which is always worth saving. You can see why the C programmer might call these subroutines "functions" or "methods" as they carry out a function, or they are a method for achieving something. Well, I am old school and I will continue to call them subroutines.

The Analysis of the Delay Subroutine

I will do this analysis line by line to try to explain how they work.

Line 1 void delay (unsigned char t)

The term "void" is a keyword, and, as the text editor is more than just a simple text editor, it will be written in blue in MPLAB X.

The term "void" means the subroutine will not be sending any data back to the main program.

Next, you simply write a suitable name for the subroutine. This time, I have called it "delay250," as it suggests the correct purpose for the subroutine. The name will be written in bold in MPLAB X's editor.

Next, we insert a normal opening bracket. When you do this, inside MPLAB X, the IntelliSense will take over and insert the closing normal bracket, then insert the cursor between the two brackets. This is because the IntelliSense thinks you will want a variable sent to the subroutine when it is called.

Here, I have inserted the phrase "unsigned char t." The unsigned char will be written in blue as both words are keywords. This is declaring a variable named "t" of the type unsigned char. This is telling the main program that every time it calls the subroutine, it must supply some data of the type unsigned char that the subroutine will copy into the variable "t."

The keyword char means that this variable "t" will be an 8-bit area of the PIC's data memory. The keyword "unsigned" means that all 8 bits will be used to represent the value that can be stored in the memory location. This is opposed to a signed char, in which bit 7 is used to tell the PIC if the variable was negative (bit 7 is a logic '1') or positive (bit 7 is a logic '0').

62

Note when declaring a signed char as opposed to an unsigned char, we don't write the word "signed." This is because the char will be either signed or unsigned. With an unsigned char, the number will always be positive, so bit 7 can be used as part of the number. This concept of using the MSB, Most Significant Bit, that is, bit 7 in an 8-bit variable, to represent the sign, positive or negative, of a variable is called "signed number representation."

Before we leave this term "unsigned char t," we must consider the term "local variable" or "global variable." A local variable is one that is defined, as we are doing so with this subroutine, that is, we declare it within the normal brackets when we create the subroutine. The importance of this is that a local variable can only be used within the subroutine in which it was declared. The variable cannot be used anywhere else in the program.

This is opposed to a "global variable." These are variables that are declared at the top of the program listing, that is, they are not declared in the main program or any subroutine. Global variables are those that can be used anywhere in the program, that is, they can be used in the main program and any subroutines that the main program uses.

This delay subroutine will use both types of variables.

Line 2 {

This is the opening curly bracket that sets out the confines of the instructions that make up the subroutine. Note line 1 does not have a semicolon at the end of it. The semicolon signifies the end of the current instruction. That is why it is not placed at the end of line 1, as it is not the end of the instruction.

Line 3 for (n = 0; n < t; n++)

This line is setting up a very useful type of instruction that you will use in most of your C programs. It is the "for do loop" instruction. The word "for" sets up the loop. The normal brackets encase three small instructions written inside them.

The first small instruction "n = 0;" is using a global variable which has been declared at the top of the main program listing. This small instruction simply loads the memory location called "n" with a value of 0. Note the semicolon is there to denote the end of the small instruction.

The next small instruction "n < t;" is of the type "test" in that it asks the question, "is n less than t?" Assuming we sent a number, say 5, for example, to be loaded into the local variable "t" when we called the subroutine, then, as we have just set the value in "n" to 0, the test must be true, that is, n is less than 5. That being the case, the micro must carry out the instructions written within the opening and closing curly brackets that define the confines of the "for do loop." We will look at the final small instruction after we have gone through the instructions of the "for do loop."

Line a {

This is the opening curly bracket of the "for do loop."

Line i TMR1 = 0;

This is loading the value 0 into the 16-bit register TMR1. This is the register that holds the current value timer1 has counted to. We set this to 0 to ensure the timer starts to count from 0.

The semicolon is there to denote the end of this current instruction.

Line ii while (TMR1 < 35160) ;

This is another very useful instruction, one that you will use in most of your programs. It is of the type "while (the test is true) do what I tell you to do." When the test becomes untrue, carry on with the rest of the program. The test is described inside the normal brackets. The test is asking whether the value in TMR1 is less than 35,160. Well, as we loaded 0 into the TMR1 register with the previous instruction, then the test will be true. That means the micro must carry out the following instructions. However, in this case, this is a one-line instruction, so we don't need to encase the instructions within a set of opening and closing curly brackets. It is also a very special one-line instruction in that there are no instructions written between the closing normal bracket and the semicolon. This is because we want the micro to do nothing while the test is true, that is, while the value in TMR1 is less than 35,160, we want the PIC to do nothing. In this way, the test will be true until TMR1 has counted up to 35,160. At this point, TMR1 will not be less than 35,160, and so the test will become untrue. We know, from before, that it will take 0.2496s for TMR1 to count up to 35,160. As the micro will do nothing while this test is true, these two instructions, in lines i and ii, will create a 0.2496s delay. Note, this is with a peripheral clock running at 36MHz.

Note, in line ii, I have made the space between the closing normal bracket and the semicolon more than needed to show the concept more clearly.

Line b }

This is the closing curly bracket of the "for do loop."

Line 4 }

This is the closing curly bracket of the delay subroutine.

Now I will explain the last of the three small instructions of the "for do loop." This is "n ++". Note, there is no semicolon at the end of this small instruction.

As stated earlier, because "n" was loaded with a value 0, which is less than the value loaded into the variable "t," the micro must carry out the instructions on lines i and ii. After carrying out those two instructions, the micro will then carry out the third small instruction written inside the normal brackets of the "for do loop" in line 3. This is the n ++ instruction. This will simply increase the value in the variable "n" by one. The micro will now repeat the test written inside the normal brackets of the "for do loop." Therefore, it will ask the question, "is n less than 't'?" In this case, n will still be less than "t," and so the micro will repeat the instructions in lines i and ii.

This whole procedure will repeat until "n" is increased so that it will have a value equal to that loaded into the variable "t." When "n" does equal the value in "t," the test, is n < t, will become untrue, and so the micro will come out of the "for do loop" and carry on with the rest of the program.

The instructions in lines i and ii will create a delay of around 0.2496s. If the value in the variable "t" is, for example, 5, as stated earlier, then the micro will repeat this 0.249s delay five times, making a total delay of approximately 1.25s. This means we have created a variable delay, whose length of time is set by the number loaded into the variable "t," but a delay that has a resolution of 250ms, that is, 1/4 of a second.

To call this subroutine from within the main program, we simply have to write the following instruction:

```
delay250 (5);
```

In general, to call any subroutine, we simply have to write out the name of the subroutine with any parameter that the subroutine may want sending to it, written inside the normal brackets. This principle is shown here:

```
subroutine name (any parameter);
```

If the subroutine does not want a parameter sending up to it, then the normal brackets in the call instruction are left blank, as would be the normal brackets in the setting up instruction of the subroutine. We will see examples of this in later program listings.

Creating a 1ms Delay

The variable delay subroutine discussed earlier has a resolution of 0.25s. This might be OK for most applications, but it might be useful to create a delay with a better resolution. The 1ms delay can give us just that.

The programming is exactly the same as the delay we have just created, except that we will restrict the value that timer1 has to count up to. The value can be calculated using the following expression:

$$value = \frac{resolution}{count\ interval}$$

Equation 2-1. The Count Value for a Delay Resolution

The resolution is 1ms or 0.001 or $1E^{-3}$.

The count interval has been set by the timer control register to be 7.111µs or 0.000007111 or $7.111E^{-6}$. Again, you need to ensure your PBCLK is running at 36MHz.

Putting these values into Equation 2-1 gives

$$value = \frac{1E-3}{7.111E-6} = 140.627$$

Equation 2-2. The Value for 1ms Resolution

This will have to be rounded down to 140, as we know the time taken to carry out the instructions in the subroutine has to be accounted for. The complete listing for the 1ms delay subroutine is shown in Listing 2-2.

Listing 2-2. The 1ms Delay Listing

```
1  void 1msdelay (unsigned char x)
2  {
3  for (n = 0; n < x; n++)
       a  {
               i   TMR1 = 0;
               ii  while (TMR1 < 140) ;
       b  }
4  }
```

I hope there is no need to analyze the instructions, as they are the same as before. The only differences are the name changed to 1msdelay, the local variable changed to x, and the count value changed to 140. Note I could have kept the name of the local variable as "t," but if we have too many variables with the same name, we can get confused – us, not the PIC.

We can now move on to our next program. However, before we do that, we should consider doing things properly. There are good reasons why we should follow tried and trusted procedures.

Good Programming Practice

All programs should be planned. The programmer should not just start writing code in the IDE. A good programmer should write an algorithm, then construct a flowchart. After that, they can write the program listing.

The Algorithm

This is really simply putting your thoughts of how you are going to get the PIC to do what is asked of it down on paper. The purpose is to focus your mind on how to complete the task. It will also allow you to choose the right PIC for the job. The algorithm should cover at least the following:

- You should explain the sequence of events you want to control.

- You should then identify all the input and output devices you will need.

- You should identify any modules, such as the ADC or interrupts, etc., that you may need.

- You should then create an allocation list for the control and identify any special inputs, outputs, or controls you will need, such as analog inputs, PWM outputs, and any timers.

The Flowchart

This is a diagram, using standard symbols, to show how the program will flow through the instructions and so complete the task. They are very useful diagrams for designing computer programs. All flowcharts use five basic symbols; there are more, but the five most common symbols are shown in Figure 2-7.

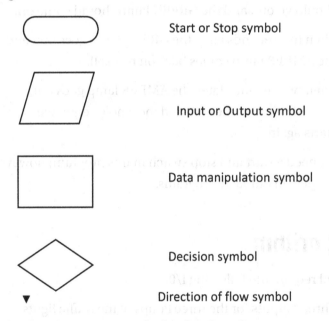

Start or Stop symbol

Input or Output symbol

Data manipulation symbol

Decision symbol

Direction of flow symbol

Figure 2-7. *The Five Basic Symbols of a Flowchart*

Our First Useful Program

We are now ready to consider our first useful program. This will be to control one set of lights – red, amber, and green – to mimic a single set of traffic lights.

The first thing we need is a sequence of events:

- The RED lamp should come on when the program starts.

- Then five seconds later, the AMBER lamp should come on as well.

- Then two seconds later, the RED and AMBER lamps should go out, and the GREEN lamp should come on.

- Then five seconds later, the GREEN lamp goes out, and the AMBER lamp comes back on by itself.

- Then two seconds later, the AMBER lamp goes out, the RED lamp comes on, and the whole sequence starts again.

We don't need a start and stop switch in this program; however, we will look at this aspect in our later programs.

The Algorithm

This task will require the following I/0:

- Three outputs for the three lamps of the traffic lights.

- It will use one timer to create a variable delay.

- We will use the explorer 16 development board, which means we will use PORTA for the LEDs and PORTD if we want to add some switches. If you are using another development board, then you may have to alter the allocation list.

- We will use the external oscillator which is set to 8MHz.

- There is no need for the WDT, Watch Dog Timer, as the watch dog timer is something that an industrial production line would need, not the sort of programs we will be writing.

The main process of the program will be to set up the PIC and the ports, oscillator, and timer0.

The program will continually go through the following sequence:

- Light the RED lamp.

- Call a five-second delay.

- Light the AMBER lamp.

- Call a two-second delay.

- Turn off the RED and AMBER lamps and turn on the GREEN lamp.

- Call a five-second delay.

- Turn off the GREEN lamp and turn on the AMBER lamp.

- Call a two-second delay.

- Then turn off the AMBER lamp and repeat the sequence again.

The Allocation List

As we are using the explorer 16 development board, we will use PORTA for the three outputs. Therefore, the allocation list will be

- Red lamp on RA0

- Amber lamp on RA1

- Green lamp on RA2

The Flowchart for the Program

This is shown in Figure 2-8.

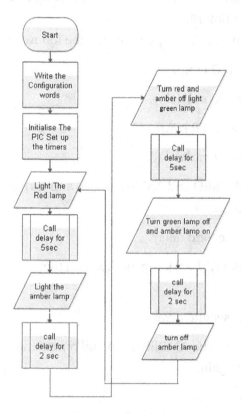

Figure 2-8. *The Flowchart for the Single Traffic Light*

Flowcharts are an aid to designing programs, as they split up the program into smaller sections that can be completed either with existing blocks of program or by different programmers.

They show how the program should flow from one part to the other. The connecting arrows should show the direction of flow from one block to the next. Each shape of the block has a special meaning.

When a flowchart extends across a page, then connecting symbols, which are circles with letters in them, can be used.

You should construct a flowchart for every program you design, as, if constructed fully, each block in the flowchart links into its own section of the program listing and instructions.

However, to save space, I will only show the flowchart for this program.

With respect to the configuration words, we are going to use the same words for all our projects, so we will use the header file we created in Chapter 1.

Creating the Project

You should create a new project every time you write a new program; don't just modify an existing project. This keeps everything separate, and the more you go through a process, the quicker you will really learn it.

Since writing Chapter 1 in this book, I have updated my IDE to Microchip's latest version which is now version 5.40. There is not a great deal of difference, but I will show you some of the changes. You don't really need to update to the latest version, but this next bit might help you if you do update. One problem you will find, if you do update, is that if you open a project from the old version, you might not be able to reopen it again in the old version. You will be given a choice though.

You create the project in the normal way, but when you get to the second window, choose a device, there is an additional small window. In this window, you are asked to select which tool you want to use. The IDE will detect the tools that you have connected and are so available to you.

73

If you don't have any connected, the window will give you the option of no tool or simulator. The window is shown in Figure 2-9. You can see that, because I have my ICD3 can connected, I am given three choices.

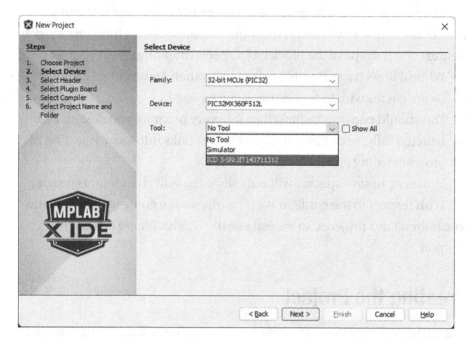

Figure 2-9. *The New Select Device Window*

This means that the "Select Tool Window" has been incorporated into the "Select Device Window," and the "Select Tool Window" is not used in this version of the IDE.

The rest of the process is just the same as before, so you should be able to complete creating the project. I have given the project the name 32bitSingleTrafficLights, but you can name it something different if you want.

The next step is to create the source file. The process is just the same as before. I have named the C file 32bitSingleTrafficLightsProg.

Now you can insert the program listing into the open editing window. As before, I have deleted all the text that Microchip automatically inserted into the editor.

The complete program listing can now be written, and it is shown in Listing 2-3.

Listing 2-3. The Single Set of Traffic Lights

```
1   /*This is a program to control a single set of
    traffic lights.
2   It is written by Mr H.H.Ward for the 32MX360512L PIC
3   Dated 08/07/2020*/
4   #include <xc.h>
5   #include <config72M36MNoWDTNoJTAG.h>
6   //Declare any definitions
7   #define REDlamp      _RA0
8   #define AMBERlamp    PORTAbits.RA1
9   #define GREENlamp    _RA2
10  //Declare any global variables
11  unsigned char n;
12  //set up all subroutines
13  void delay (unsigned char t)
14  {
15  for (n = 0; n < t; n ++ )
16  {
17  TMR1 = 0;
18  while (TMR1 <35160);
19  }
20  }
21  void main ()
22  {
23  PORTA = 0;
```

```
24  PORTB = 0;
25  PORTC = 0;
26  PORTD = 0;
27  PORTE = 0;
28  TRISA = 0;
29  T1CON = 0X8030;
30  AD1CON1 = 0;
31  DDPCONbits.JTAGEN = 0;
32  while (1)
33  {
34  REDlamp = 1;
35  delay (20);
36  AMBERlamp = 1;
37  delay (8);
38  REDlamp = 0;
39  AMBERlamp = 0;
40  GREENlamp = 1;
41  delay (20);
42  GREENlamp = 0;
43  AMBERlamp = 1;
44  delay (8);
45  AMBERlamp = 0;
46  }
47  }
```

Analysis of Listing 2-3

There are no real new instructions, so the analysis can be brief. The program is using the variable delay subroutine that has a resolution of 0.25s. This is fine as we are using a 5s and a 2s delay.

The only new items are the definitions on lines 7, 8, and 9. With these definitions, we are declaring suitable phrases to be associated with particular inputs. For example:

```
#define REDlamp _RA0
```

This tells the compiler software that wherever the phrase "REDlamp" is used in the program, it really stands for the bit 0 of PORTA. There is no semicolon at the end of the definition as this is not a program instruction. Also, I have used two methods of identifying individual bits on the ports. The "_RA0" identifies bit 0 of PORTA. An alternative method is with "PORTAbits.RA1". This identifies bit 1 of PORTA.

This idea of using definitions makes the program more readable and also makes it easier to change the inputs if we want to. All we need to do is change them in these definitions, instead of finding all instances, in the program, where the inputs have been used. As we go further into our experience of programming PICs, we will use this definition aspect for interesting applications.

You will also see that lines 23–27 simply load the value "0" to all the ports. This is just a bit of safety, in that all the bits are set to logic '0', so as to make sure nothing is accidentally turned on when we first turn the PIC on. This is just good practice.

Downloading the Program to a Prototype Board

It would be useful, at this point, to show you how to download your program to an actual PIC on a prototype board. There are a range of prototype boards you can use. One that I use for my programs is from Microchip, and it is the explorer 16 development board. To connect to the board, I normally use the ICD3 can. These can be found on the Microchip website. However, to use any programming tool, you must specify which hardware tool you want to use, as shown in Figure 2-9, if you are using version 5.40, when you create your project in the first place. However, if you have already created your project, you can change the hardware tool by right-clicking the project name in the project view tree. You should then see a fly-out window appear, from which you can select the option Set Configuration. Then select the Customize option from the fly-out window that appears, as shown in Figure 2-10.

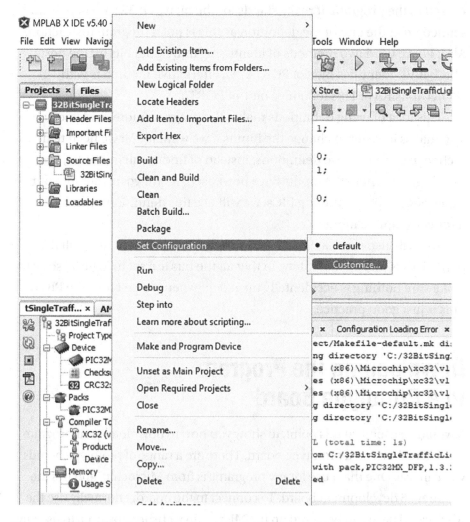

Figure 2-10. *The Project Properties Window in Version 5.5*

You will then be presented with the Project Properties window, as shown in Figure 2-11. You should be able to select the tool you are using as shown in Figure 2-11. This assumes you have already connected it to the laptop.

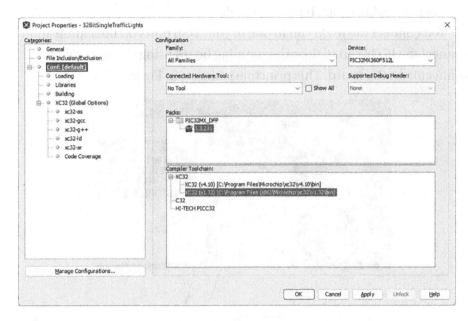

Figure 2-11. *The Project Properties Window in MPLAB X 5.40*

Having made sure you have selected your programming tool and connected it to your prototype board, you can download the program to the PIC by clicking the green down arrow from the main menu bar as shown in Figure 2-12. When we were using the simulator tool, these two arrows were not available to us before.

Figure 2-12. *The Download Arrow*

The following picture should help show how to connect the ICD3 can to the PIC prototype board and the laptop. For most of my practical downloads, I use the explorer 16 development board from Microchip. There are other boards you can use, but I know this one is very useful. You will have to decide which board you prefer.

You connect the ICD3 can to one of your USB ports on the laptop and connect the ICD3 can to the programming board using the RJ11 cable connector on the board. This principle is shown in Figure 2-13.

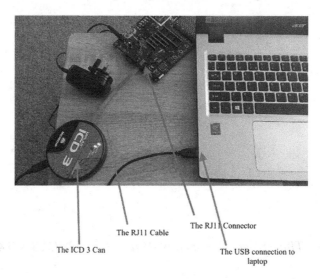

The RJ11 Cable

The RJ11 Connector

The ICD 3 Can

The USB connection to laptop

Figure 2-13. *Downloading to a Prototype Board*

Extending the Program to the Crossroads Traffic Lights

The natural extension to this single traffic light program would be to write a program that models the full crossroads set of traffic lights, that is, both the North-South and the East-West set of lights. The timing sequence for this task is shown in Figure 2-14.

The sequence would be as follows:

Note N/S lamps are numbered Red1, Amber1, and Green1, whereas E/W lamps are numbered Red2, Amber2, and Green2.

- The sequence starts with both red lamps on.

- Then five seconds later, Amber1 comes on as well.

- Then two seconds later, Red1 and Amber1 go out, and Green1 comes on.

- Then five seconds later, Green1 goes out, and Amber1 comes back on.

- Then two seconds later, Amber1 goes out, and Red1 comes back on.

- Note all this time Red2 has been on.

- Now one second later, Amber2 comes on as well.

- Then two seconds later, Red2 and Amber2 go out, and Green2 comes on.

- Then five seconds later, Green2 goes out, and Amber2 comes back on.

- Then two seconds later, Amber2 goes out, and Red2 comes back on.

- Note all this time Red1 has been on.

- The cycle now repeats.

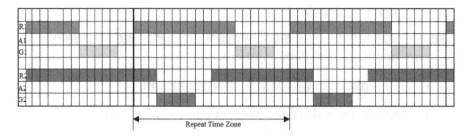

Figure 2-14. *The Timing Diagram for the Crossroads Traffic Lights*

The Algorithm

The diagram shown in Figure 2-14 was created from the sequence for the traffic lights. Each of the rectangles represents one second in time. Once the timing diagram had been created, it became clear that the 20-second period shown in Figure 2-14, as repeat time zone, was, as its name suggests, repeated every 20 seconds. This then means that the only sequence that needed to be programmed was the sequence listed between these repeat time zone periods.

The next step was to list all the important time steps and what we need to have happened at those times. The list is as follows:

- **Time0**: This is the start time in the sequence, and at this time, both Red1 and Red2 should come on.

- **Time1**: This is one second later, and at this time, Amber2 should come.

- **Time2**: This is two seconds after time1, and at this time, Amber2 and Red2 should go out, and Green2 should turn on.

- **Time3**: This is five seconds after time2, and at this time, Green2 turns off, and Amber2 comes back on again.

- **Time4**: This is two seconds after time3, and at this time, Amber2 turns off, and Red2 turns back on again.

- **Time5**: This is one second after time4, and at this time, Amber1 is turned on.

- **Time6**: This is two seconds after time5, and this is when Red1, which has been lit all this time, is turned off, and Amber1 turns off. At the same time, Green1 is turned on.

- **Time7**: This is five seconds after time6, and at this time, Green1 turns off, and Amber1 turns back on again.

- **Time8**: This is two seconds after time7, and at this time, Amber1 turns off, and the cycle goes back to time0 and starts to repeat the whole sequence.

The program has to create these time steps and turn on and off the appropriate lights at those times.

The program needs six outputs to connect the six lamps. Note there will actually be 12 lamps, but the North and South work together, and so do the East and West lamps.

There is no real need for an input, but we will include a start switch that starts the whole sequence.

The program will make use of a variable delay to create the various time steps.

The next step is to draw the flowchart that is shown in Figure 2-15.

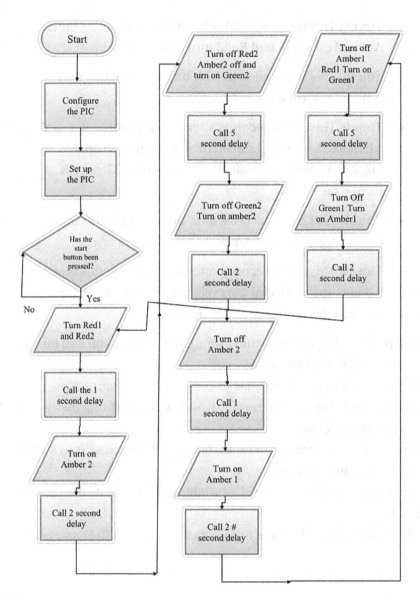

Figure 2-15. *The Flowchart for the Crossroads Traffic Light Program*

The program listing for the crossroads traffic light is shown in
Listing 2-4.

Listing 2-4. The Crossroads Traffic Lights

```
1   /*This is a program to control a crossroads set of
    traffic lights.
2   It is written by Mr H.H.Ward for the 32MX360512L PIC
3   Dated 08/07/2020*/
4   #include <xc.h>
5   #include <config72M36MNoWDTNNoJTAG.h>
6   //Declare any definitions
7   #define RED1      _RA0
8   #define AMBER1    _RA1
9   #define GREEN1    _RA2
10  #define RED2      _RA3
11  #define AMBER2    _RA4
12  #define GREEN2    _RA5
13  #define startButton    _RD6
14  //Declare any global variables
15  unsigned char n;
16  //set up all subroutines
17  void delay (unsigned char t)
18  {
19  for (n = 0; n < t; n ++ )
20  {
        a   TMR1 = 0;
        b   while (TMR1 <35050);
21  }
22  }
```

```
23  void main ()
24  {
25  PORTA = 0;
26  PORTB = 0;
27  PORTC = 0;
28  PORTD = 0;
29  PORTE = 0;
30  TRISA = 0;
31  TRISD = 0X00FF;
32  T1CON = 0X8030;
33  AD1CON1 = 0;
34  DDPCONbits.JTAGEN = 0;
35  while (startButton);
36  while (1)
37  {
         a   RED1 = 1;
         b   RED2 = 1;
         c   delay (4);
         d   AMBER2 = 1;
         e   delay (8);
         f   RED2 = 0;
         g   AMBER2 = 0;
         h   GREEN2 = 1;
         i   delay (20);
         j   GREEN2 = 0;
         k   AMBER2 = 1;
         l   delay (8);
         m   AMBER2 = 0;
         n   RED2 = 1;
         o   delay (4);
         p   AMBER1 = 1;
```

```
      q  delay (8);
      r  RED1 = 0;
      s  AMBER1 = 0;
      t  GREEN1 = 1;
      u  delay (20);
      v  GREEN1 = 0;
      w  AMBER1 = 1;
      x  delay (8);
      y  AMBER1 = 0;
38  }
39  }
```

Analysis of Listing 2-4

There is not much that is new in this program. The only items worth
discussing are

Line 13 #define startButton _RD6

This simply uses the #define statement to associate the phrase
"startButton" with bit 6 of PORTD. I have used this bit as the start button
because the three of the four buttons on the explorer 16 development
board are connected to PORTD, bits 6, 7, and 13. The other button is
connected to bit 7 of PORTA. If the switches on your board are connected
to different inputs, then you would have to change these bit allocation
types of instructions accordingly.

Line 31 TRISD = 0XFFFF;

This sets all the bits of PORTD as inputs.

Line 35 while (startButton);

This is using the phrase "startButton," which the compiler reads as bit 6 of PORTD. As there is no other reference within the normal brackets, then this means the test is true while the logic on bit 6 of PORTD is a logic '1'. This will be so if we do not press the button connected to bit 6 of PORTD. The way the switches are wired on the explorer 16 development board is that if you press the switch, you will take the input down to 0V, which is a logic '0'. If they are not pressed, the logic on the input will be a logic '1'. Therefore, with this instruction, we are getting the PIC to do nothing while the "startButton" has not been pressed. Note, there are no instructions between the closing normal bracket and the semicolon ";". We are waiting for the start button to go low.

Line 36 while (1)

This sets up a forever loop which will prevent the PIC from carrying out the instructions from lines 23 to 36 again, as there is no need for the PIC to carry out these instructions again.

I hope you can understand how the instructions work and how the program does model a set of traffic lights at a simple crossroads.

Simulating the Program Within MPLAB X

It is difficult to simulate programs that use subroutines within MPLAB X. However, if we comment out all the calls to the subroutines in this crossroads traffic lights, then we can get a good idea of how the program would work.

To comment out the call to the delay subroutine, all we need to do is add the two forward slashes in front of all the call instructions. This is done as shown here:

```
// delay (4);
```

The compiler will now ignore these instructions.

Indeed, you can comment out any instruction in this way. This may be a helpful thing to do when debugging a program.

When we started this project, we set the tool to the ICD3 can; see Figure 2-9. Now we need to change the tool that we have selected for the project to "simulator." The process for doing this is described here. However, if you are not using version 5.40 of MPLAB X, the properties window will be slightly different. The new window is shown in Figure 2-16.

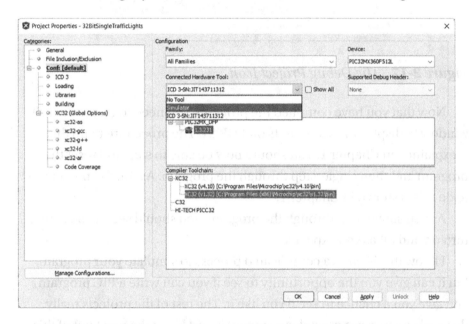

Figure 2-16. *The Project Properties Window in Version 5.40*

To select the properties window, you need to click the right-hand mouse while placing the mouse on the project name in the project tree window. You should then see a fly-out window from which you can select the term "properties." However, since writing this chapter, I have moved to version 5.50, and now you need to select the term "Set Configuration" and then customize from the second fly-out window.

To change the tool, you simply need to select the tool you want to use, which in this case would be the simulator, as highlighted in Figure 2-16; you simply need to select Apply and then OK.

Note with this properties window, you can also change other properties such as the compiler.

Once you have changed the tool and commented out the subroutine calls, you should compile the program using the Debug Project icon on the main menu. This is shown in Figure 2-17.

Figure 2-17. *The Debug Project Icon*

Now that you have compiled the program, you need to create the I/O window to display the six outputs on PORTA. The procedure to do this is explained in Chapter 1. You should now be able to stop and reset the program and then single-step through the program. Again, the procedure to do this is shown in Chapter 1.

As you single-step through the program, you should see the outputs turn on and off as you expected.

I know this is quite a complicated process to simulate your program, but it can give you the opportunity to see if you can write a PIC program and give you a chance to see if you like it. The rest of the projects really do need you to buy a good development board to get the most out of this book. However, if you like what you have done, so far, then I think the cost would be a very good investment, as there are lots of opportunities for embedded programmers, and it can be very well paid.

Figure 2-18 shows the traffic light program working with a pair of LED boards I have made on the veroboard. They are connected to the explorer 16 development board using the expansion boards I have purchased to extend the explorer 16 development board.

Figure 2-18. *The Traffic Light Program Working with a Set of LEDS on the Veroboard*

Summary

In this chapter, we have learned how to create a delay – a very useful process. We have studied the difference between local and global variables. We then learned how the "for do loop" works and how we can use both local and global variables, in a subroutine, to make a variable delay.

We have learned how we can use the keyword #define to define phrases to represent useful I/O in a PIC program. We have studied how to create a program controlling a set of traffic lights and how to download that program to a development board.

In the next chapter, we will look at using the seven-segment display.

CHAPTER 3

The Seven-Segment Display

In this chapter, we will look at using the PIC to control the display on a seven-segment display. We will look at what the seven-segment display is and the principle upon which it works.

We will then write a program to display a count going from 0 to 9 and then showing the hexadecimal characters A, B, C, D, E, and F. We will look at creating an array and learn why and how we use them.

After reading this chapter, you will understand what a seven-segment display is. You will know the difference between the common anode and common cathode and how to use the PIC to control both types.

Controlling a Seven-Segment Display

The Seven-Segment Display

This is a device that can be used to display numbers, so it can be used to create a display for a digital clock. A typical seven-segment display is shown in Figure 3-1.

© Hubert Ward 2023
H. Ward, *Introductory Programs with the 32-bit PIC Microcontroller*,
Maker Innovations Series, https://doi.org/10.1007/978-1-4842-9051-4_3

Figure 3-1. *A Typical Seven-Segment Display*

There are seven LEDs, light-emitting diodes, in a display, hence the name seven-segment display. Some displays have an extra LED for the decimal place, or dot. The LEDs can be switched on in different arrangements to display the numbers 0–9 and, if required, the letters A, B, C, D, E, and F, as in the hexadecimal number system. We can get red, green, blue, yellow, and white LEDs, as well as extra bright LEDs.

LEDs have an anode terminal and a cathode terminal. These terminals are sometimes labeled "A" and "K," as C can stand for capacitance or coulomb. Electrical current can only flow one way through the diode, and conventional current flows from the anode to cathode. To make the current flow through the LED, the anode voltage must be around 2.2V higher than the cathode.

There are two main types of seven-segment displays which are common anode and common cathode.

Common Anode Seven-Segment Display

With this type of seven-segment display, the anodes of all seven LEDs are usually connected to a +5V supply. To turn an LED on, the cathode must be connected, independently, to ground or 0V. A resistor is inserted between the cathode and ground to limit the current that flows through the LEDs, to prevent it from destroying itself. This arrangement is shown in Figure 3-2.

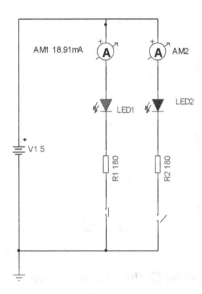

Figure 3-2. *The Basic Circuit to Turn on an LED in Common Anode*

In Figure 3-2, LED1 is shown illuminated as its cathode is switched to ground. LED2 is off as its cathode is not switched to ground. The 180Ω resistor is there to limit the current flowing through the LEDs.

Common Cathode Seven-Segment Display

With this type of seven-segment display, the cathodes of all seven LEDs are usually connected to a 0V supply. To turn each LED on, the anode of each LED can be connected, independently, to a +5V supply. This arrangement is shown in Figure 3-3.

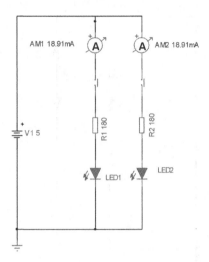

Figure 3-3. *The Common Cathode Arrangement*

We will use the PIC to control when each LED is switched on. However, some seven-segment displays come with their own driver circuit that takes a 4-bit binary count and sets the display accordingly.

We will connect the display to PORTA and use the output from PORTA to turn on and off the LEDs appropriately.

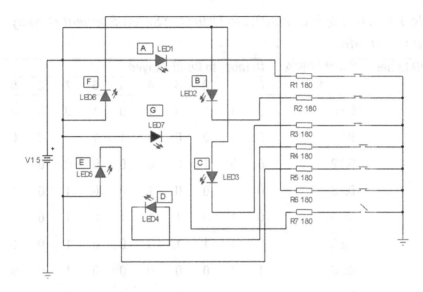

Figure 3-4. *The Circuit of a Common Anode Seven-Segment Display*

Figure 3-4 is an attempt to show you the circuitry of the common anode display. The seven LEDs are laid out to form a ring, going from LED "A" to LED "F" in six LEDs. Then there is the seventh LED, LED "G," that lies central to the display. Figure 3-4 shows the six outer LEDs turned on by closing their respective switches to connect their respective cathodes to ground, or 0V, via the series resistor. This means those six LEDs are switched on, and current flows through them. It is hoped that you can see that this forms the number zero.

Controlling the Display with the PIC

When we use the PIC to control the display, there would be no switches, and we would connect R1 to bit 0 of PORTA, R2 to bit 1, and so on, with R7 connected to bit 6. To turn on the respective LED, we would load a logic '0', or 0V, onto the bit. To switch the respective LED off, we would load a logic '1', or +5V, onto the bit. In this way, the numbers 0–9 can be controlled from PORTA as shown in Table 3-1. Table 3-2 shows the binary values to display the letters A to F on the seven-segment display.

Table 3-1. *The Logic at PORTA to Drive the Seven-Segment Display Common Anode*

LED ID Letter	Bit of PORTA	Number to Be Displayed									
		0	1	2	3	4	5	6	7	8	9
A	Bit 0	0	1	0	0	1	0	1	0	0	0
B	Bit 1	0	0	0	0	0	1	1	0	0	0
C	Bit 2	0	0	1	0	0	0	0	0	0	0
D	Bit 3	0	1	0	0	1	0	0	1	0	1
E	Bit 4	0	1	0	1	1	1	0	1	0	1
F	Bit 5	0	1	1	1	0	0	0	1	0	0
G	Bit 6	1	1	0	0	0	0	0	1	0	0
DOT	Bit 7	0	0	0	0	0	0	0	0	0	0

If the display has a decimal point, then bit 7 would turn it on or off. The table shows how the PIC can control the display.

Table 3-2. *The Logic to Display the Letters A–F*

LED ID Letter	Bit of PORTA	A	B	C	D	E	F
A	Bit 0	0	0	0	0	1	0
B	Bit 1	0	0	1	0	0	1
C	Bit 2	0	0	1	0	0	0
D	Bit 3	1	1	0	0	1	0
E	Bit 4	0	1	0	1	1	1
F	Bit 5	0	1	0	1	0	0
G	Bit 6	0	1	1	0	0	0
DOT	Bit 7	0	0	0	0	0	0

The Seven-Segment Display Program

This program is simply to get a seven-segment display to count up from 0 to 9. The count will increment every two seconds.

The Algorithm

There is no defined format of how you construct the algorithm. I just like to create a bullet list as follows:

- We will need to write a subroutine to create a delay. We will make it a variable delay. The program will simply increment the number displayed on the display every two seconds from 0 to 9.

- The delay subroutine will require a global variable "n" and a local variable "t."

- When the display gets to 9, the display will go back to 0 at the next increment.

- To initiate the start of the count, the program will wait for a start button to be momentarily pressed to logic '0'. The program will start the count with the display set at 0.

- There will be a stop button that if pressed will halt the count at the current value on the display.

- The program will include the header file for the configuration words that we have already created in Chapter 2.

- We will need two digital inputs for the two switches and seven outputs to control the seven-segment display. We will connect the display to PORTA.

- There is no need for any analog inputs; therefore, we don't need to turn the ADC on.

- We will use the 8MHz crystal for the clock source.

- There is no need for anything else, so really a basic 8-pin PIC will do the job. However, this book is based on the 32-bit PIC, so we will be using the 32MX360F512L PIC.

Note, I have added the last item in the list to try and show you that you can use the algorithm to decide which PIC you should use for your project. This could save money. You must remember that in the industry, your project could go into production, and if you can save 10p by choosing a more basic PIC, then you should.

The Flowchart

It is always a good idea to construct a flowchart for your programs. However, as this book is really aimed at explaining how the C code works, this will be the last flowchart in this book. This flowchart uses the decision box to ask if the start or stop button has been pressed. If written correctly, each block of the flowchart should link clearly to its corresponding set of instructions in the program listing.

The flowchart for this program is shown in Flowchart 3-1.

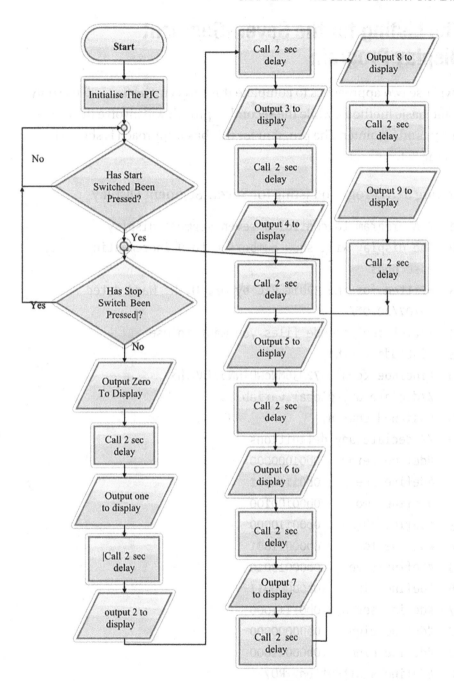

Flowchart 3-1. *The Flowchart for Listing 3-1*

The Listing for the Seven-Segment Display Program

I will use two approaches to complete this project. The first will use only some basic methods, while the second approach will involve the use of arrays and a pointer. The program for this basic approach is shown in Listing 3-1.

Listing 3-1. Program Listing for Seven-Segment Display

```
1   /*A program to control a seven segment display
2   The display will show numbers 0 to 9 incrementing every
    2 seconds
3   Written for the 32bit PIC by Mr. H. H. Ward dated
    09/07/2020*/
4   //List any include files you want to use
5   #include <xc.h>
6   #include <config72M36MNoWDTNNoJTAG.h>
7   //declare any global variables
8   unsigned char n;
9   // declare any definitions
10  #define zero      0b01000000
11  #define one       0b01111001
12  #define two       0b00100100
13  #define three     0b00110000
14  #define four      0b00011001
15  #define five      0b00010010
16  #define six       0b00000011
17  #define seven     0b01111000
18  #define eight     0b00000000
19  #define nine      0b00011000
20  #define startButton _RD7
```

```
21   #define stopButton _RD6
22   //declare any subroutines
23   void delay250 (unsigned char t)
24   {
25   for (n = 0; n < t; n++)
26   {
27   TMR1 = 0;
28   while (TMR1 < 35160);
29   }
30   }
31   void main ()
32   {
33   PORTA = 0;
34   PORTB = 0;
35   PORTC = 0;
36   PORTD = 0;
37   PORTE = 0;
38   TRISA = 0;
39   TRISD = 0x00FF;
40   T1CON = 0X8030;
41   AD1CON1 = 0;
42   DDPCONbits.JTAGEN = 0;
43   start: while (startButton);
44   while (1)
45   {
46   if (!stopButton) goto start;
47   PORTA = zero;
48   delay250 (8);
49   PORTA = one;
50   delay250 (8);
51   PORTA = two;
```

```
52  delay250 (8);
53  PORTA = three;
54  delay250 (8);
55  PORTA = four;
56  delay250 (8);
57  PORTA = five;
58  delay250 (8);
59  PORTA = six;
60  delay250 (8);
61  PORTA = seven;
62  delay (8);
63  PORTA = eight;
64  delay250 (8);
65  PORTA = nine;
66  delay250 (8);
67  }
68  }
```

Analysis of Listing 3-1

I hope you can appreciate that there is only one new instruction. This will be analyzed here.

Lines 10–19 are used to define the phrases "zero" to "nine" to represent the binary values that need to be sent to the seven-segment display to show the appropriate number. Wherever the compiler sees these phrases, in the program listing, it will know to use the appropriate binary value, instead of the actual phrase, when it downloads the program. This will make the listing easier to read and program. For example, the phrase "one" is easier to understand than 0b01111001, and there is less chance of making a mistake than with the binary value. These phrases are used as in line 47, etc.

It is good practice to use these definitions in this way. We will see more use of the #define in later programs.

Line 48 and others call the delay250(8) subroutine and send the value "8." This will create the two-second delay we want, as 8 quarters make 2.

Line 43 start: while (startButton);

The colon ":" after the word "start" is used to show the compiler that this is a label. We will get the PIC to go back to this label, later in the program; see line 46. The instruction here will simply make the PIC wait until the "startButton" has been pressed. The principle is that while the logic on the "startButton" is high, at a logic '1', the PIC does nothing.

Line 46 if (!stopButton) goto start;

This is using the "if (this test is true) do what I say." There could also be an "else do this" type of statement, but, as in this case, it is not always required. If we don't include an "else statement," then the program just carries on with the rest of the program.

The test, which can either be true or untrue, is described between the normal set of brackets. The test "!stopButton" is using the NOT symbol, which, in C, is the exclamation mark "!". So it reads NOT "stopButton," and it is really testing to see if the logic on the "stopButton," which has been defined on line 21 as bit 6 of PORTD, has gone to a logic '0'. If it is a logic '0', then the test will be true, and the PIC should carry out the one-line instruction, that is, "goto start." This will force the PIC to go to the label "start" which has been declared on line 43.

Figure 3-5. *The Seven-Segment Display*

Figure 3-5 shows the seven-segment display program working. I
have used a board, upon which I have built four seven-segment displays.
However, I am just using one of the displays. The board includes the
220Ω resistors that are used to limit the current flowing through each of
the LEDs.

Improving the Seven-Segment Display Program

There is an issue with this program in how it works. If you run the program,
you may determine what the issue is. It should become apparent when you
press the stop button to stop the display. Try running the program a few
times and see if you do recognize the problem.

Not to worry, I will explain what the problem is and go through a
program that avoids it, or at least is an improvement for it, in this section of
the chapter.

The Problem with the Program

I hope that after running the program a few times, you would have realized that you have to hold the stop button for at least 2 seconds, if not 20 seconds, before the program stops the display from incrementing. Also, the display always stops with the display showing the number 9.

The reason why this happens is because the instruction that looks as the stop button is on line 46, and if you are not pressing the stop button, when the micro carries out the instruction on this line, then the micro will not notice you have pressed the stop button. Also, it won't look at this instruction again until it has gone through all the other lines. Then, after reaching line 66, it loops back to line 46 via lines 44 and 45. The micro will then see that you have pressed the stop button, assuming you are still pressing it, and go to the label "start:". Not very good programming.

One way around this issue would be to insert this instruction, if (!stopButton) goto start;, after each of the calls to the delay subroutine. This method is called software polling, where you continually keep asking the same question. This approach is not the most efficient as it wastes a lot of time checking the stop switch, in this case, even if it hasn't been pressed. It also wastes a lot of memory in writing the same instruction many times.

One solution we will look at involves some new instructions using arrays and pointers. It will save memory and speed up the response of the program.

Arrays

This is a method by which you can create a list of variables and store them in locations one after the other. Then use them sequentially one at a time or randomly. It is very much like a lookup table. It is very important to appreciate the memory locations are set up one after the other, in order, when the program is compiled and downloaded to the PIC. The array can store a variable using all the common data types, that is, unsigned char, integer, float, etc.

To create an array, you simply declare it using the data type you want to use, then give it a sensible name followed by the "[5]" square bracket. Inside the square bracket, you state how many memory locations you want to place in your array. When the compiler compiles the program, it will place the start of the array in a memory location and then create the total number of memory locations, immediately after the start location, one after the other. Each location will have its own reference number with the first location having the reference 0. If, as in this example, the array had five memory locations, they would be referenced as 0, 1, 2, 3, and 4.

You can use any variable, of the correct data type, and load it with a copy of the contents in the array by making reference to it as follows:

```
data5 = inputStore [3];
```

The term "data5" is a global variable of the same type in the array. You would have declared, earlier, the term "inputStore" as the name of the array. Assuming the array has the following values stored in the array:

Array Reference	Data Stored
0	0b11000001
1	0b00011111
2	0b11100000
3	0b11111111
4	0b00011110

Then, after this instruction, the value in data5 would be 0b11111111.

Loading Values into an Array

You can set up an array and then load the array with values by making reference to the location in the array. An example of this would be

```
inputStore [3] = 0b11111111;
```

This would load the fourth location of the array with the value 0b11111111, or 0xFF.

Another approach would be to assign values to the array when you declare it. An example of this would be

```
inputStore [5] =
{
    0b11000001,
    0b00011111,
    0b11100000,
    0b11111111,
    0b00011110,
};
```

It is the "=" equal sign after the declaration of the array that tells the compiler we want to load each location with the data that follows. Each item has to be placed between the two curly brackets, and the closing bracket finishes with the semicolon. This is because this denotes the end of the complete instruction.

Also, each item finishes with a comma, as this is a list of values. You could place the complete instruction on the same line, but I prefer to write it out as shown.

I think it is appropriate that I should inform you that when you declare an ordinary variable, you could load it with an initial value also, using a similar approach. An example would be

```
unsigned char data1 = 8;
```

This creates an 8-bit memory location for the variable which we will call "data1" and loads an initial value of 8 into it. This 8-bit value would be 0b00001000 in 8-bit binary. There is a section in the appendix that goes through how to change a decimal to binary and hexadecimal and more.

Using Pointers

Pointers can be used to point to locations inside an array. To create a pointer, it is best to create an array, then create the pointer with the same name and type as the array. This is best explained by going through an example instruction as shown in Listing 3-2. With this example, we will create an array called "inputDataStore" that has eight locations. We will create a pointer to point to locations within the array. We will use two global variables that we will load with data from the array. The listing for the array example is shown in Listing 3-2.

Listing 3-2. The Listing for the Array and Pointer Example

```
1   unsigned int inputDataStore [8] =
2   {
3       0,
4       1,
5       2,
6       3,
7       4,
8       5,
9       6,
10  7,
11  };
12  unsigned int *inputDataPointer;
13  unsigned int info0, info1;
14      inputDataPointer = inputDataStore;
```

```
15  info0 = *inputDataPointer;
16  inputDataPointer++;
17  info1 = *inputDataPointer;
18      inputDataPointer++;
```

Analysis of Listing 3-2

Line 1 unsigned int inputDataStore [8]=;

This creates an array of eight locations one after the other, each being a 16-bit memory location, as we are using the data type unsigned int. The "=" at the end of the instruction tells the compiler that we want to load the eight locations in the array with the data that is listed between the opening and closing curly brackets on lines 2 and 11.

Lines 3–10 list the initial data we want to store in the eight locations in the array. Note, we place a comma after each value, as this is a list of data. The values are stated using the default radix of decimal, as no indication of any other radix is shown.

Line 12 unsigned int *inputDataPointer;

This creates a memory location that can be loaded with the particular address of a location in the array "inputDataStore." The "*" is to tell the compiler that this is not a simple variable; it is a "pointer" that will point to an address in an array.

Line 13 unsigned int info0, info1;

This creates two global variables that are 16-bit long. We will load these variables with copies of data from the array.

Line 14 inputDataPointer = inputDataStore;

This tells the compiler to load the pointer "inputDataPointer" with the address of the first location in the array "inputDataStore."

Line 15 info0 = inputDataPointer;

With this instruction, the micro will load a copy of what is stored in the first location of the array "inputDataStore" into "info0." This is because in the previous instruction, we made the pointer, "inputDataPointer," point to that memory location in the array.

Line 16 inputDataPointer ++;

This increments the value in the "inputDataPointer" by one. This means that as the information in the "inputDataPointer," before this instruction, was the address of the first location in the array "inputDataStore," then by incrementing it, the pointer "inputDataPointer" is now pointing to the second memory location in the array "inputDataStore."

Line 17 info1 = inputDataPointer;

With this instruction, the micro will load a copy of what is stored in the second location of the array "inputDataStore" into "info1."

Line 18 inputDataPointer ++;

This does the same as line 16, in that it simply adds 1 to the value stored in the "inputDataPointer." This means that the pointer is now pointing to the next location in the array.

This is a simple one-dimensional array. You can create two-dimensional arrays that have columns and rows, but we will look at that in Chapter 5.

I hope this goes some way to explaining what an array is. The following program is an example of how to set up and use an array.

The Improved Program

In this program, we will see how, by using arrays, we can program the counting sequence from before in a more efficient manner.

The listing for the program is shown in Listing 3-3.

Listing 3-3. The Improved Seven-Segment Listing

```
1   /*An improved program to control a seven segment display
2   The display will show numbers 0 to 9 incrementing every
    2 seconds
3   Written for the 32bit PIC by Mr. H. H. Ward dated 09/07/2020*/
4   //List any include files you want to use
5   #include <xc.h>
6   #include <config72M36MNoWDTNoJTAG.h>
7   //declare any global variables
8   unsigned char n, m;
9   // declare any definitions
10  #define zero     0b01000000
11  #define one      0b01111001
12  #define two      0b00100100
13  #define three    0b00110000
14  #define four     0b00011001
15  #define five     0b00010010
16  #define six      0b00000011
17  #define seven    0b01111000
18  #define eight    0b00000000
19  #define nine      0b00011000
20  #define startButton _RD6
21  #define stopButton _RD7
22  unsigned int sevenDisplay [10] =
23  {
```

```
24   zero,
25   one,
26   two,
27   three,
28   four,
29   five,
30   six,
31   seven,
32   eight,
33   nine,
34   };
35   unsigned int *displayPointer;
36   //declare any subroutines
37   void delay250 (unsigned char t)
38   {
39   for (n = 0; n < t; n++)
40   {
41   TMR1 = 0;
42   while (TMR1 < 35050);
43   }
44   }
45   void main ()
46   {
47   PORTA = 0;
48   PORTB = 0;
49   PORTC = 0;
50   PORTD = 0;
51   PORTE = 0;
52   TRISA = 0;
53   TRISD = OX00FF;
54   T1CON = OX8030;
55   AD1CON1 = 0;
```

```
56  DDPCONbits.JTAGEN = 0;
57  start: while (startButton);
58  while (1)
59  {
60  displayPointer = sevenDisplay;
61  for (m = 0; m <10; m ++ )
62  {
63  if (!stopButton) goto start;
64  PORTA = *displayPointer;
65  displayPointer ++;
66  delay250 (8);
67  }
68  }
69  }
```

I hope you can appreciate that the only new instruction starts at line 22 which is

Line 22 unsigned int sevenDisplay [10] =

This sets up an array, called "sevenDisplay," which has ten memory locations. However, the equal sign "=" means that the following lines dictate what is initially loaded into those ten memory locations.

The values to be used are listed between the following two curly brackets. However, to make them more readable, we are using the phrases defined in lines 10–19 before.

In line 24, we are placing a copy, in the first location in the array, of the 8-bit binary number to display "zero" on the seven-segment display, as defined on line 10.

The remaining values are stored in the following lines.

One more thing you should note is that line 34 is

```
};
```

where the semicolon is added to indicate this is the end of the instruction, as this is a list of values to be stored in the array. That is also why there is a comma after each of the phrases in the list.

Line 35 unsigned int *displayPointer;

This is where we create the pointer that we will use to point to individual memory locations in the array. Note you don't have to use the phrase Pointer as part of the name, it is just my preference.

Lines 37–44 create our variable delay, which we have created previously.

Line 58 creates the forever loop, and line 59 is the opening curly bracket of that loop.

Line 60 displayPointer = sevenDisplay;

This loads the "displayPointer" with the address of the first memory location in the array "sevenDisplay." This gets the displayPointer ready for the instruction on line 64.

Line 61 for (m = 0; m <10; m ++)

This sets up the "for do loop" that controls what data is sent to the display connected to PORTA. Note we must use a different variable than "n" as "n" is used in the "delay" subroutine that this "for do loop" calls within it. Note, in line 8, we declared the variable "m" as an unsigned char.

Line 62 {

This is the opening curly bracket of the "for do loop."

Line 63 if (stopButton) goto start;

Here, we are checking to see if the stop button has been pressed. If it has been pressed, the program will jump back to the "start" label on line 57, where the program then waits for the start button to be pressed. If the stop button has not been pressed, the program moves on to the next line.

Line 64 PORTA = *displayPointer;

This loads a copy of the data in the memory location in the array "sevenDisplay," which the pointer, "displayPointer," is pointing to, into PORTA. As this is the first run through the "for do loop," then the data will be the 8-bit binary value for "zero" (see lines 24–33), and so the display will show the number 0. As we run through the "for do loop" until n = 10, we will display the numbers 0–9 on the seven-segment display.

Line 64   displayPointer ++;

This increments the value in the "displayPointer" by 1. This means that the pointer will now be pointing to the next memory location in the array "sevenDisplay." This then gets the data for "one" to be displayed next.

Line 65   delay250 (8);

This calls the "delay" subroutine and sends the value 8 to be copied into the local variable "t" in the subroutine. This creates a two-second delay.

Line 66   }

This is the closing bracket of the "for do loop."

You should create a new project named "sevenSegImproved" with a source file also named "sevenSegImproved.c". Then write the instructions listed in Listing 3-3. You should see that as you run it, there is an improvement on the first program. Note you can stop the display on any number possible.

I hope you can see that we are actually checking the stop button after each time we display a number on the seven-segment display. This is the software polling that I mentioned earlier. This is not the most efficient method of doing this. It would be more efficient if we used interrupts. We will look at using interrupts in Chapter 8.

Exercise 3-1

I want you to speed up the change of display so that it takes around 30ms for the numbers to change. You might need to use a delay with a better resolution, that is, the 1ms delay from Chapter 2. Also, restrict the count to go from 1 to 6. Then run the new program. Having done that can you suggest what this new program may be used for.

Solution to Exercise 3-1

I hope you can see that this program could be used as an electronic dice.

Summary

In this chapter, we have learned about the seven-segment display and how you can use a PIC to control one. You have also become more familiar with the "while" and the "if" instructions. You have also learned how to use definitions to make the program more readable.

We have also looked at using arrays and the "for do loop" to reduce the number of instructions in a program.

In the next chapter, we will look at using a Liquid Crystal Display (LCD) to display messages and special characters.

CHAPTER 4

The LCD

In this chapter, we will look at using a Liquid Crystal Display (LCD) to display messages we want to send to it. We will then go on to learn how to create our own special characters and display them on the LCD.

After reading this chapter, you will understand what an LCD is and how we can use the PIC to write characters to it.

The 1602 LCD

We will use the LCD that is connected to the explorer 16 development board. This LCD is of the type 1602 as shown in Figure 4-1. We will use PORTE, as this is where the LCD is connected to the PIC with the explorer 16 development board. However, if you use a different PORT to connect your LCD to the PIC, then you would have to make some small changes to the header file for the LCD that we will create in this chapter. I will point them out to you as we analyze the program listings.

Figure 4-1. *The 1602 LCD, Liquid Crystal Display*

© Hubert Ward 2023
H. Ward, *Introductory Programs with the 32-bit PIC Microcontroller,*
Maker Innovations Series, https://doi.org/10.1007/978-1-4842-9051-4_4

The connections are listed in Table 4-1.

Table 4-1. *The Pin Usage for the 1602 LCD Module*

PIN N$_0$	PIN Usage
1	This is the ground or VSS pin
2	This is the +5V or VDD pin
3	This is the contrast pin which is the output of a variable resistor. Really, I set this pin to 0.3V via a voltage divider circuit
4	This is the RS pin. The logic on this pin allows the LCD to determine if the information being sent is an instruction (the RS pin is a logic '0') or data to be displayed (the RS pin is a logic '1')
5	This is the R/W pin. I simply connect this to ground for the "W" or write operation
6	This is the "E" pin. This is sent high and then low to tell the LCD new information has been sent
7	This is data pin D0
8	This is data pin D1
9	This is data pin D2
10	This is data pin D3
11	This is data pin D4
12	This is data pin D5
13	This is data pin D6
14	This is data pin D7
15	This is the anode of the LED
16	This is the cathode of the LED

Like most LCDs, it uses either the Samsung KS0066U or Hitachi HD44780 driver, which converts your binary digits into the required signals. It can be set up to use eight data lines or just four data lines. We will use it using eight data lines, as with this 32-bit PIC, the number of I/O, input and output, is not really a problem.

We can communicate with the LCD in either instruction mode or data mode.

Instruction or Command Mode

This is used to firstly initialize the LCD, that is, decide if we will operate it in 8-bit or 4-bit data mode, and other operational aspects. We then use the instruction mode to move the cursor positions, such as

- Send the cursor to line two.

- Shift the cursor to the right or left a number of characters.

- Move the cursor one bit to the right after each character or not.

- Send the cursor to the home position.

- Clear the screen.

- Blink or not blink the cursor.

Data Mode

The LCD is programmed to recognize characters using ASCII code for each character. Basically, the LCD has memory locations, which are nonvolatile; that is, the memory keeps the data even when the power is removed. In these memory locations, the pixel information to draw any one of the

ASCII characters is stored. The address of each of these memory locations, with the pixel maps for a character, corresponds to the same address found in the ASCII character standard table, shown in the appendix, for that particular character. For example, the address in the LCD's memory, where it stores the pixel map for the number "3," is 0x33 or 0b00110011. If you look at the ASCII character set, you will see that 0x33 is the ASCII for the number "3." Also, to display the character "a," you would send the information 0b01100001 to open up that location in the LCD's memory and find the pixel map for the letter "a." The number 0b01100001 is the ASCII for the letter "a." This is to make it a more logical action to display any character on the LCD.

In another program, in this chapter, that uses the LCD, we will look at creating our own characters to display on the LCD. We will need this level of understanding to be able to create our own characters.

The Control Pins of the LCD

There are four control pins on the LCD:

- RS pin
- E pin
- R/W pin
- VEE or V0 pin

The RS pin on the LCD is used to distinguish between instructions to the LCD and data to be displayed on the LCD. The RS pin goes to logic '0' for instructions and to a logic '1' for data to be displayed. We must make this happen with the instructions we write in our program.

The "E" pin is used to tell the driver inside the LCD that some new information has been sent to the LCD, and it should deal with it. This is done by simply sending this pin high, then back to low, with no delay, every time information is sent to the LCD.

The R/W pin is simply connected to 0V, as the W, or write, function is active low. This means that to write to the LCD, we need to set this pin to 0V. The "R" means "read," but there is no real need to use this function.

A variable voltage can be connected to the VEE pin of the LCD to control the contrast of the LCD. However, I find that using two resistors to divide the voltage down to around 300mV works fine.

The LCD on the explorer 16 development board is connected to PORTE. It is also connected to the Parallel Master Port, the PMP. However, with this first LCD program, we will not use the PMP. We will use the PMP in Chapter 6.

As we may use the LCD, connected to PORTE, with other projects with the 32-bit PIC, we will create a header file for it. We will make it a local header file and then save it in the compiler's include folder to make it global.

The LCD Header File for PORTE

We should create a new project for these LCD programs. Therefore, using the approach as described in Chapter 1, create a new project and call it "ourFirstLCDProject." You could use any name you think appropriate, but if you use my name, then it would be easier to refer to in the book. I will save it on the root directory, and I have used the XC32 version 1.32 compiler software. You could use the latest version, as we are not using any interrupts. However, when we move on to using interrupts, in Chapter 8, you may need this earlier version of the XC32 compiler. You should be able to download these earlier versions of the compiler software from the "Archive Section" of the Microchip website.

Once you have created the project, you will need to create a header file, by right-clicking the mouse on the term "Header Files" in the project tree. Then select "New" and then xc32_header... from the fly-out menus that appear. In the window that appears, give the file the name "LCDPORTE" and simply click "Finish" to accept the default location and close the window.

A new header file will appear in the text editing window. Microchip will include a lot of text and material that, for our purposes, we don't need. Therefore, you should delete all that content to give an empty file. You should then write the program listing in Listing 4-1 into the editing window.

Listing 4-1. The Header File for the LCD on PORTE

```
1  /*This is a header file for the 32bit to use an LCD
2  The LCD will be set up to use the full 8bit mode
3  It will display the cursor and increment it's position
   after each character is displayed
4  It will be connected to PORTE using RB15 as the RSPIN and
   RD4 as the E Bit
5  The R/W pin is connected to RD5
6  It was written By Mr G. H. Ward dated 26/07/2021 for the
   32MX360F512l
7  */
8  #define entryMode        0b00000110
9  #define displayCtl       0b00001110
10 #define functionSet      0b00111000
11 #define Clear_Screen     0b00000001
12 #define Return_Home      0b00000010
13 #define Line_2           0b11000000
14 #define ShiftLeft        0b00010000
15 #define ShiftRight       0b00010100
16 #define ShDisRight       0b00011100
17 #define lcdPort          PORTE
18 #define RSpin            PORTBbits.RB15
19 #define eBit             PORTDbits.RD4
20 #define LCDrwPin         PORTDbits.RD5
21 //variables
```

```
22  unsigned char lcdData, n,m;
23  unsigned char lcdInitialis [4] =
24  {
25  functionSet,
26  entryMode,
27  displayCtl,
28  Clear_Screen,
29  };
30  //subroutines
31  void sendData ()
32  {
33  lcdPort = lcdData;
34  eBit = 1;
35  eBit = 0;
36  TMR1 = 0; while (TMR1 < 380);
37  }
38  void setUpTheLCD ()
39  {
40  TMR1 = 0;
41  while( TMR1<6000);
42  RSpin = 0;
43  n = 0;
44  while (n < 4)
45  {
46  lcdData = lcdInitialis [n];
47  sendData ();
48  n ++;
49  }
50  RSpin = 1;
51  }
```

```
52  void line2 ()
53  {
54  RSpin = 0;
55  lcdData = Line_2;
56  sendData ();
57  RSpin = 1;
58  }
59  void goHome ()
60  {
61  RSpin = 0;
62  lcdData = Return_Home;
63  sendData ();
64  RSpin = 1;
65  }
66  void writeString (unsigned char *print)
67  {
68  while (*print)
69  {
70  lcdData = *print;
71  sendData ();
72  *print ++;
73  }
74  }
75  void clearTheScreen ()
76  {
77  RSpin = 0;
78  lcdData = Clear_Screen;
79  sendData ();
80  RSpin = 1;
81  }
```

```
82   void shiftcurleft ( unsigned char l)
83   {
84   RSpin = 0;
85   for (n = 0; n < l; n ++)
86   {
87   lcdData = ShiftLeft;
88   sendData ();
89   }
90   RSpin = 1;
91   }
92   void shiftcurright (unsigned char r)
93   {
94   RSpin = 0;
95   for (n = 0; n < r; n ++)
96   {
97   lcdData = ShiftRight;
98   sendData ();
99   }
100  RSpin = 1;
101  }
102  void cursorPos (unsigned char row, unsigned char col)
103  {
104  switch (row)
105  {
106  case 1:
107  {
108  goHome ();
109  shiftcurright (col);
110  break;
111  }
```

```
112  case 2:
113  {
114  line2 ();
115  shiftcurright (col);
116  break;
117  }
118  case 3:
119  {
120  goHome ();
121  shiftcurright (col+ 20);
122  break;
123  }
124  case 4:
125  {
126  line2 ();
127  shiftcurright (col + 20);
128  break;
129  }
130  }
131  }
```

Analysis of Listing 4-1

Lines 1–7 are the comments that give a brief description of what the header file is for and who wrote it.

Lines 8–16 define the phrases that are used for the instructions to set up the LCD. The binary numbers for these instructions have been derived from the instruction set for the LCD, shown in the appropriate data sheet.

To understand how I have arrived at the binary values for these instructions, we need to appreciate what the LCD is expecting in order to set the display up. It will normally expect three main types of instructions in its setup routine, and they are as follows:

- **Entry mode**: The LCD recognizes this as the entry mode setup instruction, as bits 3 to 7 are logic '0' and bit 2 is a logic '1'. It is then bits 1 and 0 that determine the entry mode.

  - These two bits are labeled: I/D for bit 1 and S/H for bit 0.

  - I/D stands for increment or decrement. A logic '1' means we shift one place to the right, that is, incrementing, after the data has been displayed. A logic '0' means we will move one place to the left, that is, decrementing. As we write from left to right, then we normally set this bit to a logic '1'.

    - The increment or decrement relates to the address in the DDRAM pointer that keeps track of what position the cursor is in. If we shift to the right, then we increment this pointer. If we shift to the left, then we decrement this pointer.

    - For all these shift operations, it is the S/H bit that determines if it is just the cursor or the whole display.

  - S/H stands for shift, and with this bit, we can decide if we want to shift the entire display or just the cursor in the direction set by the I/D bit.

    - A logic '1' in this bit means we will shift the display. The direction is then controlled with the I/D bit. A logic '1' in that bit as well means the display will be shifted right.

    - A logic '0' means we will just shift the cursor. Again, the direction of the shift is controlled by the logic on the I/D bit.

- For example, the binary value 0b00000110 is the normal setting, and the cursor will shift one place to the right once the character has been displayed.

- **Display control**: The LCD recognizes this as the display control setup instruction, as bits 4 to 7 are logic '0' and bit 3 is a logic '1'. It is then bits 2, 1, and 0 that determine the display mode. Bit 2 is labeled D, bit 1 is C, and bit 0 is B.

  - If D is a logic '1', then the display will be turned on. If it is a logic '0', then the display will be turned off.

  - If C is a logic '1', the cursor will be displayed as a simple dash in the current position. If C is a logic '0', then the cursor is not displayed.

  - If B is a logic '1', then the cursor will blink. It is normally displayed as a block in the current position. If B is a logic '0', then the cursor will not blink.

    - For example, if the binary data is 0b00001110, then the display and cursor will be turned on. The cursor will not blink. With this setting, you will be able to see where the cursor is currently positioned. It will be displayed as a steady dash on the screen.

- **Function set**: The LCD recognizes this as the function setup instruction, as bits 6 and 7 are logic '0' and bit 5 is a logic '1'. It is then bits 4, 3, and 2 that determine the function mode of the display; bits 1 and 0 have no effect.

- Bit 4 is labeled DL, and this determines if the LCD is working in 4-bit or 8-bit data mode. A logic '1' in the DL bit sets the LCD to work in 8-bit mode. A logic '0' sets it to 4-bit mode.

  - Using the LCD in 4-bit mode does save four I/O lines, so if you are short of I/O, then you may want to use this mode. I have used the LCD in this mode with my 8-bit PICs. The drawback is the process is a bit more involved.

- Bit 3 is labeled "N," and this is used to set the LCD to operate with one or two lines of characters. A logic '1' means the LCD is set for two lines. A logic '0' means just one line.

  - Bit 2 is labeled "F," and this sets the height of each character. A logic '1' means the characters are 5x10, high height. A logic '0' means they are 5x8, low height. However, if, as we will do, you use the LCD in two lines of characters, then the 5x8 pixel size is the simplest to use.

These three instructions must be in the setup routine for the LCD. In Listing 4-1, they are defined in lines 9–11. With the definitions, I am setting up the LCD to move the cursor one place to the right when a character is displayed. Then turn the display on and turn the cursor on with no blink. Finally, I am setting the LCD to work in 8-bit mode using two lines of characters with a size of 5x8 pixels. These are the minimum instructions that I will store in the "lcdInitialis" array.

Line 11 #define Clear_Screen   0b00000001

This is an LCD control instruction that is used to clear the display of any characters and return the cursor to the start of the first line, going from left to right.

Line 12 #define Return_Home   0b00000010

This instruction simply returns the cursor to the start of the first line, but leaves any characters that were currently on the display.

Line 13 #define Line_2   0b11000000

This instruction forces the LCD to set the cursor to go to the start of line 2 on the display.

Line 14 #define ShiftLeft   0b00010000

This is the cursor or display shift control instruction. The LCD recognizes this type of setup instruction, as bits 5 to 7 are logic '0' and bit 4 is a logic '1.' The control of the shifting operation is set by bits 3 and 2, according to Table 4-2. This operation will also increment or decrement the DDRAM pointer, that is, shifting left decrements and shifting right increments the pointer.

Table 4-2. Setting the Shift Operation

Bit 3 S/C	Bit 2 R/L	Shift Operation
0	0	Shift the cursor to the left
0	1	Shift the cursor to the right
1	0	Shift all the display to the left
1	1	Shift all the display to the right

With the definition on line 14, we are shifting the cursor to the left, as bits 3 and 2 are both logic '0.'

Line 15 #define ShiftRight   0b00010100

This simply shifts the cursor to the right; note, bit 3 is a logic '0', and bit 2 is a logic '1'; see Table 4-2.

Line 16 #define ShDisRight   0b00011100

This instruction will cause the whole display to shift to the right, as bits 3 and 2 are both at a logic '1'; see Table 4-2.

Line 17 #define lcdPort   PORTE

This sets out which PORT the LCD is connected to. Using a define in this way, instead of just referring to PORTE in all the instructions that send information to the LCD, makes the process of changing the PORT in the program easier. We only need to change the PORT reference in this line here, instead of finding every reference to PORTE in our program listing.

If you are connecting your LCD to a different PORT, you should change the PORT name here to the one you are using. You should be aware that with this header file, we will be using the LCD in 8-bit mode. This means we will need 8 bits for the data and 2 or 3 more bits for some control functions.

Line 18 #define RSpin   PORTBbits.RB15

This tells the compiler that wherever it sees the phrase RSpin, it knows we mean bit 15 of PORTB. The logic on the RSpin allows the LCD to distinguish if the information being sent is an instruction, when the logic on the RSpin would be a logic '0', or the address of the data to be displayed on the LCD, when the logic on the RSpin would be a logic '1.'

Line 19 #define ebit   PORTDbits.RD4

This does the same for the phrase "ebit." The "ebit" is sent high, then back to low, without a delay between the action, to inform the LCD some information has just been sent to the display, and it should deal with it.

Line 20 #define LCDrwPin   PORTDbits.RD5

This does the same for the phrase "LCDrwPin." It is bit 5 of PORTD that is connected to the R/W pin of the LCD on the explorer 16 development board. Connecting the R/W pin of the LCD to an output pin of the PIC enables us to change the function of this pin from read to write and vice versa. However, we will normally be simply writing to the LCD, so we should set the logic on the "LCDrwPin," or bit 5 of PORTD, to 0V, that is, a logic '0'. This is because the write function on this pin is active low. This is indicated by the var written above the letter "W" in the data sheet for that pin.

If you are using a different development board, you will need to set these 3 bits to the appropriate ones that your board uses to connect to the relevant pins on the LCD.

Line 21 //variables

Here, I am just using comments to split the listing up into useful sections. The following section is declaring any global variables.

Line 22 unsigned char lcdData, n,m;

This is simply creating three 8-bit memory locations that will be used to store the value of three global variables. These variables can be used anywhere in the program. We only need 8 bits for the memory locations, as they are set to the data type "unsigned char." With this data type, all 8 bits are used as part of the value. This means we can store a value from 0 to 255 in these memory locations. We will look at the other 8-bit data type, which is a "char," when we use it later in the book.

There is a section in the appendix that lists all the data types used in this book.

Line 23 unsigned char lcdInitialis [4] =

This is creating an array of four memory locations. We have looked at how arrays work in Chapter 3, so we will just look at the data here. They are only 8-bit memory locations as they are being used to store data of the type unsigned char. With this instruction, there is the "=" equal sign after the square brackets. This means that we are going to tell the compiler what data it must load into the four memory locations of the array. That is why there is no semicolon at the end of this line. This is not the end of the instruction; that is on line 29.

Line 24 {

This is the opening curly bracket that encases the list of data to be stored in the array.

Line 25   functionSet,

This is the phrase that was defined in line 10. The binary value defined for the phrase "functionSet" is 0b00111000, which will be the data stored in the first location in the array. The important bits are bits 4, 3, and 2. As bit 4 is a logic '1', then the LCD is set for 8-bit operation. As bit 3 is a logic '1', then it is set for two lines of 16 characters. As bit 2 is a logic '0', then the resolution of the display is set for 5 by 8.

Line 26 entryMode,

This represents the binary value 0b00000110. This simply shifts the cursor one place to the right after each character has been displayed on the screen. As bit 1 is a logic '1', we are shifting to the right after a character has been displayed. As bit 0 is a logic '0', then it means it is the cursor, and not the display, that is shifted.

Line 27 displayCtl,

135

This represents the binary value 0b00001110. This simply turns the display on and turns the cursor on, with no blinking of the cursor.

Line 28 Clear_Screen,

This represents the binary value 0b00000001. This simply clears all characters from the screen and returns the cursor to the beginning of the first line.

These are the basic four instructions that we use to set up the LCD display.

Line 29 };

This is the closing curly bracket of the list that details the data to be stored in the four memory locations in the array. The opening curly bracket is on line 24. Note, there is a semicolon at the end of line 29. This is because this is the end of the instruction. Also, there is a comma after each declaration of the data to be stored in the array. You must be aware of the correct syntax for these declarations and instructions and use them accordingly.

Line 30 // subroutines

This sets up the section of the listing for any subroutines that we might use. I find it best to state all the subroutines in order that they will be called before we write the main routine of the program. As an alternative to writing them here, they can be written after the main section, or even in another file, but you need to make reference to them first. I think the process that I am using here is simpler.

Line 31 void sendData ()

This creates a subroutine that will be used to send information, be it instruction or data, to the LCD. The instructions for the subroutine are enclosed between the opening curly bracket on line 32 and the closing curly bracket on line 37.

Line 33 lcdPort = lcdData;

The phrase "lcdPort" has been defined as PORTE on line 17. Therefore, the compiler knows we mean the SFR, Special Function Register, PORTE. The variable "lcdData" is an 8-bit variable that would have been loaded previously with the binary value we want to send to the LCD. This then simply loads PORTE with the value that is in the variable "lcdData."

Line 34 ebit = 1;

This simply loads the "ebit," which is actually bit 4 of PORTD (see line 19) with a logic '1.'

Line 35 ebit = 0;

This now loads the same bit with a logic '0.' It is the setting of the "ebit" to a logic '1' and then a logic '0' with no delay that signifies to the LCD new information has arrived at its input, and it should deal with it.

Line 36 TMR1 = 0; while (TMR1 < 380);

This is actually two instructions written on the same line. Note they are separated by the semicolon. The semicolon is used to indicate the end of an instruction. I prefer to write instructions on their own separate lines as it makes them easy to see separately. I just wanted to show you that you could do it this way.

The first instruction is TMR1 = 0;. This simply loads the TMR1 register with a value of zero. The TMR1 register is used to keep track of what value timer1 has counted to. Therefore, this instruction is just making sure timer1 starts to count from zero again.

The second instruction is while (TMR1 < 380);. This is of the type "while (the test is true) do what I say;" instruction. The test is written inside the normal brackets. In this instruction, the test is "(is the value in TMR1 less than 380)." If the test is true, then the PIC must carry out the instruction, or instructions, that is written between the normal closing bracket and the semicolon. This does explain the importance of the semicolon. However, in this case, there is nothing written between the normal closing bracket and the semicolon. This is because we want the PIC to do nothing while the test is true.

Eventually, the value in the TMR1 register will get to a value of 380 and above. When the value in TMR1 reaches 380, the test will be untrue, and the PIC can move on to the next instruction. This means that these two instructions are being used to create a simple delay. The length of the delay is $380 \times 7.11\mu s = 2.7ms$. This delay is there to give the LCD time to deal with the information we have just sent to it. There are different delay times required for different information; see the instruction set for the LCD in the data sheet for the LCD. However, I have just created the one delay that is long enough for all types of information.

Note, the keyword "void" at the beginning of the declaration of the subroutine means that this subroutine will not be sending any data back to the main program or to wherever it was called from. Also, the normal brackets are empty, which means the subroutine does not expect any data to be passed up to it when it is called.

Line 38 void setUpTheLCD ()

This creates a subroutine that is called when we want to set up the LCD. Note this subroutine is called only once in the program, so, really, we do not need to put the instructions into a subroutine. However, we are going to create a header file that includes these instructions, so we are setting them out here as a subroutine. The main program will call this later in the listing.

Again, this subroutine will not send any data back, hence the keyword "void." Also, it does not expect any data to be sent up to it, hence the empty normal brackets. Some people put the word void inside the normal brackets to indicate the subroutine does not expect any data being sent to it. However, I think that is unnecessary, and so I just leave the brackets empty. Both approaches work the same.

The instructions for the subroutine are between the opening and closing curly brackets between lines 39 and 51.

Line 40 TMR1 = 0;

This simply resets the TMR1 register back to zero. This is to ensure timer1 starts to count from zero.

Line 41 while (TMR1 < 6000);

This ensures the PIC does nothing while the value in TMR1 is less than 6000. These two instructions create a simple delay of 6000 x 7.11µs = 42.66ms. This delay is to ensure we send nothing to the LCD until after 40ms after the power has been applied to the LCD. This is to give the LCD time for the internal circuitry to settle down.

Line 42 RSpin = 0;

This simply loads the "RSpin," which has been defined as bit 15 of PORTB (see line 18) with a logic '0'. We are sending instructions to the LCD; therefore, we set this pin to a logic '0'.

Line 43 n = 0;

This loads the variable "n," which was declared in line 22 as an unsigned char, with the value zero. This is to get it ready for the next instruction on line 44.

Line 44 while (n < 4)

This is another "while (the test is true) do what I say here;" instruction. The test is simply testing if the value in the variable "n" is less than 4. If it is, the test is true and the PIC should carry out the instructions written between the opening and closing brackets between lines 45 and 49. We need to use the curly brackets as there is more than just one line instruction. Of course, as we have just loaded "n" with 0 on line 43, then the result of the test will be true, and so the PIC must carry out the following instructions.

Line 46 lcdData = lcdInitialis [n];

This will load the variable "lcdData" with the contents of the memory location in the array "lcdInitialis," indicated by the value in the variable "n." As this is the first run through the while loop, then n = 0. This means that the PIC will load the variable "lcdData" with the contents of the first memory location in the array. This will be the instruction "functionSet"; see line 25.

Line 47 sendData ();

This calls the subroutine "sendData" which will send the instruction "functionSet" to the LCD.

Line 48 n++;

This simply increments the variable "n" by one. It will now have the value of "1" in it.

The PIC will now go back to the while test on line 44 and test to see if "n" is still less than 4.

In this way, the PIC will carry out the instructions on lines 46, 47, and 48 a total of four times. This ensures the PIC will send the four instructions from the array "lcdInitialis" to the LCD and so set it up as we want.

Line 50 RSpin = 1;

This loads the "RSpin" with the logic '1'. This is done to tell the LCD that any information that is sent up to it, from now on, is data to be displayed.

Line 52 void line2 ()

This creates a subroutine that will send the instruction to move the cursor to the beginning of line 2 on the LCD screen.

Line 54 RSpin = 0;

This is to tell the LCD that the next information that will be sent to it is an instruction.

Line 55 lcdData = Line_2;

This loads the variable "lcdData" with the instruction "Line_2". This will send the cursor to the beginning of line 2 on the LCD.

Line 56 sendData ();

This calls the subroutine "sendData" to send the instruction, loaded into the variable "lcdData," to the LCD.

Line 57 RSpin = 1;

This tells the LCD that any information sent from now on is data to be displayed.

Line 59 void goHome ()

This creates a subroutine that works in exactly the same way as the previous subroutine, except that it is sending the instruction "returnHome." This instruction will simply send the cursor back to the beginning of the first line on the LCD screen. Note, it does not clear the screen of characters that are already on the screen.

Line 66 void writeString (unsigned char *print)

This creates a subroutine that will display a string of characters on the LCD. It works, in a rather complex way, in conjunction with the instruction that calls the subroutine. The first call is on line 32 in the main program listing.

This subroutine, on line 66, is expecting a value to be sent up to it when it is called. This value will be loaded into a special variable that is of the type unsigned char. The variable is called "print," and it has an asterisk "*" in front of it. This tells the compiler that it is a pointer, and the contents of the variable will actually point to a location within an array. However, unlike the array "lcdInitialis" we created earlier, we do not create this array directly. This array is automatically created and filled when the PIC carries out the instruction that calls the subroutine. If we look at the first call instruction from line 32 of the main program (see Listing 4-2) now, we can determine how it works. We will look at that instruction here.

Line 32 writeString ("Hello World");

This calls the "writeString" subroutine. However, more importantly, it automatically creates an array of type unsigned char and stores in it the ASCII, American Standard Code for Information Interchange, for all 11 characters written between the two quotation marks. Note the space is also a character. These 11 ASCII values will be loaded one after the other, beginning with the first character in the array. However, the PIC will also store the ASCII for a very important character that we have not put between the two quotation marks. This will be the ASCII for the "null character." This is put into the array to signify the end of the list of characters. Note we cannot set the length of the array, as we did with the "lcdInitialis" array, because we don't know how many characters we will want to display. Therefore, using this "null character" allows the compiler software to signify the end of the array. This null character will not be displayed on the LCD, it is there just to signify the end of the array.

Now we know how the array is automatically created, and about the important null character, we can look at how the subroutine deals with the array.

Line 68 while (*print)

This is another "while (the test is true) do what I say" type of instruction. The test is a special test in that it is testing to see if the pointer, *print, is **not** pointing to the address in the array that contains the important "null character." If the pointer is not pointing to the null character, then the test will be true, and the PIC must carry out the instructions between lines 69 and 73. When the PIC first called this subroutine, the contents of the pointer will have been loaded with the address of the first memory location in the array. Therefore, the PIC must carry out the following instructions, as the null character is in the last memory location in the array.

Line 70 lcdData = *print;

This will load the variable "lcdData" with the contents of the memory location in the array that the pointer *print is pointing to. If we assume this is the first run from when the PIC ran the call instruction on line 32 in the main program (see Listing 4-2), then the variable "lcdData" will be loaded with the ASCII for "H," that is, capital H which is 72 in decimal or 0b01001000 in binary.

Line 71 sendData ();

This will call the subroutine "sendData" and send the contents of the variable "lcdData" to the LCD.

Line 72 *print ++;

This simply increments the value in the pointer *print by one. This makes the pointer point to the next memory location in the array.

The PIC now goes back to line 68, where it checks to see if the pointer, *print, is still not pointing to the memory location in the array that has the ASCII for the null character. If it is not, then the PIC will carry out the instructions again.

In this way, the PIC will repeat the instructions until the pointer is pointing to where the null character is in the array. At this point, the test on line 68 will be untrue, and the PIC will break out of the loop without displaying the important null character.

This is a very wordy explanation of a rather complex set of instructions. However, I hope that, after a couple of readings, you will understand how they work. I believe that it is important you fully understand how your program works. Only then can you truly say you have written your programs, and you are well on your way to becoming that experienced embedded programmer.

Line 75 void clearTheScreen ()

This creates a subroutine that will make the PIC clear the screen of the LCD and send the cursor to the beginning of the first line. The instructions work in the same way as the "line_2" subroutine, except that the instruction sent to the LCD is "Clear_Screen".

Line 82 void shiftcurleft (unsigned char l)

This creates a subroutine that is used when we want to shift the current cursor position back to the left a number of places. The instructions for the subroutine are between the curly brackets on lines 83 and 91. This subroutine is expecting a value to be sent up to it when it is called. This value will be copied into the local variable "l" which is declared as an unsigned char within the normal brackets of the subroutine declaration on line 82.

Line 84 RSpin = 0;

This sets the RSpin to a logic '0' which tells the LCD that what will follow is an instruction that the LCD must carry out, not data to be displayed.

Line 85 for (n = 0; n < l; n ++)

This sets up another for do loop that controls how many times the PIC carries out the instructions between the curly brackets that follow on lines 86 and 89. The number of times the PIC carries out these instructions is set by the value copied into the local variable "l."

Line 87 lcdData = shiftLeft;

This loads the variable lcdData with the instruction for the LCD "shiftLeft." This is defined on line 14.

Line 88 sendData () ;

This calls the subroutine sendData which will send the contents of the variable lcdData to the LCD.

Line 90 RSpin = 1;

This sets the RSpin back to a logic '1' which gets the LCD ready to receive data to be displayed, as that is what will most likely be sent next to the LCD.

You should be able to appreciate that this subroutine will shift the current position of the cursor on the LCD a controlled number of places back to the left. This can be used to allow the user to correct some value already displayed on the screen without having to change the whole display.

Line 92 void shiftcurright (unsigned char r)

This does exactly the same, but shifts the cursor a controlled number of places to the right. The local variable "r" controls how many places the cursor is shifted.

Line 102 void cursorPos (unsigned char row, unsigned char col)

This creates a normal subroutine which will expect two values to be passed up to it. The values will be passed up with the call instruction cursorPos (1,3); as in line 31 in the main program. The first value, a 1 in this case, will be loaded into the local variable "row." The second value will be loaded into the local variable "col."

It is the instructions between lines 104 and 129 that are really new.

Line 104 switch (row)

This type of instruction is used to allow the PIC to choose, or switch, what it does from a list of actions, controlled by a value loaded into the control variable, which is stated inside the normal brackets. In this case, this control variable is the variable "row." The PIC will then choose which instructions it carries out from the case statements that follow, selecting the case statement that has the same value as that in the control variable.

Line 106   case 1:

This is the first case statement from the list that the PIC could choose from. If the value in the control variable was "1," then the PIC would carry out the instructions associated with this case statement. Note the use of the colon ":" as this is not the end of the instruction. The instruction associated with the case statement will be written between the following opening and closing curly brackets, that is, between lines 107 and 111 in this case.

Line 108 goHome ();

This calls the subroutine "goHome," which will send the cursor to the first position on the LCD display.

line 109 shiftcurright (col);

This calls the subroutine to shift the cursor right a number of positions controlled by the value stored in the variable "col." Note this value will be copied into the local variable "r" in the subroutine "shiftcurright." You should also appreciate that when the main program calls the subroutine "cursorPos," the main program would pass up two values that will be copied into the local variables "row" and "col."

Line 110 break;

This is a keyword that makes the PIC break out of the switch routine at this point in the case. The PIC will then leave the "cursorPos" subroutine and return to the main program or to where the subroutine was called from.

Lines 112–129 do exactly the same but for the other three case statements.

I have used four case statements as this subroutine can be used with LCD displays that have four lines of characters. You can see that case 2 shifts the cursor a number of places starting from the first position on the second line of the display. This is because we have called the subroutine line 2 in the instruction previous to this shift.

Case 3 is a repeat of case 1 except that the cursor is shifted 20 positions extra to the value in the variable "col." This is because line 3, on the four-line LCD, is simply a continuation of line 1 after the first 20 positions have been used. However, the next cursor position starts at the beginning of the line under line 2 on the display.

The case 4 statement works in the same way except that it is a continuation of line 2 on the display, hence the addition of the 20 positions in the instruction to shift the cursor.

However, this is assuming that the four-line LCD has 20 characters in each line of its display. We will be using this concept when we look at the larger LCD in Chapter 6.

The program listing for the basic LCD is shown in Listing 4-2. The program will set the LCD up to work in 8-bit mode. Then it will send two separate messages to the LCD.

Listing 4-2. The Listing for the Basic LCD Program

```
1  /*File:    LCDPORTEProg.c
2  Author: H. H. Ward
3  *A program for the 32bit PIC to write two simple messages
   to a LCD display
4  Created on 26 July 2021, 15:51
5  */
6  #include <xc.h>
7  #include <config72M36MNoWDTNoJTAG.h>
8  #include <LCDPORTE.h>
9  #define startButton      _RA7
10 void main()
11 {
12 // set up the timers and PORTS
13 T1CON = 0x8030;
14 TRISA = 0x0080;
15 TRISB = 0x00FF;
16 TRISC = 0X00FF;
17 TRISD = 0X0000;
18 TRISE = 0x0000;
19 PORTA = 0;
20 PORTB = 0;
21 PORTC = 0;
22 PORTD = 0;
23 PORTE = 0;
24 AD1PCFG = 0XFFFF;
25 AD1CON1 = 0;
26 DDPCONbits.JTAGEN = 0;
27 LCDrwPin = 0;
28 setUpTheLCD ();
29 //the main part of the program
```

```
30  while (startButton);
31  cursorPos (1,3);
32  writeString ("Hello World");
33  cursorPos (2,2);
34  writeString ("8Bit PORTE");
35  while (1);
36  }
```

Analysis of Listing 4-2

Lines 1–5 are the basic comments for a program.

Lines 6 and 7 are the usual include files that we use.

Line 8 #include <LCDPORTE.h>

This includes the header file, which we have just looked at, that has the instruction for using the LCD on PORTE.

Line 9 #define startButton   _RA7

This defines the phrase "startButton," but here we are using an alternative method to indicate which bit of which PORT we mean. It means the start button has been allocated to bit 7 of PORTA. This is one of the three main switches on the explorer 16 development board that I use. Note we need to make sure that bit 7 of PORTA is set as an input.

These lines with the keyword "define" do not end with a semicolon ";" as they are not program instructions. They are commands to the compiler.

Line 10 void main()

This is the main loop of the program. It is not a subroutine, it is the main part of the program. All C programs must have this main loop, hence its name.

Line 12 // set up the timers and PORTS

This is just to split the main program into different sections. You don't have to do it this way, it is just a personal choice.

Lines 13–26 have been looked at in Chapter 2.

Line 27 LCDrwPin = 0;

This simply ensures that this pin is set to a logic '0', that is, a logic low. This is because the "write" function of the LCD is active low. The "LCDrwPin" is allocated to bit 5 of PORTD (see line 20) in the header file for the LCD. This is connected to the R/W pin on the LCD. This means we are telling the LCD that we want to write to it.

Line 28 setUpTheLCD ();

This calls the subroutine "setUpTheLCD" and sets the LCD up as we have planned.

Line 29 //the main part of the program

Here, I am splitting the main loop up into another section. The previous section was just organizing the PIC in terms of any timers, etc., and setting the direction of the I/O. This next section is the real workings of the program.

Line 30 while (startButton);

This is a very useful "while (the test is true) do what I say" test. It has been looked at in Chapter 2 already. Really, we are simply making the PIC wait until someone presses the start button.

Line 31 cursorPos (1,3);

This calls the subroutine "cursorPos" to send the cursor to column 3 of the first row on the LCD. This gets it ready to start writing characters to the current position on the LCD.

Line 32 writeString ("Hello World");

This calls the subroutine "writeString" and sends the ASCII for the characters between the two quotation marks, " ", to the LCD.

Line 33 cursorPos (2,2);

This calls the subroutine "cursorPos" to send the cursor to column 2 of the second row on the LCD.

Line 34 writeString ("8bit PORTE");

This calls the subroutine "writeString" again to send the characters to be displayed on the LCD.

Line 35 while(1);

This is a very useful instruction; however, it is not one that you normally see in a C program. It is one way of stopping the program at this point. There is no "halt" instruction in C. However, we have used the while(1) test loop. It is termed the forever loop, as the test described between the normal brackets will forever be true, as the test is simply "1," which basically sets the result bit to true, that is, a logic '1'. However, there are no curly brackets within which we write the instructions that the PIC must forever do. There is just the semicolon that signifies the end of the instruction. There is nothing between the closing normal bracket and the semicolon, as we want the PIC to do nothing forever. In this way, we are simply stopping the PIC from moving away from this instruction. The PIC will continually loop around this one-line instruction forever and so stop here.

This program is simply about showing you how you can set up the LCD and write some text to it on both of the lines on the LCD, Figure 4-2 shows the LCD displaying two lines of text. Before we move on to do some more work with the LCD, we will make a header file for the LCD, as we will be using it with a lot of our programs in this book. However, we will initially keep it as it is, which means the LCD must be connected to PORTE, and the "RSpin" and "ebit" must be allocated as shown in the listing. Also, as we might use the LCD connected to PORTD, instead of PORTE, we will make a second header file for using the LCD while connected to PORTD.

Figure 4-2. *The LCD Program Working*

Creating Your Own Symbols to Display on the LCD

We will now move on to an interesting aspect of using the LCD. If you look at the extract of the data sheet for the LCD, you should see there are two memory areas, which are

> CGRAM from 0b00000000 to 0b00001111

> DDRAM from 0b00100000 to 0b11111111

This means there are 16 CGRAM addresses and 192 DDRAM addresses. Both these types of addresses are used to store a 5x8 pixel map of the characters that you can display on the LCD. However, the DDRAM addresses are preloaded with the pixel map for the 192 ASCII characters you might want to display on the LCD. We cannot change the pixel maps in these DDRAM addresses. However, the 16 CGRAM do not have a predefined pixel map. Indeed, they are available to us, as programmers, to create our own pixel maps for the characters we want to display. This means that there is the possibility to create our own characters to display on the LCD. This part of this chapter will show you how to do just that.

The addresses of the DDRAM correspond to the ASCII values for the normal character set. This is so that we can access the correct memory location in the DDRAM by simply sending the desired ASCII for the character we want to display to the LCD.

For example, the address of where we can find the pixel map to display the character H in capitals is 0b01001000. This is also the ASCII for the capital H.

To access the address for the pixel map to display the number 9, we would use the address in the DDRAM of 0b00111001 which is the ASCII for the number 9.

However, when accessing the CGRAM, we need to send the appropriate binary address value. This is because we don't know what character the pixel maps in those locations represent, as we need to design the maps ourselves.

The Pixel Maps

The size of the pixel grid depends on the resolution of the LCD display. The resolution of the LCD in this exercise is set to a 5 by 8 grid. The empty grid is shown in Figure 4-3.

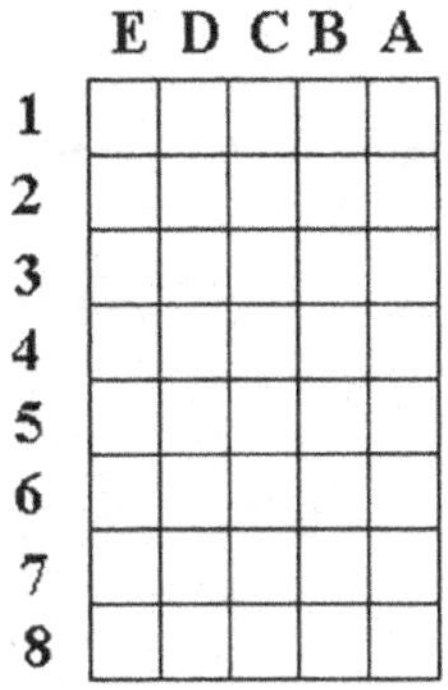

Figure 4-3. *The 8 Rows by 5 Columns Grid of a Pixel Map*

To create a character, we have to turn on or off the particular cells in the grid. A logic '1' in the cell reference turns it on and a logic '0' turns it off. Therefore, if we said that in row 1 columns A, B, D, and E were logic '0' and column C was a logic '1', then the pixel map would be as shown in Figure 4-4.

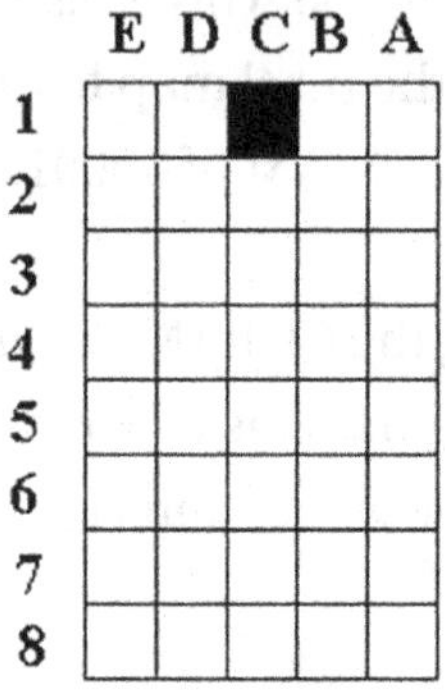

Figure 4-4. *The Pixel Map with Row 1*

The process by which we create the pixel map in code is to write 8 bytes, one for each row, to control the cells accordingly for all the rows in the map. However, it will only be bits 0 to 4 of each byte that control the pixel map. As an example, to display a single line down the middle of the map, the 8 bytes would be

Row 1 0b00000100
Row 2 0b00000100
Row 3 0b00000100
Row 4 0b00000100
Row 5 0b00000100
Row 6 0b00000100
Row 7 0b00000100
Row 8 0b00000100

The map would be as shown in Figure 4-5.

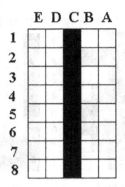

Figure 4-5. *The Full Pixel Map for Example 1*

We need to be able to load the memory areas in the CGRAM with the data for the pixel maps we want to display. To access the CGRAM, we need to send the following instruction to the LCD: 0b01000000 or 0x40. This will tell the LCD we want to write the following data to the CGRAM. When we have finished writing the data, we need to send the following instruction: 0b10000000 or 0x80. This tells the LCD we have finished writing to the CGRAM and will simply access the DDRAM from now on.

Note when we send the instruction 0x40, the LCD will load the pointer inside the LCD with the first address of the CGRAM. When the LCD has finished receiving the eight binary values for the pixel map, the address pointer will automatically point to the next address in the CGRAM.

The whole process will be best explained by writing a program that will send the pixel maps for the four characters shown in Figure 4-6 to the CGRAM. Then after displaying a simple message on line 1 of the LCD, the program will display the four characters from the CGRAM on line 2 of the display. I will not say that my approach is the only method or indeed the best for displaying some special characters, but it does the job well.

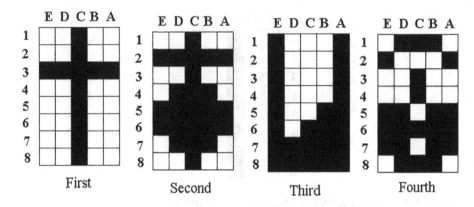

Figure 4-6. *The Pixel Maps for the Four Characters*

We need to be able to determine the binary value for the pixel maps for the characters shown in Figure 4-6. I will list the four binary values for the four maps in the next section. However, why not try working them out first and then read the list in the next section to see if you have got it right? To help you, here is the 8-bit binary value for the first three rows of the first character map:

Row 1 0b00000100

Row 2 0b00000100

Row 3 0b00011111

Now try writing the maps for all four characters.

The 8-Bit Binary Values for the Four Special Characters

First character

Row 1 0b00000100

Row 2 0b00000100

Row 3 0b00011111

Row 4 0b00000100

Row 5 0b00000100
Row 6 0b00000100
Row 7 0b00000100
Row 8 0b00000100
Second character
Row 1 0b00000100
Row 2 0b00011111
Row 3 0b00000100
Row 4 0b00001110
Row 5 0b00011111
Row 6 0b00011111
Row 7 0b00001110
Row 8 0b00000100
Third character
Row 1 0b00010001
Row 2 0b00010001
Row 3 0b00010001
Row 4 0b00010001
Row 5 0b00010011
Row 6 0b00010111
Row 7 0b00011111
Row 8 0b00011111
Fourth character
Row 1 0b00001110
Row 2 0b00010001
Row 3 0b00000100
Row 4 0b00000100
Row 5 0b00011011
Row 6 0b00011111
Row 7 0b00011011
Row 8 0b00001110

The Program "Pixel to Matrix"

To try and make the process easier, we could use a program that will generate the 8-bit binary values for us. One such program is the "pixel to matrix" that can be found on the Internet for free. I will use it here to generate the binary data for the second map in Figure 4-7.

The opening screen for the software is shown in Figure 4-7.

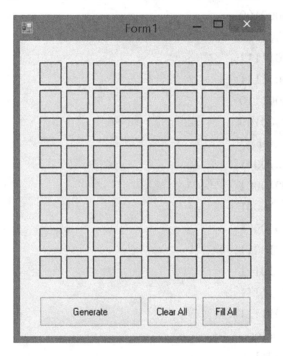

Figure 4-7. *Form1, the Opening Screen of the Pixel to Matrix Software*

You now simply click the mouse on the squares in each row that you want to turn on. This is shown in Figure 4-8.

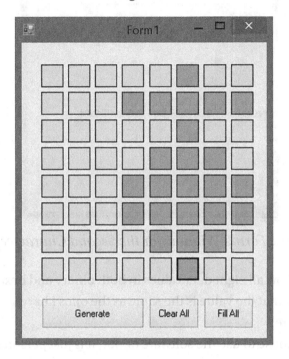

Figure 4-8. *The Filled-In Screen for the Second Character*

If you now click the mouse on the Generate tab, the form2 window will appear as shown in Figure 4-9.

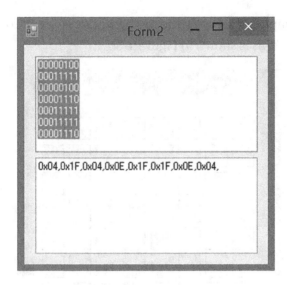

Figure 4-9. *The Form2 Window for the Second Character*

This will show all eight data values in both binary and hexadecimal. You should see that the value is the same as the ones I have produced before.

You can choose to use the software or not; it is just personal preference. However, when we look at programming a matrix display in the next chapter, we will use this software again.

The Special Character Program

We will look at a program that will initially write the data for the four special characters, shown in Figure 4-7, to the CGRAM. It will then display a simple message on line 1 of the LCD, then the special characters, followed by some ASCII characters on line 2 of the LCD.

I will miss out the algorithm and flowchart for this, and any other programs in the future, as I want to teach you how the C instructions work. I will assume you have done both the algorithm and flowchart yourselves.

The Program Listing for the Special Character Program

This is shown in Listing 4-3.

Listing 4-3. The Program to Display Some Special Characters

```
1  /*File:    LCDPORTESpecialChars.c
2  This is a basic program to control the LCD using the PIC
   32MX360F512L
3  Written by H H Ward dated 26/07/21.
4  It writes to the CGRAM in the LCD
5  The display the four characters we have saved in
   the CGRAM*/
6  //some includes
7  #include <xc.h>
8  #include <config72M36MNoWDTNoJTAG.h>
9  #include <LCDPORTE.h>
10 //variables
11 char firstCharacter [8] =
12 {
13 0b00000100,
14 0b00000100,
15 0b00011111,
16 0b00000100,
17 0b00000100,
18 0b00000100,
19 0b00000100,
20 0b00000100,
21 };
```

```
22   char secondCharacter [8] =
23   {
24   0b00000100,
25   0b00011111,
26   0b00000100,
27   0b00001110,
28   0b00011111,
29   0b00011111,
30   0b00001110,
31   0b00000100,
32   };
33   char thirdCharacter [8] =
34   {
35   0b00010001,
36   0b00010001,
37   0b00010001,
38   0b00010001,
39   0b00010011,
40   0b00010111,
41   0b00011111,
42   0b00011111,
43   };
44   char fourthCharacter [8] =
45   {
46   0b00001110,
47   0b00010001,
48   0b00000100,
49   0b00000100,
50   0b00011011,
51   0b00011111,
52   0b00011011,
```

```
53  0b00001110,
54  };
55  //subroutines
56  void writeToCGram ()
57  {
58  RSpin = 0;
59  lcdData = 0x40;
60  sendData ();
61  RSpin = 1;
62  n = 0;
63  while (n < 8)
64  {
65  lcdData = firstCharacter [n];
66  sendData ();
67  n ++;
68  }
69  n = 0;
70  while (n < 8)
71  {
72  lcdData = secondCharacter [n];
73  sendData ();
74  n ++;
75  }
76  n = 0;
77  while (n < 8)
78  {
79  lcdData = thirdCharacter [n];
80  sendData ();
81  n ++;
82  }
83  n = 0;
```

```
84   while (n < 8)
85   {
86   lcdData = fourthCharacter [n];
87   sendData ();
88   n ++;
89   }
90   RSpin = 0;
91   lcdData = 0x80;
92   sendData ();
93   RSpin = 1;
94   }
95   void main ()
96   {
97   // set up the timers and PORTS
98   T1CON = 0x8030;
99   TRISA = 0x0080;
100  TRISB = 0x00FF;
101  TRISC = 0X00FF;
102  TRISD = 0X0000;
103  TRISE = 0x0000;
104  PORTA = 0;
105  PORTB = 0;
106  PORTC = 0;
107  PORTD = 0;
108  PORTE = 0;
109  AD1PCFG = 0XFFFF;
110  AD1CON1 = 0;
111  DDPCONbits.JTAGEN = 0;
112  setUpTheLCD ();
113  //the main part of the program
114  writeToCGram ();
```

```
115   while (1)
116   {
117   writeString ("Using the CGRAM");
118   line2 ();
119   lcdData = 0x00;
120   sendData ();
121   lcdData = 0x20;
122   sendData ();
123   lcdData = 0x01;
124   sendData ();
125   lcdData = 0x20;
126   sendData ();
127   lcdData = 0x02;
128   sendData ();
129   lcdData = 0x20;
130   sendData ();
131   lcdData = 0x03;
132   sendData ();
133   lcdData = 0x20;
134   sendData ();
135   lcdData = 0x48;
136   sendData ();
137   lcdData = 0x2E;
138   sendData ();
139   lcdData = 0x57;
140   sendData ();
141   lcdData = 0x2E;
142   sendData ();
143   lcdData = 0x31;
144   sendData ();
145   lcdData = 0x32;
```

```
146  sendData ();
147  lcdData = 0x33;
148  sendData ();
149  RSpin = 0;
150  lcdData = Return_Home;
151  sendData ();
152  RSpin = 1;
153  }
154  }
```

Analysis of Listing 4-3

Lines 1–5 are the usual comments, and lines 7–9 are the normal include directives. Note line 9 includes the header file for using the LCD in 8-bit mode on PORTE. Also, I am using a line of comments to split the program listing up into different sections.

Line 11 char firstCharacter [8] =

This is setting up an array of eight locations with 8 bits of data. We can use the type char instead of unsigned char, as we know the MSB will always be a logic '0'. That is because it is only the first 5 bits that are used to create the design of the characters to be displayed. We are defining what is stored in the eight locations as we add the "=" sign with the instruction, and there is no semicolon to denote the end of the instruction. The following eight binary values, written between the opening and closing curly brackets, will be stored in the memory locations, one after the other, in the array. Each binary number is followed by a comma as this is really a list of numbers.

In this way, lines 12–22 create an array named "firstCharacter" that stores the binary values to create the first special character.

Note, the whole program will be using some global variables named "n" and "m". However, we do not need to declare them in this listing as they are declared in the listing for the LCD header file.

Lines 23–54 create the arrays for the remaining special characters we want to display.

Line 56 void writeToCGram ()

This creates a subroutine that will write the data for the special characters to the area of the LCD memory open for us to use. The instructions for the subroutine are between the curly brackets on lines 57 and 94.

Line 58 RSpin = 0;

This tells the LCD that the following are commands to the LCD.

Line 59 lcdData = 0x40;

This is the value that instructs the LCD to go to the first memory location in the CGRAM area of the LCD.

Line 60 sendData ();

This sends the instruction to the LCD.

Line 61 RSpin = 1;

This tells the LCD that what is to follow is data to be stored in the current memory location, which is the first location in the CGRAM area.

Line 62 n = 0;

This loads the global variable "n" with 0 ready for the following while loop.

Line 63 while (n < 8)

This sets up a "while (test is true) do what I say" type of loop. The test written between the normal brackets is "is n less than 8." At this point, n is less than 8, as we have just loaded it with 0 in line 62. As there are a number of instructions that the PIC must do while the test is true, they are written between the curly brackets on lines 64 and 68. Note we don't need the semicolon at the end of line 63 as it is not the end of the instruction.

Line 65 lcdData = firstCharacter [n];

This loads the variable "lcdData" with the contents of the array "firstCharacter," as indicated by the value in the variable "n." As this would be zero, then the "lcdData" will be loaded with a copy of the first memory location in the array.

Line 66 sendData ();

This sends the contents of the variable "lcdData" to the LCD.

Line 67n ++;

This simply adds one to the value in the variable "n." After this instruction, the PIC will carry out the while test written in line 63. The result will still be true, as n now has a value of 2 in it. The PIC must then carry out the instructions on lines 65–67. This looping action will carry on eight times until the variable "n" has a value of 8 in it. At that point, the while test on line 63 will be untrue, and the PIC will then jump to line 69.

This first while loop will have stored the binary values for the first special character in the first area of the CGRAM. The address pointer of the LCD will now move on to the second area of the CGRAM.

Line 69 n = 0;

This loads the variable "n" with zero ready for the next "while (test is true) do what I say" test.

Lines 70–94 carry out the same type of instructions to load the next three areas of the CGRAM with the data for the remaining three special characters.

Line 95 void main ()

This creates the important main section of the program listing.

Lines 98–112 are the usual instructions for setting up the PIC. We have looked at these instructions already.

Line 114 writeToCGram ();

This calls the subroutine to load the CGRAM area with the data for the four special characters we want to display.

Lines 115–153 have been looked at before. The only new ones that need analyzing are

Line 119 lcdData = 0x00;

This loads the variable "lcdData" with the value 0x00 or 0. This is to tell the LCD to go to the first memory location, that is, location 0. This is the first location in the CGRAM area. There, it will find the eight binary values for the first special character we have stored in the CGRAM area.

Line 120 sendData ();

This sends the data in "lcdData" to the LCD. In this way, the LCD will go to the very first memory location. There, it will find the pixel map we have previously loaded into that memory area. This means that the first special character will be displayed on the LCD.

Line 121 lcdData = 0x20;

This loads the variable "lcdData" with the value 0x20. This is the address that will hold the binary data 0x20 which is the ASCII for the space. This is so that the LCD will display a space between the first special character and the next character to be displayed.

Line 122 sends this data to the LCD and so opens up the memory area where the pixel map for the "space" is stored.

Line 124 lcdData = 0x01;

This loads the variable "lcdData" with the address of the second memory area in the CGRAM area. This gets the LCD ready to display the second special character on the LCD.

Lines 124–134 send this and the remaining special characters to the LCD. Note, there is a "space" between each character.

Lines 135–148 send the ASCII for H.W.123 to the LCD.

Line 149 RSpin = 0;

This tells the LCD that what is to follow is an instruction to the LCD.

Line 150 lcdData = returnHome;

This loads the "lcdData" with the value for the instruction to send the cursor back to the beginning of the first line on the LCD. Line 151 sends it to the LCD.

I hope this analysis does explain how we can create our own special characters on the LCD.

Line 152 RSpin = 1;

This tells the LCD that the next data that will be sent to the LCD will be data to be displayed on the screen. This is because the program will now loop back to line 115, which is the start of the forever loop. The PIC will then move on to line 117 where it resends the message to the LCD.

Figure 4-10 shows the special character program working as expected.

Figure 4-10. *The Special Characters on the LCD*

Summary

In this chapter, we have studied how to use an LCD with two lines of 16 characters. We have also studied how to create our own characters to display on the LCD.

We have also looked at using the switch directive with the case statement to get the PIC to choose what action it should carry out from a list of different operations.

In the next chapter, we will learn how to use a dot matrix display to display characters on a single matrix display and then a simple message on a combination of four matrix displays.

In Chapter 6, we will extend our experience with LCD displays to controlling an LCD with four lines of 20 characters.

CHAPTER 5

The Dot Matrix Display

The 8 by 8 Dot Matrix Board

In this chapter, we will look at another method of displaying characters.
We will look at using a dot matrix board. Initially, we will use just a single
matrix display, and then we will move on to controlling four matrix
displays cascaded together. Finally, we will write a program that scrolls
some text along the four dot matrix displays.

After reading this chapter, you will be able to use the Max7219 driver
IC to control a single 8 by 8 dot matrix display and a series of four matrix
displays cascaded together.

We will also learn how to set up and use a two-dimensional array.

The Single Dot Matrix Display

The dot matrix board that we will use in the first program is shown in
Figure 5-1.

© Hubert Ward 2023
H. Ward, *Introductory Programs with the 32-bit PIC Microcontroller*,
Maker Innovations Series, https://doi.org/10.1007/978-1-4842-9051-4_5

Figure 5-1. *The 8 by 8 Dot Matrix Display*

The dot matrix can be bought as a separate item, but you will need to drive it directly. It can also be bought, as shown in Figure 5-1, with a Max7219 driver IC connected to it. The Max7219 can be used to enable the matrix to be driven from just five wires from the PIC. There are also five more terminals on the other side of the board. These can enable the board to be cascaded with other matrix boards.

The Max7219 Driver IC

Before we look at the program listing, it would be useful to look at this IC. To make it easier to use the 8 by 8 matrix display, the IC has been built into the PCB board as shown in Figure 5-1. This does mean we can use just five wires to use the matrix display. They are

- VCC for the +5V

- GND for the 0V

- DIN for the data to be sent to the display

- CS or Load to synchronize the latching of the 16 bits of data

- Clk to synchronize the operation of the display

Communicating with the Max7219 is done serially with the DIN and DOUT lines. The load and clock lines are used to synchronize when the data is latched in the IC. Communication can be achieved by using the SPI protocol or by controlling the input of the individual bits. We will use the latter method, as we will not be looking at the SPI protocol until Chapter 6 in the book. We will connect the DIN, Load/CS, and the Clk inputs of the driver to three outputs from the PIC, and they will be used to control the sending of data to the Max7219.

Writing to the Max7219

When using the Max7219, we must first send some control information that sets the 7219 up as we want to use it. Then, once we have set up the IC, we will simply send the data that tells the 7219 which LEDs, in the matrix, we want to turn on to create our display.

All information is sent in two bytes of 8 bits, making a total of 16 bits of data. Each bit is latched into the internal shift register in the 7219 when the clk signal goes high. This also means that the clock signal must be low before each bit is sent to the 7219. This clock signal will be a pseudo simulated clock created in software.

When the second of the two bytes has been sent, that is, when all 16 bits have arrived in the 7219, the load signal is sent high to signify that all 16 bits have been sent, and the IC must latch the two bytes into the 7219. This then means that the load signal must be low when we start to send the 16 bits to the 7219. How we achieve this should become apparent when we analyze the program listing.

Just a few more concepts before we look at the program. Inside the 7219, there are five control registers:

- **Shutdown register**: This puts the IC into shutdown or not shutdown.

- **Mode register**: This sets up how the IC decodes the data being sent to be displayed.

- **Intensity register**: This sets up how we control the brightness of the display.

- **Scan-limit register**: This sets up how the digits are scanned to be displayed.

- **Display test register**: This is used to put the display into normal mode or test mode.

When we are writing control information to the registers, we must firstly tell the 7219 which register we are writing to and then which command byte we want to write to that register.

When we are sending data as to what we want to display, it will be sent again in two bytes. These will control which LEDs on which column we want to turn on. Again, how we achieve this should become clearer as we analyze the program listing. The program listing is shown in Listing 5-1.

Listing 5-1. The Program Listing for the 8 by 8 Dot Matrix Display

```
1  /* File:    64DotMatrixBoard.c
2  Author: H. H. Ward
3  Using the 7219 matrix controller
4  Created on 01 February 2019, 16:36
5  */
6  #include <xc.h>
7  #include <config72M36MNoWDTNoJTAG.h>
8  #define decodeModeReg        0b00001001
```

```
 9  #define intensityReg        0b00001010
10  #define scanLimitReg        0b00001011
11  #define shutdownReg         0b00001100
12  #define displayTestReg      0b00001111
13  #define disableDecode       0b00000000
14  #define codeB0              0b00000001
15  #define codeB4              0b00001111
16  #define codeB8              0b11111111
17  #define brightMax           0b00001111
18  #define brightMin           0b00000001
19  #define scanAll             0b00000111
20  #define normalOperation     0b00000001
21  #define shutdown            0b00000000
22  #define noTest              0b00000000
23  #define maxin               _RA0
24  #define maxload             _RA1
25  #define maxclk              _RA2
26  #define nzero        maxWrite (0,0x00); maxWrite(1,0x08);
    maxWrite(2,0x14); maxWrite(3,0x22); maxWrite(4,0x26);
    maxWrite(5,0x2A); maxWrite(6,0x32); maxWrite(7,0x14);
    maxWrite(8,0x08);
27  #define none         maxWrite (0,0x00); maxWrite (1,0x08);
    maxWrite (2,0x18); maxWrite (3,0x28); maxWrite (4,0x08);
    maxWrite (5,0x08); maxWrite (6,0x08); maxWrite (7,0x08);
    maxWrite (8,0x3E);
28  #define ntwo         maxWrite (0,0x00); maxWrite(1,0x1C);
    maxWrite(2,0x22); maxWrite(3,0x22); maxWrite(4,0x02);
    maxWrite(5,0x3C); maxWrite(6,0x20); maxWrite(7,0x20);
    maxWrite(8,0x3E);
29  #define nthree       maxWrite (0,0x00); maxWrite (1,0x38);
    maxWrite (2,0x04); maxWrite (3,0x04); maxWrite (4,0x04);
```

```
        maxWrite (5,0x1C); maxWrite (6,0x04); maxWrite(7,0x04);
        maxWrite(8,0x38);
30   #define nfour        maxWrite (0,0x00); maxWrite (1,0x04);
        maxWrite (2,0x0C); maxWrite (3,0x14); maxWrite (4,0x24);
        maxWrite (5,0x7C); maxWrite (6,0x04); maxWrite (7,0x04);
        maxWrite (8,0x3F);
31   unsigned char n, row, col;
32   unsigned const char show [62][9]=
33   {
34   {0x00,0x08,0x14,0x22,0x26,0x2A,0x32,0x14,0x08}, //0
35   {0x00,0x08,0x18,0x28,0x08,0x08,0x08,0x08,0x3E}, //1
36   {0x00,0x1C,0x22,0x22,0x02,0x3C,0x20,0x20,0x3E}, //2
37   {0x00,0x3C,0x04,0x04,0x04,0x1C,0x04,0x04,0x3C}, //3
38   {0x00,0x04,0x0C,0x14,0x24,0x7C,0x04,0x04,0x3F}, //4
39   {0x00,0x3C,0x20,0x20,0x3C,0x04,0x04,0x04,0x3C}, //5
40   {0x00,0x3C,0x20,0x20,0x3C,0x24,0x24,0x24,0x3C}, //6
41   {0x00,0x7F,0x01,0x02,0x04,0x08,0x10,0x20,0x40}, //7
42   {0x00,0x1C,0x22,0x22,0x1C,0x1C,0x22,0x22,0x1C}, //8
43   {0x00,0x1C,0x22,0x22,0x22,0x1E,0x02,0x02,0x1E}, //9
44   {0x00,0x10,0x28,0x44,0x44,0x7C,0x44,0x44,0x44}, //A
45   {0x00,0x70,0x48,0x48,0x70,0x48,0x44,0x44,0x78}, //B
46   {0x00,0x1C,0x20,0x40,0x40,0x40,0x40,0x20,0x1C}, //C
47   {0x00,0x78,0x24,0x22,0x22,0x22,0x22,0x24,0x78}, //D
48   {0x00,0x7E,0x40,0x40,0x7C,0x40,0x40,0x40,0x7E}, //E
49   {0x00,0x7E,0x40,0x40,0x7C,0x40,0x40,0x40,0x40}, //F
50   {0x00,0x3E,0x41,0x80,0x80,0x8E,0x91,0x41,0x3E}, //G
51   {0x00,0x42,0x42,0x42,0x7E,0x42,0x42,0x42,0x42}, //H
52   {0x00,0x7E,0x08,0x08,0x08,0x08,0x08,0x08,0x7E}, //I
53   {0x00,0x7E,0x08,0x08,0x08,0x08,0x08,0x48,0x30}, //J
54   {0x00,0x44,0x48,0x50,0x60,0x50,0x48,0x44,0x42}, //K
55   {0x00,0x70,0x20,0x20,0x20,0x20,0x22,0x22,0x3C}, //L
56   {0x00,0x81,0xC3,0xA5,0x99,0x81,0x81,0x81,0x81}, //M
```

```
57   {0x00,0x81,0xC1,0xA1,0x91,0x89,0x85,0x83,0x81}, //N
58   {0x00,0x18,0x24,0x42,0x42,0x42,0x42,0x24,0x18}, //O
59   {0x00,0xF8,0x44,0x44,0x48,0x70,0x40,0x40,0x40}, //P
60   {0x00,0x3C,0x42,0x81,0x81,0x81,0x4A,0x24,0x1A}, //Q
61   {0x00,0xF0,0x48,0x44,0x48,0x70,0x50,0x48,0xE4}, //R
62   {0x00,0x7C,0x80,0x80,0x78,0x04,0x04,0x04,0xF8}, //S
63   {0x00,0xFF,0x89,0x08,0x08,0x08,0x08,0x08,0x1C}, //T
64   {0x00,0x81,0x81,0x81,0x81,0x81,0x81,0x42,0x3C}, //U
65   {0x00,0x41,0x41,0x41,0x41,0x41,0x22,0x14,0x08}, //V
66   {0x00,0x81,0x81,0x42,0x5A,0x24,0x24,0x24,0x00}, //W
67   {0x00,0x82,0x44,0x28,0x10,0x28,0x44,0x82,0x00}, //V
68   {0x00,0x82,0x44,0x28,0x10,0x20,0x40,0x80,0x00}, //Y
69   {0x00,0xFE,0x04,0x08,0x10,0x20,0x40,0xFE,0x00}, //Z
70   {0x00,0x30,0x48,0x04,0x3C,0x44,0x44,0x3E,0x00}, //a
71   {0x00,0x40,0x40,0x40,0x78,0x44,0x44,0x78,0x00}, //b
72   {0x00,0x00,0x18,0x20,0x40,0x40,0x20,0x18,0x00}, //c
73   {0x00,0x08,0x08,0x08,0x18,0x28,0x28,0x18,0x00}, //d
74   {0x00,0x30,0x48,0x48,0x30,0x40,0x48,0x30,0x00}, //e
75   {0x00,0x18,0x24,0x20,0x78,0x20,0x20,0x70,0x00}, //f
76   {0x00,0x18,0x24,0x24,0x18,0x04,0x24,0x18,0x00}, //g
77   {0x00,0x20,0x20,0x20,0x38,0x24,0x24,0x24,0x00}, //h
78   {0x00,0x20,0x00,0x20,0x20,0x20,0x20,0x70,0x00}, //i
79   {0x00,0x08,0x00,0x08,0x08,0x08,0x48,0x38,0x10}, //j
80   {0x00,0x20,0x20,0x24,0x28,0x30,0x28,0x24,0x00}, //k
81   {0x00,0x20,0x60,0x20,0x20,0x20,0x20,0x78,0x00}, //l
82   {0x00,0x00,0x00,0x00,0x66,0x5A,0x42,0x42,0x00}, //m
83   {0x00,0x00,0x00,0x18,0x64,0x42,0x42,0x42,0x00}, //n
84   {0x00,0x00,0x00,0x18,0x24,0x24,0x24,0x18,0x00}, //o
85   {0x00,0x00,0x00,0x38,0x24,0x38,0x20,0x20,0x20}, //p
86   {0x00,0x00,0x18,0x24,0x24,0x1C,0x04,0x06,0x04}, //q
87   {0x00,0x00,0x58,0x24,0x20,0x20,0x20,0x20,0x00}, //r
88   {0x00,0x00,0x18,0x24,0x20,0x18,0x04,0x38,0x00}, //s
```

```
89  {0x00,0x10,0x38,0x10,0x10,0x10,0x14,0x08,0x00}, //t
90  {0x00,0x00,0x64,0x24,0x24,0x24,0x14,0x0A,0x00}, //u
91  {0x00,0x00,0x00,0xC2,0x44,0x28,0x10,0x00,0x00}, //v
92  {0x00,0x00,0x00,0x82,0x44,0x54,0x28,0x28,0x00}, //w
93  {0x00,0x00,0x00,0x44,0x28,0x10,0x28,0x44,0x00}, //x
94  {0x00,0x00,0x00,0x44,0x28,0x10,0x20,0x40,0x00}, //y
95  {0x00,0x00,0x00,0x78,0x08,0x10,0x20,0x78,0x00}  //z
96  };
97  void delay (unsigned char t)
98  {
99  for (n = 0; n < t; n ++)
100 {
101 TMR1 = 0;
102 while (TMR1 < 35050);
103 }
104 }
105 void sendByte(char info)
106 {
107 for(n = 0 ; n < 8 ; n ++ )
108 {
109 maxclk = 0;
110 maxin = ( (info << n) & 0x80 ) ? 1 : 0;
111 maxclk = 1;
112 }
113 }
114 void maxWrite(char add,char data)
115 {
116 maxload = 0;
117 sendByte(add);
118 sendByte(data);
119 maxload = 1;
120 }
```

```
121  void maxSetup()
122  {
123  maxWrite(decodeModeReg,disableDecode);
124  maxWrite (intensityReg,brightMax);
125  maxWrite(scanLimitReg,scanAll);
126  maxWrite(shutdownReg,normalOperation);
127  maxWrite(displayTestReg,noTest);
128  }
129  void main ()
130  {
131  // set up the timers and PORTS
132  T1CON = 0x8030;
133  TRISA = 0x0080;
134  TRISB = 0x00FF;
135  TRISC = 0X00FF;
136  TRISD = 0X0000;
137  TRISE = 0x0000;
138  PORTA = 0;
139  PORTB = 0;
140  PORTC = 0;
141  PORTD = 0;
142  PORTE = 0;
143  AD1PCFG = 0XFFFF;
144  AD1CON1 = 0;
145  DDPCONbits.JTAGEN = 0;
146  maxSetup ();
147  while (1)
148  {
149  maxWrite( 0, 0x00);
150  maxWrite( 1, 0x66);
151  maxWrite( 2, 0x66);
152  maxWrite( 3, 0x66);
```

```
153  maxWrite( 4, 0x7E);
154  maxWrite( 5, 0x7E);
155  maxWrite( 6, 0x66);
156  maxWrite( 7, 0x66);
157  maxWrite( 8, 0x66);
158  delay (60);
159  maxWrite( 0, 0x00);
160  maxWrite( 1, 0xC3);
161  maxWrite( 2, 0xC3);
162  maxWrite( 3, 0xC3);
163  maxWrite( 4, 0xDB);
164  maxWrite( 5, 0x5A);
165  maxWrite( 6, 0x7E);
166  maxWrite( 7, 0x66);
167  maxWrite( 8, 0x24);
168  delay (60);
169  nzero;
170  delay (60);
171  none;
172  delay (60);
173  ntwo;
174  delay (60);
175  nthree;
176  delay (60);
177  nfour;
178  delay (60);
179  for (row = 0; row < 62; row  ++)
180  {
181  for(col = 0; col < 9; col++)
182  {
183  maxWrite( col, show[row][col]);
184  }
```

```
185   delay (60);
186   }
187   }
188   }
```

Analysis of Listing 5-1

The first item we should look at, before we go too far into the analysis, is the two-dimensional array set up between lines 32 and 96. We create the array on line 32 and fill the array with data when we set it up.

The reason why we need a two-dimensional array is because we want to store the information to display 62 different characters to the dot matrix display. Each character will require 9 bytes of data to enable the matrix display to show the character. Therefore, the array will have 62 rows, one for each character, that holds 9 bytes, that is, 9 columns. The instruction to create and fill the array is on line 32 in the listing.

Line 32   unsigned const char show [62] [9] =

This instruction creates the array. It is done in a similar fashion to the single array we created in Chapters 3 and 4. However, the difference is that we have added a second square bracket. The two dimensions of the array correspond to rows and columns in the array. The first square bracket [62] sets up the number of rows in the array. The second square bracket [9] sets up the number of columns in the array. We are again including the "=" equal sign with the instruction. That is because we are going to define what is stored in the array with this instruction. The contents of each row in the array are listed within the opening and closing curly brackets on lines 33 and 96 that follow. We are using the term "const" as in const char to ensure that the contents in the array cannot be changed.

Line 34   {0x00,0x08,0x14,0x22,0x26,0x2A,0x32,0x14,0x08}, //0

This is defining what is stored in the first row of the array. The 9 hexadecimal numbers are what is stored in the 9 columns of the first row of the array. These 9 bytes will get the matrix to display the character "0," hence the comment //0 at the end of the line.

Lines 35–95 define what is stored in the remaining rows of the two-dimensional array.

Creating the Data for Each Row in the Two-Dimensional Array

We could determine the data for the 8 bits in each column, using a similar process as we did in Chapter 4, when we worked out the binary data for the four special characters. In Chapter 4, we also looked at using the software "pixel to matrix." As there are going to be 62 sets of nine different binary values to determine, we will use the software "pixel to matrix" to create the pixel maps for the matrix display. This can be freely downloaded from the Internet. The only real difference here is that bits 7, 6, and 5 could be both logic '1' and logic '0', whereas in Chapter 4, they were always a logic '0'.

The concept of how we relate the matrix to the two-dimensional array is shown in Figure 5-2.

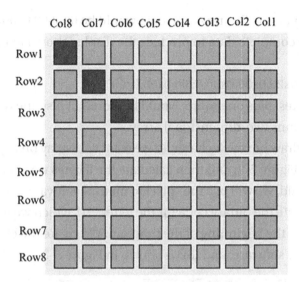

Figure 5-2. *The 8 by 8 Dot Matrix Grid*

The data for the whole display, in Figure 5-2, is for just one character we want to display on the matrix. We would create 8 bytes of data – note a byte is made up of 8 bits – that would be the data to display one character on the matrix display. Each byte would make up the 8 bits for one row on the display shown in Figure 5-2. The whole 8 bytes plus a ninth byte would make up the data to be stored in just one of the 62 rows in the two-dimensional array.

With respect to the grid shown in Figure 5-2, the top row is row1, and each row has eight cells. We can turn each cell on by indicating a logic '1' in the cell we want to light and a logic '0' in those we don't want to light. This means to light just the last cell, that is, cell 8, in row1, as shown in Figure 5-2, the 8-bit binary number would be 0b1000 0000 or 0x80 in hexadecimal.

The data for row2 would be 0b0100 0000 or 0x40.

For row3, it would be 0b0010 0000 or 0x20.

For the remaining five rows, the data would be 0b0000 0000 or 0x00. Therefore, the complete data to produce the display shown in Figure 5-2 would be

0x80,0x40,0x20,0x00,0x00,0x00,0x00,0x00

These 8 bytes, plus one more, would be stored in just one row of the 62 rows by 9 columns two-dimensional array.

We could draw out each character we want to display on a grid, such as that shown in Figure 5-2, and then calculate the 8 bytes we need, but, as I have already said, we will use the "pixel to matrix" software. I have used the program to create the binary code for the letter "H," which we will display on the matrix at the beginning of the program. We create the character in the form1 of the software, and this is shown in Figure 5-3.

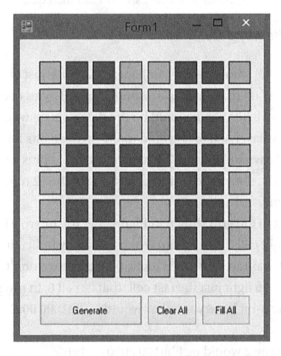

Figure 5-3. *The Form1 Drawn by Me in the Pixel to Matrix Program*

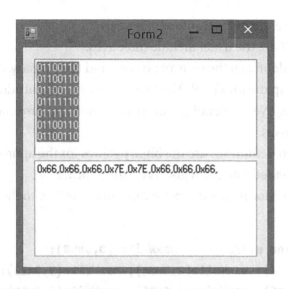

Figure 5-4. *The Form2 with the 8 Bytes of Data to Display the "H"*

Figure 5-4 shows the form2 that is created when you click the Generate button on the form1 display. This will list the 8-bit binary and hexadecimal values to create the symbol you want, the H in this case, for you to store in one of the rows in the array. There is one issue I have found when using this array, and that is that you need to add an extra byte at the beginning of the list. This is the 0x00 that I have added here, shown in bold:

0x00,0x66,0x66,0x66,0x7E,0x7E,0x66,0x66,0x66

I have used this pixel to matrix program to create a list of 9 bytes for the 62 rows in the array "show." When the program accesses this array, the display will show the numbers 0–9 and then go through the alphabet in capital letters and then go through the alphabet in small letters. I have used comments, at the end of the lines, to indicate what character that row will display. That is why there are 62 rows in the array: 10 for the numbers 0–9, 26 for the uppercase letters of the alphabet, and 26 for the lowercase letters.

I hope this description of how we create the two-dimensional array and use the pixel to matrix software to create the data to fill the array is helpful. We can now carry on with the analysis of the program listing.

Lines 1–5 are the normal comments we use.

Line 6 and 7 are the usual include directives.

Lines 8–22 define all the control phrases and their binary values that are used to set up the Max7219. The first five are the actual addresses of the control registers. We are defining phrases with some appropriate wording for these addresses.

The next ten definitions are the binary values for the appropriate settings to be loaded into the registers defined earlier.

Lines 23–25 allocate the three inputs to the Max7219 to the bits on PORTA.

Line 26 #define nzero   maxWrite (0,0x00);
maxWrite(1,0x08); maxWrite(2,0x14); maxWrite(3,0x22);
maxWrite(4,0x26); maxWrite(5,0x2A); maxWrite(6,0x32);
maxWrite(7,0x14); maxWrite(8,0x08);

This is defining what the phrase "nzero" means. When the compiler sees the phrase "nzero" in the program listing, it knows I mean the program should carry out the list of nine instructions, with their bytes of data, that are defined here, on line 25. These nine instructions call the subroutine "maxWrite" and send the 9 bytes needed to display a "0" with a line through the nought on the matrix.

On line 169, there is the phrase "nzero." This gets the PIC to carry out the nine instructions, defined here, on line 25. The nine instructions call the subroutine "maxWrite" and send the parameters defined on line 25 to the subroutine "maxWrite" for each of the 9 bytes of data. Inside the normal brackets of the instructions, there are two values. The first indicates the particular row on the matrix display, and the next value is the data to turn on or off the LEDs on that row. For example, the instruction maxWrite (1,0x08); sends the data 0x08 to turn on or off the LEDs in row1 of the matrix display. In this instance, it will turn on just the one LED on column 4 of row1.

This is quite a powerful use of the define aspect of the C compiler. It allows us to list, in this case, nine instructions, with just a single phrase. It works in a similar fashion as a "macro" in a word processing software, where just one special key stroke could write a predefined set of words or characters. As you become more experienced in C programming, you could make more use of this concept.

Lines 27–30 do the same for the numbers 1, 2, 3, and 4.

Line 31 creates the three unsigned char global variables used in the program.

Lines 32–95 create the two-dimensional array as described earlier.

Lines 97–104 create our usual variable delay subroutine.

Line 105 void sendByte (char info)

This is creating a subroutine that will be used to send a byte to the DIN pin of the Max7219. I have called the output of the PIC that connects to this DIN pin of the matrix display, "maxin"; see line 23 of the listing. This subroutine expects the PIC to send a byte to it when it is called from the program. The subroutine will then load this byte into the local variable "info" to be used in the subroutine.

Line 107 for (n = 0; n < 8; n ++)

This sets up a normal for do loop that is carried out eight times, once for each bit in the byte that has been loaded into "info."

Line 109 maxclk = 0;

This puts a logic '0' onto the output pin RA2 on PORTA; see line 25. This is connected to the "clk" input of the Max7219. This means we are sending the clock to a logic '0', ready to go back to a logic '1', which is the signal to latch the first bit into the 7219.

Line 110 maxin = ((info << n) & 0x80) ? 1 : 0;

189

This is quite an involved instruction. It is performing an action detailed within the normal brackets, then testing if the action results in a true outcome. It then tells the PIC what logic to put onto the output pin "maxin" depending upon the outcome of the test.

The action that is listed between the outer brackets is **(info << n) & 0x80**. What this does is perform a logic AND with the contents of the variable "info" and the number 0X80, but only *after* the contents in that variable have been shifted to the left. The number of bits that the contents of the variable are shifted is controlled by the value in the variable "n."

To help explain the operation of this instruction, we will assume that the information loaded into the variable "info," when the subroutine was called, is 0x66 or 0b01100110 in binary.

If we now assume this is the first run through the "for do loop" in the subroutine, then n = 0.

This means we will not shift the data in the variable "info," that is, shift it 0 places to the left.

This then means the two bytes that will be ANDed will be as shown in Table 5-1.

Table 5-1. *The Logical AND Operation When n = 0*

	Bit 7	Bit 6	Bit 5	Bit 4	Bit 3	Bit 2	Bit 1	Bit 0
Info After being shifted	0	1	1	0	0	1	1	0
0x80	1	0	0	0	0	0	0	0
Result	**0**	**0**	**0**	**0**	**0**	**0**	**0**	**0**

This will result in the test being untrue. You should appreciate that we are only testing the bit 7 of the variable "info" as the data 0x80 is 0b10000000 in binary. Really, only when bit 7 of the variable "info" is a logic '1' will the test be true. This is because a logical AND operation will only produce a "1" when both bits are a logic '1'. So, what happens now that the result is untrue? A good question. You can see that there is the following after the brackets:

```
? 1 : 0
```

The question mark relates to the test part of the instruction. The "1" is the logic that the pin "maxin" goes to if the test was true. The "0" after the colon is what the pin "maxin" goes to if the test was untrue. This means that the pin "maxin" goes to a logic '0', in this case, as the result of the test was untrue.

After the PIC has carried out this instruction once, the PIC carries out the next instruction on line 111.

Line 111 maxclk = 1;

This will set the "clk" pin high which is the signal for the Max7219 to latch the data at the DIN pin to the register in the 7219. Note, at this moment in time, this will be the MSB, bit 15, of the 16-bit data register inside the 7219.

Now the PIC goes back to line 107, where it increments the value in "n." Now n = 1, which is still less than 8, so the PIC goes to line 109, where it resets the "clk" line to logic '0'.

Now, when we carry out the instruction on line 110, the data in "info" is shifted one place to the left. This means that the logical AND operation is as shown in Table 5-2.

Table 5-2. *The Logical AND Operation When n = 1*

	Bit 7	Bit 6	Bit 5	Bit 4	Bit 3	Bit 2	Bit 1	Bit 0
Info After being shifted	1	1	0	0	1	1	0	0
0x80	1	0	0	0	0	0	0	0
Result	1	0	0	0	0	0	0	0

This time, the AND operation produces a true result, which means the pin "maxin" is sent to a logic '1'. This means that the logic on DIN on the 7219 is sent to a logic '1'. Now when the PIC sends the "clk" high, as with line 111, the 7219 latches the logic '1', but now into bit 14 of the data register inside the 7219. The cycle repeats until n = 8. The final result would be that bits 15 to 8 of the data register in the 7129 have the same data as was loaded into the variable info. In this case, it would be

0b01100110xxxxxxxx

Note the remaining 8 lower bits have not been loaded yet.

So, this instruction will split a byte of data up into its 8 single bits and send them one at a time to the DIN pin of the 7219. This is a very complex instruction which has required a detailed explanation of how it works. I hope you can follow the explanation without too much trouble.

Line 114 void maxWrite(char add,char data)

This sets up a subroutine that will write two bytes of data to the 7219. It expects the PIC to send up two bytes of info to the subroutine. These will be loaded into the two local variables "add" and "data."

The first variable, "add," will be the address of the control register the "data" is to be written to, if the info is for a control command. However, if the info is a character to be displayed, then the "add" will be the "row" number of the matrix. If we are sending a command to the 7219, then the "data" will be the command we want to send. However, if we are sending a character, then the "data" will be the column number.

Line 116 maxload = 0;

This sets the logic on the "maxload" pin to logic '0'. This is to get the load pin of the 7216 ready to go to a logic '1', which is the signal to latch the full 16 bits to the 7219 and get it to respond to them.

Line 117 sendByte (add);

This calls the subroutine "sendByte" to send the first byte of the two bytes required to the 7219. This sends the information loaded into the variable "add" when the "maxWrite" subroutine was called. We have looked at how this subroutine, "sendByte," splits a byte up into the single 8 bits and sends them to the 7219. This will be the high byte.

Line 118 sendByte (data);

This calls the subroutine "sendByte" a second time to send the second byte of the two bytes required to the 7219. This sends the information loaded into the variable "data" when the "maxWrite" subroutine was called. This uses the "sendByte" subroutine again. This time, it will be the low byte.

With these two instructions, we can send the full 16 bits of the command instruction or the "data to be displayed instruction" to the 7219.

Line 119 maxload = 1;

This sets the logic on the "maxload" pin of the 7219 to a logic '1'. This is the action needed to get the 7219 to latch the 16 bits into the register and respond to them.

Line 121 void maxSetup ()

This sets up a subroutine that is used to send the commands to set up the Max7219 as we want to use it.

Lines 123–127 send the commands for the following actions:

- Set up the 7219 to disable the decode

- Set for maximum brightness

- Set to scan all inputs

- Set to use normal operation

- Have no test action

These five subroutine calls send two bytes. The first is the address of the particular register to be written to. The second is the binary value for the particular command.

Lines 129–145 create the main loop and set up the PIC as normal.

Line 146 maxSetup ();

This is the first real action of the program, and it is to call the setup subroutine and set up the 7219 as per that subroutine.

Line 147 while (1)

This sets up a "for every loop" so that the PIC does not carry out the instructions on lines 131–146 again.

Lines 149–157 call the subroutine "maxWrite" and send the information to display the symbol "H" on the dot matrix.

Line 158 delay (60);

This just creates a delay of approximately two seconds.

Lines 159–168 do the same for the symbol "W."

Line 169 nzero;

This is the phrase that was defined in line 26. The PIC will now carry out the instructions listed in that line which sends the symbol 0 to the display.

Lines 170–178 do the same for the numbers 1, 2, 3, and 4 but with a two-second delay between them.

Line 179 for (row = 0; row < 62; row ++)

This sets up an outer loop that will be used to access the two-dimensional array "show," created between lines 32 and 96.

Line 181 for(col = 0; col < 9; col++)

This sets up the inner loop that will be used to access the columns for each of the rows in the array "show."

Line 183 maxWrite(col, show[row][col]);

This accesses the array "show" and sends the information to the subroutine "maxWrite." The value of "row" varies from 0 to 62 and so accesses all rows in the array. The value of "col" varies from 0 to 9, so that the PIC can access each of the columns in the array as the "row" value changes from 0 to 62.

Line 183 sends the "col" number to control which column in the matrix display we are writing to. Then with the "show[row][col]", it selects which byte from the array "show" it will display on the current column in the matrix display. The "row" number stays initially at 0, while the "col" number increments until it reaches the value of 9, as the PIC cycles through the inner loop. This ensures that the PIC retrieves the 9 bytes of data for the first character to be displayed on the matrix display. Then the PIC goes to the outer loop where it increments the value in "row" to 1. The PIC then repeats the inner loop where it gets the 9 bytes from the array "show" to display the next character. The PIC then goes back to line 179 and so repeats the whole process 62 times. In this way, the PIC can cycle through all the rows in the array and so get all the 9 bytes from all 62 rows of the array "show."

Line 185 delay (60);

This calls a two-second delay between displaying each character.

I hope you have been able to follow the analysis of this program, as it is quite a complex program, which is covering some new and challenging concepts.

Controlling Four 64-Bit Dot Matrix Boards

In this next program, we will look at controlling four of these dot matrix boards together. This is so that we can display a message made up of four characters. We will then extend this program to create a scrolling type message that can use more than four characters in any number of words.

The program listing for this new matrix program is shown in Listing 5-2.

Listing 5-2. The Four Dot Matrix Displays

```
1   /* File:    64BitMatrixCaseSmallProg.c
2   Author: H. H. Ward
3   Using the 7219 matrix controller with four matrix boards
4   Created on 01 October 2021, 16:36
5   */
6   #include <xc.h>
7   #include <con72Meg36Meg32Bit.h>
8   #define decodeModeReg       0b00001001
9   #define intensityReg        0b00001010
10  #define scanLimitReg        0b00001011
11  #define shutdownReg         0b00001100
12  #define displayTestReg      0b00001111
13  #define disableDecode       0b00000000
14  #define codeB0              0b00000001
15  #define codeB4              0b00001111
16  #define codeB8              0b11111111
17  #define brightMax           0b00001111
18  #define brightMin           0b00000001
19  #define scanAll             0b00000111
20  #define normalOperation     0b00000001
21  #define shutdown            0b00000000
```

```
22  #define noTest              0b00000000
23  #define maxin               _RA0
24  #define maxload             _RA1
25  #define maxclk              _RA2
26  #define nzero      maxWrite (0,0x00); maxWrite(1,0x08);
    maxWrite(2,0x14); maxWrite(3,0x22); maxWrite(4,0x26);
    maxWrite(5,0x2A); maxWrite(6,0x32); maxWrite(7,0x14);
    maxWrite(8,0x08);
27  #define none       maxWrite (0,0x00); maxWrite (1,0x08);
    maxWrite (2,0x18); maxWrite (3,0x28); maxWrite (4,0x08);
    maxWrite (5,0x08); maxWrite (6,0x08); maxWrite (7,0x08);
    maxWrite (8,0x3E);
28  #define ntwo       maxWrite (0,0x00); maxWrite(1,0x1C);
    maxWrite(2,0x22); maxWrite(3,0x22); maxWrite(4,0x02);
    maxWrite(5,0x3C); maxWrite(6,0x20); maxWrite(7,0x20);
    maxWrite(8,0x3E);
29  #define nthree     maxWrite (0,0x00); maxWrite (1,0x38);
    maxWrite (2,0x04); maxWrite (3,0x04); maxWrite (4,0x04);
    maxWrite (5,0x1C); maxWrite (6,0x04); maxWrite(7,0x04);
    maxWrite(8,0x38);
30  #define nfour      maxWrite (0,0x00); maxWrite (1,0x04);
    maxWrite (2,0x0C); maxWrite (3,0x14); maxWrite (4,0x24);
    maxWrite (5,0x7C); maxWrite (6,0x04); maxWrite (7,0x04);
    maxWrite (8,0x3F);
31  #define nfive      maxWrite (0,0x00); maxWrite (1,0x7C);
    maxWrite (2,0x40); maxWrite (3,0x40); maxWrite (4,0x40);
    maxWrite (5,0x7C); maxWrite (6,0x04); maxWrite (7,0x04);
    maxWrite (8,0x7C);
32  #define nsix       maxWrite (0,0x00); maxWrite (1,0x7C);
    maxWrite (2,0x40); maxWrite (3,0x40); maxWrite (4,0x40);
    maxWrite (5,0x7C); maxWrite (6,0x44); maxWrite (7,0x44);
    maxWrite (8,0x7C);
```

```
33  #define nseven        maxWrite (0,0x00); maxWrite (1,0xFF);
    maxWrite (2,0x02); maxWrite (3,0x04); maxWrite (4,0x08);
    maxWrite (5,0x10); maxWrite (6,0x20); maxWrite (7,0x40);
    maxWrite (8,0x80);
34  #define neight        maxWrite (0,0x00); maxWrite (1,0x1C);
    maxWrite (2,0x22); maxWrite (3,0x22); maxWrite (4,0x22);
    maxWrite (5,0x1C); maxWrite (6,0x22); maxWrite (7,0x22);
    maxWrite (8,0x1C);
35  #define nnine         maxWrite (0,0x00); maxWrite (1,0x1C);
    maxWrite (2,0x22); maxWrite (3,0x22); maxWrite (4,0x22);
    maxWrite (5,0x1E); maxWrite (6,0x02); maxWrite (7,0x02);
    maxWrite (8,0x02);
36  #define letA          maxWrite (0,0x00); maxWrite (1,0x10);
    maxWrite (2,0x28); maxWrite (3,0x44); maxWrite (4,0x44);
    maxWrite (5,0x7C); maxWrite (6,0x44); maxWrite (7,0x44);
    maxWrite (8,0x44);
37  #define letB          maxWrite (0,0x00); maxWrite (1,0x70);
    maxWrite (2,0x48); maxWrite (3,0x48); maxWrite (4,0x70);
    maxWrite (5,0x48); maxWrite (6,0x44); maxWrite (7,0x44);
    maxWrite (8,0x78);
38  #define letC          maxWrite (0,0x00); maxWrite (1,0x1C);
    maxWrite (2,0x20); maxWrite (3,0x40); maxWrite (4,0x40);
    maxWrite (5,0x40); maxWrite (6,0x20); maxWrite (7,0x1C);
    maxWrite (8,0x00);
39  #define letD          maxWrite (0,0x00); maxWrite (1,0x70);
    maxWrite (2,0x48); maxWrite (3,0x44); maxWrite (4,0x44);
    maxWrite (5,0x44); maxWrite (6,0x48); maxWrite (7,0x70);
    maxWrite (8,0x00);
40  #define letE          maxWrite (0,0x00); maxWrite (1,0x78);
    maxWrite (2,0x40); maxWrite (3,0x40); maxWrite (4,0x70);
    maxWrite (5,0x40); maxWrite (6,0x40); maxWrite (7,0x78);
    maxWrite (8,0x00);
```

```
41  #define letF        maxWrite (0,0x00); maxWrite (1,0x78);
    maxWrite (2,0x40); maxWrite (3,0x40); maxWrite (4,0x70);
    maxWrite (5,0x40); maxWrite (6,0x40); maxWrite (7,0x40);
    maxWrite (8,0x00);
42  #define letG        maxWrite (0,0x00); maxWrite (1,0x38);
    maxWrite (2,0x44); maxWrite (3,0x40); maxWrite (4,0x58);
    maxWrite (5,0x44); maxWrite (6,0x44); maxWrite (7,0x38);
    maxWrite (8,0x00);
43  #define letH        maxWrite (0,0x00); maxWrite (1,0x44);
    maxWrite (2,0x44); maxWrite (3,0x44); maxWrite (4,0x7C);
    maxWrite (5,0x44); maxWrite (6,0x44); maxWrite (7,0x44);
    maxWrite (8,0x00);
44  #define letI        maxWrite (0,0x00); maxWrite (1,0x7C);
    maxWrite (2,0x10); maxWrite (3,0x10); maxWrite (4,0x10);
    maxWrite (5,0x10); maxWrite (6,0x10); maxWrite (7,0x7C);
    maxWrite (8,0x00);
45  #define letJ        maxWrite (0,0x00); maxWrite (1,0x00);
    maxWrite (2,0x3E); maxWrite (3,0x08); maxWrite (4,0x08);
    maxWrite (5,0x08); maxWrite (6,0x48); maxWrite (7,0x38);
    maxWrite (8,0x10);
46  #define letK        maxWrite (0,0x00); maxWrite (1,0x44);
    maxWrite (2,0x48); maxWrite (3,0x50); maxWrite (4,0x60);
    maxWrite (5,0x50); maxWrite (6,0x48); maxWrite (7,0x44);
    maxWrite (8,0x00);
47  #define letL        maxWrite (0,0x00); maxWrite (1,0x70);
    maxWrite (2,0x20); maxWrite (3,0x20); maxWrite (4,0x20);
    maxWrite (5,0x20); maxWrite (6,0x22); maxWrite (7,0x3C);
    maxWrite (8,0x00);
48  #define letM        maxWrite (0,0x00); maxWrite (1,0x41);
    maxWrite (2,0x63); maxWrite (3,0x55); maxWrite (4,0x49);
    maxWrite (5,0x41); maxWrite (6,0x41); maxWrite (7,0x41);
    maxWrite (8,0x00);
```

```
49  #define letN        maxWrite (0,0x00); maxWrite (1,0x42);
    maxWrite (2,0x62); maxWrite (3,0x52); maxWrite (4,0x4A);
    maxWrite (5,0x46); maxWrite (6,0x42); maxWrite (7,0x42);
    maxWrite (8,0x00);
50  #define letO        maxWrite (0,0x00); maxWrite (1,0x18);
    maxWrite (2,0x24); maxWrite (3,0x42); maxWrite (4,0x42);
    maxWrite (5,0x42); maxWrite (6,0x24); maxWrite (7,0x18);
    maxWrite (8,0x00);
51  #define letP        maxWrite (0,0x00); maxWrite (1,0xF8);
    maxWrite (2,0x44); maxWrite (3,0x44); maxWrite (4,0x78);
    maxWrite (5,0x40); maxWrite (6,0x40); maxWrite (7,0xE0);
    maxWrite (8,0x00);
52  #define letQ        maxWrite (0,0x00); maxWrite (1,0x18);
    maxWrite (2,0x24); maxWrite (3,0x42); maxWrite (4,0x42);
    maxWrite (5,0x42); maxWrite (6,0x24); maxWrite (7,0x1C);
    maxWrite (8,0x02);
53  #define letR        maxWrite (0,0x00); maxWrite (1,0xF0);
    maxWrite (2,0x48); maxWrite (3,0x44); maxWrite (4,0x48);
    maxWrite (5,0x70); maxWrite (6,0x50); maxWrite (7,0x48);
    maxWrite (8,0xE4);
54  #define letS        maxWrite (0,0x00); maxWrite (1,0x30);
    maxWrite (2,0x48); maxWrite (3,0x40); maxWrite (4,0x30);
    maxWrite (5,0x08); maxWrite (6,0x48); maxWrite (7,0x30);
    maxWrite (8,0x00);
55  #define letT        maxWrite (0,0x00); maxWrite (1,0x7C);
    maxWrite (2,0x94); maxWrite (3,0x10); maxWrite (4,0x10);
    maxWrite (5,0x10); maxWrite (6,0x10); maxWrite (7,0x38);
    maxWrite (8,0x00);
56  #define letU        maxWrite (0,0x00); maxWrite (1,0xE4);
    maxWrite (2,0x64); maxWrite (3,0x64); maxWrite (4,0x64);
    maxWrite (5,0x64); maxWrite (6,0x24); maxWrite (7,0x18);
    maxWrite (8,0x00);
```

```
57  #define letV        maxWrite (0,0x00); maxWrite (1,0x41);
    maxWrite (2,0x41); maxWrite (3,0x22); maxWrite (4,0x22);
    maxWrite (5,0x14); maxWrite (6,0x14); maxWrite (7,0x08);
    maxWrite (8,0x00);
58  #define letW        maxWrite (0,0x00); maxWrite (1,0x81);
    maxWrite (2,0x81); maxWrite (3,0x42); maxWrite (4,0x5A);
    maxWrite (5,0x24); maxWrite (6,0x24); maxWrite (7,0x24);
    maxWrite (8,0x00);
59  #define letX        maxWrite (0,0x00); maxWrite (1,0x82);
    maxWrite (2,0x44); maxWrite (3,0x28); maxWrite (4,0x10);
    maxWrite (5,0x28); maxWrite (6,0x44); maxWrite (7,0x82);
    maxWrite (8,0x00);
60  #define letY        maxWrite (0,0x00); maxWrite (1,0x82);
    maxWrite (2,0x44); maxWrite (3,0x28); maxWrite (4,0x10);
    maxWrite (5,0x20); maxWrite (6,0x40); maxWrite (7,0x80);
    maxWrite (8,0x00);
61  #define letZ        maxWrite (0,0x00); maxWrite (1,0xFE);
    maxWrite (2,0x04); maxWrite (3,0x08); maxWrite (4,0x10);
    maxWrite (5,0x20); maxWrite (6,0x40); maxWrite (7,0xFE);
    maxWrite (8,0x00);
62  #define sma         maxWrite (0,0x00); maxWrite (1,0x38);
    maxWrite (2,0x44); maxWrite (3,0x04); maxWrite (4,0x04);
    maxWrite (5,0x3C); maxWrite (6,0x44); maxWrite (7,0x44);
    maxWrite (8,0x3F);
63  #define smb         maxWrite (0,0x00); maxWrite (1,0x40);
    maxWrite (2,0x40); maxWrite (3,0x40); maxWrite (4,0x40);
    maxWrite (5,0x78); maxWrite (6,0x44); maxWrite (7,0x44);
    maxWrite (8,0x78);
64  #define smc         maxWrite (0,0x00); maxWrite (1,0x00);
    maxWrite (2,0x00); maxWrite (3,0x00); maxWrite (4,0x1C);
    maxWrite (5,0x20); maxWrite (6,0x20); maxWrite (7,0x20);
    maxWrite (8,0x1C);
```

```
65  #define smd           maxWrite (0,0X00); maxWrite (1,0x04);
    maxWrite (2,0x04); maxWrite (3,0x04); maxWrite (4,0x04);
    maxWrite (5,0x3C); maxWrite (6,0x44); maxWrite (7,0x44);
    maxWrite (8,0x3C);
66  #define sme           maxWrite (0,0x00); maxWrite (1,0x00);
    maxWrite (2,0x1C); maxWrite (3,0x22); maxWrite (4,0x42);
    maxWrite (5,0x7C); maxWrite (6,0x40); maxWrite (7,0x20);
    maxWrite (8,0x1E);
67  #define smf           maxWrite (0,0x00); maxWrite (1,0x00);
    maxWrite (2,0x0C); maxWrite (3,0x10); maxWrite (4,0x10);
    maxWrite (5,0x38); maxWrite (6,0x10); maxWrite (7,0x10);
    maxWrite (8,0x38);
68  Write (0,0x00); maxWrite (1,0x00); maxWrite (2,0x1E);
    maxWrite (3,0x24); maxWrite (4,0x24); maxWrite (5,0x3C);
    maxWrite (6,0x04); maxWrite (7,0x24); maxWrite (8,0x18);
69  #define smh           maxWrite (0,0x00); maxWrite (1,0x00);
    maxWrite (2,0x00); maxWrite (3,0x20); maxWrite (4,0x20);
    maxWrite (5,0x20); maxWrite (6,0x38); maxWrite (7,0x24);
    maxWrite (8,0x24);
70  #define smi           maxWrite (0,0x00); maxWrite (1,0x00);
    maxWrite (2,0x00); maxWrite (3,0x10); maxWrite (4,0x00);
    maxWrite (5,0x30); maxWrite (6,0x10); maxWrite (7,0x10);
    maxWrite (8,0x38);
71  #define smj           maxWrite (0,0x00); maxWrite (1,0x00);
    maxWrite (2,0x00); maxWrite (3,0x04); maxWrite (4,0x00);
    maxWrite (5,0x1C); maxWrite (6,0x04); maxWrite (7,0x04);
    maxWrite (8,0x1C);
72  #define smk           maxWrite (0,0x00); maxWrite (1,0x00);
    maxWrite (2,0x20); maxWrite (3,0x20); maxWrite (4,0x24);
    maxWrite (5,0x28); maxWrite (6,0x30); maxWrite (7,0x28);
    maxWrite (8,0x00);
```

```
73  #define sml           maxWrite (0,0x00); maxWrite (1,0x00);
    maxWrite (2,0x00); maxWrite (3,0x00); maxWrite (4,0x10);
    maxWrite (5,0x10); maxWrite (6,0x10); maxWrite (7,0x10);
    maxWrite (8,0x3C);
74  #define smm           maxWrite (0,0x00); maxWrite (1,0x00);
    maxWrite (2,0x00); maxWrite (3,0x00); maxWrite (4,0x40);
    maxWrite (5,0x68); maxWrite (6,0x54); maxWrite (7,0x54);
    maxWrite (8,0x54);
75  #define smn           maxWrite (0,0x00); maxWrite (1,0x00);
    maxWrite (2,0x00); maxWrite (3,0x00); maxWrite (4,0x40);
    maxWrite (5,0x70); maxWrite (6,0x48); maxWrite (7,0x48);
    maxWrite (8,0x48);
76  #define smo           maxWrite (0,0x00); maxWrite (1,0x00);
    maxWrite (2,0x00); maxWrite (3,0x00); maxWrite (4,0x38);
    maxWrite (5,0x44); maxWrite (6,0x44); maxWrite (7,0x44);
    maxWrite (8,0x38);
77  #define smp           maxWrite (0,0x00); maxWrite (1,0x00);
    maxWrite (2,0x00); maxWrite (3,0x00); maxWrite (4,0x38);
    maxWrite (5,0x24); maxWrite (6,0x38); maxWrite (7,0x20);
    maxWrite (8,0x70);
78  #define smq           maxWrite (0,0x00); maxWrite (1,0x00);
    maxWrite (2,0x00); maxWrite (3,0x38); maxWrite (4,0x48);
    maxWrite (5,0x48); maxWrite (6,0x38); maxWrite (7,0x08);
    maxWrite (8,0x3C);
79  #define smr           maxWrite (0,0x00); maxWrite (1,0x00);
    maxWrite (2,0x00); maxWrite (3,0x00); maxWrite (4,0x58);
    maxWrite (5,0x20); maxWrite (6,0x20); maxWrite (7,0x20);
    maxWrite (8,0x78);
80  #define sms           maxWrite (0,0x00); maxWrite (1,0x00);
    maxWrite (2,0x00); maxWrite (3,0x18); maxWrite (4,0x24);
    maxWrite (5,0x20); maxWrite (6,0x18); maxWrite (7,0x04);
    maxWrite (8,0x38);
```

```
81  #define smt          maxWrite (0,0x00); maxWrite (1,0x00);
    maxWrite (2,0x00); maxWrite (3,0x20); maxWrite (4,0x20);
    maxWrite (5,0x78); maxWrite (6,0x20); maxWrite (7,0x20);
    maxWrite (8,0x38);
82  #define smu          maxWrite (0,0x00); maxWrite (1,0x00);
    maxWrite (2,0x00); maxWrite (3,0x00); maxWrite (4,0x00);
    maxWrite (5,0x64); maxWrite (6,0x24); maxWrite (7,0x24);
    maxWrite (8,0x1A);
83  #define smv          maxWrite (0,0x00); maxWrite (1,0x00);
    maxWrite (2,0x00); maxWrite (3,0x00); maxWrite (4,0x63);
    maxWrite (5,0x22); maxWrite (6,0x22); maxWrite (7,0x14);
    maxWrite (8,0x08);
84  #define smw          maxWrite (0,0x00); maxWrite (1,0x00);
    maxWrite (2,0x00); maxWrite (3,0x00); maxWrite (4,0x80);
    maxWrite (5,0x49); maxWrite (6,0x49); maxWrite (7,0x55);
    maxWrite (8,0x22);
85  #define smx          maxWrite (0,0x00); maxWrite (1,0x00);
    maxWrite (2,0x00); maxWrite (3,0x00); maxWrite (4,0x42);
    maxWrite (5,0x24); maxWrite (6,0x18); maxWrite (7,0x24);
    maxWrite (8,0x42);
86  #define smy          maxWrite (0,0x00); maxWrite (1,0x00);
    maxWrite (2,0x00); maxWrite (3,0x00); maxWrite (4,0x22);
    maxWrite (5,0x14); maxWrite (6,0x08); maxWrite (7,0x10);
    maxWrite (8,0x20);
87  #define smz          maxWrite (0,0x00); maxWrite (1,0x00);
    maxWrite (2,0x00); maxWrite (3,0x00); maxWrite (4,0x3E);
    maxWrite (5,0x04); maxWrite (6,0x08); maxWrite (7,0x10);
    maxWrite (8,0x3E);
88  unsigned char n, row, col,display, rdatain;
89  void delay (unsigned char t)
```

```
90  {
91  for (n = 0; n < t; n ++)
92  {
93  TMR1 = 0;
94  while (TMR1 < 35050);
95  }
96  }
97  void sendByte(char info)
98  {
99  for(n = 0 ; n < 8 ; n ++ )
100 {
101 maxclk = 0;
102 maxin = ( (info << n) & 0x80 ) ? 1 : 0; //send bits to max
    MSB of byte first this test to see if the bit ANDED with
    0X80 is true. If it is then bit is '1' if not bit is '0'
103 maxclk = 1;
104 }
105 }
106 void maxWrite(char add,char data)
107 {
108 switch (display)
109 {
110 case 0:
111 {
112 maxload = 0;
113 sendByte(add);
114 sendByte(data);
115 sendByte(0x00);
116 sendByte(0x00);
117 sendByte(0x00);
118 sendByte(0x00);
119 sendByte(0x00);
```

```
120   sendByte(0x00);
121   maxload = 1;
122   break;
123   }
124   case 1:
125   {
126   maxload = 0;
127   sendByte(0x00);
128   sendByte(0x00);
129   sendByte(add);
130   sendByte(data);
131   sendByte(0x00);
132   sendByte(0x00);
133   sendByte(0x00);
134   sendByte(0x00);
135   maxload = 1;
136   break;
137   }
138   case 2:
139   {
140   maxload = 0;
141   sendByte(0x00);
142   sendByte(0x00);
143   sendByte(0x00);
144   sendByte(0x00);
145   sendByte(add);
146   sendByte(data);
147   sendByte(0x00);
148   sendByte(0x00);
149   maxload = 1;
150   break;
151   }
```

```
152  case 3:
153  {
154  maxload = 0;
155  sendByte(0x00);
156  sendByte(0x00);
157  sendByte(0x00);
158  sendByte(0x00);
159  sendByte(0x00);
160  sendByte(0x00);
161  sendByte(add);
162  sendByte(data);
163  maxload = 1;
164  break;
165  }
166  }
167  }
168  void gotdata (unsigned char rdata, unsigned char dn)
169  {
170  switch (rdata)
171  {
172  case 48:
173  {
174  display = dn;
175  nzero;
176  delay(16);
177  break;
178  }
179  case 49:
180  {
181  display = dn;
182  none;
```

```
183   delay(16);
184   break;
185   }
186   case 50:
187   {
188   display = dn;
189   ntwo;
190   delay(16);
191   break;
192   }
193   case 51:
194   {
195   display = dn;
196   nthree;
197   delay(16);
198   break;
199   }
200   case 52:
201   {
202   display = dn;
203   nfour;
204   delay(16);
205   break;
206   }
207   case 53:
208   {
209   display = dn;
210   nfive;
211   delay(16);
212   break;
213   }
```

```
214  case 54:
215  {
216  display = dn;
217  nsix;
218  delay(16);
219  break;
220  }
221  case 55:
222  {
223  display = dn;
224  nseven;
225  delay(16);
226  break;
227  }
228  case 56:
229  {
230  display = dn;
231  neight;
232  delay(16);
233  break;
234  }
235  case 57:
236  {
237  display = dn;
238  nnine;
239  delay(16);
240  break;
241  }
242  case 101:
243  {
244  display = dn;
```

```
245   letA;
246   delay(16);
247   break;
248   }
249   case 102:
250   {
251   display = dn;
252   letB;
253   delay(16);
254   break;
255   }
256   case 103:
257   {
258   display = dn;
259   letC;
260   delay(16);
261   break;
262   }
263   case 104:
264   {
265   display = dn;
266   letD;
267   delay(16);
268   break;
269   }
270   case 105:
271   {
272   display = dn;
273   letE;
274   delay(16);
275   break;
276   }
```

```
277  case 106:
278  {
279  display = dn;
280  letF;
281  delay(16);
282  break;
283  }
284  case 107:
285  {
286  display = dn;
287  letG;
288  delay(16);
289  break;
290  }
291  case 110:
292  {
293  display = dn;
294  letH;
295  delay(16);
296  break;
297  }
298  case 111:
299  {
300  display = dn;
301  letI;
302  delay(16);
303  break;
304  case 112:
305  {
306  display = dn;
307  letJ;
```

```
308   delay(16);
309   break;
310   }
311   case 113:
312   {
313   display = dn;
314   letK;
315   delay(16);
316   break;
317   }
318   case 114:
319   {
320   display = dn;
321   letL;
322   delay(16);
323   break;
324   }
325   case 115:
326   {
327   display = dn;
328   letM;
329   delay(16);
330   break;
331   }
332   case 116:
333   {
334   display = dn;
335   letN;
336   delay(16);
337   break;
338   }
```

```
339  case 117:
340  {
341  display = dn;
342  letO;
343  delay(16);
344  break;
345  }
346  case 120:
347  {
348  display = dn;
349  letP;
350  delay(16);
351  break;
352  }
353  case 121:
354  {
355  display = dn;
356  letQ;
357  delay(16);
358  break;
359  }
360  case 122:
361  {
362  display = dn;
363  letR;
364  delay(16);
365  break;
366  }
367  case 123:
368  {
369  display = dn;
```

```
370   letS;
371   delay(16);
372   break;
373   }
374   case 124:
375   {
376   display = dn;
377   letT;
378   delay(16);
379   break;
380   }
381   case 125:
382   {
383   display = dn;
384   letU;
385   delay(16);
386   break;
387   }
388   case 126:
389   {
390   display = dn;
391   letV;
392   delay(16);
393   break;
394   }
395   case 127:
396   {
397   display = dn;
398   letW;
399   delay(16);
400   break;
401   }
```

```
402  case 130:
403  {
404  display = dn;
405  letX;
406  delay(16);
407  break;
408  }
409  case 131:
410  {
411  display = dn;
412  letY;
413  delay(16);
414  break;
415  }
416  case 132:
417  {
418  display = dn;
419  letZ;
420  delay(16);
421  break;
422  }
423  case 141:
424  {
425  display = dn;
426  sma;
427  delay(16);
428  break;
429  }
430  case 142:
431  {
432  display = dn;
433  smb;
```

```
434   delay(16);
435   break;
436   }
437   case 143:
438   {
439   display = dn;
440   smc;
441   delay(16);
442   break;
443   }
444   case 144:
445   {
446   display = dn;
447   smd;
448   delay(16);
449   break;
450   }
451   case 145:
452   {
453   display = dn;
454   sme;
455   delay(16);
456   break;
457   }
458   case 146:
459   {
460   display = dn;
461   smf;
462   delay(16);
463   break;
464   }
```

```
465  case 147:
466  {
467  display = dn;
468  smg;
469  delay(16);
470  break;
471  }
472  case 150:
473  {
474  display = dn;
475  smh;
476  delay(16);
477  break;
478  }
479  case 151:
480  {
481  display = dn;
482  smi;
483  delay(16);
484  break;
485  }
486  case 152:
487  {
488  display = dn;
489  smj;
490  delay(16);
491  break;
492  }
493  }
494  case 153:
495  {
496  display = dn;
```

```
497  smk;
498  delay(16);
499  break;
500  }
501  case 154:
502  {
503  display = dn;
504  sml;
505  delay(16);
506  break;
507  }
508  case 155:
509  {
510  display = dn;
511  smm;
512  delay(16);
513  break;
514  }
515  case 156:
516  {
517  display = dn;
518  smn;
519  delay(16);
520  break;
521  }
522  case 157:
523  {
524  display = dn;
525  smo;
526  delay(16);
527  break;
528  }
```

```
529  case 160:
530  {
531  display = dn;
532  smp;
533  delay(16);
534  break;
535  }
536  case 161:
537  {
538  display = dn;
539  smq;
540  delay(16);
541  break;
542  }
543  case 162:
544  {
545  display = dn;
546  smr;
547  delay(16);
548  break;
549  }
550  case 163:
551  {
552  display = dn;
553  sms;
554  delay(16);
555  break;
556  }
557  case 164:
558  {
559  display = dn;
560  smt;
```

```
561  delay(16);
562  break;
563  }
564  case 165:
565  {
566  display = dn;
567  smu;
568  delay(16);
569  break;
570  }
571  case 166:
572  {
573  display = dn;
574  smv;
575  delay(16);
576  break;
577  }
578  case 167:
579  {
580  display = dn;
581  smw;
582  delay(16);
583  break;
584  }
585  case 170:
586  {
587  display = dn;
588  smx;
589  delay(16);
590  break;
591  }
```

```
592  case 171:
593  {
594  display = dn;
595  smy;
596  delay(16);
597  break;
598  }
599  case 172:
600  {
601  display = dn;
602  smz;
603  delay(16);
604  break;
605  }
606  }
607  }
608  void maxSetup()
609  {
610  display = 0;
611  maxWrite(decodeModeReg,disableDecode);
612  maxWrite (intensityReg,brightMin);
613  maxWrite(scanLimitReg,scanAll);
614  maxWrite(shutdownReg,normalOperation);
615  maxWrite(displayTestReg,noTest);
616  display = 1;
617  maxWrite(decodeModeReg,disableDecode);
618  maxWrite (intensityReg,brightMin);
619  maxWrite(scanLimitReg,scanAll);
620  maxWrite(shutdownReg,normalOperation);
621  maxWrite(displayTestReg,noTest);
```

```
622  display = 2;
623  maxWrite(decodeModeReg,disableDecode);
624  maxWrite (intensityReg,brightMin);
625  maxWrite(scanLimitReg,scanAll);
626  maxWrite(shutdownReg,normalOperation);
627  maxWrite(displayTestReg,noTest);
628  display = 3;
629  maxWrite(decodeModeReg,disableDecode);
630  maxWrite (intensityReg,brightMin);
631  maxWrite(scanLimitReg,scanAll);
632  maxWrite(shutdownReg,normalOperation);
633  maxWrite(displayTestReg,noTest);
634  }
635  void mess1 ()
636  {
637  rdatain = 101;
638  gotdata (rdatain, 0);
639  rdatain = 102;
640  gotdata (rdatain, 1);
641  rdatain = 102;
642  gotdata (rdatain, 2);
643  rdatain = 101;
644  gotdata (rdatain, 3);
645  }
646  void mess2 ()
647  {
648  rdatain = 141;
649  gotdata (rdatain, 0);
650  rdatain = 142;
651  gotdata (rdatain, 1);
652  rdatain = 143;
```

```
653  gotdata (rdatain, 2);
654  rdatain = 144;
655  gotdata (rdatain, 3);
656  }
657  void main ()
658  {
659  // set up the timers and PORTS
660  T1CON = 0x8030;
661  TRISA = 0x0080;
662  TRISB = 0x00FF;
663  TRISC = 0X00FF;
664  TRISD = 0X0000;
665  TRISE = 0x0000;
666  PORTA = 0;
667  PORTB = 0;
668  PORTC = 0;
669  PORTD = 0;
670  PORTE = 0;
671  AD1PCFG = 0XFFFF;
672  AD1CON1 = 0;
673  DDPCONbits.JTAGEN = 0;
674  maxSetup ();
675  rdatain  = 102;
676  while (1)
677  {
678      mess1 ();
679      delay(16);
680      mess2 ();
681      delay(16);
682  }
683  }
```

The main concept in controlling which of the displays shows the correct character is to send the data to the display that you want to show the current character on and, in the same operation, send a no action control instruction to the other three displays. In this way, only one display will change, while the other three don't change their display. It is the switch directive instructions, between lines 108 and 166, within the void maxWrite(char add,char data) subroutine, declared on line 106, that control which display shows the new character and which displays are unchanged. To help explain this switch directive, we will look at some of the instructions of the maxWrite subroutine in Listing 5-2. The partial code in Listing 5-3 lists the first case for the switch directive. The key variable that is used to determine which case the PIC carries out is the variable "display," written between the normal brackets.

Listing 5-3. The Switch and Case Listing

```
1  switch (display)
2  {
     a   case 0:
     b   {
            i    maxload = 0;
           ii    sendByte(add);
          iii    sendByte(data);
           iv    sendByte(0x00);
            v    sendByte(0x00);
           vi    sendByte(0x00);
          vii    sendByte(0x00);
         viii    sendByte(0x00);
           ix    sendByte(0x00);
            x    maxload = 1;
           xi    break;
     c   }
```

Analysis of Listing 5-3

Line 1 switch (display)

This is the actual "switch" directive. The word "switch" is a keyword, and so it is written in blue in the IDE editor. It allows the programmer to get the PIC to switch, or choose, the action it takes from a number of options that are listed below. To enable the PIC to choose which action it carries out, the switch directive needs a number that dictates which choice, out of the cases listed, it takes. That is why the normal brackets include the name of a global variable, in this case called "display," that will contain the number of the choice the PIC must take.

Line 2 {

This is the opening curly bracket that defines the boundaries of this switch directive.

Line a. case 0:

This now uses another directive, that is, "case," that is used with the "switch" directive. These two directives go hand in hand to create this list of choices. The "case" directive lists what must happen if the value sent to the switch directive within the associated variable, that is, the variable "display," has the value which is the same as that alongside the "case" directive. In this instance, if the variable "display" had the number "0" in it, then the PIC must carry out the instructions listed within the boundaries of the following opening and curly brackets. Note the use of the colon ":" at the end of the case directive.

Line b. {

This is the opening curly bracket for the case 0.

Line i. maxload = 0;

This sends the logic on this input to the 7219 low – ready to send it high when the full 16 bits have been sent to the 7219.

Line ii sendByte(add);

This calls the subroutine "sendByte" and sends the value in the variable "add."

When the main program called the "maxWrite(char add,char data)" subroutine, it would have sent two values to the subroutine. This particular subroutine is used within the maxSetUp subroutine on line 608. The first call to the maxWrite subroutine is on line 612 with maxWrite(dec odeModeReg,disableDecode);. This is used to set up the 7219, and the first variable sent up to the subroutine is the "decodeModeReg." This will contain the actual address of the register we want to write to. This value will be loaded into the first local variable "add." The second variable sent up to the subroutine, in this call instruction, is "disableDecode." This will contain the binary value defined on line 8. This will be copied into the local variable "data." Before this first call instruction, the value in the variable "display" was set to "0." This is on line 610. This value in "display" is used in this "switch and case" directive to ensure we are sending these two local variables to the first display. See lines ii and iii in this analysis of Listing 5-3.

Line iii sendByte(data);

This now calls the "sendByte" subroutine a second time, but now it sends the data for the LEDs in that address line. Note as the display variable has not changed, then only display 0 will be affected.

Lines iv–ix send the no change instruction and zero data to the other three displays.

Line x maxLoad = 1;

This sends the logic on the PIN high to a logic '1' which is the signal for the 7219 to latch the data into the 7219.

Line x1 break;

This is the directive to get the PIC to break out of the case and switch directive and return to the main program.

I hope, as you examine the other case directives, that it is the placing of the variables "add" and "data" that selects which of the four displays does change its display and show the correct data. We will do some more analysis as we go through the instructions of the program listing.

The four case choices in this switch directive in lines 108–166 are used to set up the four displays in the format we want to use them.

Analysis of Listing 5-2

Lines 1–5 are the usual comments.

Lines 6 and 7 are our usual includes.

Lines 8–22 define phrases for the commands and their associated binary numbers to the 7219.

Lines 23–25 allocate the control pins to the PIC.

Lines 26–35 define the phrases and the set of instructions to display the characters for "nzero" to "nnine" on the matrix. These are the numbers 0–9.

Lines 36–61 define the phrases and the set of instructions to display the characters for "letA" to "letZ" on the matrix.

Lines 62–87 define the phrases and the set of instructions to display the characters for "sma" to "smz" on the matrix.

In this way, I have created macros to display the characters 0–9 and all the capital and lowercase letters of the alphabet on the dot matrix display.

Line 88 unsigned char n, row, col,display, rdatain;

This simply creates the global variables we will use in the program.

Lines 89–96 create the variable delay that has a resolution of approximately 250ms.

Lines 97–105 create the "sendByte" subroutine which we have looked at in Listing 5-1.

Line 106 void maxWrite(char add,char data)

This creates a new subroutine which controls what is written to which of the four matrix displays. The instructions for the subroutine are listed within the opening and closing curly brackets between lines 107 and 167.

Line 108 switch (display)

This sets up the switch and case directive that we have looked at earlier. This switch directive uses the instructions between lines 109 and 166 to set up the four matrix displays.

Line 168 void gotdata (unsigned char rdata, unsigned char dn)

This creates the subroutine "gotdata" which uses the instructions between lines 168 and 607. We will come back to this subroutine when we look at the subroutine "mess1."

Line 608 void maxSetup()

This creates a subroutine that is used to initially set up the dot matrix using the appropriate commands.

Line 610 display = 0;

This loads the variable "display" with the value "0." It is the contents of the variable "display" that makes the PIC choose the appropriate case statement in the switch directive inside the subroutine " maxWrite(char add,char data)" on line 106. This makes the PIC choose "case" 0.

Line 611 maxWrite(decodeModeReg,disableDecode);

This sends the two bytes defined by the phrases decodeModeReg and disableDecode. These were defined in lines 8 and 13. The "decodeModeReg" is the address of the first control register we want to write a command to. The "disableDecode" is the command we want to write to that register.

Lines 612–615 send the other four commands to the other four control registers we need to write to. Note the variable "display" has the value 0 in it. These five control commands will be sent to the first display.

Lines 616 display = 1;

This loads the variable "display" with the value "1." This is so that we can write the same five commands to the second display.

Lines 617–634 send the same five commands to the remaining matrix displays. In this way, all four displays are set up in the same way. They are now all ready to receive characters to be displayed.

Line 635 void mess1 ()

This creates a subroutine that will be used to send the first message to the four matrix displays.

Line 637 rdatain = 101;

This loads the variable "rdatain" with the value 101. This is, by design, the ASCII for the character "A" in decimal. I am using the variable "rdatain" to allow the PIC to choose which "case" statement in the "switch" directive that is set up within the subroutine "gotdata" it will carry out.

Line 638 gotdata (rdatain, 0);

This calls the subroutine "gotdata" and sends the two values "rdatain" and "0" up to the subroutine. The value in the variable "rdatain," at this moment in the program, is 101. This makes the PIC choose " case 101:" which is on line 242. Here, the PIC carries out the following instructions:

Line 244 display = dn;

This loads the variable "display" with the value that has been loaded into the local variable "dn" when this subroutine was called. At this point of the program, the variable "dn" would have been loaded with "0."

Line 245 letA;

This is the macro "letA" which is on line 36. This will get the PIC to carry out the nine instructions that are on that line. In this way, the PIC will now call the subroutine "maxWrite" and send the 9 bytes to display the letter "A" to the dot matrix. Note as the variable "display" currently has the value "0" in it, then this character will be displayed on the first matrix. The other three won't change from what, if anything, was displayed on them already.

After displaying the character "A" on the display, the PIC returns to line 246.

Line 246 delay(16);

This simply calls the subroutine "delay" and creates a four-second delay. This is to allow us to see the display.

Line 247 break;

This makes the PIC break away from the instructions listed in the switch directive and return to the instructions in the subroutine "mess1."

Lines 639–645 send the characters "B," "B," then "A" to the dot matrix displays 1, 2, and 3, that is, the remaining displays of the four in total.

This then should spell out the message "ABBA" on the display.

Line 646 void mess2 ()

This subroutine has the instructions to send the message "abcd" to the dot matrix display.

This creates a subroutine to send out a second message to the four matrix displays. It works in exactly the same way except this time it displays the message "abcd."

Lines 657–675 are the normal instructions in the "main" loop to set up the PIC.

Line 676 while (1)

This creates the forever loop that keeps the PIC carrying out the instructions between the opening and closing curly brackets on lines 677 and 682.

Line 678 mess1 ();

This calls the subroutine to display the message 1 on the display.

Line 679 delay (16);

This calls the subroutine "delay" and creates a four-second delay.

Line 680 mess2 ();

This calls the subroutine to display the message 2 on the display.

Line 679 delay (16);

This creates another four-second delay.

Line 683 is the closing curly bracket of the main loop.

I have created the different macros and the switch and case statements to hopefully extend this program so that the display will show the characters that can be inputted from a terminal connected to the PIC via a

UART module. We will look at using the UART module in the next chapter. I hope that after reading that chapter you should be able to extend this program to use the dot matrix display to read characters inputted from a terminal.

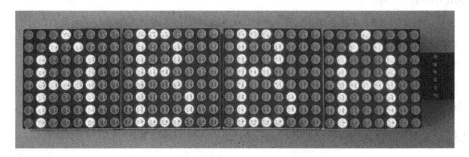

Figure 5-5. *The Mess1 on the Dot Matrix Display*

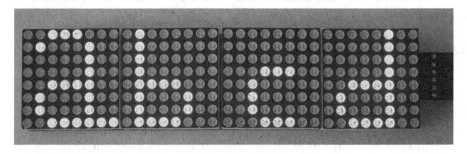

Figure 5-6. *The Mess2 on the Dot Matrix Display*

Figures 5-5 and 5-6 show the two messages being displayed on the dot matrix display.

A Program to Scroll Text on the Matrix Display

With this program, the display starts by scrolling the numbers 1–4, going from right to left. It then goes on to scroll the name "Hubert." This will hopefully show you how you can create any message and scroll it on the matrix display.

The listing for this program is shown in Listing 5-4.

Listing 5-4. The Scrolling Program

```
1  /* File:    64BitMatrixScrollingDisplayProg.c
2  Author: H. H. Ward
3  Using the 7219 matrix controller with four matrix boards
4  Created on 01 October 2021, 16:36
5  */
6  #include <xc.h>
7  #include <config72M36MNoWDTNoJTAG.h>
8  #define decodeModeReg      0b00001001
9  #define intensityReg       0b00001010
10  #define scanLimitReg       0b00001011
11  #define shutdownReg        0b00001100
12  #define displayTestReg     0b00001111
13  #define disableDecode      0b00000000
14  #define codeB0             0b00000001
15  #define codeB4             0b00001111
16  #define codeB8             0b11111111
17  #define brightMax          0b00001111
18  #define brightMin          0b00000001
19  #define scanAll            0b00000111
20  #define normalOperation    0b00000001
21  #define shutdown           0b00000000
```

```
22   #define noTest                 0b00000000
23   #define maxin                  _RA0
24   #define maxload                _RA1
25   #define maxclk                 _RA2
26   #define blank        maxWrite (0,0x00); maxWrite(1,0x00);
     maxWrite(2,0x00); maxWrite(3,0x00); maxWrite(4,0x00);
     maxWrite(5,0x00); maxWrite(6,0x00); maxWrite(7,0x00);
     maxWrite(8,0x00);
27   #define nzero        maxWrite (0,0x00); maxWrite(1,0x08);
     maxWrite(2,0x14); maxWrite(3,0x22); maxWrite(4,0x26);
     maxWrite(5,0x2A); maxWrite(6,0x32); maxWrite(7,0x14);
     maxWrite(8,0x08);
28   #define none         maxWrite (0,0x00); maxWrite (1,0x08);
     maxWrite (2,0x18); maxWrite (3,0x28); maxWrite (4,0x08);
     maxWrite (5,0x08); maxWrite (6,0x08); maxWrite (7,0x08);
     maxWrite (8,0x3E);
29   #define ntwo         maxWrite (0,0x00); maxWrite(1,0x1C);
     maxWrite(2,0x22); maxWrite(3,0x22); maxWrite(4,0x02);
     maxWrite(5,0x3C); maxWrite(6,0x20); maxWrite(7,0x20);
     maxWrite(8,0x3E);
30   #define nthree       maxWrite (0,0x00); maxWrite (1,0x38);
     maxWrite (2,0x04); maxWrite (3,0x04); maxWrite (4,0x04);
     maxWrite (5,0x1C); maxWrite (6,0x04); maxWrite(7,0x04);
     maxWrite(8,0x38);
31   #define nfour        maxWrite (0,0x00); maxWrite (1,0x04);
     maxWrite (2,0x0C); maxWrite (3,0x14); maxWrite (4,0x24);
     maxWrite (5,0x7C); maxWrite (6,0x04); maxWrite (7,0x04);
     maxWrite (8,0x3F);
32   #define nfive        maxWrite (0,0x00); maxWrite (1,0x7C);
     maxWrite (2,0x40); maxWrite (3,0x40); maxWrite (4,0x40);
     maxWrite (5,0x7C); maxWrite (6,0x04); maxWrite (7,0x04);
     maxWrite (8,0x7C);
```

```
33   #define nsix        maxWrite (0,0x00); maxWrite (1,0x7C);
     maxWrite (2,0x40); maxWrite (3,0x40); maxWrite (4,0x40);
     maxWrite (5,0x7C); maxWrite (6,0x44); maxWrite (7,0x44);
     maxWrite (8,0x7C);
34   #define nseven      maxWrite (0,0x00); maxWrite (1,0xFF);
     maxWrite (2,0x02); maxWrite (3,0x04); maxWrite (4,0x08);
     maxWrite (5,0x10); maxWrite (6,0x20); maxWrite (7,0x40);
     maxWrite (8,0x80);
35   #define neight      maxWrite (0,0x00); maxWrite (1,0x1C);
     maxWrite (2,0x22); maxWrite (3,0x22); maxWrite (4,0x22);
     maxWrite (5,0x1C); maxWrite (6,0x22); maxWrite (7,0x22);
     maxWrite (8,0x1C);
36   #define nnine       maxWrite (0,0x00); maxWrite (1,0x1C);
     maxWrite (2,0x22); maxWrite (3,0x22); maxWrite (4,0x22);
     maxWrite (5,0x1E); maxWrite (6,0x02); maxWrite (7,0x02);
     maxWrite (8,0x02);
37   #define letA        maxWrite (0,0x00); maxWrite (1,0x10);
     maxWrite (2,0x28); maxWrite (3,0x44); maxWrite (4,0x44);
     maxWrite (5,0x7C); maxWrite (6,0x44); maxWrite (7,0x44);
     maxWrite (8,0x44);
38   #define letB        maxWrite (0,0x00); maxWrite (1,0x70);
     maxWrite (2,0x48); maxWrite (3,0x48); maxWrite (4,0x70);
     maxWrite (5,0x48); maxWrite (6,0x44); maxWrite (7,0x44);
     maxWrite (8,0x78);
39   #define letC        maxWrite (0,0x00); maxWrite (1,0x1C);
     maxWrite (2,0x20); maxWrite (3,0x40); maxWrite (4,0x40);
     maxWrite (5,0x40); maxWrite (6,0x40); maxWrite (7,0x20);
     maxWrite (8,0x1C);
40   #define letD        maxWrite (0,0x00); maxWrite (1,0x70);
     maxWrite (2,0x48); maxWrite (3,0x44); maxWrite (4,0x44);
     maxWrite (5,0x44); maxWrite (6,0x44); maxWrite (7,0x48);
     maxWrite (8,0x70);
```

```
41  #define letE        maxWrite (0,0x00); maxWrite (1,0x78);
    maxWrite (2,0x40); maxWrite (3,0x40); maxWrite (4,0x70);
    maxWrite (5,0x40); maxWrite (6,0x40); maxWrite (7,0x40);
    maxWrite (8,0x78);
42  #define letF        maxWrite (0,0x00); maxWrite (1,0x78);
    maxWrite (2,0x40); maxWrite (3,0x40); maxWrite (4,0x70);
    maxWrite (5,0x40); maxWrite (6,0x40); maxWrite (7,0x40);
    maxWrite (8,0x40);
43  #define letG        maxWrite (0,0x00); maxWrite (1,0x38);
    maxWrite (2,0x44); maxWrite (3,0x40); maxWrite (4,0x58);
    maxWrite (5,0x44); maxWrite (6,0x44); maxWrite (7,0x44);
    maxWrite (8,0x38);
44  #define letH        maxWrite (0,0x00); maxWrite (1,0x44);
    maxWrite (2,0x44); maxWrite (3,0x44); maxWrite (4,0x7C);
    maxWrite (5,0x44); maxWrite (6,0x44); maxWrite (7,0x44);
    maxWrite (8,0x44);
45  #define letI        maxWrite (0,0x00); maxWrite (1,0x7C);
    maxWrite (2,0x10); maxWrite (3,0x10); maxWrite (4,0x10);
    maxWrite (5,0x10); maxWrite (6,0x10); maxWrite (7,0x10);
    maxWrite (8,0x7C);
46  #define letJ        maxWrite (0,0x00); maxWrite (1,0x00);
    maxWrite (2,0x3E); maxWrite (3,0x08); maxWrite (4,0x08);
    maxWrite (5,0x08); maxWrite (6,0x48); maxWrite (7,0x38);
    maxWrite (8,0x10);
47  #define letK        maxWrite (0,0x00); maxWrite (1,0x44);
    maxWrite (2,0x48); maxWrite (3,0x50); maxWrite (4,0x60);
    maxWrite (5,0x50); maxWrite (6,0x48); maxWrite (7,0x44);
    maxWrite (8,0x00);
48  #define letL        maxWrite (0,0x00); maxWrite (1,0x70);
    maxWrite (2,0x20); maxWrite (3,0x20); maxWrite (4,0x20);
    maxWrite (5,0x20); maxWrite (6,0x22); maxWrite (7,0x3C);
    maxWrite (8,0x00);
```

```
49  #define letM        maxWrite (0,0x00); maxWrite (1,0x41);
    maxWrite (2,0x63); maxWrite (3,0x55); maxWrite (4,0x49);
    maxWrite (5,0x41); maxWrite (6,0x41); maxWrite (7,0x41);
    maxWrite (8,0x00);
50  #define letN        maxWrite (0,0x00); maxWrite (1,0x42);
    maxWrite (2,0x62); maxWrite (3,0x52); maxWrite (4,0x4A);
    maxWrite (5,0x46); maxWrite (6,0x42); maxWrite (7,0x42);
    maxWrite (8,0x00);
51  #define letO        maxWrite (0,0x00); maxWrite (1,0x18);
    maxWrite (2,0x24); maxWrite (3,0x42); maxWrite (4,0x42);
    maxWrite (5,0x42); maxWrite (6,0x24); maxWrite (7,0x18);
    maxWrite (8,0x00);
52  #define letP        maxWrite (0,0x00); maxWrite (1,0xF8);
    maxWrite (2,0x44); maxWrite (3,0x44); maxWrite (4,0x78);
    maxWrite (5,0x40); maxWrite (6,0x40); maxWrite (7,0xE0);
    maxWrite (8,0x00);
53  #define letQ        maxWrite (0,0x00); maxWrite (1,0x18);
    maxWrite (2,0x24); maxWrite (3,0x42); maxWrite (4,0x42);
    maxWrite (5,0x42); maxWrite (6,0x24); maxWrite (7,0x1C);
    maxWrite (8,0x02);
54  #define letR        maxWrite (0,0x00); maxWrite (1,0xF0);
    maxWrite (2,0x48); maxWrite (3,0x44); maxWrite (4,0x48);
    maxWrite (5,0x70); maxWrite (6,0x50); maxWrite (7,0x48);
    maxWrite (8,0xE4);
55  #define letS        maxWrite (0,0x00); maxWrite (1,0x30);
    maxWrite (2,0x48); maxWrite (3,0x40); maxWrite (4,0x30);
    maxWrite (5,0x08); maxWrite (6,0x48); maxWrite (7,0x30);
    maxWrite (8,0x00);
56  #define letT        maxWrite (0,0x00); maxWrite (1,0x7C);
    maxWrite (2,0x94); maxWrite (3,0x10); maxWrite (4,0x10);
    maxWrite (5,0x10); maxWrite (6,0x10); maxWrite (7,0x10);
    maxWrite (8,0x38);
```

```
57  #define letU        maxWrite (0,0x00); maxWrite (1,0xE4);
    maxWrite (2,0x64); maxWrite (3,0x64); maxWrite (4,0x64);
    maxWrite (5,0x64); maxWrite (6,0x24); maxWrite (7,0x24);
    maxWrite (8,0x18);
58  #define letV        maxWrite (0,0x00); maxWrite (1,0x41);
    maxWrite (2,0x41); maxWrite (3,0x22); maxWrite (4,0x22);
    maxWrite (5,0x14); maxWrite (6,0x14); maxWrite (7,0x08);
    maxWrite (8,0x00);
59  #define letW        maxWrite (0,0x00); maxWrite (1,0x81);
    maxWrite (2,0x81); maxWrite (3,0x42); maxWrite (4,0x5A);
    maxWrite (5,0x24); maxWrite (6,0x24); maxWrite (7,0x24);
    maxWrite (8,0x00);
60  #define letX        maxWrite (0,0x00); maxWrite (1,0x82);
    maxWrite (2,0x44); maxWrite (3,0x28); maxWrite (4,0x10);
    maxWrite (5,0x28); maxWrite (6,0x44); maxWrite (7,0x82);
    maxWrite (8,0x00);
61  #define letY        maxWrite (0,0x00); maxWrite (1,0x82);
    maxWrite (2,0x44); maxWrite (3,0x28); maxWrite (4,0x10);
    maxWrite (5,0x20); maxWrite (6,0x40); maxWrite (7,0x80);
    maxWrite (8,0x00);
62  #define letZ        maxWrite (0,0x00); maxWrite (1,0xFE);
    maxWrite (2,0x04); maxWrite (3,0x08); maxWrite (4,0x10);
    maxWrite (5,0x20); maxWrite (6,0x40); maxWrite (7,0xFE);
    maxWrite (8,0x00);
63  #define sma         maxWrite (0,0x00); maxWrite (1,0x38);
    maxWrite (2,0x44); maxWrite (3,0x04); maxWrite (4,0x04);
    maxWrite (5,0x3C); maxWrite (6,0x44); maxWrite (7,0x44);
    maxWrite (8,0x3F);
64  #define smb         maxWrite (0,0x00); maxWrite (1,0x40);
    maxWrite (2,0x40); maxWrite (3,0x40); maxWrite (4,0x40);
    maxWrite (5,0x78); maxWrite (6,0x44); maxWrite (7,0x44);
    maxWrite (8,0x78);
```

```
65  #define smc           maxWrite (0,0x00); maxWrite (1,0x00);
    maxWrite (2,0x00); maxWrite (3,0x00); maxWrite (4,0x1C);
    maxWrite (5,0x20); maxWrite (6,0x20); maxWrite (7,0x20);
    maxWrite (8,0x1C);
66  #define smd           maxWrite (0,0X00); maxWrite (1,0x04);
    maxWrite (2,0x04); maxWrite (3,0x04); maxWrite (4,0x04);
    maxWrite (5,0x3C); maxWrite (6,0x44); maxWrite (7,0x44);
    maxWrite (8,0x3C);
67  #define sme           maxWrite (0,0x00); maxWrite (1,0x00);
    maxWrite (2,0x1C); maxWrite (3,0x22); maxWrite (4,0x42);
    maxWrite (5,0x7C); maxWrite (6,0x40); maxWrite (7,0x20);
    maxWrite (8,0x1E);
68  #define smf           maxWrite (0,0x00); maxWrite (1,0x00);
    maxWrite (2,0x0C); maxWrite (3,0x10); maxWrite (4,0x10);
    maxWrite (5,0x38); maxWrite (6,0x10); maxWrite (7,0x10);
    maxWrite (8,0x38);
69  #define smg           maxWrite (0,0x00); maxWrite (1,0x00);
    maxWrite (2,0x1E); maxWrite (3,0x24); maxWrite (4,0x24);
    maxWrite (5,0x3C); maxWrite (6,0x04); maxWrite (7,0x24);
    maxWrite (8,0x18);
70  #define smh           maxWrite (0,0x00); maxWrite (1,0x00);
    maxWrite (2,0x00); maxWrite (3,0x20); maxWrite (4,0x20);
    maxWrite (5,0x20); maxWrite (6,0x38); maxWrite (7,0x24);
    maxWrite (8,0x24);
71  #define smi           maxWrite (0,0x00); maxWrite (1,0x00);
    maxWrite (2,0x00); maxWrite (3,0x10); maxWrite (4,0x00);
    maxWrite (5,0x30); maxWrite (6,0x10); maxWrite (7,0x10);
    maxWrite (8,0x38);
72  #define smj           maxWrite (0,0x00); maxWrite (1,0x00);
    maxWrite (2,0x00); maxWrite (3,0x04); maxWrite (4,0x00);
    maxWrite (5,0x1C); maxWrite (6,0x04); maxWrite (7,0x04);
    maxWrite (8,0x1C);
```

```
73  #define smk          maxWrite (0,0x00); maxWrite (1,0x00);
    maxWrite (2,0x20); maxWrite (3,0x20); maxWrite (4,0x24);
    maxWrite (5,0x28); maxWrite (6,0x30); maxWrite (7,0x28);
    maxWrite (8,0x00);
74  #define sml          maxWrite (0,0x00); maxWrite (1,0x00);
    maxWrite (2,0x00); maxWrite (3,0x00); maxWrite (4,0x10);
    maxWrite (5,0x10); maxWrite (6,0x10); maxWrite (7,0x10);
    maxWrite (8,0x3C);
75  #define smm          maxWrite (0,0x00); maxWrite (1,0x00);
    maxWrite (2,0x00); maxWrite (3,0x00); maxWrite (4,0x40);
    maxWrite (5,0x68); maxWrite (6,0x54); maxWrite (7,0x54);
    maxWrite (8,0x54);
76  #define smn          maxWrite (0,0x00); maxWrite (1,0x00);
    maxWrite (2,0x00); maxWrite (3,0x00); maxWrite (4,0x40);
    maxWrite (5,0x70); maxWrite (6,0x48); maxWrite (7,0x48);
    maxWrite (8,0x48);
77  #define smo          maxWrite (0,0x00); maxWrite (1,0x00);
    maxWrite (2,0x00); maxWrite (3,0x00); maxWrite (4,0x38);
    maxWrite (5,0x44); maxWrite (6,0x44); maxWrite (7,0x44);
    maxWrite (8,0x38);
78  #define smp          maxWrite (0,0x00); maxWrite (1,0x00);
    maxWrite (2,0x00); maxWrite (3,0x00); maxWrite (4,0x38);
    maxWrite (5,0x24); maxWrite (6,0x38); maxWrite (7,0x20);
    maxWrite (8,0x70);
79  #define smq          maxWrite (0,0x00); maxWrite (1,0x00);
    maxWrite (2,0x00); maxWrite (3,0x38); maxWrite (4,0x48);
    maxWrite (5,0x48); maxWrite (6,0x38); maxWrite (7,0x08);
    maxWrite (8,0x3C);
80  #define smr          maxWrite (0,0x00); maxWrite (1,0x00);
    maxWrite (2,0x00); maxWrite (3,0x00); maxWrite (4,0x58);
    maxWrite (5,0x20); maxWrite (6,0x20); maxWrite (7,0x20);
    maxWrite (8,0x78);
```

```
81  #define sms          maxWrite (0,0x00); maxWrite (1,0x00);
    maxWrite (2,0x00); maxWrite (3,0x18); maxWrite (4,0x24);
    maxWrite (5,0x20); maxWrite (6,0x18); maxWrite (7,0x04);
    maxWrite (8,0x38);
82  #define smt          maxWrite (0,0x00); maxWrite (1,0x00);
    maxWrite (2,0x00); maxWrite (3,0x20); maxWrite (4,0x20);
    maxWrite (5,0x78); maxWrite (6,0x20); maxWrite (7,0x20);
    maxWrite (8,0x38);
83  #define smu          maxWrite (0,0x00); maxWrite (1,0x00);
    maxWrite (2,0x00); maxWrite (3,0x00); maxWrite (4,0x00);
    maxWrite (5,0x64); maxWrite (6,0x24); maxWrite (7,0x24);
    maxWrite (8,0x1A);
84  #define smv          maxWrite (0,0x00); maxWrite (1,0x00);
    maxWrite (2,0x00); maxWrite (3,0x00); maxWrite (4,0x63);
    maxWrite (5,0x22); maxWrite (6,0x22); maxWrite (7,0x14);
    maxWrite (8,0x08);
85  #define smw          maxWrite (0,0x00); maxWrite (1,0x00);
    maxWrite (2,0x00); maxWrite (3,0x00); maxWrite (4,0x80);
    maxWrite (5,0x49); maxWrite (6,0x49); maxWrite (7,0x55);
    maxWrite (8,0x22);
86  #define smx          maxWrite (0,0x00); maxWrite (1,0x00);
    maxWrite (2,0x00); maxWrite (3,0x00); maxWrite (4,0x42);
    maxWrite (5,0x24); maxWrite (6,0x18); maxWrite (7,0x24);
    maxWrite (8,0x42);
87  #define smy          maxWrite (0,0x00); maxWrite (1,0x00);
    maxWrite (2,0x00); maxWrite (3,0x00); maxWrite (4,0x22);
    maxWrite (5,0x14); maxWrite (6,0x08); maxWrite (7,0x10);
    maxWrite (8,0x20);
88  #define smz          maxWrite (0,0x00); maxWrite (1,0x00);
    maxWrite (2,0x00); maxWrite (3,0x00); maxWrite (4,0x3E);
    maxWrite (5,0x04); maxWrite (6,0x08); maxWrite (7,0x10);
    maxWrite (8,0x3E);
```

```
89   unsigned char n, row, col,display, rdatain;
90   void delay (unsigned char t)
91   {
92   for (n = 0; n < t; n ++)
93   {
94   TMR1 = 0;
95   while (TMR1 < 35050);
96   }
97   }
98   void sendByte(char info)
99   {
100  for(n = 0 ; n < 8 ; n ++ )
101  {
102  maxclk = 0;
103  maxin = ( (info << n) & 0x80 ) ? 1 : 0; //send bits to max
     MSB of byte first this test to see if the bit ANDED with
     0X80 is true. If it is then bit is '1' if not bit is '0'
104  maxclk = 1;
105  }
106  }
107  void maxWrite(char add,char data)
108  {
109  switch (display)
110  {
111  case 0:
112  {
113  maxload = 0;
114  sendByte(add);
115  sendByte(data);
116  sendByte(0x00);
117  sendByte(0x00);
118  sendByte(0x00);
```

```
119  sendByte(0x00);
120  sendByte(0x00);
121  sendByte(0x00);
122  maxload = 1;
123  break;
124  }
125  case 1:
126  {
127  maxload = 0;
128  sendByte(0x00);
129  sendByte(0x00);
130  sendByte(add);
131  sendByte(data);
132  sendByte(0x00);
133  sendByte(0x00);
134  sendByte(0x00);
135  sendByte(0x00);
136  maxload = 1;
137  break;
138  }
139  case 2:
140  {
141  maxload = 0;
142  sendByte(0x00);
143  sendByte(0x00);
144  sendByte(0x00);
145  sendByte(0x00);
146  sendByte(add);
147  sendByte(data);
148  sendByte(0x00);
149  sendByte(0x00);
```

```
150  maxload = 1;
151  break;
152  }
153  case 3:
154  {
155  maxload = 0;
156  sendByte(0x00);
157  sendByte(0x00);
158  sendByte(0x00);
159  sendByte(0x00);
160  sendByte(0x00);
161  sendByte(0x00);
162  sendByte(add);
163  sendByte(data);
164  maxload = 1;
165  break;
166  }
167  }
168  }
169  void maxSetup()
170  {
171  display = 0;
172  maxWrite(decodeModeReg,disableDecode);
173  maxWrite (intensityReg,brightMin);
174  maxWrite(scanLimitReg,scanAll);
175  maxWrite(shutdownReg,normalOperation);
176  maxWrite(displayTestReg,noTest);
177  display = 1;
178  maxWrite(decodeModeReg,disableDecode);
179  maxWrite (intensityReg,brightMin);
180  maxWrite(scanLimitReg,scanAll);
181  maxWrite(shutdownReg,normalOperation);
```

```
182  maxWrite(displayTestReg,noTest);
183  display = 2;
184  maxWrite(decodeModeReg,disableDecode);
185  maxWrite (intensityReg,brightMin);
186  maxWrite(scanLimitReg,scanAll);
187  maxWrite(shutdownReg,normalOperation);
188  maxWrite(displayTestReg,noTest);
189  display = 3;
190  maxWrite(decodeModeReg,disableDecode);
191  maxWrite (intensityReg,brightMin);
192  maxWrite(scanLimitReg,scanAll);
193  maxWrite(shutdownReg,normalOperation);
194  maxWrite(displayTestReg,noTest);
195  }
196  void main ()
197  {
198  // set up the timers and PORTS
199  T1CON = 0x8030;
200  TRISA = 0x0080;
201  TRISB = 0x00FF;
202  TRISC = 0X00FF;
203  TRISD = 0X0000;
204  TRISE = 0x0000;
205  PORTA = 0;
206  PORTB = 0;
207  PORTC = 0;
208  PORTD = 0;
209  PORTE = 0;
210  AD1PCFG = 0XFFFF;
211  AD1CON1 = 0;
212  DDPCONbits.JTAGEN = 0;
213  maxSetup ();
```

```
214   while (1)
215   {
216   display = 0;
217   blank;
218   display = 1;
219   blank;
220   display = 2;
221   blank;
222   display = 3;
223   none;
224   delay (3);
225   display = 0;
226   blank;
227   display = 1;
228   blank;
229   display = 2;
230   none;
231   display = 3;
232   ntwo;
233   delay (3);
234   display = 0;
235   blank;
236   display = 1;
237   none;
238   display = 2;
239   ntwo;
240   display = 3;
241   nthree;
242   delay (3);
243   display = 0;
244   none;
```

```
245  display = 1;
246  ntwo;
247  display = 2;
248  nthree;
249  display = 3;
250  nfour;
251  delay (3);
252  display = 0;
253  blank;
254  display = 1;
255  blank;
256  display = 2;
257  blank;
258  display = 3;
259  letH;
260  delay (3);
261  display = 0;
262  blank;
263  display = 1;
264  blank;
265  display = 2;
266  letH;
267  display = 3;
268  letU;
269  delay (3);
270  display = 0;
271  blank;
272  display = 1;
273  letH;
274  display = 2;
275  letU;
```

```
276  display = 3;
277  letB;
278  delay (3);
279  display = 0;
280  letH;
281  display = 1;
282  letU;
283  display = 2;
284  letB;
285  display = 3;
286  letE;
287  delay (3);
288  display = 0;
289  letU;
290  display = 1;
291  letB;
292  display = 2;
293  letE;
294  display = 3;
295  letR;
296  delay (3);
297  display = 0;
298  letB;
299  display = 1;
300  letE;
301  display = 2;
302  letR;
303  display = 3;
304  letT;
305  delay (3);
306  }
307  }
```

I hope there are no new instructions that need further analysis. However, I think it is worth explaining how this program gets the display to scroll the text on the display. The program should help show the advantage of creating the macros, between lines 26 and 88, that define how the phrases used relate to the nine calls to the "maxWrite" subroutine to display the individual characters. This approach makes the process of displaying the text on the display easier. All we need to do is state the display number we are writing to, followed by the macro for the character we want to display. The first example of this is the two instructions on lines 216 and 217:

- display (0);

- blank;

The macro "blank" has been defined on line 26. This turns off all LEDs on all the rows on each display.

To get the display to scroll, we write to all four displays, sending the character we want to display on the particular matrix. The first run through should send the "blank" display to displays 0, 1, and 2. Display 3 should show the number 1, that is, using the "none" macro. This is programmed using lines 216–223.

Now we call a ¾ second delay on line 224.

Then we shift the number 1 one display to the left and show the number 2 on the third matrix display. This is done with lines 225–232.

Again, we call a ¾ second delay on line 233. Then we shift the numbers 1 and 2 one display to the left and show the number 3 on the third matrix display.

I hope you can see that the instructions between lines 215 and 306 do display the scrolling text as we want. They are all within a forever "while loop," which gets the PIC to keep on repeating this scrolling text.

I hope you have found these three programs useful and you can go on to use them in your projects in the future.

Summary

In this chapter, we have studied how to use the Max7219 driver IC to send data to an 8 by 8 dot matrix display. We have studied how to create macros that we used to define a phrase that represents a series of instructions for the PIC. We have then gone on to learn how to cascade four dot matrix displays together and send messages of four characters to it. Finally, we have studied how to display a scrolling text message on the four dot matrix displays.

In the next chapter, we will learn how the PIC can communicate with other devices using the SPI and UART modules in the PIC.

I hope you have found this chapter useful and you will look forward to reading the next chapter.

CHAPTER 6

Communication

In this chapter, we will look at how the PIC can communicate with different devices, such as another PIC, some extra EEPROM, a terminal device, a Real-Time Clock (RTC), and many others. There are three main methods for communicating with these devices that PICs use and they are

- SPI, Serial Peripheral Interface

- I²C or IIC which stands for Inter-Integrated Circuit

- UART, Universal Asynchronous Receiver/ Transmitter system

In this chapter, we will study how we can use the SPI module, within the PIC, to communicate with a device. Also, as we will be displaying data on the LCD, we will learn how to use the Parallel Master Port, the PMP, to communicate with the LCD.

After reading this chapter, you will be able to use the SPI module in the PIC to communicate with peripherals. You will also be able to communicate with the EEPROM IC on the explorer 16 development board. You will also have learned how to use the PMP.

The Serial Peripheral Interface (SPI) Module

This is a module within the PIC that allows the PIC to communicate with a range of external peripheral devices, including another PIC or microcontroller. It uses a synchronous interface, which means it generates a clock signal with which all actions are synchronized. There has to be a

© Hubert Ward 2023
H. Ward, *Introductory Programs with the 32-bit PIC Microcontroller*,
Maker Innovations Series, https://doi.org/10.1007/978-1-4842-9051-4_6

master that generates the clock signal and at least one slave that receives the data from the master. There are four connections that connect the master to the slave, and they are as follows:

1. **SDOx, serial data out**: This is an output, and the data is transmitted to the slave on this line. At the slave end, this is connected to the SDI of the slave. The "x" is added to the SDO as there are two SPI modules with the PIC32. Therefore, we simply replace the "x" with either "1" or "2," depending upon which SPI module we will be using.

2. **SDIx, serial data in**: This is an input at the PIC as the PIC receives data from the slave on this pin. Note, this is connected to the SDO of the slave device.

3. **SCKx, serial clock**: This is an output from the PIC, and it becomes an input at the slave which is connected to the SCK pin at the slave. This carries the clock signal, generated by the master, which synchronizes the operation.

4. **SSx, slave select**: This is an output from the PIC that is used if the master is to be connected to more than one slave. The PIC will use any one of its general input/output pins for this purpose. There can be one or more SS pins depending upon how many slaves the master is communicating with. These outputs from the PIC will be connected to the chip select of the slave devices used. In this way, the master can select which of the slaves needs to respond to the communication. This is required because the data must go to all the slaves that are connected to the master's SDO line.

This arrangement of the connections is shown in Figure 6-1.

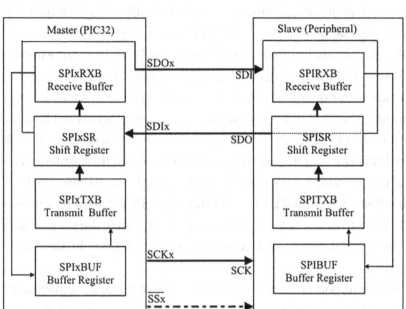

Figure 6-1. *The Connections Between the Master and the Slave on the SPI Bus*

The master must initialize the transmission cycle. This will happen when we load data onto the SPIxBuff, the SPI Buffer Register in the master. When the master is transmitting data, the data goes into the SPI Buffer and into the SPI Transmit Buffer, SPIxTXB, at the same time. From there, it goes into the SPIxSR which is the Serial Shift Register. This action of loading the SPI Buffer and the SPIxSR allows the master to start the clock signal, and data is sent out of the SPIxSR one bit at a time, starting with the MSB, the Most Significant Bit. As the new data, from the SDOx pin, starts to enter the slave, at its SDI pin, the slave must start to push the current data in the slave's SPISR out of it. This is done one bit at a time, starting with the MSB. The data from the slave's SPISR moves into the master's SPIxSR, to be received by the master, while the transmitted data from the master moves into the slave's SPISR. This circulating action continues until the master has sent out all of the data bits that were in its buffer. This then means that the data bits that were in the master's SPIxSR have gone into the slave's SPISR, and the data bits that were in the slave's SPISR have gone into the master's SPIxSR, via their respective shift registers. This means that as the master sends out data to the slave, the slave will send some data to the master. This data that the slave has sent out may or may not be useful data from the slave, but the master will receive it, and it must decide what to do with it. Once all the data has been circulated, in this fashion, the master can then load the Serial Receive Buffer (SPIxRXB) with the data that has just been shifted into the master's SPIxSR. From there, it goes into the SPIxBUF to be read by the PIC's program. It is up to the programmer to decide if this is nonsense that has just come back from the slave or useful data.

Another important thing to become aware of is that if the slave needs to send data to the master, that is, if the master wants to read data from the slave, the master must send some data bits first to the slave to start the clock signal and so start this circulating action. These first data bits that have been sent from the master would be useless information, and the slave would simply ignore it. The slave cannot initiate any communication, but when the master sends this useless information, the slave will push the data that was in the slave's SPISR out. This is how the slave can send data to the master.

It is important that the programmer understands this circulating action so that they can decide whether or not the data from the slave is useful or not.

We should appreciate that the PIC32 can support data in 8 bits, 16 bits, or even 32 bits in length. The size of the data is controlled by bits 10 and 11 of the SPIxCON register. Table 6-1 shows how these bits control the data length. Note, the "X" means the logic can be either a "1" or a "0"; the PIC does not care.

Table 6-1. *The MODE 32, 16, or 8 Data Bit Selection*

Bits	11	10	Data size
	0	0	8
	0	1	16
	1	X	32

As the data is shifted out of the shift registers, one at a time, on a single clock cycle, then the clock cycle can have 8 pulses or 16 or 32, depending upon the data length that is being set.

With the PIC32, the SPI modules can be operated in a variety of modes:

1. Master mode, where the PIC is the master SPI device.

2. Slave mode, where the PIC is actually one of the slaves and another device, typically another PIC, is the master.

3. It can operate with four different clock modes.

4. It can operate in framed support mode.

5. It can operate with 8, 16, or 32 bits of data.

6. Programmable interrupts with any of the bit width transfer.

We will use the SPI module in its basic mode which is as a master using 8 bits of data.

The 25LC256 EEPROM

This device is supplied with the explorer 16 development board so that we can use it to test our ability to use the SPI module in the 32-bit PIC. It is a 256Kbit device, which is organized in 32,768 one-byte memory locations. It is manufactured by microchip and uses the SPI mode of communication. This makes it a suitable device for our first implementation of the SPI module. The EEPROM is a storage device that can retain its data even after the power is removed. This is termed nonvolatile memory. It can be electrically erased and its memory locations overwritten with new data, hence the "EE" in its name. This makes it an ideal device for storing important data that needs saving even when the power is removed.

What Is an EEPROM Device

Originally, the EEPROM was just a PROM device, which stands for Programmable Read-Only Memory. This type of memory was nonvolatile, but, once written to, its contents could not be changed. It was used for BIOS programs. However, advancement meant that it could be erased and so reprogrammed. To erase it, the device had to be exposed to ultraviolet light. This type of memory was called EPROM, Erasable Programmable Read-Only Memory.

Further advancements were made which meant the device could be erased electrically; hence, we have EEPROM, Electrically Erasable Programmable Read-Only Memory. This now means that the memory is no longer read only, but the name has stuck.

To use any device, we need to understand how it communicates with other systems and devices. We have already stated that it uses the SPI format of communication, but we need to know the process that the EEPROM uses to communicate. It is an eight-pin device that comes in a variety of packages. The pin allocation is shown in Table 6-2.

Table 6-2. The Pin Usage for the 25LC256 EEPROM

Pin Name	Function
$\overline{CS}$	Chip select: Used to turn the device on, i.e., select it. This pin is active low, indicated by the bar across the CS. This means it must go to a logic '0' to turn the device on
SO	Serial data out: This is connected to the SDI of the master. Data being sent to the master goes out on this pin
$\overline{WP}$	Write protect: This pin is used to prevent data from being overwritten. If the logic on this pin is a logic '0', the device cannot be written to
VSS	This is the ground pin of the device
SI	Serial in: This pin is connected to the SDO pin of the master. It is on this pin that data is sent from the master to this device
SCK	Serial clock: This is connected to the SCK pin on the master. It is on this pin that the master sends the synchronizing clock signal
$\overline{HOLD}$	Hold input
VCC	The positive power supply

There are no actual pin numbers in Table 6-2 as the actual pin numbers vary for the different types of packages. Some typical packages are shown in Figure 6-2.

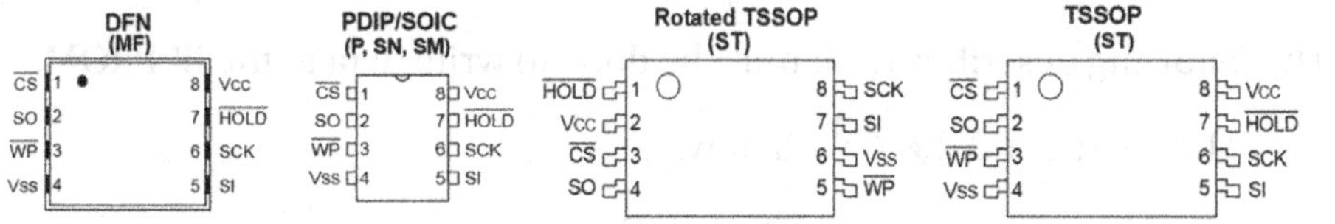

Figure 6-2. The Packages for the 25LC256 EEPROM

The 25LC256 contains an 8-bit instruction register that can be used to put the device into a read mode, ready for the master to read from its memory, or into a write mode, ready for the master to write data to the device. The master must write to this register to put the device into the correct mode. Information, be it instruction or data, is clocked into the device on the rising edge of the clock signal. This is termed positive edge triggering, and the master must put the SPI into this mode of triggering. The $\overline{CS}$ must be kept low to select the EEPROM, and the $\overline{HOLD}$ pin must be kept high to disable the "Hold" option during the whole operation. Table 6-3 lists the instructions for the device.

Table 6-3. *The Six Instructions for the 25LC256 EEPROM*

Name	Binary Value	Function
Read	0000 0011	Read data from the EEPROM starting at the address supplied
Write	0000 0010	Write data to the EEPROM starting at the address supplied
WRDI	0000 0100	Reset the write enable latch (disable write operations)
WREN	0000 0110	Set the write enable latch (enable write operations)
RDSR	0000 0101	Read the STATUS register
WDSR	0000 0001	Write to the STATUS register

Writing to the EEPROM

The following describes what must be done to write data to the EEPROM:

1. First, send the $\overline{CS}$ pin low.

2. Now send the instruction WREN to the EEPROM. Note the EEPROM will fill the SPIxSR with nonsense. The master must then read this from its SPIxBUF register and dispose of it.

3. After all 8 bits of the instruction have been sent, send the $\overline{CS}$ high. This is to allow the EEPROM to set the write enable latch in the EEPROM.

4. Now send the $\overline{CS}$ pin back low again.

5. Send a write instruction to the EEPROM. Note the EEPROM will fill the SPIxSR with nonsense. The master must then read this from its SPIxBUF register and dispose of it.

6. Now send the high byte of the 16-bit address we want to start writing to. Note we only need 15 bits to address 32,768 memory locations, that is, $2^{15} = 32,768$. This means that the MSB, Most Significant Bit, of this high byte has no meaning, and it can be either a logic '0' or logic '1'. I will set it to a logic '0'.

7. Now send the low byte of the 16-bit address we want to start writing to. Note, as each byte of the address is sent to the EEPROM, the EEPROM will fill the SPIxSR with nonsense. The master must then read this from its SPIxBUF register and dispose of it.

8. Now send the actual data to be written to the EEPROM. You can write up to 64 bytes of data without having to restart a write cycle, as long as the 64 memory locations are on the same page. Note as each byte of data is sent to the EEPROM, the EEPROM will fill the SPIxSR with nonsense. The master must then read this from its SPIxBUF register and dispose of it.

9. Now, after the last bit of the data has been sent to the EEPROM, the $\overline{CS}$ can be sent high. This will end the write cycle, and the write enable latch is reset.

Reading from the EEPROM

The following describes what must be done to read data from the EEPROM:

1. Firstly, send the $\overline{CS}$ must be sent low.

2. Now send the READ instruction to the EEPROM.

3. Send the 16-bit address of where you want to start the read process from, sending the high byte first. Note, as each byte of the address is sent to the EEPROM, the EEPROM will fill the SPIxSR with nonsense. The master must then read this from its SPIxBUF register and dispose of it.

4. The EEPROM will be ready to send the data to the master, but because of the circulating action of the SPI process, the master must put some information on the SDO line. This will start the clocking signal and so synchronize the process. Note the slave cannot create the clock signal. This information the master puts on the SDO pin can be anything; it is only used to start the clocking.

5. Once the master has received all the data it requires from the slave, the master must send the $\overline{CS}$ high to stop the read process.

Note, as with the write sequence, every time the master sends information to the EEPROM, the EEPROM will send information back to the master, and the programmer must decide if the information is useless or not. This is due to the circulating action of the SPI process.

Now we have a good idea of the process to write and read from the EEPROM, we can start to think about the program.

The Connections of the EEPROM on the Explorer 16 Development Board

You need to know how your EEPROM will be connected to your PIC so that you know what pins can be used.

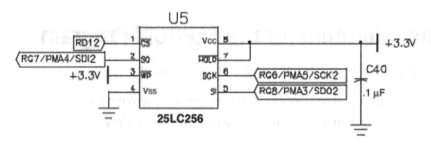

Figure 6-3. *The Connections of the 25LC256 to the PIC32 on the Explorer 16 Development Board*

Figure 6-3 shows the connections of the EEPROM on the explorer 16 development board. The $\overline{CS}$ is connected to bit 12 of PORTD. This bit must be set as an output and used to control the $\overline{CS}$ of the EEPROM.

1. The $\overline{HOLD}$ is permanently tied to VCC, so this is something we don't need to bother with.

2. The $\overline{WP}$ is also permanently tied to VCC, so this is something we don't need to bother with; this is because we will be writing to the EEPROM, and the $\overline{WP}$ is the write protect which stops you from writing to the EEPROM.

3. The SO pin is connected to the SDI2 pin of the PIC. This means we are using the second SPI module, so we must write to the SPI2CON register to set up the SPI.

4. The SCK is connected to the SCK2 pin, and so this must be set as an output.

5. The SI pin is connected to the SDO2 pin, and so this must be set as an output.

The Algorithm for the EEPROM Program

The algorithm is simply a list of the things we need to do:

- We need to know what it is we are trying to get the program to do. This can be described as follows.

- The basic idea is to write the following data to the EEPROM:

  - "Ann Ward".

- We will send the data to the first eight memory locations starting at address 0x0000.

  - We won't send the two quotation marks and the full stop.

- We will then get the PIC to read the data back from the EEPROM and display it on the LCD.

- As we will be displaying the data from the EEPROM on the LCD, we must use an LCD header file. We will use the header file for the PORTD, as this is where we will connect the LCD; we will not use the LCD supplied with the explorer 16 development board.

- We will use a start button to control when we start the whole process. This will be connected to bit 7 of PORTA as this is where one of the three buttons on the explorer 16 development board is connected. They are connected as going low when the switch is pressed. We must set bit 7 of PORTA as an input.

That is most likely all we need for this program. As we progress, we might have to add some items, but we will see.

The listing for the program is shown in Listing 6-1.

Listing 6-1. Writing a Message to the EEPROM

```
1   /*
2   * File:    LCD1Prog.c
3   Author: H. H. Ward
4   *A program for the 32bit PIC to write two simple messages
    to a LCD display
5   Created on 17 July 2021, 15:51
6   */
7   #include <xc.h>
8   #include <config72M36MNoWDTNoJTAG.h>
9   #include <8BitLCDPortD.h>
10  //some definitions
11  #define WRSR            0b00000001
12  #define WRITE           0b00000010
13  #define READ            0b00000011
14  #define WRDI            0B00000100
15  #define RDSR            0b00000101
16  #define WREN            0b00000110
17  #define CS              _RD12
18  #define startButton     _RA7
```

```
19  //variables
20  unsigned char dummy;
21  unsigned char EEdata [10];
22  unsigned char EEdisplay [10];
23  //some subroutines
24  int  EEPWRIGHT(int infow)
25  {
26  SPI2BUF = infow;
27  while (!SPI2STATbits.SPIRBF);
28  return SPI2BUF;
29  }
30  int EEPREAD(int infor)
31  {
32  SPI2BUF = infor;
33  while (!SPI2STATbits.SPIRBF);
34  return SPI2BUF;
35  }
36  void main()
37  {
38  // set up the timers and PORTS
39  T1CON = 0x8030;
40  TRISA = 0x0080;
41  TRISB = 0x00FF;
42  TRISC = 0X00FF;
43  TRISD = 0X0000;
44  TRISE = 0x0000;
45  PORTA = 0;
46  PORTB = 0;
47  PORTC = 0;
48  PORTD = 0;
49  PORTE = 0;
```

```
50   AD1PCFG = 0XFFFF;
51   AD1CON1 = 0;
52   //SPI2CONbits.ON = 0;
53   SPI2CONCLR = 0X8000;
54   SPI2BRG = 17;
55   SPI2CON = 0x0060;
56   SPI2CONSET = 0X8000;
57   //SPI2CONbits.ON = 1;
58   DDPCONbits.JTAGEN = 0;
59   CS = 1;
60   setUpTheLCD();
61   CS = 0;
62   EEPWRIGHT(WREN);
63   CS = 1;
64   TMR1 = 0;
65   while (TMR1 < 60);
66   CS = 0;
67   EEPWRIGHT(WRITE);
68   dummy = SPI2BUF;
69   EEPWRIGHT(00);
70   dummy = SPI2BUF;
71   EEPWRIGHT(00);
72   dummy = SPI2BUF;
73   EEPWRIGHT(0x41);
74   dummy = SPI2BUF;
75   EEPWRIGHT(0x6E);
76   dummy = SPI2BUF;
77   EEPWRIGHT(0x6E);
78   dummy = SPI2BUF;
79   EEPWRIGHT(0x20);
80   dummy = SPI2BUF;
```

```
81   EEPWRIGHT(0x57);
82   dummy = SPI2BUF;
83   EEPWRIGHT(0x61);
84   dummy = SPI2BUF;
85   EEPWRIGHT(0x72);
86   dummy = SPI2BUF;
87   EEPWRIGHT(0x64);
88   dummy = SPI2BUF;
89   EEPWRIGHT(0x31);
90   dummy = SPI2BUF;
91   CS = 1;
92   //read sequence
93   TMR1 = 0;
94   while (TMR1 < 600);
95   CS = 0;
96   dummy = EEPREAD(READ);
97   dummy = EEPREAD(00);
98   dummy = EEPREAD(00);
99   EEdata [0] = EEPREAD(0);
100  EEdata [1] = EEPREAD(0);
101  EEdata [2] = EEPREAD(0);
102  EEdata [3] = EEPREAD(0);
103  EEdata [4] = EEPREAD(0);
104  EEdata [5] = EEPREAD(0);
105  EEdata [6] = EEPREAD(0);
106  EEdata [7] = EEPREAD(0);
107  EEdata [8] = EEPREAD(0);
108  CS = 1;
109  //the main part of the program
110  while (startButton);
```

```
111  while (1)
112  {
113  writeString("EEPROM Data out");
114  line2();
115  for (n = 0; n < 8; n++)
116  {
117  lcdData = EEdata [n];
118  sendData();
119  for (m = 0; m < 10; m++)
120  {
121  TMR1 = 0;
122  while (TMR1 < 6000);
123  }
124  }
125  goHome();
126  }
127  }
```

Analysis of Listing 6-1

Lines 1–6 are the usual comments. Lines 7 and 8 are the normal include, and line 9 includes the header file for the LCD to be used in 8-bit mode on PORTD.

Lines 11–16 define some sensible phrases to represent the binary values for the six instructions for the EEPROM.

Line 17 #define CS   _RD12

This defines the term "CS" as being allocated to bit 12 of PORTD. This bit is connected to the $\overline{CS}$ pin on the EEPROM; see Figure 6-3.

Line 18 #define startButton   _RA7

This is the usual definition and allocation of the "startButton" to bit 7 of PORTA.

Line 20 unsigned char dummy;

This creates a byte of memory location referred to as "dummy." This is the global variable that is used to store the unimportant data that is sent from the slave to the master.

Line 21 unsigned char EEdata [10];

This creates an array of ten locations that can be used to store 8 bits of data, that is, of type char. This might be used in an extended program.

Line 22 unsigned char EEdisplay [10];

This creates another array of ten locations to store up to ten integers. This is used to store the data retrieved from the EEPROM ready to be displayed on the LCD.

Line 24 int   EEPWRIGHT(int infow)

This creates a subroutine that we can use for writing data to the EEPROM. It expects some data of the type int or integer, that is, 16 bits, to be sent up to the subroutine when it is called. When the subroutine finishes, it will send some data of the type int back to where it was called from. I did think that we could use unsigned chars instead of integers as we are sending 8 bits at a time. However, the only data type that worked successfully was int. This is probably because the registers in the SPI module are 16 bits. However, I have been able to make the global variable "dummy" and the two arrays unsigned char, that is, 8 bits, as we are using just 8 bits of data. The integer data that is sent up to the subroutine will be copied into the local variable "infow," which is the "information to write." The 8 bits sent up to the subroutine will be copied into the low byte of the local variable "infow."

Line 26   SPI2BUF = infow;

This copies the data in the variable infow into the SPI2BUF. This action starts the SPI circular action and the clock.

Line 27 while (!SPI2STATbits.SPIRBF);

This waits for the SPIRBF of the SPI2 module to go to a logic '1'. This will happen when the module receives data from the slave and moves it into the SPI2RXB register. With this instruction, we are making the PIC wait until the slave sends a reply back to the master. Note, this will be useless data, and it will most likely be 0xFF.

Line 28   return SPI2BUF;

This ends the subroutine and copies the contents of the SPI2BUF into the variable linked to the subroutine call. This would clear the SPIRBF bit and set it back to a logic '0'.

Line 30 int EEPREAD(int infor)

This creates a subroutine that is used to read data from the EEPROM. Just like the EEWRITE subroutine, it is expecting data to be sent up to the subroutine, and it will be sending data back from the subroutine when it ends. The data that is to be sent up to the subroutine is the nonsense data from the master that enables the master to start the clock and so start the circulating action of the SPI. This is because we want to read from the slave. Note the master must send some nonsense to the slave to push the data out of the slave SPISR.

Line 32   SPI2BUF = infor;

This copies the nonsense data into the SPI2BUF and so starts the SPI process.

Line 33 while (!SPI2STATbits.SPIRBF);

This gets the PIC to wait until the slave has sent some data back to the master. However, this time, the data will be useful.

Line 34 return SPI2BUF;

This ends the subroutine and copies the contents of the SPI2BUF into the variable linked to the subroutine call. This would clear the SPIRBF bit back to a logic '0'.

Line 36 void main()

This is the main loop of the program.

Lines 38–51 have been looked at already.

Line 52 //SPI2CONbits.ON = 0;

I am including this line, even though it is commented out by placing the two forward slashes in front of it, because I want to explain the use of the new instruction on line 53. Note, because this instruction is commented out, the compiler will not include this instruction in the program. This idea of commenting out an instruction is a useful procedure for debugging your programs. If we were to use this instruction, then it would simply load the "ON" bit, that is, bit 15, of the SPI2CON register with a logic '0'. This would turn the SPI module off.

Line 53 SPI2CONCLR = 0x8000;

This is an alternative method of clearing a bit, that is, setting it to a logic '0', to the method shown in line 52. In line 52, we have identified the particular bit of the register and then stated what logic we want to set that bit to. With this alternative method, we state that we want to clear bits in the register. We identify the particular bit, or bits, we want to clear by stating the value for the register, but with a logic '1' in the bit, or bits, we want to clear. All bits with a logic '0' at their respective position will be unaffected by this instruction. The hex value 0x8000 means that only bit 15 of the value has a logic '1' in it. So, only this bit, in the SPI2CON register, will be affected by this instruction and so cleared; this is indicated by the term "CLR" after the name of the register we want the instruction to affect. It is supposed to be a faster acting type of instruction. It is up to you which method you use. Note this instruction will turn the SPI module off.

Line 54 SPI2BRG = 17;

This is used to set the frequency of the clock signal used by the SPI module. In this case, we will choose to use a frequency of 1MHz for the clock signal. We now need to know what value to load into the BRG register that will set the SPI module to operate at this frequency. Microchip gives us an equation for calculating the clock frequency, which is shown in Equation 6-1. I have rearranged this for the BRG value as shown in Equation 6-2.

$$fck = \frac{PBCK}{2*(BRG+1)} \qquad \text{(Equation 6-1)}$$

$$BRG = \frac{PBCK}{2*fck} - 1$$
$$\therefore BRG = \frac{36Mhz}{2*1Mhz} - 1 = 17 \qquad \text{(Equation 6-2)}$$

There is no set frequency you should use, but 1MHz is a typical frequency.

Line 55 SPI2CON = 0x0060;

This loads the SPI2CON register with the data 0x0060. To appreciate what this instruction does, we must look at the SPI2CON register. This is the register that controls how we use the SPI2 module, refer to Table 6-4. There are 32 bits in that register, and the bits set a lot of parameters. The bits control the following aspects of the SPI2 module.

Table 6-4. *The Bit Usage for the SPIxCON Register*

Bits	Area of Control
31–24	Control the framed SPI process
23	MCLKSel: Master Clock Select bit Logic '1': MCLK is used by the baud rate generator Logic '0': PBCLK is used by the baud rate generator
22–18	Not used; read as logic '0'
17	SPIFE: Frame Sync Pulse Edge Select bit (framed SPI mode only) 1 = Frame synchronization pulse coincides with the first bit clock 0 = Frame synchronization pulse precedes the first bit clock
16	ENHBUF: Enhanced Buffer Enable bit 1 = Enhanced Buffer mode is enabled 0 = Enhanced Buffer mode is disabled
15	ON: SPI Peripheral On bit 1 = SPI Peripheral is enabled 0 = SPI Peripheral is disabled
14	Unimplemented: Write '0'; ignore read
13	SIDL: Stop in Idle Mode bit 1 = Discontinue operation when the CPU enters in idle mode 0 = Continue operation in idle mode
12	DISSDO: Disable SDOx pin bit 1 = SDOx pin is not used by the module (pin is controlled by the associated PORT register) 0 = SDOx pin is controlled by the module
11–10	See Table 6-5

(*continued*)

Table 6-4. (*continued*)

Bits	Area of Control
9	SMP: SPI Data Input Sample Phase bit Master mode (MSTEN = 1): 1 = Input data sampled at the end of data output time 0 = Input data sampled at the middle of data output time Slave mode (MSTEN = 0): SMP value is ignored when SPI is used in slave mode. The module always uses SMP = 0
8	CKE: SPI Clock Edge Select bit 1 = Serial output data changes on transition from active clock state to idle clock state (see CKP bit) 0 = Serial output data changes on transition from idle clock state to active clock state (see CKP bit) The CKE bit is not used in the framed SPI mode. The user should program this bit to "0" for the framed SPI mode (FRMEN = 1)
7	SSEN: Slave Select Enable (slave mode) bit 1 = SSx pin used for slave mode 0 = SSx pin not used for slave mode, pin controlled by the port function
6	CKP: Clock Polarity Select bit 1 = Idle state for clock is a high level; active state is a low level 0 = Idle state for clock is a low level; active state is a high level
5	MSTEN: Master Mode Enable bit 1 = Master mode 0 = Slave mode

(*continued*)

Table 6-4. (*continued*)

Bits	Area of Control
4	DISSDI: Disable SDI bit 1 = SDIx pin is not used by the SPI module (pin is controlled by the PORT function) 0 = SDIx pin is controlled by the SPI module
3–2	See Table 6-6
1–0	See Table 6-7

Table 6-5. *The Options for Bits 11 and 10*

Bit 11–10 MODE<32,16>: 32/16-Bit Communication Select Bits		
11 **Mode 32**	**10** **Mode 16**	**Communication**
1	x	32 bits
0	1	16 bits
0	0	8 bits

Table 6-6. *Options for Bits 3 and 2*

STXISEL<1:0>: SPI Transmit Buffer Empty Interrupt Mode Bits		
Bit 3	**Bit 2**	**Usage**
1	1	SPIxTXIF is set when the buffer is not full (has one or more empty elements)
1	0	SPIxTXIF is set when the buffer is empty by one-half or more
0	1	SPIxTXIF is set when the buffer is completely empty
0	0	SPIxTXIF is set when the last transfer is shifted out of SPISR and transmit operations are complete

Table 6-7. *Options for Bits 1 and 0*

SRXISEL<1:0>: SPI Receive Buffer Full Interrupt Mode Bits		
Bit 1	**Bit 0**	**Usage**
1	1	SPIxRXIF is set when the buffer is full
1	0	SPIxRXIF is set when the buffer is full by one-half or more
0	1	SPIxRXIF is set when the buffer is not empty
0	0	SPIxRXIF is set when the last word in the receive buffer is read (i.e., buffer is empty)

This is a very complicated control register, and we will look at the more complex bits later. In this first program, we are not using the SPI in the framed protocol, so bits 31 to 24 can be set at logic '0'.

We will be using the PBCLK for the baud rate generator, so set bit 23 to a logic '0'.

Bits 22 to 18 are set to a logic '0'.

We are not using a framed protocol, so bit 17 can be set to a logic '0'.

We will not be using the enhanced buffer mode, so bit 16 can be set to a logic '0'.

This means that the upper 16 bits can all be set to a logic '0' or left at their default setting of logic '0'.

We need to turn the SPI on, so bit 15 must be set to a logic '1' when we are ready to turn it on. However, it is good practice to turn a module off until you have completed setting it up ready for use.

Bit 14 is a logic '0'.

We will let the SPI continue operating when the PIC is placed in idle mode, so set bit 13 to a logic '0'.

We will let the SPI control the SD0 pin, so set bit 12 to a logic '0'.

We will be using 8-bit data, so set both bits 11 and 10 to logic '0'.

We will sample the data at the middle of data output time, so set bit 9 to a logic '0'.

As we are looking for a positive edge triggering at the slave, we will try changing from idle to active at the master. So set bit 8, the CKE bit, to a logic '0'.

We don't need the SSX pin as the PIC will be the master mode, and we will be using bit 12 on PORTD to control the CS. Therefore, set this bit 7 to a logic '0'.

As we want a positive edge triggering at the slave, and we are using idle to active for the change at the master, then we will try setting the idle state to be high and the active state to be low. Therefore, set bit 6, the CKP bit, to a logic '1'. This will produce a negative edge triggering at the master, but a positive edge triggering at the slave.

As we want the PIC to be the master, we must set bit 5 to a logic '1'.

The final 5 bits, 4 to 0, will be set to a logic '0'.

This means that the lower 16 bits written to the SPI2CON register will be shown in Table 6-8.

Table 6-8. *The Data to Be Written to the SPI2CON Register*

B15	B14	B13	B12	B11	B10	B9	B8	B7	B6	B5	B4	B3	B2	B1	B0
1	0	0	0	0	0	0	0	0	1	1	0	0	0	0	0
	8				0				6				0		

The Setting of the CKE and CKP Bits

I have stated that the process is synchronized to a clock signal created by the master. However, we need to appreciate what a clock signal is and how we can use it to synchronize operations. A typical clock signal is shown in Figure 6-4.

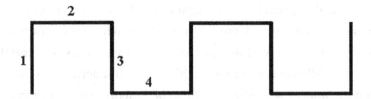

Figure 6-4. *A Typical Clock Signal*

The purpose of this clock signal is to synchronize when the master and the slave will be triggered or told to carry out their actions. Figure 6-4 shows that there are four points on the clock signal when this triggering can happen. They are identified as follows:

- Trigger point 1 is termed positive edge triggering.

- Trigger point 2 is termed high-level triggering.

- Trigger point 3 is termed negative edge triggering.

- Trigger point 4 is termed low-level triggering.

It should be clear that the edge triggering is the more precise triggering point as it lasts for only an instant. That is why it is the most common type to be used, either positive or negative edge triggering. The programmer must set the trigger point of the clock signal to ensure the slave device will use the correct data when it latches the data in. Some slave devices can work with any trigger point, and so the master can set it to whatever the master wants. However, we will look at using the positive edge of the clock signal, as this is when the 25LC256 EEPROM will attempt to latch the data in. Therefore, the master, controlling the operations, must set up its clock synchronization accordingly.

The CKE and the CKP are the two bits that are used together to set what type of triggering is used for the SPI module. These two bits give four options, and I have difficulty in defining exactly how they work. I will, however, use Table 6-9 to try and explain my understanding of what they achieve.

We can use these two bits to control when the master allows changes of the data on the data line. If we set the CKE = 0, where serial output data changes on transition from idle clock state to active clock state, and the CKP = 1, where idle state for clock is a high level and active state is a low level, then the master will allow a change of data on a transition from high to low, as shown in Figure 6-5. This is known as negative edge triggering; see Figure 6-5. We know that the 25LC256 EEPROM will latch the data in at the time when the clock signal changes from low to high, as shown in Figure 6-5. This is known as positive edge triggering.

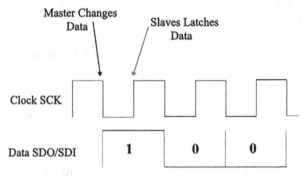

Figure 6-5. *CKE = 0 and CKP = 1*

If, on the other hand, we set CKE = 0 as before but set CKP = 0, where idle state for clock is a low level and active state is a high level, then the master would change the data at the point of the clock signal, as shown in Figure 6-6. This would mean that at the next positive edge of the clock, when the slave tries to latch the data, there would be some ambiguity as to whether or not the logic would be a "1" or a "0" and the data could be wrong. This is shown in Figure 6-6.

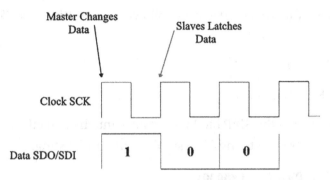

Figure 6-6. *CKE = 0 and CKP = 0*

As there are only two bits to consider, that is, if we don't consider the SMP bit, then we can try the four different settings and see what happens with the program. I have tried all four possibilities with this program, and the settings I have chosen work fine. I know this is not a precise method, but I have found it difficult to find a definitive process for choosing the settings of these two pins.

Table 6-9 lists the results of each of the settings for CKE and CKP. Note I have also indicated what happens if the logic on the SMP bit is changed.

Table 6-9. *The Triggering Action of the CKE and CKP Bits*

CKE Bit 8	CKP Bit 6	Mode	Master Trigger	Slave Response
0	0	0	Positive	Error as expected No change when SMP = 1
0	1	1	Negative	Good No change when SMP = 1
1	0	2	Negative	Good No change when SMP = 1
1	1	3		Error as expected Different error when SMP = 1

This shows that we could use the following two settings for CKE and CKP:

- CKE = 0, CKP = 1

- CKE = 1, CKP = 0

We can see that the SMP bit does not have much of an effect.

Now we can return to the analysis of the program listing.

Line 56 SPI2CONSET = 0x8000;

This is using the SET and CLR instructions for any control register. This instruction will set the actual bit indicated by the logic '1s' in the data stated in the instruction. It works in the same way as the instruction on line 53 except that it is setting the actual bit instead of clearing it; note the "SET" term. There is only one bit indicated as a logic '1' in the data 0x8000, and this is bit 15 of the SPIxCON control register. Line 53 turns the SPI module off, whereas this instruction turns the SPI module on. Microchip does advise you to turn most modules off while you set them up and then turn them back on again when they have been correctly configured.

Line 57 //SPI2CONbits.ON = 1;

This is the alternative way of setting the same bit and so turn on the SPI module. It is simply down to personal preference which method you use. The SET and CLR methods may be better if you want to SET or CLR a number of bits in a control register without affecting any of the other bits.

Line 58 DDPCONbits.JTAGEN = 0;

This is just freeing up the bits of PORTA for us to use.

Line 59 CS = 1;

This disables the EEPROM. I am including it here as just a precaution so that nothing is sent out accidentally to the EEPROM.

Line 60 setUpTheLCD();

This calls the subroutine "setUpTheLCD" which is in the header file for the LCD. This sets up the LCD ready for us to use.

Line 61 CS = 0;

This enables the EEPROM as we are ready to write to it.

Line 62 EEPWRIGHT(WREN);

This calls the subroutine to write to the EEPROM. It sends the data defined by the phrase "WREN." This is defined on line 16 as 0b00000110. This is the data for the instruction "WREN" which tells the EEPROM we want to set the EEPROM up so that it is ready to be written to.

Line 63 CS = 1;

This disables the EEPROM. This action is required to ensure the EEPROM latches the instruction we have just sent into its instruction register.

Line 64 TMR1 = 0;

This loads the TMR1 register, that is, TIMER1 register, which holds the current value that timer1 has currently counted to with the value 0. This is done to ensure timer1 starts counting from 0.

Line 65 while (TMR1 < 60);

This makes the PIC do nothing while the value in the TMR1 register is less than 60. These two instructions make the PIC do nothing for approximately 420μ seconds. This short delay is required to ensure the EEPROM has latched the instruction correctly.

Line 66 CS = 0;

This reenables the EEPROM as we want to write to it again.

Line 67 EEPWRIGHT(WRITE);

This sends the instruction "WRITE" as we will be writing the following data to the EEPROM.

Line 68 dummy = SPI2BUF;

This loads the variable "dummy" with what the EEPWRITE subroutine sends back to the main program. This is done as we know the circulating action of the SPI module will send data back to the master, but we know it is simple nonsense and so does not need saving. The program might work just as well without loading the variable dummy, with this nonsense sent from the slave. However, I prefer to ensure the receive buffer of the SPI has gone to a logic '0'. Emptying the SPI2BUF, in this way, ensures the SPIRBF bit does go to a logic '0'. This then ensures the while (!SPI2STATbits. SPIRBF); instructions do make the PIC wait until the slave has sent its data, useful or not.

Line 69 EEPWRIGHT(00);

This sends the high byte of the memory address we are writing to in the EEPROM.

Line 70 dummy = SPI2BUF;

This does the same as line 68.

Line 71 EEPWRIGHT(00);

This sends the low byte of the memory address.

Line 72 dummy = SPI2BUF;

This does the same as line 68.

Lines 73–90 send the ASCII values to store the message "Ann Ward" in the first eight locations in the EEPROM. Note after each ASCII character has been sent, we are loading the variable "dummy" with the data the slave sends back due to the circulating action of the SPI mode.

Line 91 CS = 1;

This disables the EEPROM to tell it we have ended the write operation.

Line 92 //read sequence

I tend to use simple comments like this to separate the listing into different sections; see lines 10, 19, 23, etc.

Lines 93 and 94 set up a 4.2ms delay to ensure the EEPROM has settled down before I read the data back.

Line 95 CS = 0;

This reenables the EEPROM ready for the read operation.

Line 96 dummy = EEPREAD(READ);

This calls the subroutine to read from the EEPROM. It sends the instruction to tell the EEPROM we are wanting to read from the EEPROM. We will read the data starting from the memory location we send next. Note, the instructions for the EEPREAD and EEPWRITE are the same. This is because we have to write to the EEPROM when we are sending the instruction "READ" and sending the high and low bytes of the address we want to start reading from to the EEPROM. This means we could have saved some memory if we had used the EEPWRITE subroutine. However, it seems more logical if we have a separate subroutine for WRITE and READ.

The instruction says "dummy = ". This is done to get the PIC to load the variable "dummy" with the data that is sent back when the subroutine finishes. Line 34 return SPI2BUF; will end the subroutine and send back the value in the SPI2BUF register, which, in this case, will be loaded into the variable "dummy." Note, in this instance, we know the data sent back from the slave, due to the circulating action of the SPI, will be nonsense, and so we can dispose of it.

Lines 97 and 98 do the same but send the high and low bytes of the address we want to start reading from. Again, we know the data sent back from the slave will be nonsense.

Line 99 EEdisplay [0] = EEPREAD(0);

This now calls the EEPREAD subroutine, but this time we know the data the slave will send back will be useful. It will be the data stored in the address 0x0000, which is the first address of the EEPROM. This is where we wrote the ASCII 0x41 for the letter "A" to be stored in the EEPROM. We have to send a value up to the subroutine to ensure the master starts the SPI clock and so the SPI cycle, hence the "0" between the normal brackets. The slave will simply ignore this data, and that is why it could be any value. In this case, I have used "0."

The PIC will store the value the slave sends back into the first memory location in the "EEdisplay" array. It is in this array that we will store the data ready to display it on the LCD.

Lines 100–107 do the same for the remaining seven characters we want to read from the EEPROM.

Line 108 CS = 1;

This ends the read sequence by disabling the EEPROM.

Line 110 while (startButton);

This simply gets the PIC to wait until the user presses the start button, which will drive the logic to a logic '0.'

Line 111 while (1)

This sets up a forever loop. This is used to ensure the PIC never carries out any of the previous instructions again. The PIC will only carry out the instructions listed between the opening and closing curly brackets that follow on lines 112 and 126.

Line 113 writeString("EEPROM Data out");

This simply displays the message "EEPROM Data out" on the LCD.

Line 114 line2();

This calls the subroutine to send the cursor to the beginning of the second line on the LCD.

Line 115 for (n = 0; n < 8; n++)

This sets up a "for do loop" of the type we have looked at before, which makes the PIC carry out the instructions listed between the following set of curly brackets eight times.

Line 117 lcdData = EEdisplay [n];

This loads the variable "lcdData" with the contents of the memory location in the array "EEdisplay," indicated by the value in the variable "n." As this is the first run through the "for do loop," "n" will be equal to 0. Therefore, this will load the variable "lcdData" with the ASCII 0x41, as this is what has been stored in the first location of the array; see line 99.

Line 118 sendData();

This calls the subroutine "sendData" which displays the contents of the variable "lcdData" on the LCD.

Line 119 for (m = 0; m < 10; m++)

This sets up a second "for do loop" which loops for ten times. This runs inside the first "for do loop," created on line 115. This process is termed "nested loop," as the loops are nested within an outer loop.

Lines 121 and 122 create a delay of approximately 42ms. This is just to create a delay between displaying the characters of the message.

Line 125 goHome();

This calls the subroutine to send the cursor back to the beginning of the first line of the LCD.

The PIC will now loop back to line 113 where it will write the messages again.

I hope this analysis has helped you to understand how these instructions work and how they carry out the requirements of this program.

The Message "Ann Ward"

To keep the program simple, as we are looking at the SPI module, I have just listed the ASCII for the eight characters to display the message "Ann Ward". These are listed in Table 6-10. Note the space is also listed as a character in ASCII.

Table 6-10. *The ASCII for the Message "Ann Ward"*

Character	ASCII
A	0x41
n	0x6E
n	0x6E
space	0x20
W	0x57
a	0x61
r	0x72
d	0x64

Figure 6-7 shows the program working with an LCD connected to PORTD.

Figure 6-7. *The EEPROM Program Working on the Explorer 16 Development Board with the LCD Connected to PORTD*

Using the Parallel Master Port

The 32-bit PIC has a parallel port module termed the PMP. It can be used in 8-bit or 16-bit mode, and the bits can be set as inputs or outputs. The PMP can be used to communicate with a variety of peripherals that can accept data in parallel, that is, all 8 or 16 bits at once, as opposed to serial, one bit at a time. The most common peripheral device we use is the LCD. We know the LCDs can work in 4-bit or 8-bit mode. However, as we have previously connected the LCD to an output board, the data has been sent all 4 or 8 bits at once, that is, in parallel. This means we could have used the PMP, Parallel Master Port. That is what we will look at now.

The PMP has 16 data bits available to it, which are PMD0 to PMD15. The first 8 bits, PMD0 to PMD7, are multiplexed with bits 0 to 7 of PORTE. The LCD on the explorer 16 development board is connected to bits 0 to 7 of PORTE. That is why we can use the PMP to write to the LCD, as opposed to using PORTE directly, as we have done in previous programs.

As with all the modules in the PIC, there is a control register that is used to configure how we use the PMP. This is the PMCON register, and it is the lower 16 bits of it that we need to use. We will look at the important control bits as we use them in the program. The following program will send some simple messages to the LCD, but the only difference is that it will use the PMP to communicate with the LCD on the explorer 16 development board.

The Data for the PMMODE Control Register

- We will ensure the Busy Flag is reset, disable the interrupt facility, and disable the automatic address increment function. This is done by setting bits 15 to 11 all to logic '0'.

- We will set the data bus to be 8 bits as opposed to 16 bits. This is achieved by setting bit 10, the "Mode16" bit, to a logic '0'.

- We will be using the PMP in master mode. There are two master modes available to us, and we will be using master mode1. To select this, we must set both bits 9 and 8 of the PMMODE register to logic '1'.

- There are a variety of different "wait" configurations we can use with the PMP.

- Bits 7 and 6 set the "WAITB" period, which sets the delay between loading the data onto the bus and sending the "E," or "Strobe Bit," pin high. We will set this to a maximum of 4xTPB, by setting these two bits to a logic '1'.

- Bits 5 to 2 set the "WAITM" period, which determines how long we keep the "E" pin high. Again, we will initially set this to the maximum period of 16xTPB. Therefore, set these bits to a logic '1'.

- Bits 1 and 2 set the "WAITE" period, which determines how long the data is kept on the bus after the "E" pin has gone low. We will set this to the maximum period as well, which is done by setting these two bits to a logic '1'.

The term "TPB" stands for the periodic time of the peripheral clock. This means that the data to be written to the PMMODE register is 0x03FF; see Table 6-11.

Table 6-11. *The Logic for the Bits in the PMMODE Control Register*

Bits	15	14	13	12	11	10	9	8	7	6	5	4	3	2	1	0
Logic	0	0	0	0	0	0	1	1	1	1	1	1	1	1	1	1

The PMCON Control Register

With respect to the PMCON register, we will set it up accordingly:

- Initially turn the PMP module off, so set bit 15 to a logic '0'. It is good practice to set up the module first before we turn it on.

- We will keep the module operating while the PIC is in "Freeze" or "Idle" mode, so set bits 14 and 13 to a logic '0'.

- We will not multiplex any of the PMD pins with the addressing function and use other pins for addressing. Therefore, we must set pins 12 and 11 to logic '0'.

- We will use the "Schmitt Input Buffers," so set bit 10 to logic '0'.

- We will enable PM write and read strobes, so set bits 9 and 8 to logic '1'.

- We will set PMCS2 and PMCS1 to act as the address pins for the PMP. Therefore, we must set bits 7 and 6 to logic '0'.

- We will set the polarity for the CS pins to be active low, so we must set bits 5, 4, and 3 to logic '0'.

- Bit 2 is not used, so we don't care what it is set to.

- We will set the write and read strobes to active high, so set bits 1 and 0 to logic '1'.

Therefore, the data we need to write to the PMCON register is 0x0303, which is shown in Table 6-12.

Table 6-12. *The Logic for the Bits in the PMCON Control Register*

Bits	15	14	13	12	11	10	9	8	7	6	5	4	3	2	1	0
Logic	0	0	0	0	0	0	1	1	0	0	0	0	0	0	1	1

The PMAEN Control Register

The final control register we need to write to is the PMAEN register. As we are not multiplexing the PMD pins as address lines, then we need to enable the PMA1 and PMA0 to be available as address lines. This is because the "RS" pin of the LCD is connected to the PMA0 pin of the PMP. Therefore, the data we need to write to the PMAEN register is 0x0001.

Before we leave the control pins of the PMP, we should note that the "E" pin of the LCD is connected to the PMWR. Also, the "R/W" pin of the LCD is connected to the PMRD pin of the PMP; see Figure 6-8. The logic on these two pins, the PMWR and PMRD, is controlled by the PMP module itself. It is only the "WAIT" timing of the PMWR, or "E" bit, that we have control over.

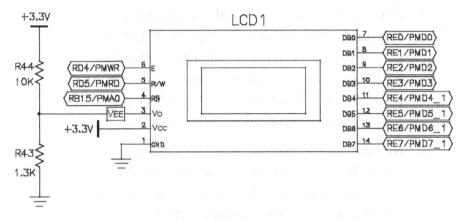

Figure 6-8. *The PMP and PORTE Connections to the LCD*

Now that we have determined what data should be written to the various registers of the PMP, we can think about creating a header file for using the LCD with the PMP:

1. First, we should consider how the PMP will send data to the device, the LCD in this case, that it is connected to. The operation is as follows.

2. The PMP will address the particular device it wants to talk to. This is done by setting the appropriate logic on the pins used for addressing the device. In our case, we are only using the PMA0 bit, so set this bit accordingly. However, you must appreciate that this pin is connected to bit 15 of PORTB, which is connected to the "RS" pin of the LCD. The "RS" pin is used to help the LCD distinguish between

instructions and data sent to the LCD. This means that the PMA0 bit is used in this case to set the appropriate logic on the "RS" pin of the LCD.

3. Next, load the PM data bus with the appropriate data. In our case, this will mean loading PMD0 to PMD7 with the correct data. This action of loading the PM data bus with data should ensure the R/W pin, that is, the PMRD pin or bit 5 of PORTD, is set to a logic '0' as we will be writing to the LCD.

4. Now wait for the first wait period, the "WAITB" period, before we send the "E" pin, which is the PMWR pin, or bit 4 of PORTD, high. In our case, the "WAITB" is set to the maximum of 4xTPB.

5. Now wait for the "WAITM" period before we return the "E" pin back to a logic '0'. In our case, we have set this "WAITM" to be the maximum of 16xTPB.

6. Finally, wait for the "WAITE" period before we remove the data from the PMP data bus.

This procedure should enable safe writing of instructions and data to the LCD. However, we should remember that we must enable the LCD to distinguish between instructions and data by setting the RS bit to a logic '0' for instructions and a logic '1' for data. This then means we must set the logic on the PMA0 bit correctly as it is the PMA0 that is connected to the "RS" pin.

Once we have set up the LCD, we can use the reading facility of the LCD to read the status register. This will enable us to check the "Busy Flag" of the LCD to ensure we don't start to write to the LCD while it is still dealing with the last instruction or data we sent to it. This approach will avoid the use of timers to give the LCD time to end what it was doing. It is a more efficient approach. Up until now, I have not used the facility to be able to read the status register of the LCD. Indeed, in wiring up the LCD, I have usually tied the R/W pin to ground, as I would only be writing to the LCD. This new approach does mean that we will be switching the R/W pin of the LCD to logic '1' or logic '0' as the need arises. However, with the PMP module, this action is controlled by the PMRD pin, as this is connected to the R/W pin of the LCD; see Figure 6-8.

With the different "WAIT" states set to their maximums, we should note that the complete sequence for one write will take at least 24 cycles of the PBCLK. This means it will take approximately 0.67µs, as we have set the PBCLK to run at 36MHz. However, this is not long compared with the time period between sending new data to the LCD.

If we look at our normal header files for sending data to the LCD direct, we will see that the strobe bit, or "E" bit, is sent high and then immediately sent back low. This action is done to inform the LCD that a new piece of data has been sent to the LCD, and it should deal with it. The PMP does the same, but, as we have shown, it will take approximately 0.67µs longer than the direct approach. Well, the PMP gives us a range of different "WAIT" periods as different peripherals will require different "waits." The PMP offers a wide range of flexibility in setting these wait states to meet a wide range of peripherals. Indeed, using the PMP for writing to the LCD is not the best use of the PMP. However, I am using it here to introduce you to the PMP. The PMP has the possibility of using 16 address lines to address separate peripherals connected to the PMP data bus. This suggests that it could address 65,536 different peripherals, a huge number of peripherals. However, each of the 16 address lines must use up some of the I/O pins of the PIC. Therefore, the programmer can use multiplexing to determine which of the I/O pins are used as address lines and when they are used. This can get very complex, but the ability to create this parallel data bus, which can be 8 bits or 16 bits wide, does make this PMP module very useful as your experience with the PIC32 grows. For now, we will just use it to control the LCD.

The program listing for this use of the PMP program is shown in Listing 6-2.

Listing 6-2. The PMP Program Listing

```
1  /*
2  * File:   PMPbasicLCD.c
3  Author: H. H. Ward
4  *A program for the 32bit PIC to write two simple messages
   to a LCD display using the PMP
5  Created on 18 April 2022, 18:11
6  */
7  #include <xc.h>
8  #include <config72M36MNoWDTNoJTAG.h>
9  #include "LCDPMP.h"
10 void main()
11 {
12 // set up the timers and PORTS
13 T1CON = 0x8030;
14 T4CON = 0x8070;
15 TRISA = 0x0080;
16 TRISB = 0x00FF;
17 TRISC = 0X00FF;
18 TRISD = 0X0000;
19 TRISE = 0x0000;
20 PORTA = 0;
21 PORTB = 0;
22 PORTC = 0;
23 PORTD = 0;
24 PORTE = 0;
25 AD1PCFG = 0XFFFF;
26 AD1CON1 = 0;
```

```
27  DDPCONbits.JTAGEN = 0;
28  setupPMP ();
29  setupLCD();
30  while (1)
31  {
32  writeString("Using The");
33  line2 ();
34  writeString("PMP");
35  cursorPos (2,6);
36  sendChar(0x39);
37  goHome ();
38  }
39  }
```

Analysis of Listing 6-2

There are no real new instructions to look at with this listing. Line 28 calls the subroutine "setupPMP ();" which is in the header file LCDPMP.h. At present, this is just a local header file. I am not sure if I will make it a global one later. The listing for this header file is shown in Listing 6-3.

The only other newish instruction is on line 36 where we call the subroutine "sendChar (0x39);". This subroutine is also in the header file LCDPMP.h. This instruction is sending the value "0x39" up to the subroutine. This is the ASCII for the character "9" to be displayed on the LCD.

Listing 6-3. The Listing for the PMP Header File

```
1  /*
2  * File:    LCDPMP.h
3  Author: HubertWard
4  A Header File to control the LCD using the PMP
```

```
 5  Created on 10 October 2014, 13:09
 6  */
 7  #define entryMode        0b00000110
 8  #define displayCtl       0b00001110
 9  #define functionSet      0b00111000
10  #define clearScreen      0b00000001
11  #define returnHome       0b00000010
12  #define lineTwo          0b11000000
13  #define shiftLeft        0b00010000
14  #define shiftRight       0b00010100
15  #define shDisRight       0b00011100
16  #define Gohome           0b00000010
17  #define Notblink         0b00001110
18  #define Doblink          0b00001111
19  #define               Inc_Position 0b00000110
20  //define some macros
21  #define BusyFlag() readStatus() & 0x80
22  #define sendChar(d)  writeLCD( 1,d)
23  #define sendInst(c)  writeLCD( 0,c)
24  //some variables
25  unsigned char n, LCDrubbish, LCDstatus;
26  unsigned char lcdInitialise [5] =
27  {
28  functionSet,
29  entryMode,
30  displayCtl,
31  clearScreen,
32  returnHome,
33  };
34  void setupPMP ()
35  {
```

```
36   PMCON = 0x0303;
37   PMMODE = 0x3FF;
38   PMAEN = 0x0001;
39   PMCONSET = 0x8000;
40   }
41   //Subroutines for LCD
42   void setupLCD()
43   {
44   TMR4 = 0; while( TMR4<6000);
45   PMADDR = 0;
46   n = 0;
47   while (n < 5)
48   {
49   PMDIN = lcdInitialise [n];
50   TMR4 = 0; while( TMR4<8);
51   n ++;
52   }
53   TMR4 = 0; while( TMR4<300);
54   }
55   //Subroutine to read status register from LCD
56   unsigned char readStatus()
57   {
58   while( PMMODEbits.BUSY);
59   PMADDR = 0;
60   LCDrubbish = PMDIN;
61   while( PMMODEbits.BUSY);
62   return( PMDIN);
63   }
64   //Subroutine to read data register from LCD
65   unsigned char readData()
66   {
```

```
67   while( PMMODEbits.BUSY);
68   PMADDR = 1;
69   LCDrubbish = PMDIN;
70   while( PMMODEbits.BUSY);
71   return( PMDIN);
72   }
73   void writeLCD( unsigned char RSbit, char info)
74   {
75   while( BusyFlag());
76   while( PMMODEbits.BUSY);
77   PMADDR = RSbit;
78   PMDIN = info;
79   }
80   void writeString (unsigned char *print)
81   {
82   while( *print) sendChar( *print++);
83   }
84   void line2 ()
85   {
86   sendInst (lineTwo);
87   }
88   void goHome ()
89   {
90   sendInst (returnHome);
91   }
92   void clearTheScreen ()
93   {
94   sendInst (clearScreen);
95   }
96   void shiftcurleft (unsigned char n)
97   {
```

```
98   while (n!=0)
99   {
100  sendInst (shiftLeft);
101  n--;
102  }
103  };
104  void shiftcurright (unsigned char n)
105  {
106  while (n!=0)
107  {
108  sendInst (shiftRight);
109  n--;
110  }
111  };
112  void cursorPos (unsigned char line, unsigned char pos)
113  {
114  switch (line)
115  {
116  case 1:
117  {
118  goHome ();
119  shiftcurright (pos);
120  break;
121  }
122  case 2:
123  {
124  line2 ();
125  shiftcurright (pos);
126  break;
127  }
128  }
129  }
```

Analysis of Listing 6-3

Lines 1–6 are the usual comments.

Lines 7–19 are defining some of the phrases for the control of the LCD.

Line 21 #define BusyFlag() readStatus() & 0x80

This creates a macro called "BusyFlag" that is used in line 75. The macro calls the subroutine "readStatus()". This will read the current value that is in the "status" register of the LCD. Then the macro will perform a logical AND operation with the contents of the status register and the number 0x80. This will only result in a logic '1' if bit 7 of the status register is also a logic '1'. Bit 7 of the status register is the "Busy Flag" of the LCD. If bit 7 is a logic '1', which means the LCD is busy, then the macro call will return a true result. If bit 7 is not a logic '1', then the macro will return an untrue result.

Line 22 #define sendChar(d) writeLCD(1, (d))

This creates the macro called "sendChar(d)" that is used in line 82. The macro calls the subroutine "writeLCD(1,d)". The "1" inside the normal brackets loads the "RS" with a logic '1'. This is because this macro will send a character to be displayed on the LCD.

Line 23 #define sendInst(c) writeLCD(0, (c))

This creates the macro called "sendInst(c)" that is used in line 86. The macro calls the subroutine "writeLCD(0,c)". The "0" inside the normal brackets loads the "RS" pin with a logic '0'. This is because this macro will send a new instruction to the LCD.

Line 25 simply declares some global variables to use in the program.

Lines 26–33 declare the array with its contents that holds the control data to set up the LCD. We have looked at these instructions in Chapter 4.

Line 34 void setupPMP ()

This creates a subroutine to set up the PMP. The instructions for the subroutine are between lines 35 and 40.

Line 36 PMCON = 0x0303;

This loads the PMCON register with the value 0x0303. This ensures the PMP is turned off and enables the write and the write/read strobe bits setting them to active high.

Also, as bits 12, 11, 7, and 6 are set at logic '0', the PMP will use just PMA0 and PMA1 as the address lines. However, in this instance, they are not being used to address the LCD, as the LCD is the only device connected to the PMP. The address line PMA0 is being used to control the logic on the "RS" pin of the LCD. This is because the PMA0 bit is multiplexed with bit 15 of PORTB, which is connected to the "RS" pin of the LCD; see Figure 6-8. The PMA1 is not used with the LCD.

Line 37 PMMODE = 0x3FF;

This loads the PMMODE register with the data 0x3FF.

Setting bit 10 to a logic '0' makes the PMP work in 8-bit mode.

Setting bits 9 and 8 to logic '1' puts the PMP into master mode 1.

Setting all the remaining bits to a logic '1' sets all three wait states to their maximums as explained earlier. I have tried various other settings for these wait states, and I have found that the LCD works fine with the minimum settings of 1TPB for the "WAITB" and "WAITE" periods, but we need a minimum setting of 8TPB for the middle wait "WAITM." This means that we could load the PMMODE register with the data 0x0320. As stated earlier, there are a wide range of wait settings, and you can either use the maximum setting with confidence or see what the specification for the device says or do some trial and error. I have chosen to leave them at the maximum settings.

Line 38 PMAEN = 0x0001;

This loads the PMAEN register with the value 0x0001, which enables the function of the PMA1 and PMA0 to be set by bits 12 and 11 of the PMPCON register. In this case, these are set as address lines; see line 36.

Line 39 PMCONSET = 0x8000;

This uses the "SET" Special Function Register for the PMPCON register. This will get the PIC to "SET," that is, force to a logic '1', any corresponding bit in the PMPCON register that matches where there is a logic '1' in the PMCONSET register. This means that bit 15 of the PMPCON register will go to a logic '1', and all other bits in the PMPCON register will be unaffected. This is because the value 0x8000 means that only bit 15 is a logic '1'. This action of setting bit 15 of the PMPCON register to a logic '1' will enable the PMP module.

Line 42 void setupLCD()

This creates a subroutine to set up the LCD. The instructions are between lines 43 and 54.

Line 44 TMR4 = 0; while(TMR4<6000);

This is two instructions on one line. The first instruction simply resets the value in the timer4 count register to 0. This makes sure timer4 starts counting from 0.

The second instruction makes the PIC do nothing while the count in timer4 is less than 6000. These two instructions create a 6000 x 7.1µs delay, which is the 43ms delay before we can send any data to the LCD.

Line 45 PMADDR = 0;

This loads the PM address register with "0." Really, as we are only using PMAD0, this puts a logic '0' on the PMAD0 pin which sends the "RS" pin of the LCD to logic '0'. This is to tell the LCD that what follows are instructions that the LCD must carry out, not characters to be displayed.

Line 46 n = 0;

This loads the variable "n" with "0" ready for the following while loop.

Line 47 while (n<5)

This gets the PIC to carry out the instructions, between lines 48 and 52, five times.

Line 49 PMDIN = lcdInitialise [n];

This loads the PMDIN bus, which is the 8 bits PMD0 to PMD7, with the contents of the memory location of the array "lcdInitialise," as indicated by the variable "n" in the square brackets. As this would be the first run through the while loop, then "n" will be "0" and so this instruction will load the PMDIN bus with the first content of the array. This would be the phrase " functionSet,"; see line 28. This will be the instruction as defined on line 9.

Line 50 TMR4 = 0; while(TMR4<8);

This is again two instructions on one line which creates a delay of around 57µs this time. This is to give the LCD time to process the instruction.

Line 51 n ++;

This simply increments the value in the variable "n" by 1.

In this way, the PIC will go through the while loop until n is incremented to the value "5." This will make the PIC send the five instructions to the LCD that are needed to set it up appropriately.

Line 53 TMR4 = 0; while(TMR4<300);

This creates another small delay, but this time it is around 2ms.

Line 56 unsigned char readStatus()

This creates a subroutine that is used to read the "Status" register of the LCD. We need to do this so that we can check to see if the "Busy Flag," that is, bit 8 of the "Status" register, is set. We need to make sure the LCD is not busy before we attempt to read from it.

Line 58 while(PMMODEbits.BUSY);

This checks to see if the "Busy" bit of the PMMODE register is set to a logic '1'. If it is, the test would be true, and the PIC should do nothing. This makes the PIC wait until the PMP is no longer busy.

Line 59 PMADDR = 0;

This loads the PMAD0, and so the "RS" pin of the LCD, with a logic '0'; see line 45.

Line 60   LCDrubbish = PMDIN;

This loads the variable "LCDrubbish" with what data is currently on the PMP data bus. It will not be useful, so we will not use it.

Line 61 while(PMMODEbits.BUSY);

This makes sure the PMP has finished with the last operation.

Line 62 return(PMDIN);

This is the last instruction in this subroutine, and, as the subroutine will be sending a variable of type unsigned char (see line 56), it will send back the contents of the PMP data bus to be copied into the variable associated with the subroutine call instruction.

Line 65 unsigned char readData()

This creates a similar subroutine to the last one. The instructions for the subroutine are between lines 66 and 72. The only difference between this subroutine and the other one between lines 57 and 64 is that in line 68

PMADDR = 1;, we load the PMAD0 with a logic '1', and this sets the "RS" pin to a logic '1'; see line 45. This tells the LCD that we want to read the "data register" within the LCD.

Line 73 void writeLCD(unsigned char RSbit, char info)

This creates a subroutine that allows us to write instructions to the LCD or write characters that we want to display on the LCD. The subroutine expects two pieces of data to be sent to it. The first piece of data will be copied into the local variable "RSbit," and this will be used to tell the LCD the information being sent is either an instruction, RSbit = 0, or a character to be displayed, RSbit = 1. The second piece of data will be copied into the local variable "info." This is the actual data, be it an instruction for the LCD or a character to be displayed.

Line 75   while(BusyFlag());

This calls the macro defined on line 21. This instruction is of the type "while (test is true) do what I tell you to do." The test will respond to the macro instruction "BusyFlag ()", which calls the subroutine to "readStatus" and ANDs the Status register with 0x80. In this way, the PIC simply tests to see if the "Busy Flag" in the LCD is a logic '1'. If the test result is true, then the PIC will do nothing. If the test result is untrue, then the PIC moves on to the next instruction. Therefore, this instruction simply makes the PIC wait while the LCD is busy. This is to ensure we don't try to write to the LCD while it is busy.

Line 76 while(PMMODEbits.BUSY);

This makes the PIC wait while the Busy bit in the PMMODE register is a logic '1'. Note the syntax of the instruction; there is no NOT symbol "!" which means we are testing to see if the bit is a logic '1'. If there was a NOT symbol "!", then we would be testing for a logic '0'.

We must ensure we don't try to use the PMP while it is busy. This is really repeating the action of the previous instruction. But there is no real problem in being overprotective. Any electronic system can be subjected to noise on the signal lines.

Line 77   PMADDR = RSbit;

This loads the PMADDR register with the data that was copied into the local variable "RSbit" when the subroutine was called. This will actually load the PMAD0 bit with the logic that is currently in bit 0 of the "RSbit." In this way, we can tell the LCD if this will be an instruction for the LCD or a character to be displayed.

Line 78 PMDIN = info;

This simply loads the PMP data bus with the data to be written to the LCD.

Line 80 void writeString (unsigned char *print)

This creates a subroutine to write a string of characters to the LCD. It is expecting some data to be sent up to it of type unsigned char. This will be copied into a local pointer called *print.

Line 82 while(*print) sendChar(*print++);

This makes the PIC test to see if the character that the pointer "*print" is pointing to is not the important Null character. The Null character signifies the end of the string of characters being sent to the subroutine. This Null character will not be displayed. While the character is not the Null character, the PIC must carry out the instruction that follows the while test. That instruction is "sendChar(*print++);" which calls the macro defined on line 22. This macro calls the subroutine "writeLCD" and sends the number "1" to set the "RS" pin of the LCD to a logic '1'. This is because, with this instruction on line 82, we are sending a character to be displayed on the LCD. It will also send the data, which is the ASCII for the character that the pointer "*print" is currently pointing to, to be displayed. This subroutine works in conjunction with the subroutine call, firstly used on line 32, of the main program listing shown in Listing 6-2. The instruction for that subroutine call is

```
writeString("Using The ");
```

This instruction will call the subroutine "writeString" and create an array at the same time. It will fill this array with the ASCII for all the characters in the string written between the two quotation marks. It will also append the important Null character to the end of the array. This is the Null character that denotes the end of the string that we want to display on the LCD.

Line 84 void line2 ()

This creates a subroutine that sends the instruction to move the cursor to the beginning of line 2 on the LCD.

Line 86 sendInst (lineTwo);

This is the only instruction in this subroutine. The instruction calls the macro "sendInst," on line 25, sending the instruction "lineTwo," which has been defined on line 12, to be sent to the subroutine "writeLCD." You should note that this macro sends the value "0" to be sent to the "RS" pin of the LCD, as this is an instruction for the LCD to carry out.

Line 88 creates a subroutine to return the cursor to the beginning of line 1 on the LCD.

Line 92 creates a subroutine to clear all the characters from the display of the LCD and return the cursor to the beginning of the first line on the LCD.

Line 96 void shiftcurleft (unsigned char n)

This creates a subroutine to shift the cursor a number of places to the left. It is expecting a number to be passed up to the subroutine which will control the number of places the cursor is shifted. This will be copied into the local variable "n." Note this is not the same as the global variable "n" created on line 27. Really, I should not have used the same name for the two variables, but I wanted to make you aware of the possible problem.

Line 98 while (n!=0)

This test is testing to see if the value in the local variable "n" is not equal to 0. The test will be true while this variable is not equal to 0. While the test is true, the PIC must carry out the following instructions listed between the opening and closing curly brackets on lines 99 and 102.

Line 100 sendInst (shiftLeft);

This calls the macro "sendInst" and sends the instruction "shiftLeft" as defined on line 13 to the LCD.

Line 101 n --;

This instruction decrements the contents of the local variable "n" by 1. Then the PIC goes back to the instruction on line 98. This makes the PIC test to see if the variable "n" is still not equal to 0. If it isn't, then the PIC must repeat the instructions, on lines 100 and 101, again. This allows the variable "n" to control the number of places we shift the cursor.

Lines 104–111 create a subroutine to shift the cursor a set number of places to the right. It works in the same way as the last subroutine.

Lines 112–129 create a switch and case statement to move the cursor to a set position on the LCD display. These instructions have been analyzed in Chapter 4. The only difference is that there are only two case statements. This is because the LCD on the explorer 16 development board has only two lines of 16 characters.

I hope the analysis of these two listings, Listings 6-2 and 6-3, do help you appreciate how you can use the PMP module. It is a very useful module that could make communicating with peripherals quicker. However, the peripherals will need to be able to accept parallel communication, and you need to have such peripheral devices. The LCD is such a peripheral.

Summary

In this chapter, we have looked at using the first and simplest method of serial communication available on 32-bit PICs, that is, the SPI module. We have also learned how to use an EEPROM device to permanently store data externally to the PIC. We then moved on to study how to use the PMP module, which allows us to use a parallel bus to communicate with devices connected to the PIC. I hope you have found this chapter informative and useful.

In the next chapter, we will look at using the I^2C protocol to communicate with peripheral devices connected to the PIC.

CHAPTER 7

The I²C Communication

The I²C Protocol

In the last chapter, we looked at using the SPI module of the PIC. This is probably the simplest method of serial communication, as it does not use a protocol. In this chapter, we will look at a process, which does use an industrial protocol, that is termed I²C. We will also study how we can use an I²C expander module and program it, with the 32-bit PIC, to send messages to an LCD.

   After reading this chapter, you will be able to use the I²C module of the 32-bit PIC to control an LCD using the I²C expander module.

I²C Communication Protocol

This stands for Inter-Integrated Circuit, and it is a protocol designed by Philips back in 1982. A protocol is simply a recognized process by which a transmitter and receiver can recognize how to interpret the logic '1s' and '0s' passed between them. The I²C is a synchronous serial communication protocol that only uses two wires. These wires are termed the SDA and

© Hubert Ward 2023
H. Ward, *Introductory Programs with the 32-bit PIC Microcontroller*,
Maker Innovations Series, https://doi.org/10.1007/978-1-4842-9051-4_7

the SCL lines. That is why it is sometimes referred to as "TWI" (Two-Wire Interface). It can be served by multiple masters and have multiple slaves on the bus. A simple setup is shown in Figure 7-1.

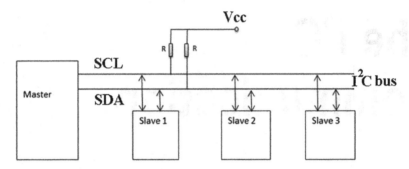

Figure 7-1. *A Typical I²C Bus*

The SDA is the line on which the data is sent from the master to the slave and from the slave to the master. The SCL line is the line on which the master sends the clock signal that synchronizes the process. Both these lines have pull-up resistors to ensure that when the signal is not switched low, that is, to 0V, the logic does go high, that is, to +VCC. The resistors are used to limit the current flowing through the switches when the lines are switched low.

The fact that it only requires two wires is an advantage over the SPI communication system we looked at in Chapter 6. However, there are some extra aspects that make this protocol more rigorous. The following is my attempt to describe what the I²C protocol requires and how it works.

Once communication has been set up, the master can be the transmitter, as when the master is simply writing to the slave. However, it can also be the receiver, as when the master is reading from the slave.

The slave can be the receiver, as when the master is just writing to the slave, but it can also be the transmitter, as when the master is reading from the slave.

To try and fully explain the I²C protocol, we will look at the process when the master is just writing to the slave and then when it is reading from the slave.

Writing to the Slave

The following describes what happens when the master is writing to the slave.

The Start Bit

The first thing the master must do is send a "start" bit to the slave. This means the master must drive the SDA line from high to low, while the SCL line is held high. This means that the SDA line must already be held high, that is, at a logic '1', before we send the start signal.

The Address Bits and Control Bit in the First Byte

The master will then send a byte that contains the address of the particular slave it wants to write to and a control bit that tells the slave it wants to write to it or read from it. This byte is b7, b6, b5, b4, b3, b2, b1, and b0.

Bits 1 to 7 contain the actual address of the slave the master wants to write to. This gives the master the ability to address 2^7 slaves, that is, 128, addresses 0 to 127.

The final bit, bit 0, is used to tell the slave whether or not the master wants to read or write to it. A logic '1' in bit 0 means the master wants to read from the slave, and a logic '0' means the master wants to write to the slave.

The address of the I²C expander board we will use in this project is 0x27, which is 0b00100111. Therefore, assuming we want to write to this device, the first byte will be 0b01001110 or 0x4E. You need to appreciate that we would have moved the bits of the data 0x27 one bit to the left. This is so that we can change the value of bit 0 to either a logic '1' or a logic '0'. Note bit 0 is set to a logic '0', in this case, as we are writing to the LCD connected to the expander board.

The Acknowledgment Bit

Then, as the slave is in receiving mode, it must send an acknowledgment bit to confirm to the master it has received the byte. This means the slave must pull the SDA line low while the clock is high. The slave will do this by switching the SDA line to 0V via a transistor switch inside the slave. This is known as the "acknowledgment bit (ACK)."

The Data Byte

The master must now write to the slave a byte of data that contains the memory location in the slave which the master wants to write to first. The slave will load this data into an address pointer inside it. The slave uses this address pointer to point to the address the master wants to write to. The slave will then send another acknowledgment bit to the master.

The master will now send the data that it wants to write to the address it has just sent to the slave. The slave will write the data to that address. Then the slave will increment its address pointer so that it now points to the next memory address in the slave. The slave will then send another acknowledgment bit to the master.

The master will send any more data to the slave that it wants to write to it. The slave will respond as before.

The Stop Bit

When the master wants to tell the slave it has finished writing to it, the master must send a stop bit. This is when the master changes the SDA line from low to high when the SCL line is high.

Table 7-1 shows the process that is required for I^2C communication when writing to the slave.

314

Table 7-1. *The Process for Writing to the Slave*

Start Bit	Slave Address	R/W Bit	ACK	Memory Address	ACK	Data	ACK	Last Data	ACK	Stop Bit
H to L	0b0100111x	0	Low	xxxxxxxx	Low	xxxxxxxx	Low	xxxxxxxx	Low	L to H

The shaded cells are the responses from the slave.

When we look at the program listing, we will see how the program conforms to this protocol.

Reading from the Slave

Before the master can read from the slave, the master must send to the slave the address of where the master wants to start reading from. This address would be loaded into the address pointer in the slave as before. This would be a write operation; therefore, to start the read sequence, the master must do the following:

- Put a start bit on the SDA line.

- Send the address and control byte to tell the correct slave the master will be writing to it. In our case, assuming we want to read from the I^{2}C expander module, this would be the following 8 bits:

  - 0b01001110.

  - Bits 7 down to 1 are the correct address of the slave, but shifted one bit to the left, and bit 0 is a logic '0' as we are writing to the slave.

- The slave will then respond with the acknowledgment bit.

- The master will then send the 8 bits that detail the start
  address of where the master wants to start reading
  from. The slave will load its address pointer with this
  address.

- The slave will respond with the acknowledgment bit.

- The master will then send the stop bit to finish this
  initial write operation.

The master will now tell the slave it wants to read from the start
address it has just sent. This will involve the following operations:

- The master will send another start bit.

- The master then sends the address and control bit as
  follows:

  - 0b01001111.

  - Bits 7 down to 1 are the correct address of the slave,
    but shifted one bit to the left, and bit 0 is a logic '1'
    as the master is now reading from the slave.

- The slave will send the acknowledgment bit.

- The slave now sends the first byte of data from the
  requested address. Note if the master did not send an
  address via an initial write operation, then the slave will
  send the data from the address that its address pointer
  is currently pointing to. The slave then increments its
  address pointer.

- Now, as the master is receiving the data, the master
  must put an acknowledgment on the SDA.

- After seeing the acknowledgment, the slave will put the data from the next location on the SDA line to send it to the master. The slave increments its address pointer again.

- The master after receiving this new data from the slave must put an acknowledgment bit on the SDA line again.

The NACK or Not Acknowledgment Bit

This process for reading from the slave carries on until the master gets the last byte of data it wants from the slave. When the master gets this last byte of data, it will put a not acknowledgment bit on the SDA line. The NACK is recognized as the SDA line being held high while the ninth clock signal is high. This ninth clock cycle is generated by the master after all 8 bits have been transmitted. This ninth cycle is reserved for the reception of either the acknowledgment bit or NACK bit.

When the slave sees this NACK bit on the SDA line, it knows not to transmit any more data.

To complete the action, the master will put a stop bit on the SDA line.

This whole read action can be summed up in Tables 7-2 and 7-3.

Table 7-2. *The Initial Write to the Slave to Set Up the Read Operation*

Start Bit	Slave Address	R/W Bit	ACK	Memory Address	ACK	Stop Bit
H to L	0b0100111x	0	Low	xxxxxxxx	Low	L to H

317

Table 7-3. *The Read from the Slave Operation*

Start Bit	Slave Address	R/W Bit	ACK	Data from Slave	ACK from Master	Last Data	Not ACK from Master	Stop Bit
H to L	0b0100111x	1	Low	xxxxxxxx	Low	xxxxxxxx	High	L to H

The shaded cells are the responses from the slave.

I know this is rather a lot to read through, but once you have got your thorough understanding correct, you know you now have a firm basis for writing your program instructions to implement the I²C protocol.

As we will be using the I²C protocol in a couple of projects, I will create a header file that complies with this protocol. The PIC32 has two I²C modules, and we will be using the first module, that is, module 1. That is why we are using the I²C1 control registers. The program listing for this header file is shown in Listing 7-1.

Listing 7-1. The I²C Protocol Header File

```
1  /* A header file to implement the I2C
2   protocol on a 32bit Pic
3   Written by Mr H. H. Ward
4   Dated 25 November 2021*/
5  void I2CInit()
6  {
7  I2C1CON = 0;
8  I2C1BRG = 178;
9  I2C1CONbits.ON = 1;
10 TRISGbits.TRISG2 = 1;
11 TRISGbits.TRISG3 = 1;
12 }
```

```
13  void I2Cidle()
14  {
15  while ((I2C1STATbits.TBF) || (I2C1CON & 0x1F));
16  }
17  void I2Cwait()
18  {
19  while(I2C1CON & 0x1F);
20  while(I2C1STATbits.TRSTAT);
21  }
22  void I2CStart()
23  {
24  I2Cwait();
25  I2C1CONbits.SEN = 1;
26  while (I2C1CONbits.SEN );
27  }
28  void I2CStop()
29  {
30  I2Cwait();
31  I2C1CONbits.PEN = 1;
32  while (I2C1CONbits.PEN );
33  }
34  void I2CRestart()
35  {
36  I2Cwait();
37  I2C1CONbits.RSEN = 1;
38  while (I2C1CONbits.RSEN == 1);
39  }
40  void I2CNACK()
41  {
42  I2Cwait();
43  I2C1CONbits.ACKDT = 1;
44  I2C1CONbits.ACKEN = 1;
```

```
45  while(I2C1CONbits.ACKEN);
46  }
47  void I2CWrite(unsigned char data)
48  {
49  I2Cwait();
50  send: I2C1TRN = data;
51  while (I2C1STATbits.TBF);
52  I2Cwait();
53  while (I2C1STATbits.TRSTAT);
54  while(I2C1STATbits.ACKSTAT)
55  {
56  I2C1CONbits.RSEN = 1;
57  goto send;
58  }
59  }
60  unsigned int I2Cread()
61  {
62  I2C1CONbits.RCEN = 1;
63  while (I2C1CONbits.RCEN);
64  while(!I2C1STATbits.RBF);
65  I2C1CONbits.ACKDT = 0;
66  I2C1CONbits.ACKEN = 1;
67  while(I2C1CONbits.ACKEN);
68  I2C1CONbits.RCEN=0;
69  return I2C1RCV;
70  }
71  unsigned char I2CreadNAck()
72  {
73  I2C1CONbits.RCEN=1;
74  while (I2C1CONbits.RCEN);
75  while(!I2C1STATbits.RBF);
76  I2C1CONbits.ACKDT=1;
```

```
77  I2C1CONbits.ACKEN=1;
78  while(I2C1CONbits.ACKEN);
79  I2C1CONbits.RCEN=0;
80  return I2C1RCV;
81  }
```

Analysis of the I²C Protocol Header File

Lines 1–4 are the normal set of comments.

Line 5 void I2CInit()

This creates a subroutine that will set up the I²C1 module ready to be used.

Line 7 I2C1CON = 0;

This turns the I²C1 module off, as it is best to set up the control bits while the module is turned off.

Line 8 I2C1BRG = 178;

This loads the I2C1BRG register with the decimal value 178. This register is used to set the frequency of the clock signal used to synchronize the module. However, it is normal to use a frequency for the SCL, that is, the FSCL frequency, of 100kHz or 400kHz. We will use the 100kHz for the FSCL. Knowing that, the value in the BRG register can be calculated according to the following expression:

$$BRG = \left(\frac{PBCLK}{FSCL*2} \right) - 2$$

$$BRG = \left(\frac{36E^6}{100E^3 * 2} \right) - 2 \therefore BRG = 178$$

This is currently all we need to do with the I²C module, so we can now simply turn the module on.

Line 9 I2C1CONbits.ON = 1;

This simply turns the I²C module on.

Line 10 TRISGbits.TRISG2 = 1;

This sets bit 2 of PORTG to an input. This bit is the SCL1 bit for the I²C1 module; see the data sheet. It is on this bit that the master will send out the clock signal to synchronize the module. This will be controlled by the module and be set as an output when it is required to send out the clock signal.

Line 11 TRISGbits.TRISG3 = 1;

This sets bit 3 of PORTG to an input. This bit is the SDA1 bit for the I²C1 module; see the data sheet. It is on this bit that the master sends out data to the slave or receives data from the slave. The I²C module will control the direction of the data through the bit as required. However, to initialize the module, we must set these two bits to input as we have done here.

Line 13 void I2Cidle()

This creates a subroutine that is used to check that the module is idle, that is, doing nothing.

Line 15 while ((I2C1STATbits.TBF) || (I2C1CON & 0x1F));

This is a "while test is true" instruction that makes the PIC do nothing if any of the two tests described inside the normal brackets results in a logic '1' being present. This is because we are using the logical OR "||" symbol. This takes two conditions, and if any of the two conditions is not at a logic '0', then the OR test will result in a true response. With this instruction, while the test is true, the PIC will do nothing.

The first of the two tests, inside the normal brackets, is looking at the TBF bit in the I2C1Status register. This TBF is the transmit buffer full bit, and it will be a logic '1' if the I²C module is currently transmitting data. This bit will go to a logic '0' once all 8 bits have been transmitted. Therefore, this test is simply testing if we are currently transmitting data.

The second condition is the result of a logical AND operation on the individual bits of the I2C1CON register and the value 0x1F. This is really testing if any of the first 5 bits of the I2C1CON register is at a logic '1'. These first 5 bits are as follows:

- **Bit 4 ACKEN**: Acknowledge Sequence Enable bit

  - This will be a logic '1' if the I²C module has initiated an acknowledge signal.

  - It will be a logic '0' if the acknowledge sequence is idle.

- **Bit 3 RCEN**: Receive Enable bit

  - This will be a logic '1' if the module has been put into receive mode as it is ready to receive data.

  - It will be a logic '0' if the module is not ready to receive data.

- **Bit 2 PEN**: Stop Condition Enable bit

  - This will be a logic '1' if the master has initiated a stop signal.

  - It will be a logic '0' if there is no stop signal activated.

- **Bit 1 RSEN**: Restart Condition Enable bit

  - This will be a logic '1' if the master has initiated a restart signal.

  - It will be a logic '0' if there is no restart signal activated.

- **Bit 0 SEN**: Start Condition Enable bit

  - This will be a logic '1' if the master has initiated a start signal.

  - It will be a logic '0' if there is no start signal activated.

This means that if either the TBF bit is a logic '1', that is, the PIC is currently transmitting data, or any of the first 5 bits in the I2C1CON is a logic '1', then the PIC must do nothing. This instruction does test to see if the I²C module is idle.

Line 17 void I2Cwait()

This creates a subroutine that makes the PIC wait until the I²C module has finished what it is currently doing.

Line 19 while(I2C1CON & 0x1F);

This is doing the same job as the second condition in line 15. It is getting the PIC to do nothing while any of the first 5 bits in the I2C1CON register is at a logic '1'.

Line 20 while(I2C1STATbits.TRSTAT);

This gets the PIC to do nothing while the I2C1CON is transmitting data. While the I²C module is transmitting data, the TRSTAT bit in the status register will be a logic '1'.

This means that these two instructions are making the PIC wait if it is transmitting or receiving data.

Line 22 void I2CStart()

This creates a subroutine that sends out the start signal from the master to the slave.

Line 24 I2Cwait();

The first thing we do is call the I²Cwait subroutine that makes the PIC wait if the module is busy; see lines 19 and 20.

Line 25 I2C1CONbits.SEN = 1;

This simply sets this bit to a logic '1.' This gets the master to send a start signal to the slave. When the master has finished the start signal, this bit will automatically go back to a logic '0.'

Line 26 while (I2C1CONbits.SEN);

This gets the PIC to do nothing while the SEN bit is a logic '1.' This ensures the PIC waits for the start signal to finish.

Line 28 void I2CStop()

This creates a subroutine that sends out a stop signal from the master to the slave.

Line 30 I2Cwait();

This just calls the subroutine to make sure the PIC waits while the module is doing something.

Line 31 I2C1CONbits.PEN = 1;

This sets the PEN bit which starts the sequence to put the stop signal on the data line SDA.

Line 32 while (I2C1CONbits.PEN);

This waits for the PEN to go back to a logic '0'. This will happen automatically at the end of the stop sequence.

Line 34 void I2CRestart()

This creates a subroutine to initiate a restart sequence on the data line. It works in the same way as the stop subroutine but uses the RSEN bit.

Line 40 void I2CNACK()

This creates a subroutine to initiate the NACK, not acknowledged, sequence on the SDA line.

line 42 I2Cwait();

This calls the wait subroutine as before.

Line 43 I2C1CONbits.ACKDT = 1;

This sets the ACKDT bit to a logic '1'. This needs to be a logic '1' for the not acknowledged signal.

Line 44 I2C1CONbits.ACKEN = 1;

This sets the ACKEN bit to a logic '1'. This then enables the acknowledgment sequence. However, as the ACKDT bit is set to a logic '1', the slave will see this as the NACK and so know the master has finished sending data.

Line 45 while(I2C1CONbits.ACKEN);

This makes the PIC wait for the logic on the ACKEN bit to go to a logic '0'. This will happen automatically at the end of the NACK or ACK sequence.

Line 47 void I2CWrite(unsigned char data)

This creates a subroutine to write data to the slave. It will expect a value to be passed up to the subroutine which it will copy into the local variable "data" to be used in this subroutine.

Line 49 I2Cwait();

This is simply checking, in the usual way, that the module is not doing something.

Line 50 send: I2C1TRN = data;

With this instruction, we are creating a label "send" which we might get the PIC to go to later in the subroutine.

The instruction at this label is I2C1TRN = data. This simply loads the I2C1TRN register with a copy of the value in the local variable "data." This action will automatically get the module to transmit the data in this register.

Line 51 while (I2C1STATbits.TBF);

This makes the PIC do nothing while the logic on the TBF, transmit buffer flag, is a logic '1'. Once the transmit cycle has started, this bit will be a logic '1' until the last bit has been transmitted. When the last bit has been transmitted, this bit will automatically go back to a logic '0'. Therefore, this instruction gets the PIC to wait until all 8 bits have been transmitted.

Line 52 I2Cwait();

This calls the wait subroutine. This is just an extra check to make sure the module is not doing something, in this case transmitting. This may not be needed, but it is not a problem being overcautious.

Line 53 while (I2C1STATbits.TRSTAT);

This gets the PIC to do nothing while the TRSTAT bit is a logic '1'. This bit will be set to a logic '1' when the master is transmitting data. This bit will return back to a logic '0' automatically when the module has finished transmitting the ACK or NACK. Again, this may seem overprotective, but it's not a problem.

Line 54 while(I2C1STATbits.ACKSTAT)

This gets the PIC to carry out the following instructions while the ACKSTAT bit is a logic '1'. The ACKSTAT bit will be set to a logic '1' when the master is expecting an acknowledgment from the slave, but it has not yet got one. When the slave sends the acknowledgment, this bit will automatically go back to a logic '0'. This bit would only be a logic '1' if the slave did not receive the data the master had just sent to it. Therefore, try sending it again.

Line 56 I2C1CONbits.RSEN = 1;

This sets the RSEN bit which is used to get the module ready to resend the data.

Line 57 goto send;

This gets the PIC to go back to the label "send" which is on line 46. This then starts the write cycle again with the same data.

Line 60 unsigned int I2Cread()

This creates a subroutine which will read data from the slave, and it will then send an acknowledgment, ACK, back to the slave. The subroutine will send data back to where it was called from using the data type unsigned int.

Line 62 I2C1CONbits.RCEN = 1;

This sets the RCEN bit. This is required to allow the master to receive data from the slave.

Line 63 while (I2C1CONbits.RCEN);

This gets the PIC to do nothing while the RCEN bit is set to a logic '1'. This bit will automatically be reset back to a logic '0' once all the data bits have been received by the master. Therefore, this instruction makes the PIC wait until the data has been received from the slave.

Line 64 while(!I2C1STATbits.RBF);

This bit will go to a logic '1' once all the data has been received and placed in the receive register ready to be read by the program. This gets the PIC to do nothing while the RBF bit is a logic '0'.

Line 65 I2C1CONbits.ACKDT = 0;

The master, which is the receiver at this point in the process, must send an acknowledgment, which means it must pull the SDA line low while the clock is high. This instruction puts a logic '0' on the SDA line.

Line 66 I2C1CONbits.ACKEN = 1;

This starts the acknowledgment process and so sends the acknowledgment to the slave. However, as we have set the ACKDT, the acknowledge data bit, to a logic '0' with the previous instruction, the slave will see this action as the ACK action, not the NACK action. See the description of the ACK and NACK bits earlier.

Line 67 while(I2C1CONbits.ACKEN);

This gets the PIC to do nothing while the ACKEN bit is a logic '1'. Note this bit will automatically reset back to a logic '0' once the acknowledgment sequence has finished. Therefore, this instruction makes the PIC wait until the acknowledgment sequence has completed.

Line 68 I2C1CONbits.RCEN=0;

This disables the receive aspect of the master as it has finished.

Line 69 return I2C1RCV;

This makes the PIC exit the subroutine and loads a copy of the contents of the receive register into the variable that was linked to the call of the subroutine.

Line 71 unsigned char I2CreadNAck()

This creates a subroutine that will read the data being sent from the slave, but it will then send a not acknowledgment, NACK, back to the slave. The subroutine will send data back to where it was called from using the data type unsigned int.

The instructions are the same as the previous subroutine except that in line 76 I2C1CONbits.ACKDT=1; we are setting the ACKDT data bit to a logic '1'. This is the requirement for the master to send the NACK to the slave.

This completes the analysis of the header file that I will use to allow the PIC to communicate with devices using the I²C protocol. I will use this header file with two programs. The first will use an I²C expander module that communicates with the PIC using the I²C protocol. The second will use the DS3231 RTC, Real-Time Clock, module to display the time and date on an LCD device. I hope you will find these two programs useful.

The I²C Expander Module

This is a module that can be used to enable the PIC to communicate with an LCD using just two lines: the SCL and SDA used with I²C. The expander module is shown in Figure 7-2.

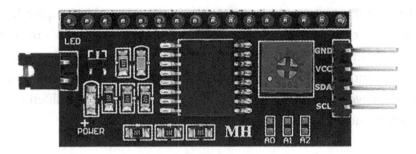

Figure 7-2. *The I²C Expander Module*

This can be used to enable the SDA and SCL lines of the I²C module to control eight I/O lines of the PIC. However, you should be aware that the drive capability of the device is very low. Therefore, if you want to use the expander to drive outputs, then you should use a driver IC such as a ULN2004. This could be useful if you were short of I/O; however, as the 32-bit PIC has plenty of I/O, I will be using the device to show how we can use the I²C module on the PIC to communicate with an LCD.

The LCD2004

As the expander has low drive capabilities, the expander is more commonly used with the LCD2004. An LCD2004 is shown in Figure 7-3.

Figure 7-3. *The LCD2004*

The LCD2004 is very similar to the 1602 LCD we used in Chapter 4. The difference is that it can display 20 characters on four lines of text. This makes it slightly more useful than the 1602 LCD. However, as we are using the I²C expander module to communicate with LCD2004, there are some differences even if we used the 1602 LCD. To appreciate those differences, we need to know how the expander is connected.

The Connections of the I²C Expander

To connect the expander to the PIC, there are just four connections:

- The SCL which is the synchronizing clock signal from the PIC as the master.

- The SDA which is the data line to receive data from the master and send data back to the master. The expander will be used as the slave to the master.

- There are also the ground and VCC connections to the expander.

There are now 16 connections from the expander to the LCD. These are made using the PC8574T IC. The pin usage of that IC is listed in Table 7-4.

Table 7-4. Pin Usage of I²C Expander PC8574T

Expander Pin		Usage
1	A0	Address line 0
2	A1	Address line 1
3	A2	Address line 2
4	P0	RS on LCD
5	P1	Not used
6	P2	E pin on LCD
7	P3	Not used
8	GND	0V
9	P4	D4, data bit 4 on LCD
10	P5	D5, data bit 5 on LCD
11	P6	D6, data bit 6 on LCD
12	P7	D7, data bit 7 on LCD
13	INT	An active low interrupt output
14	SCL	Clock signal
15	SDA	Data line
16	VCC	+5V

The expander communicates with the LCD using 4-bit format, which is why just P4, P5, P6, and P7 are connected to the data lines of the LCD. They are connected to the upper data lines of the LCD. This makes sending the high nibble of data to the LCD easier. Note, in 4-bit mode, we must send the high nibble first and then the low nibble. Also, whenever any information is sent to the LCD, the E pin must be sent high and then low.

One last thing we need to remember is that the RS pin is sent to a logic '0' when the information being sent to the LCD is an instruction and to a logic '1' when it is data to be displayed.

Knowing what we need to do, the header file for sending information to the LCD, using the I²C expander, can be written. This is shown in Listing 7-2.

Listing 7-2. The LCD2004 Header File Using the I²C Expander Module

```
 1  /*A header file to use the I2C expander module
 2  to write to a 20 character by 4 line LCD.
 3  It can also be used to write to a 16 character
 4  by 2 line LCD.
 5  Written by H H Ward dated 27/10/2021*/
 6  //some definitions
 7  #define entrymode      0b00000100
 8  #define fourBitOp      0b00110010
 9  #define twoLines       0b00101100
10  #define twoLines4bit   0b00101000
11  #define cursorNoBlink  0b00001100
12  #define clearScreen    0b00000001
13  #define returnHome     0b00000010
14  #define lineTwo        0b11000000
15  #define doBlink        0b00001111
16  #define shiftLeft      0b00010000
17  #define shiftRight     0b00010100
18  #define shdisright     0b00011100
19  // declare any variables
20  unsigned char n,s,d, lcdData, lcdTempData, rsLine, dataIn,
    ebit = 4, i2cadd = 0x27, curadd;
```

```
21  void msdelay (unsigned char m)
22  {
23  for (d = 0; d < m; d++)
24  {
25  TMR1 = 0;
26  while (TMR1 <140);
27  }
28  }
29  char lcdInitialise [5] =
30  {
31  entrymode,
32  twoLines4bit,
33  cursorNoBlink,
34  clearScreen,
35  returnHome,
36  };
37  void writeExp (unsigned char data)
38  {
39  I2Cwait();
40  I2CStart ();
41  I2CWrite ((i2cadd << 1));
42  I2CWrite (data | 0x08);
43  I2CStop();
44  }
45  void sendData1 (lcdTempData)
46  {
47  lcdTempData |= rsLine;
48  writeExp(lcdTempData|ebit);
49  writeExp(lcdTempData & 0XFB);
50  TMR1 = 0; while (TMR1 < 10);
51  }
```

```
52  void lcdOut (unsigned char LCDDATA)
53  {
54  lcdData = LCDDATA;
55  sendData1 (lcdData & 0XF0);
56  sendData1 ((lcdData << 4) & 0XF0 );
57  }
58  void setUpTheLCD ()
59  {
60  writeExp (0x00);
61  msdelay (50);
62  n = 0;
63  rsLine = 0X00;
64  while (n < 5)
65  {
66  lcdOut (lcdInitialise [n]);
67  n ++;
68  msdelay (50);
69  }
70  rsLine = 0x01;
71  }
72  void shiftcurleft ( unsigned char l)
73  {
74  for (s = 0; s < l; s ++)
75  {
76  rsLine = 0X00;
77  lcdOut (shiftLeft);
78  msdelay (50);
79  rsLine = 0x01;
80  }
81  }
```

```
82  void shiftcurright (unsigned char r)
83  {
84  for (s = 0; s < r; s ++)
85  {
86  rsLine = 0X00;
87  lcdOut (shiftRight);
88  msdelay (50);
89  rsLine = 0x01;
90  }
91  }
92  void line2 ()
93  {
94  rsLine = 0X00;
95  lcdOut (lineTwo);
96  msdelay (50);
97  rsLine = 0x01;
98  }
99  void clearTheScreen ()
100 {
101 rsLine = 0X00;
102 lcdOut (clearScreen);
103 msdelay (50);
104 rsLine = 0x01;
105 }
106 void sendcursorhome ()
107 {
108 rsLine = 0X00;
109 lcdOut (returnHome);
110 msdelay (50);
111 rsLine = 0x01;
112 }
```

```
113  void writeString (const char *words)
114  {
115  while (*words)
116  {
117  lcdOut (*words);
118  *words ++;
119  }
120  }
121  void cursorPos (unsigned char row, unsigned char col)
122  {
123  switch (row)
124  {
125  case 1:
126  {
127  sendcursorhome ();
128  shiftcurright (col);
129  break;
130  }
131  case 2:
132  {
133  line2 ();
134  shiftcurright (col);
135  break;
136  }
137  case 3:
138  {
139  sendcursorhome ();
140  shiftcurright (col + 20);
141  break;
142  }
```

```
143  case 4:
144  {
145  line2 ();
146  shiftcurright (col + 20);
147  break;
148  }
149  }
150  }
```

Analysis of Listing 7-2

Lines 1–5 are the normal comments at the start of a program.

Lines 7–18 are using definitions to give the binary values of the instructions for the LCD some meaningful, useful phrases.

Line 19 is just using some meaningful comments to split the listing up into sections.

Line 20 sets aside some 8-bit memory locations for the variables named here. The important ones are as follows:

- The "ebit" which is given the initial value of 4. This ensures that bit 2 is a logic '1.' This means that we can set bit 2 of the 8-bit value sent to the expander to a logic '1' and so set the "ebit" of the LCD high when we want to. We will look at this later with line 48.

- The "i2add" which is given the initial value of 0x27 in hexadecimal format. This is the default address of the I²C expander module. The master must send this address on the SDA when it wants to write to or read from the expander. We will look at this in line 41.

Line 21 void msdelay (unsigned char m)

This is creating a subroutine that creates a delay with a resolution of 1ms. It expects a value to be sent up to the subroutine when it is called. This value will be loaded into the local variable "m." In this way, we can create a variable delay of "m" milliseconds, set by the value sent up to the subroutine.

Line 23 for (d = 0; d < m; d++)

This sets up a "for do loop" that will control how many times the PIC carries out the following instructions written between the following opening and closing curly brackets. I think it is important that you use different global variables in the "for do loop" setup. If you use just one, say "n" or "i," then you might find that another loop that uses the same global variable could change the value of the variable. Take it from me that this could cause a problem with your program that is difficult to debug; I have experience of this problem. We did mention this in the previous chapter.

Line 25 TMR1 = 0;

This ensures that timer1 starts to count again from zero.

Line 26 while (TMR1 < 140);

This makes sure the PIC does nothing while the value in the TMR1 register is less than 140. At a resolution of 7.11µs for timer1, 140 ticks take approximately 1ms.

Line 29 char lcdInitialise [5] =

This creates an array that sets aside five memory locations, one after the other, to store variables of the type char. The array is called "lcdInitialise" as it holds the five instructions, in order, that are used to initialize the LCD. The "=" sign is there to tell the compiler we want to load the five locations with the data that is listed between the opening and closing curly brackets.

Line 31 entrymode,

This is the first instruction we use, and, as stated on line 7, this phrase, "entrymode," stands for the binary value 0b00000100. It is really bits 0, 1, and 2 that are used. These three bits set up how the LCD will move the cursor once data has been sent to display on the LCD. The three bits control the following:

- **Bit 0**: The "S" bit. This determines if the shifting works on just the cursor, that is, S = 0, or works on the whole display, that is, S = 1.

- **Bit 1**: The I/D bit. This determines if the cursor will increment its position, that is, move to the right. For this, the I/D bit is set to logic '0.' Or whether the cursor will decrement its position, that is, move to the left. For this, the I/D bit is set to a logic '1.'

- **Bit 2**: This is set to a logic '1' while all the further bits, 3 to 7, are set to a logic '0.' This identifies this instruction as the entry mode instruction.

Therefore, this instruction, "entrymode," makes the LCD shift the cursor to the right one place every time a character is displayed on the LCD.

Line 32 twoLines4bit,

This phrase is the next instruction, and as stated on line 10, the phrase stands for the binary value 0b00101000. It is sometimes referred to as the "function" set. I use the phrase "twoLines4bit" as it describes what it does better. It is bits 5, 4, 3, and 2 that control the actions as follows:

- **Bit 2**: The "F" bit. This sets the character font of the display. If this bit is a logic '0', then the characters are in a 5 column by 8 row grid. If it is a logic '1', then the font is a 5 column by 10 row grid.

- **Bit 3**: The "N" bit. This sets up how many lines you will use on the LCD display. A logic '1' means it will use two lines of characters. A logic '0' means it will use just one line.

- **Bit 4**: The "DL" bit, that is, data length. This sets up the LCD to work in 8-bit data length, that is, this bit is a logic '1', or in just 4-bit data length, that is, this bit is a logic '0'.

- **Bit 5**: This will be set to a logic '1' with bits 6 and 7 set to a logic '0'. This tells the LCD controller this is the function instruction which will set the DL, N, and F for the LCD.

Therefore, this instruction, "twoLines4bit," sets the LCD up to use two lines of text using a font of 5 by 8 and working in 4-bit data mode.

Line 33 cursorNoBlink,

This phrase is the next instruction, and as stated on line 11, the phrase stands for the binary value 0b00001100. This instruction is sometimes referred to as the "display on/off control." It is bits 3, 2, 1, and 0 that control the actions as follows:

- **Bit 0**: The "B" bit. A logic '1' means the cursor will blink. If this bit is a logic '0', then the cursor will not blink.

- **Bit 1**: The "C" bit. A logic '1' means the cursor will be displayed. A logic '0' means it won't be displayed.

- **Bit 2**: The "D" bit. A logic '1' means the display is on, and a logic '0' means the display is off.

- **Bit 3**: This will be set to a logic '1' with bits 4, 5, 6, and 7 set to a logic '0'. This tells the LCD controller this is the display on/off instruction.

Therefore, this instruction, "cursorNoBlink," turns the display on and the cursor off and sets the cursor to not blink.

Line 34 clearScreen,

This is the phrase that stands for the binary value 0b00000001 as stated on line 12. This simply gets the LCD to clear the screen of any characters that were present on the display. It also sends the cursor back to the beginning of the first line on the screen.

Line 35 returnHome,

This is the phrase that stands for the binary value 0b0000001x as stated on line 13. Note the "x" means it does not matter what logic is on this bit. This simply gets the LCD to send the cursor back to the beginning of the first line on the screen, but without deleting the current characters on the display.

Line 37 void writeExp (unsigned char data)

This creates a subroutine for writing to the I²C expander module using the I²C protocol. This subroutine expects a value to be sent to it so that a copy of it can be stored in the local variable "data."

Line 39 I2Cwait ();

This calls the subroutine "I2Cwait" to ensure the I²C module is not busy. This subroutine is within the I²C protocol header file.

Line 40 I2CStart ();

This now calls the "I2CStart" subroutine to initiate the start sequence from the master.

Line 41 I2CWrite ((i2cadd << 1));

This calls the I2CWrite subroutine and sends the contents of the variable i2cadd. However, before the value is sent to the subroutine, the bits are shifted one place to the left. To help explain what this does, we will list the data before and after the shift, this is shown in Table 7-5.

Table 7-5. *The Shift One Place to the Left*

	Bit 7	Bit 6	Bit 5	Bit 4	Bit 3	Bit 2	Bit 1	Bit 0
Before	0	0	1	0	0	1	1	1
After	0	1	0	0	1	1	1	0

- Before the shift, the value is 0x27, which is the hexadecimal for the address of the I²C expander module. It is expressed here in binary.

- After being shifted, the value is the hexadecimal value 0x4E but expressed in binary. You should see that the LSB, bit 0, is a logic '0'.

There are two reasons for shifting the data:

1. The master sends the 7 bits of the address of the slave in the top 7 bits of the data sent, that is, bit 7 down to bit 1.

2. The LSB, bit 0, of the data sent is used to tell the slave if we want to write to the slave, the LSB must be a logic '0', or read from the slave, the LSB must be a logic '1'.

Therefore, the actions of this instruction put the correct address of the slave on the SDA line in the correct position and tell the slave we want to write to it.

If you are unsure about binary and hexadecimal notation, there is a section in the appendix that explains the different number systems used in this book.

Line 42 I2CWrite (data | 0x08);

This calls the I2CWrite subroutine again, but now it sends the value in the local variable data that was loaded at the start of this "writeExp" subroutine. However, before it is sent to the I2CWrite subroutine, the data is logically ORed with 0x08. This ensures that bit 3 of the value in the variable data is set to a logic '1'. This is required for the expander to use the data.

Line 43 I2CStop();

This calls the subroutine I2CStop to initiate the stop signal on the SDA line.

Line 45 void sendData1 (lcdTempData)

This creates a subroutine to send information to the LCD via the expander module. This puts a copy of what has been sent up to this subroutine, when it was called from elsewhere in the program, into the variable "lcdTempData." We don't need to set the data type for this variable "lcdTempData" as it is the global variable that has been declared on line 20. This data that is sent to the subroutine must be of the correct data type, as it will be copied into the variable "lcdTempData." It is in lines 55 and 56 that we call this subroutine.

Line 47 lcdTempData |= rsLine;

This performs a logical OR operation with the value in "lcdTempData" and "rsLine." To appreciate what this instruction is doing, we need to understand that there are two types of information that we can send to the LCD. The information could be instructions that are used to set up the LCD or control the current position of the cursor, etc. Also, the information

345

could be data, that is, characters that we want to display on the LCD. There has to be a process by which we can tell the LCD what type of information we are currently sending to it. We can only use the logic '1s' and '0s' that are sent to the LCD. It is the logic that is sent to the RS pin of the LCD that we use to make this distinction. A logic '1' means the information is data to be displayed, whereas a logic '0', on this pin, means the information is an instruction. With the I²C expander, it is the P0 pin that is connected to the RS pin on the LCD; see Table 7-4. The P0 is allocated to bit 0 of the binary value sent to the I²C expander. Therefore, we must ensure that bit 0 of this binary value does correspond to what type of information, that is, instruction or data, we are sending to the LCD. To enable this process, we use a global variable called "rsLine." Therefore, we need to ensure that bit 0 of this variable is set to a logic '1' or '0' as required.

The instruction on line 47 performs a logical "OR" operation with the variable in "lcdTempData" and the variable "rsLine." To help explain what this does, we must appreciate that when this subroutine, "void sendData1 (lcdTempData)," is called, then the variable "lcdTempData" will be loaded with a copy of what is in the variable "lcdData"; see line 55. However, before the variable "lcdData" is sent to this subroutine, the low nibble, that is, bits 0, 1, 2, and 3, is forced to a logic '0' on all four bits. This happens with the instruction "sendData1 (lcdData & 0XF0);" on line 55. When we logically AND any bits with a logic '0', the result will always be a logic '0'. To help explain how this logical AND operation works, we will look at the following example.

For example, if the data in "lcdData" was 0b11011110, then when we AND this with 0XF0, we have the result as shown in Table 7-6.

Table 7-6. *The Logical AND Operation*

	Bit 7	Bit 6	Bit 5	Bit 4	Bit 3	Bit 2	Bit 1	Bit 0
lcdData	1	1	0	1	1	1	1	0
0XF0	1	1	1	1	0	0	0	0
Result stored in lcdTempData	1	1	0	1	0	0	0	0

We can see that the first four bits, that is, the low nibble, will all be a logic '0'. Now when we perform a logical OR operation with this result in "lcdTempData" and the variable "rsLine," we will get the result as shown in Tables 7-7 and 7-8.

Table 7-7. *The Logical OR Operation When rsLine Bit 0 Is a Logic '0'*

	Bit 7	Bit 6	Bit 5	Bit 4	Bit 3	Bit 2	Bit 1	Bit 0
lcdTempData	1	1	0	1	0	0	0	0
rsLine	0	0	0	0	0	0	0	0
Result Bit 0	1	1	0	1	0	0	0	0

Table 7-8. *Logical OR Operation When rsLine Bit 0 Is a Logic '1'*

	Bit 7	Bit 6	Bit 5	Bit 4	Bit 3	Bit 2	Bit 1	Bit 0
lcdTempData	1	1	0	1	0	0	0	0
rsLine	0	0	0	0	0	0	0	1
Result Bit 0	1	1	0	1	0	0	0	1

This shows that we can control the logic on bit 0 of the value in "lcdTempData" with the logic in the variable "rsLine." This means that what we need to do is ensure the data in the variable "rsLine" is what is needed for either an instruction or data, before this subroutine, void sendData1 (lcdTempData), is called. We will see that in all the subroutines that use this subroutine, void sendData1 (lcdTempData), the value in the variable "rsLine" is set accordingly.

This is quite an involved explanation of how this instruction achieves its purpose, but it is a complex process.

Line 48 writeExp(lcdTempData|ebit);

This performs another logical OR operation with the new value in the variable "lcdTempData," after line 47, with the variable "ebit." You should appreciate that in line 20 we declared the global variable "ebit" but loaded it with a value "4" in decimal. In 8-bit binary, this would be 0b00000100. This means bit 2 will be a logic '1'. The result of this logical OR operation will ensure that bit 2 of the variable "lcdTempData" will now be a logic '1'. If we look at Table 7-4, we will see that bit P2 of the value sent to the I²C expander is allocated to the "ebit" on the LCD. This instruction will therefore ensure that when this value is sent to the LCD, the "ebit" on the LCD will be set to a logic '1'.

Line 49 writeExp(lcdTempData & 0xFB);

This now performs a logical AND with the new data in "lcdTempData" and the value 0xFB. To understand what happens, we will use Table 7-9. Note we will use the data in "lcdTempData" from the result of Table 7-7.

Table 7-9. *Manipulating the ebit*

	Bit 7	Bit 6	Bit 5	Bit 4	Bit 3	Bit 2	Bit 1	Bit 0
lcdTempData from Table 7-7	1	1	0	1	0	0	0	0
lcdTempData after line 48	1	1	0	1	0	1	0	0
0xFB	1	1	1	1	1	0	1	1
Result	**1**	**1**	**0**	**1**	**0**	**0**	**0**	**0**

You should see that bit 2 has now gone back to a logic '0'. This means that the two instructions on lines 48 and 49 will make the logic on the "ebit" of the LCD go first high and then back to a low without any delay. This action on the "ebit" of the LCD is a signal to tell the LCD that new information has been sent to the LCD, and it should deal with it.

It is because the "RS" and "ebit" pins are on different bits of the binary information passed to the LCD that we can't use the normal 4-bit LCD header file. Also, we can't control the "ebit" independently with the I2C expander, like we do with the normal LCD header file.

Again, this is another detailed analysis, but it is a rather complex operation.

Line 50 TMR1 = 0; while (TMR1 < 10);

We have looked at a similar set of instructions in Chapter 4. This simply creates a short delay of around 71µs. This is needed to give the expander and the LCD time to process the data/instruction that has just been sent to it.

Line 52 void lcdOut (unsigned char LCDDATA)

This creates a subroutine that will send information to the LCD by calling the sendData1 subroutine. This subroutine will need a value sending up to it that will be copied into the local variable "LCDDATA." Note this variable is different from the global variable "lcdData." That is why I am using capital letters. You must be careful of changing the value of variables that are used in other parts of the program. This means you should, as we do here, use local variables instead, preferably with a unique name.

Line 54 lcdData = LCDDATA;

This loads the global variable "lcdData" with the contents of "LCDDATA."

Line 55 sendData1 (lcdData & 0xF0);

This is the instruction that calls the subroutine "sendData1" and passes up the contents of the variable "lcdData" after it has been logically ANDed with 0XF0, as explained previously. This is done to ensure the high nibble, that is, bits 7, 6, 5, and 4, is a copy of what is in the high nibble of "lcdData," but the four bits of the low nibble are all logic '0s'. This sends the high nibble of information to the LCD first.

Line 56 sendData1 ((lcdData << 4) & 0xF0);

This calls the same subroutine, but this time it sends the low nibble. This is achieved by firstly shifting the binary value in "lcdData" 4 bits to the left. This will ensure that the value in bits 3, 2, 1, and 0 is put into bits 7, 6, 5, and 4. These bits are then ANDed with 0xF0 to ensure only bits 7, 6, 5, and 4 are used. In this way, we can now send the low nibble of the data or instruction we want to send to the LCD.

Line 58 void setUpTheLCD ()

This creates a subroutine that will send the instruction to the LCD to set it up as we want to use it.

Line 60 writeExp (0x00);

This writes the value 0x00, that is, 0, to the I^{2}C expander and so the LCD to make sure everything is turned off. This is similar to the same subroutine we have looked at in Chapter 4.

Line 61 msdelay (50);

This calls the millisecond delay subroutine, "msdelay," and sends the value 50 to it. This creates a 50ms delay which gives the I^{2}C expander time to process the writeExp instruction on line 60.

Line 62 n = 0;

This loads the global variable "n" with the value "0." This gets it ready for the while loop on line 64.

Line 63 rsLine = 0x00;

This ensures that bit 0 of the variable "rsLine" is a logic '0'. This is needed because the next set of information to be sent to the LCD will be instructions.

Line 64 while (n < 5)

This forces the PIC to carry out the instructions listed between the following opening and closing curly brackets while the value in the variable "n" is less than 5.

Line 66 lcdOut (lcdInitialise [n]);

We have looked at this instruction in Chapter 4.

Line 67 n ++;

This simply increments the value of the variable "n" ready for the next loop through the while loop.

Line msdelay (50);

This creates a 50ms delay to ensure the I²C expander and LCD have time to implement the instructions being sent to them. This delay is longer than if we were just using the LCD, but we have to ensure the I²C expander has time to deal with the instructions as well as communicating with the LCD. This delay could be shorter or different for different instructions, but a 50ms delay is not that long, and it is long enough for all instructions, etc. This does make the program slightly simpler.

The while loop will repeat four more times until n = 5 and so send all five instructions to set up the LCD.

Line 70 rsLine = 0x01;

This now ensures that bit 0 of the variable "rsLine" is a logic '1'. This is done because it is most likely that any further information sent to the LCD will be data to be displayed.

Line 72 void shiftcurleft (unsigned char 1)

This creates a subroutine that will shift the current position of the cursor a set number of places to the left. It requires a value to be passed up to it that will be copied into the local variable "1."

Line 74 for (s = 0; s < 1; s ++)

This sets up a "for do loop" that will repeat a number of times controlled by the value loaded into the local variable "1." We are using a unique global variable "s" to ensure we don't get trapped in the problem by using a global variable that might be changed or used elsewhere in the program.

Line 76 rsLine = 0x00;

This ensures bit 0 of the "rsLine" is a logic '0' as we are going to send an instruction to the LCD.

Line 77 lcdOut (shiftLeft);

This calls the subroutine "lcdOut" and sends the instruction "shiftLeft" as defined on line 16. This will move the cursor one place to the left.

Line 78 msdelay (50);

This creates a 50ms delay as before.

Line 79 rsLine = 0x01;

This ensures bit 0 of the "rsLine" is set back to a logic '1' as before.

Lines 82–91 create the subroutine "void shiftcurright (unsigned char r)" that does the same but shifts the cursor to the right.

Lines 92–98 set up a subroutine, "void line2 ()," which works in a similar way but sends the cursor to the start of the second line on the LCD.

Lines 99–105 set up a subroutine, "void clearTheScreen ()," that will clear all data from the display and send the cursor to the start of the first line on the LCD.

Lines 106–112 set up a subroutine, "void sendcursorhome ()," that sends the cursor to the start of the first line but does not remove any characters from the LCD display.

Lines 113–120 set up the subroutine "void writeString (const char *words)." This has been analyzed in Chapter 4.

Lines 121–149 set up the subroutine "void cursorPos (unsigned char row, unsigned char col)." This has been analyzed in Chapter 4.

This completes the analysis of this header file. I hope I have helped you understand how these instructions work and so carry out the requirements of the program.

The Program to Use the I²C Expander to Control the LCD2004

We will now look at a program that uses the I²C protocol and the I²C expander to send messages to the LCD2004.

The listing for the program is shown in Listing 7-3.

Listing 7-3. The Listing for I²C Expander Program

```
1   /*
2   * File:    32BitI2cExpLCDprog.c
3   Author: Mr H. H. Ward
4   *A program that uses the I2C Expander module
5   Created on 25 November 2021, 16:06
6   */
7   //The includes
8   #include <xc.h>
9   #include <stdio.h>
10  #include <con72Meg36Meg32Bit.h>
11  #include "32biti2cprotocol.h"
12  #include "32bBitI2cLCDRoutine.h"
13  //some variables
14  unsigned char dm;
15  //some subroutines
16  void delay250m( unsigned char t)
17  {
18  for (dm = 0; dm < t; dm ++)
19  {
20  TMR1 = 0;
21  while (TMR1 < 35150);
22  }
23  }
```

```
24  void debounce ()
25  {
26  TMR1 = 0;
27  while (TMR1 < 1830);
28  }
29  //the main program instructions
30  void main()
31  {
32  PORTA = 0;
33  PORTB = 0;
34  PORTC = 0;
35  PORTD = 0;
36  TRISA = 0x00ff;
37  TRISB = 0;
38  TRISC = 0;
39  TRISD = 0x00FF;
40  TRISE = 0;
41  AD1PCFG = 0XFFFF;
42  AD1CON1 = 0; '
43  T1CON = 0x8030;
44  DDPCONbits.JTAGEN = 0;
45  setUpTheLCD ();
46  I2CInit();
47  again: clearTheScreen ();
48  cursorPos (1,0);
49  lcdOut (0x38);
50  shiftcurright (2);
51  writeString ("Using The I2C EXP");
52  cursorPos (2,0);
53  writeString ("Line 2 fine");
54  shiftcurright (2);
```

```
55  lcdOut (0x32);
56  cursorPos (3,0);
57  writeString ("Line 3 OK");
58  shiftcurright (2);
59  lcdOut (0X33);
60  cursorPos (4,1);
61  lcdOut (0x34);
62  shiftcurright (1);
63  writeString ("This is line 4");
64  delay250m (4);
65  while (_RD7);
66  debounce ();
67  while (!_RD7);
68  debounce ();
69  while (!_RD7);
70  clearTheScreen ();
71  cursorPos (1,1);
72  writeString ("Lets write on 1");
73  while (_RD7);
74  debounce ();
75  while (!_RD7);
76  debounce ();
77  while (!_RD7);
78  cursorPos (2,2);
79  writeString ("Lets write on 2");
80  while (_RD7);
81  debounce ();
82  while (!_RD7);
83  debounce ();
84  while (!_RD7);
85  cursorPos (3,3);
```

```
86  writeString ("Lets write on 3");
87  while (_RD7);
88  debounce ();
89  while (!_RD7);
90  debounce ();
91  while (!_RD7);
92  cursorPos (4,4);
93  writeString ("Lets write on 4");
94  while (_RD7);
95  debounce ();
96  while (!_RD7);
97  debounce ();
98  while (!_RD7);
99  goto again;
100 }
```

Analysis of Listing 7-3

This program uses the I²C protocol to communicate to the expander module and so allow the PIC to write four messages to the LCD2004. This will verify that the I²C expander module works correctly. Then the program will wait for a switch to be pressed, at which time it will display further messages to the LCD, a different message after each pressing of the switch. The program will then go back and start the whole process again.

Lines 1-6 are the normal comments.

Line 7 //The includes

This just uses comments to split the listing up into sections.

Lines 8-10 are the three usual global include files.

Line 11 #include "32biti2cprotocol.h"

This gets the compiler to include this local header file. It has all the subroutines needed to implement the I²C protocol on the 32-bit PIC. At present, this is just a local header file, hence the use of the quotation marks. I will place a copy in the relevant include folder of the compiler so as to make it a global header file, as I will use the I²C protocol in other programs.

Line 12 #include "32bBitI2cLCDRoutine.h"

This is another local header file, and it has all the subroutines to control the LCD2004 with the I²C expander module. There are some differences between the global LCD routines and controlling the LCD with the I²C expander. That is why we need this new header file.

Line 13 //some variables

Just splitting the listing up again.

Line 14 unsigned char dm;

This creates an 8-bit global variable. It will be used in the "for do loop" in the delay250m subroutine.

Line 16 void delay250m(unsigned char t)

This creates a subroutine that creates a variable delay with a resolution of 250ms, that is, a quarter of a second. This type of variable delay has been analyzed in Chapter 3 already.

Line 24 void debounce ()

This creates a subroutine that we use to overcome switch bounce. This has been looked at in Chapter 3 already.

Line 30 void main()

This creates the main loop of the program. The instructions for this loop are between the opening and closing curly brackets on lines 31 and 100.

Lines 32–44 are the usual instructions to set up the PIC as we want. Note, however, on line 39 TRISD = 0x00FF;, we are making the first 8 bits on PORTD inputs and the next 8 as outputs.

Line 45 setUpTheLCD ();

This calls the subroutine to set up the LCD.

Line 46 I2CInit();

This calls the subroutine to initialize the I^{2}C module of the PIC.

Line 47 again: clearTheScreen ();

This instruction calls the subroutine that clears the screen of all data currently displayed on it and sends the cursor back to the beginning of the first line on the LCD screen. Note it also has the label "again," which we use to force the PIC to goto with the instruction on line 99. It is the colon ":" that tells the compiler this word "again" is a label.

Line 48 cursorPos (1,0);

This calls the subroutine "cursorPos" and sends the parameters 1 and 0 up to the subroutine. This forces the cursor to line 1, as stated by the first number passed up, and places it at column 0, as stated by the second number being passed up. This sends the cursor to the start of the first line. This is using the subroutine "cursorPos" to place the cursor at any position on the LCD screen, controlled by the two numbers we pass up to the subroutine. We don't really need this instruction, as the cursor has already been sent to this position with the previous instruction on line 47. I just wanted to show you how we can use the "cursorPos" subroutine.

Line 49 lcdOut (0x38);

This calls the subroutine "lcdOut" and passes the hexadecimal value 0x38 up to it. This is the ASCII for the character 8, and so this will get the PIC to display the character 8 on the LCD at the current cursor position, that is, at the start of the first line.

Line 50 shiftcurright (2);

This calls the subroutine "shiftcurright" and passes the number 2 up to it. This will move the cursor two places to the right. After this instruction, the cursor will be at position 4 on the first row or line of the LCD. This is where it will display the next character on the screen.

Line 51 writeString ("Using The I2C EXP");

This calls the subroutine "writeString" and passes up the characters we want to write to the LCD written between the two quotation marks. We have analyzed this subroutine in Chapter 4.

Lines 52–63 are simply the same type of instructions, but with some small changes in the parameters. They work in exactly the same way.

Line 64 delay250m (4);

This calls the quarter second delay and passes the number 4 up to it. Therefore, this creates an approximately one-second delay.

Line 65 while (_RD7);

This gets the PIC to do nothing while the logic on bit 7 of PORTD is high, that is, a logic '1'. The compiler knows we mean a high state as there is no "!" exclamation mark before the identifier _RD7. The exclamation mark indicates a NOT, or logic '0'. As the logic on each bit can only be a logic '1' or a logic '0', then because we are not using the "!" or NOT symbol, we must be indicating a logic '1' or high state. The switches on the explorer 16 development board are normally at a logic '1'. They only go to a logic

'0' when they are pressed. Therefore, this instruction is getting the PIC to wait until the user presses the switch on bit 7 of PORTD. You may have to change the logic if your switches switch using the opposite logic.

Line 66 debounce ();

This calls the debounce subroutine, which deals with the issue of switch bounce as described in Chapter 3. It can also be used to eliminate issues caused by electrical noise.

Line 67 while (!_RD7);

We know the logic should now have gone to a logic '0', as the switch has now been pressed. Therefore, we are now checking to see if it is a logic '0'. However, we know that as these switches are momentary switches, then, as we let go of the switch, the logic should go back to a logic '1'. This instruction gets the PIC to wait for this to happen, that is, while the logic is a NOT, that is, a logic '0', then do nothing. Eventually, the logic will return to a logic '1', and the PIC will move on to the next instruction.

Line 68 debounce ();

We should appreciate that switch bounce can happen when you let go of a switch, as well as when you press a switch. Therefore, we now get the PIC to wait 13ms for this bouncing action to die down.

Line 69 while (!_RD7);

Here, we are just checking to make sure the logic on the switch has really gone back to a logic '1', that is, it is no longer at a logic '0'.

You might think this double bouncing check is a little too much, but it does depend upon the application and the actual switches you are using. Try commenting out the second "debounce" and see what happens. I think it is needed. It is also good practice, as it does cater for any switch bounce. It also caters for noise on any input.

Lines 70–98 have already been looked at. There are only some minor parameter changes, so I hope you can appreciate how they work and what they are doing.

Line 99 goto again;

This forces the PIC to go to line 47 where we have created the label "again." This gets the PIC to go through the whole sequence again but avoids setting up the PIC and LCD and I²C again, as we don't need to.

Figure 7-4 shows the I²C expander program working.

Figure 7-4. *The I²C Expander Program*

Summary

In this chapter, we have learned what I²C is and how we can implement the protocol with the PIC32. We have gone on to use the I²C protocol to write to an I²C expander module and control an LCD. We have used the LCD2004. However, the expander could also have been used for the 1602 LCD.

We will revisit the I²C protocol when we use it to communicate with the DS3231 IC to implement the use of a Real-Time Clock module in Chapter 10.

In the next chapter, we will investigate the use of interrupts and how they can be used within the PIC32. I hope you have found this chapter useful and that you will enjoy using the I²C protocol in your future programs.

CHAPTER 8

Interrupts

In this chapter, we are going to look at interrupts. We will learn what they are and how and why we use them.

After reading this chapter, you will be able to set up and use interrupts. You will understand what single and multivectored interrupts are and how to set them up. You will be able to apply different priorities to your interrupts and use them in your program.

I hope you will find this chapter useful and informative.

Interrupts

A typical program can carry out more than one sequence of events at a time. For example, a program could be responsible for lighting a set of lights one after the other, with a one-second delay between each light. It would then go through the reverse sequence turning the lights off. The same program could also be monitoring a fire alarm to see if it has been set off. The program needs to monitor the fire alarm switch, and this could be done with a simple instruction that asks whether the fire alarm switch has been pressed. This could be done via an instruction which is carried out every time we turn on or off a light in our normal sequence. This is called "software polling," which could work. However, we would not be monitoring the fire alarm when the program is stuck in the one-second delay routines. This could be a real problem as we might be delayed in responding to the fire alarm, or worse we might miss it altogether. Also,

© Hubert Ward 2023
H. Ward, *Introductory Programs with the 32-bit PIC Microcontroller*,
Maker Innovations Series, https://doi.org/10.1007/978-1-4842-9051-4_8

we could be wasting a lot of time by checking the fire alarm needlessly, as we check the fire alarm switch every time we operate the light, but the fire alarm may not have been set off.

It would be much better if the fire alarm could somehow tell the PIC that it had been set off when it does go off. This would mean we would not waste time, as with software polling, and we shouldn't miss the fire alarm going off. That is what interrupts do. When the fire alarm goes off, it would interrupt whatever the PIC is doing and tell the PIC the fire alarm has gone off. The PIC would then stop what it was doing and deal with a set of instructions that deals with the fire. Once it has dealt with the fire, the PIC returns back to the continued operation of the program. The set of instructions that the PIC must carry out, when the interrupt occurs, is called an "ISR, interrupt service routine." They work similarly to how a subroutine works except that the program does not have to "call" the ISR. The PIC will automatically go to the ISR when the interrupt occurs.

The benefit of the interrupt method of dealing with the "fire alarm," or whatever action causes the interrupt, over the software polling method, is that the PIC never wastes time checking to see if the fire alarm has gone off when it hasn't, and we will never miss or be delayed being told the fire alarm has been set off.

How Interrupts Are Called and How the ISR Is Found

I have stated that the program does not call the ISR as it would call a subroutine. However, the PIC must be told somehow that an interrupt has occurred. It must also be told where it can find the instructions of the ISR. I have also stated that we don't check that the interrupt has occurred as we would do with software polling. Well, we don't need to write instructions that get the PIC to check if the interrupt has occurred, but in reality, the PIC is constantly, automatically, checking if an interrupt has occurred. To appreciate how this happens, we need to consider what happens every time the PIC goes to memory to fetch and then execute any instruction.

The Fetch and Execute Cycle

The PIC will go through this cycle every time it gets an instruction from the program. The following is an approximation of what happens. It is not essential to know exactly what happens, just the essence of the process.

The Program Counter or "PC"

Before we delve too deep into the fetch and execute cycle, it would be useful to consider the "PC" or "Program Counter." Every instruction must be stored in the PIC's program memory area. Every instruction will have its own unique address in the PIC's program memory, just as every house in the country has a unique address. The PIC must be told what address it must go to, to get even the first instruction of the program. When the IDE downloads the program to the PIC, the housekeeping program of the PIC loads the "Program Counter" with the address of the memory location for the first instruction of the program. This will be the first instruction in the main loop of the program listing.

Now, when we run the program, the PIC will look at the contents of the PC to find the address it must go to, so that it can find the next instruction of the program. It will then go there to get that instruction. This is the fetch part of the cycle.

Now, before the PIC even looks at the instruction, it will automatically increment the contents of the "Program Counter." This is so that the next time the PIC looks at the contents of the PC, it will be able to find the location of the next instruction of the program. This means the PC will always be pointing to the location of the next instruction in the program.

Now the PIC must look at the instruction to see what it has to do. However, either before this next step or before it goes on to carry out the instruction, the PIC will check a bit, which may also be called a flag, termed the interrupt flag. This flag would have been set to a logic '1', by some cause, if an interrupt has happened, or cleared, to a logic '0', if no interrupt has happened. If no interrupt has happened and this flag is not set, the PIC will carry on as normal. It will check the current instruction and then look at the PC to see where it must go to so that it can find the next part of the instruction or the next instruction. The cycle will then repeat.

If an interrupt has occurred, and this interrupt flag is set, then the PIC must do the following.

It must store the current contents of the PC in a specially reserved area of memory called "the stack." This is so that when the PIC has completed the instructions of the ISR, it can retrieve this address from "the stack" and load it back into the PC, so that the PIC can find the correct address of the instruction it would be carrying out next, if the interrupt had not occurred.

Once that return address has been safely stored on "the stack," the housekeeping program of the PIC will load the PC with the address of the interrupt vector. This is a special memory location that the PIC will use to store the actual address of the ISR. This storing of the ISR address in this special vector is carried out by the "housekeeping" program of the PIC. When the PIC goes to the address of this interrupt vector, the housekeeping program will load the PC with the address of the ISR. In this way, the PIC can be directed to the instructions of the ISR.

This is one of the major aspects of what happens with the "fetch and execute cycle." The most important aspect of what happens is that the PIC will always automatically check this interrupt flag to determine if an interrupt has occurred. This is a version of software polling, but, as we don't have to write any instructions to make this happen, it is not strictly software polling.

Single Vectored Interrupts

I have stated that there is a special memory location called a "vector" location. With the 32-bit PIC, we have the facility of using just one vector location, as with "single vectored interrupts," or a range of separate vector locations, as with "multivectored interrupts."

With the option of "single vectored interrupts," there is only one interrupt vector used. This defaults to vector "0." It is in this vector location that the housekeeping program of the PIC will load the address of the ISR. With single vectored interrupts, there is only one ISR used and one vector location. This is fine if you are only using a few of the interrupt sources available to you. If you use single vectored interrupts with more than one interrupt source, you must ask a question of each source that you are using if it was them that caused the interrupt. This you can do, but it will take time, and maybe some interrupts are time critical, and so waiting to be asked could take too long.

Multivectored Interrupts

This alternative gives you a chance to overcome that time-critical issue. With the 32-bit PIC, there are a total of 64 vectors we could use, which means we could have 64 ISRs. The 64 vectors do not give us a separate ISR for the 96 sources available to the 32-bit PIC. Therefore, some of the vectors must accommodate multiple sources, which means we must determine which source caused the interrupt in these ISRs. However, if you will be using more than a few interrupt sources, then multivectored interrupts could be the better way to go.

The fact that we have these two options means we must tell the PIC which option we will be using in our program.

How Does the PIC Keep Track of Where It Must Go and Where It Must Get Back To?

This is a very interesting question, and the answer is not easy. It is an interesting challenge, but you don't really need to understand how it works. However, if you are interested, here is a very brief description of how it works.

We have already discussed the use of the Program Counter or PC. This Program Counter must always be pointing to where the PIC must go in memory to get the *next* instruction. That is why, in the fetch and execute cycle, the very first thing the PIC must do, before it even looks at the instruction it has just retrieved from memory, is increment the contents of the Program Counter.

All the instructions in the program and all the labels of the subroutines, etc., will be allocated the address of where they are in the PIC's memory. For example, the label "delay" in our second program would be given an actual address. This is so that when we call the subroutine from within the program, that address can be loaded into the Program Counter, so that the PIC knows where to go to find the instructions of the subroutine. This then leads to the question of how the PIC finds its way back to where it carried out the call instruction. We will look at that issue shortly.

Lastly, the interrupt vectors must be loaded with the address of the ISR, so that when an interrupt is triggered, the PIC can find the correct address to load into the Program Counter, so that the PIC can find the instructions of the ISR. Again, we need to know how the PIC finds its way back to the main program.

The Stack and Its Main Use

It is the stack that comes to our rescue. We now know that it is the Program Counter that tells the PIC where to go to find the next instruction. Let's consider the situation that at address 20, as an example, there is a call instruction to go to the subroutine "delay." The address of the first instruction in this subroutine delay is, for example, 100.

The PIC has just retrieved the instruction that was at address 19, that is, the instruction before the call instruction at address 20. It does not matter what that instruction was, the important thing to appreciate is that before the PIC carries out that instruction, the Program Counter would have been incremented to point to address 20.

The PIC now carries out the instruction, whatever it was, it has just fetched from location 19.

The PIC now looks at the contents of the Program Counter, and it now knows it must go to address 20.

The PIC now retrieves the instruction that is at address 20. However, before it looks at that instruction, the PIC must increment the contents of the Program Counter. The Program Counter now has 21 in its contents.

The PIC now looks at the instruction and realizes that it is a call to a subroutine. This means the PIC will break away from its normal sequential operation and go to the location of the subroutine. This means the PIC must replace the contents of the Program Counter with the number 100, the address of the start of the delay subroutine. However, it also knows it must find its way back to address 21, to get back to the main program, after it has carried out the instructions of the subroutine. This is where the stack comes in. The stack is an area of the PIC's memory that is reserved for storing important information. It works on the basis of FILO, First In Last Out. It is on this stack that the PIC must save the value 21, the current contents of the Program Counter, before it replaces the contents of the Program Counter with 100, the address of the start of the delay subroutine.

Having stored the address 21 on the stack and loaded the PC with the value 100, the PIC can now go to the correct start address of the subroutine and carry out the instructions there. When the PIC gets to the end of the subroutine, there is a special instruction that we don't normally have to write into the subroutine ourselves, the compiler software does it for us. This is the "RET" or "return" instruction, which gets the PIC to return to the main program at the correct address, which is 21 in our example. What the PIC does when it carries out this "RET" instruction is go to the stack where by now the correct address is waiting at the top of the stack. This will be 21 in our example, and this will be loaded into the Program Counter, replacing its contents with 21 in our example. This means that the PIC can find the correct address in the main program, as it has just been loaded into the Program Counter of where it must go to in the main program.

The same sort of process will be carried out if the PIC has to go to an ISR because an interrupt has been triggered.

This is getting very complex, but it is a challenging operation to accommodate. You must also appreciate that, during the normal fetch and execute cycle, the PIC *must* check to see if an interrupt has been triggered, even if the PIC is responding to a subroutine call.

Also, the stack is used to save any important data in a register that might be overwritten by instructions within the subroutine and ISR. This is an added complication.

One thing you must be aware of is that the stack is limited in its number of memory locations. I believe its default size in the PIC32 is 1k, that is, 1024 bytes of memory. If you are not careful, you could try to push too much data onto the stack, and you might get the message "stack overflow." I have not come across this issue, but it is something you need to be aware of.

I hope this brief explanation does give you some idea of how the PIC finds its way around the different memory locations. It is not a perfect description, as I am not a micro design engineer, I am a programmer, and I have built up my knowledge and interpretation of how these PICs work over many years of practice. However, I know I am not perfect, so I do apologize if there are some misconceptions in this brief analysis. I will keep trying to improve my understanding as I progress.

The Sources of Interrupts in a 32-Bit PIC

Now we have some idea of how the PIC recognizes an interrupt has occurred, we now need to know how we make the PIC set or clear that interrupt flag in the fetch and execute cycle. Most PICs have a variety of sources that set this interrupt flag. Table 8-1 lists all the interrupt sources in the 32-bit PIC.

Table 8-1. *The Sources of Interrupts for the PIC32*

IRQ No.	Vector No.	Macro	IRQ Symbol	Description
0	0	CT	_CORE_TIMER_IRQ	Core timer interrupt
1	1	CS0	_CORE_SOFTWARE_ 0_IRQ	Core Software Interrupt 0
2	2	CS1	_CORE_SOFTWARE_ 1_IRQ	Core Software Interrupt 1
3	3	INT0	_EXTERNAL_0_IRQ	External Interrupt 0
4	4	T1	_TIMER_1_IRQ	Timer 1 Interrupt
5	5	IC1	_INPUT_CAPTURE_1_IRQ	Input Capture 1 interrupt
6	6	OC1	_OUTPUT_COMPARE_1_ IRQ	Output Compare 1 interrupt
7	7	INT1	_EXTERNAL_1_IRQ	External Interrupt 1
8	8	T2	_TIMER_2_IRQ	Timer 2 Interrupt
9	9	IC2	_INPUT_CAPTURE_2_IRQ	Input Capture 2 interrupt
10	10	OC2	_OUTPUT_COMPARE_2_ IRQ	Output Compare 2 interrupt
11	11	INT2	_EXTERNAL_2_IRQ	External Interrupt 2
12	12	T3	_TIMER_3_IRQ	Timer 3 Interrupt
13	13	IC3	_INPUT_CAPTURE_3_IRQ	Input Capture 3 interrupt
14	14	OC3	_OUTPUT_COMPARE_ 3_IRQ	Output Compare 3 interrupt
15	15	INT3	_EXTERNAL_3_IRQ	External Interrupt 3
16	16	T4	_TIMER_4_IRQ	Timer 4 Interrupt
17	17	IC4	_INPUT_CAPTURE_4_IRQ	Input Capture 4 interrupt

(continued)

Table 8-1. (*continued*)

IRQ No.	Vector No.	Macro	IRQ Symbol	Description
18	18	OC4	_OUTPUT_COMPARE_4_IRQ	Output Compare 4 interrupt
19	19	INT4	_EXTERNAL_4_IRQ	External Interrupt 4
20	20	T5	_TIMER_5_IRQ	Timer 5 Interrupt
21	21	IC5	_INPUT_CAPTURE_5_IRQ	Input Capture 5 interrupt
22	22	OC5	_OUTPUT_COMPARE_5_IRQ	Output Compare 5 interrupt
23	23	SPI1E	_SPI1_ERR_IRQ	SPI 1 Fault
24	23	SPI1TX	_SPI1_TX_IRQ	SPI 1 Transfer Done
25	23	SPI1RX	_SPI1_RX_IRQ	SPI 1 Receiver Done
26	24	U1E	_UART1_ERR_IRQ	UART 1 Error
27	24	U1RX	_UART1_RX_IRQ	UART 1 Receiver
28	24	U1TX	_UART1_TX_IRQ	UART 1 Transmitter
29	25	I2C1B	_I2C1_BUS_IRQ	I2C 1 Bus Collision Event
30	25	I2C1S	_I2C1_SLAVE_IRQ	I2C 1 Slave Event
31	25	I2C1M	_I2C1_MASTER_IRQ	I2C 1 Master Event
32	26	CN	_CHANGE_NOTICE_IRQ	Input Change Interrupt
33	27	AD1	_ADC_IRQ	ADC Convert Done
34	28	PMP	_PMP_IRQ	Parallel Master Port Interrupt
35	29	CMP1	_COMPARATOR_1_IRQ	Comparator 1 Interrupt
36	30	CMP2	_COMPARATOR_2_IRQ	Comparator 2 Interrupt
37	31	SPI2E	_SPI2_ERR_IRQ	SPI 2 Fault

(*continued*)

Table 8-1. (*continued*)

IRQ No.	Vector No.	Macro	IRQ Symbol	Description
38	31	SPI2TX	_SPI2_TX_IRQ	SPI 2 Transfer Done
39	31	SPI2RX	_SPI2_RX_IRQ	SPI 2 Receiver Done
40	32	U2E	_UART2_ERR_IRQ	UART 2 Error
41	32	U2RX	_UART2_RX_IRQ	UART 2 Receiver
42	32	U2TX	_UART2_TX_IRQ	UART 2 Transmitter
43	33	I2C2B	_I2C2_BUS_IRQ	I2C 2 Bus Collision Event
44	33	I2C2S	_I2C2_SLAVE_IRQ	I2C 2 Slave Event
45	33	I2C2M	_I2C2_MASTER_IRQ	I2C 2 Master Event
46	34	FSCM	_FAIL_SAFE_MONITOR_IRQ	Fail-Safe Clock Monitor Interrupt
47	35	RTCC	_RTCC_IRQ	Real-Time Clock Interrupt
48	36	DMA0	_DMA0_IRQ	DMA Channel 0 Interrupt
49	37	DMA1	_DMA1_IRQ	DMA Channel 1 Interrupt
50	38	DMA2	_DMA2_IRQ	DMA Channel 2 Interrupt
51	39	DMA3	_DMA3_IRQ	DMA Channel 3 Interrupt
56	44	FCE		FCE – Flash Control Event

To help the programmer use this multitude of interrupt sources, there are a number of macros identified by the lowercase "m" within the plib.h header file. Using this header file, the programmer has access to a number of very useful functions and macros, some of which are identified here:

1. INTEnableSystemSingleVectoredInt ( ); enables the basic interrupt management mode whereby, as the name suggests, there is only a single interrupt vector location.

2. mXXSetIntPriority (x); assigns the required priority levels 0–7 (x) for the stated interrupt where the XX is replaced with the IRQ symbol.

3. mXXClearIntFlag ( ); is used to clear the interrupt flag for that described by the IRQ symbol that replaces the XX.

4. mXXIntEnable (x); is used to enable the interrupt described by the IRQ symbol that replaces the XX. Note the small x is used to indicate the priority of the interrupt.

5. INTEnableSystemMultiVectoredInt ( ); allows the whole range of interrupts to be reached using their own interrupt vector location.

However, this presents a problem in that Microchip is removing this plib.h header file in the compilers later than version 1.40. I believe this is because they want you to move toward their MPLAB Harmony environment for programming their 32-bit PICs. I am not happy with this, and so when I know I will be using interrupts, I use the C compiler version 1.32. This version of compiler can still be downloaded from the archive section on the Microchip website.

The interrupts can be controlled using two basic approaches. The first is the single vectored interrupt where there is only one ISR that is reached via a single vector. If you are using more than one interrupt source, the ISR must determine which interrupt source has caused the interrupt and what is its priority.

The other approach is the multicore vector approach, whereby each interrupt source has its own ISR, and there is a vector location for each of the ISRs. If you are to use more than one interrupt source, it is up to you, the programmer, which approach you use.

When using interrupts, you must do the following:

- Decide if you are using a single-core or multicore vector and enable it using the appropriate function.

- You must enable the actual interrupt using the INTEnable macro and assign the priority level for the interrupt.

- You must set the priority level for the interrupt using the mXXSetIntPriority (x).

- You must write an interrupt service routine for the interrupt and clear the interrupt flag in that ISR using the mXXClearIntFlag ( ); macro.

The following program is just to show you how to use a single interrupt with the PIC32. The main section of the program is what the PIC is doing while the program simply waits for an interrupt to occur. In this example, the main program will just make the LED on bit 7 of PORTA flash on and off at ¼ second intervals. We will be using the interrupt associated with timer2. The timer2 interrupt will happen when the value that timer2 has counted up to equals the value stored in the special register associated with timer2, that is, the PR2 register. When this match happens, the timer2 interrupt flag, T2IF, will go to a logic '1'. This will cause an interrupt to the main program, as we will have enabled the timer2 interrupt function.

The PIC will then carry out the instructions of the ISR. The ISR will make the LEDS on PORTA reflect the value stored in a variable count. This variable will be incremented once every time the PIC runs the ISR. The program will use the macros that are included in the plib header file. The instructions for this program are shown in Listing 8-1.

Listing 8-1. Timer2 Interrupt Using a Single Vector

```
1   /* Single Interrupt Vector test
2   For 32bit PIC
3   Written by H H Ward dated 07/12/2021
4   */
5   #include <xc.h>
6   #include <config72M36MNoWDTNoJTAG.h>
7   #include <peripheral/int.h>
8   int count;
9   //The Interrupt Service Routine
10  void   __ISR(0, ipl1) InterruptHandler()
11  {
12  mT2ClearIntFlag();
13  mT2IntEnable( 0);
14  count++;
15  PORTA = count;
16  mT2IntEnable( 1);
17  }
18  main()
19  {
20  // set up the timers and PORTS
21  PORTA = 0;
22  PORTB = 0;
23  PORTC = 0;
24  PORTD = 0;
```

```
25   PORTE = 0;
26   TRISA = 0;
27   TRISB = 0x00FF;
28   TRISC = 0x00FF;
29   TRISD = 0x0000;
30   TRISE = 0x0000;
31   AD1PCFG = 0xFFFF;
32   AD1CON1 = 0;
33   DDPCONbits.JTAGEN = 0;
34   count = 0;
35   PR2 = 62000;          //440.1ms
36   T2CON = 0x8070;
37   T2CONSET = 0x8000;   //140.625kHz
38   T1CON = 0x8030;
39   T1CONSET = 0x8000;   //140.625kHz
40   __builtin_disable_interrupts();
41   mT2ClearIntFlag();
42   mT2IntEnable( 1);
43   mT2SetIntPriority( 1);
44   INTEnableSystemSingleVectoredInt();
45   __builtin_enable_interrupts();
46   while( 1)
47   {
48   _RA7 = (_RA7^1);
49   TMR1 = 0;
50   while (TMR1 <35150);    //1/4sec delay
51   }
52   }
```

Analysis of Listing 8-1

Lines 1–4 are the normal comments.

Lines 5 and 6 are the normal include files.

Line 7   `<peripheral/int.h>`

This is required to include the <peripheral/int.h> header file. We need this header file as we want to use the macros that make setting up the interrupts much easier. However, it is important to realize that Microchip has not included this library in the XC32 compilers after version 1.40. I am using the XC32 compiler version 1.32 to ensure I do have access to this library, which is part of the "plib.h" header file, when using interrupts. Microchip is trying to push you into using their MPLAB Harmony 3 environment. While I can appreciate why they are doing this, I do think Harmony 3 is very heavily software dependent. For now, I will show you how to use interrupts without MPLAB Harmony 3, but you will need to use one of the earlier XC32 compilers. These are still available in the archive section of the Microchip website.

When you build the program, you will be presented with a lot of warnings. These warn you that Microchip will remove the "plib.h" from their XC32 compilers after version 1.40. If we examine this header file, "plib.h," you will see that it is just a list of includes for the different peripherals you may use with the PIC. The list is shown here:

```
#include <peripheral/adc10.h>
#include <peripheral/bmx.h>
#include <peripheral/cmp.h>
#include <peripheral/cvref.h>
#include <peripheral/dma.h>
#include <peripheral/i2c.h>
#include <peripheral/incap.h>
#include <peripheral/int.h>
```

```
#include <peripheral/nvm.h>
#include <peripheral/outcompare.h>
#include <peripheral/pcache.h>
#include <peripheral/pmp.h>
#include <peripheral/ports.h>
#include <peripheral/pps.h>
#include <peripheral/power.h>
#include <peripheral/reset.h>
#include <peripheral/rtcc.h>
#include <peripheral/spi.h>
#include <peripheral/system.h>
#include <peripheral/timer.h>
#include <peripheral/uart.h>
#include <peripheral/wdt.h>
#include <peripheral/eth.h>
#include <peripheral/CAN.h>
```

The Include Directives in the Plib.h Header File

We could have used the full header file by using <plib.h>, but this would have produced more warnings.

You might now think you can look into the <peripheral/int.h> header file to see how it works. However, Microchip is good at giving you information but not explaining how it works. As I said earlier, interrupts require a very complex set of settings in a variety of control registers. I know I believe that you should understand every instruction you use in your programs, but, although I have studied many of the interrupt control registers, I have resigned myself to using this "int.h" header file. It is quite easy to understand what it is doing, and so I will restrict my analysis to that approach.

It is a little bit annoying that Microchip has gone down this route of removing the "plib.h" header file, but you can understand why. I believe they want you to migrate to the MPLAB Harmony suite which they have invested a lot of time into. However, they still allow you to download the XC32 v1.32 compiler, so you still do have access to it. Then, if like me, you can avoid using MPLAB Harmony and learn how you can actually program the control registers to get the PIC to do what you want. In this way, you don't need to rely on blocks of code that you don't understand. I think this route will make you a better embedded programmer.

Line 8 int count;

Here, we are just setting aside a 16-bit memory location of the data type "int" for integer, which we will call "count." This will be used to hold the value that a counter has counted up to.

Line 9 //The Interrupt service Routine

I am simply splitting the listing up into sections here.

Line 10 void __ISR(0, ipl1) InterruptHandler( )

This is another macro that can be used to set up the vector that is set to vector 0 and given the priority level 1, as shown in the normal brackets. When using single vectored interrupts, you should appreciate that there is only one vector location that the PIC will use to store the actual address in memory of the first instruction of the ISR. The vector number that the PIC allocates to this vector is the number "0," the first number in the normal brackets. If you use any other number, you will see that the interrupt does not work; try it and see what happens. The second term inside the normal brackets, "ipl1," is there to set the priority level of the interrupt to level 1. Note the use of the double underscore at the beginning of the instruction.

Line 12 mT2ClearIntFlag ();

This uses one of the macros, hence the "m," that is in the peripheral/int.h header file. It is used to clear the timer2 interrupt flag, that is, set it to a logic '0.' When this was set to a logic '1,' as when the value that timer2 had matched the value in the PR2 register, the interrupt bit that is checked by the PIC in the "fetch and execute cycle" will be set to a logic '1', assuming that we have enabled the timer2 interrupt, which we do in line 40. With this instruction, we are clearing the timer2 interrupt flag so that it doesn't keep setting the interrupt flag in the fetch and execute cycle. Another reason for doing this is so that we can see the flag go to a "1" on the next match of timer2 with the PR2.

Line 13   mT2IntEnable (0);

This uses another macro within the peripheral/int.h header file. This will disable the timer2 interrupt so that it will not generate another interrupt until we are ready.

Line 14 count++;

This simply increments the value in the variable "count" by one. You should appreciate that this will only happen when the PIC is carrying out the instructions of the ISR.

Line 15 PORTA = count;

This loads the SFR PORTA with a copy of what is in the variable "count." This will display the value that is in the variable "count" on the eight LEDS connected to PORTA.

Line 16 mT2IntEnable (1);

This now uses the macro to reenable the timer2 interrupt. This means that when the value in timer2 next matches the value in the PR2 register, an interrupt will be generated.

Line 18 main ()

This sets up the normal main loop.
Lines 20–33 set up the timers and ports in the PIC as normal.

Line 34 count = 0;

This simply loads the variable "count" with 0. This is to ensure "count" starts with a value of 0.

Line 35 PR2 = 62000;

This loads the PR2 register with a value of 62000. This is the value that timer2 must count up to before it generates an interrupt, which is done by setting the timer2 interrupt flag, T2INTF, to a logic '1'. When this happens, the current value in the TMR2 register goes back to 0.

Line 36 T2CON = 0X0070;

This turns timer2 on and sets the divide rate to a maximum divide of 256. This will make the timer2 counter count at a frequency of 140.625kHz. This means one tick takes $7.11\mu s$. Therefore, it will take 62,000 x $7.11\mu s$, that is, 0.441 seconds, till the count value in timer2 matches the value in the PR2 register and so generates an interrupt. This means the count value will increment approximately every half second.

This instruction loads the T2CON register with the binary value shown in Table 8-2.

Table 8-2. *The Bits of the T2CON Register*

Bit 15	Bit 14	Bit 13	Bit 12	Bit 11	Bit 10	Bit 9	Bit 8
On	FRZ	SIDL	Not used; read as logic '0'				
0	0	0	0	0	0	0	0
Bit 7	Bit 6	Bit 5	Bit 4	Bit 3	Bit 2	Bit 1	Bit 0
TGATE	TCKPS			T32	Not used	TCS	Not used
0	1	1	1	0	0	0	0

To appreciate what this does, we will look at the bits in turn to see what they do:

- A logic '0' in bit 15 turns timer2 off while we configure the timer.

- A logic '0' in bit 14 means the operation of the CPU does not freeze when the PIC is put into debug mode.

- A logic '0' in bit 13 does not stop the operation of the CPU when the PIC is put into idle mode.

- A logic '0' in bit 7 means the gate's time accumulation is disabled. Bit 7 only affects the timer2 when the TCS bit is set to a logic '0'. If the TCS bit is a logic '1', then this TGATE bit has no effect.

- Bits 6, 5, and 4 determine what divide rate is applied to the clock before it is fed to timer2. The three bits give us the divide rates as shown in Table 8-3.

- A logic '0' in bit 3 sets timer2 up to form two separate 16-bit timers.

- A logic '0' in bit 2 sets timer2 up to use the internal peripheral clock as its source.

Table 8-3. *The Different Divide Rates*

Bit 6	Bit 5	Bit 4	Divide Rate
0	0	0	1:1
0	0	1	1:2
0	1	0	1:4
0	1	1	1:8
1	0	0	1:16
1	0	1	1:32
1	1	0	1:64
1	1	1	1:256

The instruction on line 36 sets bits 6, 5, and 4 to a logic '1'. This means we are applying the maximum divide rate. As we set the source of the clock for timer2 to the PBCLK, which runs at 36MHz, then, after dividing this by 256, the frequency at which timer2 counts is 140.625kHz. This means each tick or count takes 7.11µs.

Line 37 T2CONSET = 0x8000;

This uses the "SET" Special Function Register for timer2 to set just bit 15 of the control register to a logic '1'. This will simply turn the timer on as we have now configured it as we want to use it.

Line 38 T1CON = 0x0030;

This turns timer1 off while we configure the timer as we want to use it.

This instruction sets up timer1 in a similar fashion. It loads bits 15 to 1 with the binary value as shown in Table 8-4.

Table 8-4. *The Bits of the T1CON Register*

Bit 15	Bit 14	Bit 13	Bit 12	Bit 11	Bit 10	Bit 9	Bit 8
On	FRZ	SIDL	TMWDIS	TMWIP	Not used; read as 0		
0	0	0	0	0	0	0	0
Bit 7	**Bit 6**	**Bit 5**	**Bit 4**	**Bit 3**	**Bit 2**	**Bit 1**	**Bit 0**
TGATE	Not used	TCKPS		Not used	TYSNC	TCS	Not used
0	0	1	1	0	0	0	0

To appreciate what this does, we will look at the bits in turn to see what they do:

- A logic '0' in bit 15 turns timer1 off.

- A logic '0' in bit 14 means the operation of the CPU does not freeze when the PIC is put into debug mode.

- A logic '0' in bit 13 does not stop the operation of the CPU when the PIC is put into idle mode.

- A logic '0' in bit 12 means back-to-back writes are enabled. Note if the TYSNC bit is a logic '1', then this bit has no effect.

- A logic '0' in bit 11 is a signal to inform you that an asynchronous write to the TMR1 register is now complete.

- A logic '0' in bit 7 means the gated time accumulation is disabled. Bit 7 only affects the timer1 when the TCS bit is set to a logic '0'. If the TCS bit is a logic '1', then this TGATE bit has no effect.

- The logic in bits 5 and 4 set the divide rate for timer1 as shown in Table 8-4.

- A logic '0' in bit 2 sets the external input clock to be not synchronized.

- A logic '0' in bit 1 sets timer1 up to use the internal peripheral clock as its source.

The instruction on line 37 sets bits 5 and 4 to a logic '1'. This means we are applying the maximum divide rate. As we set the source of the clock for timer1 to the PBCLK which runs at 36MHz, then after dividing this by 256, the frequency at which timer1 counts is 140.625kHz. This means each tick or count takes 7.11µs.

Line 39 T1CONSET = 0x8000;

This simply turns timer1 on in a similar fashion to that in line 37.

Line 40 __builtin_disable_interrupts();

This uses a built-in routine to disable the interrupts. Note the use of the double underscore at the beginning of the instruction.

Line 41 mT2ClearIntFlag();

This uses a macro in the peripheral/int.h header file to clear the T2IF, timer2 interrupt flag. This is required to make sure this flag, or bit, is set to a logic '0'. If it was left at a logic '1', then the PIC will not see a transition from logic '0' to a logic '1' when there was another timer2 match with the PR2. This transition is to instigate an interrupt, so we must ensure this bit is initially at a logic '0'. Note, the data sheets state that this bit must be cleared in software.

Line 42   mT2IntEnable(1);

This uses a macro to enable the timer2 interrupt. We need to enable the interrupt so that when the T2IF is set by a match with the PR2, the PIC will actually set the interrupt flag in the fetch and execute cycle.

Line 43 mT2SetIntPriority (1);

This uses another macro from the peripheral/int.h header file. This sets the priority of the timer2 interrupt to level 1. There are seven priority levels, 1 to 7, with 7 being the highest priority. We can use priority levels with interrupts to allow those interrupts with a higher priority to interrupt an ISR for an interrupt that is running if it has a lower priority level. The PIC32 also uses some subpriority levels which allow an interrupt to interrupt an ISR for an interrupt that has the same main priority level. This is an important aspect of interrupts, and you must give your interrupt a level of priority.

Line 44 INTEnableSystemSingleVectoredInt ();

This enables the use of single vectored interrupts. This is a macro in the peripheral/int.h header file that calls a subroutine to put the PIC into single-core vector mode.

Line 45 __builtin_enable_interrupts();

This uses the built-in routine to enable all interrupts. Note the use of the double underscore at the beginning of the instruction.

Line 46 while (1)

This creates a forever loop that gets the PIC to carry out the instructions listed between the opening and closing curly brackets on lines 47 and 51 forever. This is so that the PIC does not carry out the instructions between lines 18 and 43 again, as we don't need to.

Line 48 _RA7 = (_RA7^1);

This is a clever little instruction, as it will set the logic on bit 7 of PORTA according to the result of a logical EXOR operation between the logic that is currently on bit 7 of PORTA and the logic '1'. Note, the symbol "^" in "C" means the logical EXOR operation. To help explain how this instruction works, we will look at the truth table for a logical EXOR between two bits. This is shown in Table 8-5.

Table 8-5. *The EXOR Result of the Instruction*
_RA7 = (_RA7 ^ 1);

Bit 7 of PORTA	EXOR Bit	Result
0	0	0
0	**1**	**1**
1	0	1
1	**1**	**0**

The logical EXOR stands for Exclusive OR, which is so called because it excludes the logical "AND" result. The result will only be a logic '1' if one OR the other bits are a logic '1'. The normal logical OR operation, sometimes called the Inclusive OR, does result in a logic '1' if both bits are a logic '1'. This is the logical AND operation.

In the instruction on line 48, the EXOR bit is always set to a logic '1'. This means that we are only using the two possibilities shown in bold in Table 8-5. This means that, as the result will be the logic that bit 7 of PORTA goes to with this instruction, the logic on bit 7 will change from 0 to 1 and from 1 to 0 every time we carry out this instruction. This means that this instruction will simply make the LED on bit 7 of PORTA flash on and off.

Line 49 TMR1 = 0;

This simply loads the register TMR1 with 0. This is to make timer1 start counting from 0.

Line 50 while (TMR1 < 35150);

This makes the PIC do nothing while the count in the TMR1 register is less than 35,150. It will take 35,150 x 7.11ms, that is, 0.25 seconds, before timer1 counts up to this value. Therefore, these two instructions create a ¼ second delay. This means that the LED on bit 7 of PORTA will flash on and off at ¼ second intervals.

Line 51 }

This is the closing curly bracket of the while (1) loop.

Line 52 }

This is the closing curly bracket of the main loop.

Using More Than One Interrupt Source with Single Vector Mode

The next program will look at using more than one interrupt while still using single vector mode. This is shown in Listing 8-2.

Listing 8-2. The Listing for the Program Using Two Interrupt Sources

```
1   /* Single Interrupt Vector test
2   using two external interrupts
3   For 32bit PIC
4   Written by H H Ward dated 07/12/2021
5   */
6   #include <xc.h>
7   #include <config72M36MNoWDTNoJTAG.h>
8   #include <peripheral/int.h>
9   //some variables
10  int n, count, count2, slowcount;
11  //some subroutines
12  void delay (unsigned int t)
13  {
14  for (n = 0; n < t; n++)
15  {
16  TMR1 = 0;
```

```
17   while (TMR1 < 35150);
18   }
19   }
20   //the ISR Interrupt Service Routine
21   void __ISR(0, ipl2) InterruptHandler(void)
22   {
23   if (IFSObits.INTOIF)
24   {
25   mINTOIntEnable( 0);
26   for (count = 0; count < 20; count++)
27   {
28   _RAO = (_RAO ^1);
29   delay(4);
30   }
31   IFSObits.INTOIF = 0;
32   mINTOIntEnable( 1);
33   }
34   else  if (IFSObits.INT1IF)
35   {
36   mINT1IntEnable( 0);
37   for (count2 = 0; count2 < 20; count2++)
38   {
39   _RA1 = (_RA1 ^1);
40   delay(4);
41   }
42   }
43   mINT1IntEnable( 1);
44   IFSObits.INT1IF = 0;
45   }
46   //the main loop
47   main()
```

```
48  {
49  // set up the timers and PORTS
50  PORTA = 0;
51  PORTB = 0;
52  PORTC = 0;
53  PORTD = 0;
54  PORTE = 0;
55  PORTF = 0;
56  TRISA = 0;
57  TRISB = 0x00FF;
58  TRISC = 0x00FF;
59  TRISD = 0x0000;
60  TRISE = 0x0100;
61  TRISF = 0x01F0;
62  AD1PCFG = 0xFFFF;
63  AD1CON1 = 0;
64  DDPCONbits.JTAGEN = 0;
65  count = 0;
66  PR2 = 62000;        //440.1ms
67  T2CON = 0x0070;
68  T2CONSET = 0x8000;
69  T1CON = 0x0030;
70  T1CONSET = 0x8000;//set up the interrupts
71  mINT0SetIntPriority( 2);
72  mINT1SetIntPriority( 2);
73  INTEnableSystemSingleVectoredInt();
74  mINT0IntEnable( 1);
75  mINT1IntEnable( 1);
76  while (1)
77  {
78  _RA7 = (_RA7 ^1);
```

```
79  delay(4);
80  }
81  }
```

Analysis of Listing 8-2

This program uses two external interrupts: INT0 on input RF6 and INT1 on input RE8. These two inputs are connected to two momentary switches which, when closed, will drive the input high. It is the rising edge of this action that will set the appropriate interrupt flag, either INT0F or INT1F, that will generate an interrupt. Each of the two interrupts will use their respective ISRs to make an LED on an output flash one second on and one second off for ten times. INT0 will flash the LED on RA0 and INT1 will flash the LED on RA1.

When none of the interrupts are triggered, the main program will simply flash an LED on RA7 at the same rate.

We will still use single vector mode, and so there will only be one ISR. This means the ISR has to determine which of the two sources has caused the interrupt.

Lines 1–5 are the usual comments.

Lines 6–8 are the normal includes, but note I am using the xc.h header file and the peripheral/int.h, which still requires the plib header file, but it does reduce the number of warnings when the program is compiled.

Line 10 int n, count, count2, slowcount;

This sets up four 16-bit memory locations for the variables we will use in the program.

Lines 12–19 create the usual delay subroutine which can be used to create a variable delay with a time base of 1/4 of a second.

Line 21 void __ISR(0, ipl2) InterruptHandler(void)

This uses one of the macros in the int.h header file to set up the ISR that uses the vector location 0 to store its first address, as stated with the "0" in the ISR(0, ipl2). The ipl2 sets the interrupt priority for this ISR to highest priority level 2. Any interrupts that we want to use in this ISR must be set to the same level of priority or less. If we try to use an interrupt with a higher priority level than what we set here, the interrupt won't work. However, with single vectored interrupts, a higher priority interrupt cannot interrupt a lower-level interrupt that is already running. Note, there are two underscores before the phrase ISR.

Line 23 if (IFS0bits.INT0IF)

This instruction is of the type "if (the test described in the normal brackets) is true, then do what I say." However, the test is not using a macro, it is simply testing if INT0IF, that is, the interrupt flag for INT0, has been set to a logic '1.' If it has, then the result of this test will be true. This means that it was the INT0 interrupt that caused the interrupt, and so the PIC must carry out the instructions between lines 24 and 33. Also, if the result is true, the PIC will skip line 34 and those between the opening and closing curly brackets on lines 35 and 42.

Line 25 mINT0IntEnable(0);

This is using a macro to disable the INT0 interrupt. This is done to ensure the INT0 interrupt does not generate an interrupt until we are ready. We could have used the following instruction instead of this macro:

IEC0bits.INT0IE = 0;.

This would work exactly the same and would save some memory. However, there are a lot of instructions, associated with interrupts, that are very complex. Using the macros within the plib.h header file does make the use of interrupts easier. While you can mix the approach up by using direct instructions, as suggested here, it might be more sensible to use the macro instructions all the time. It is entirely up to you which one you use.

Line 26   for (count = 0; count < 20; count++)

This sets up a "for do loop" that will run through its instructions 20 times. We have looked at this type of instruction in Chapter 2. It will carry out the instructions between lines 27 and 30, 20 times.

Line 28 _RA0 = (_RA1 ^0);

The _RA0 part of the instruction is one method of identifying bit 0 of PORTA. The other method would be to use PORTAbits.RA0.

We have looked at this type of instruction in Listing 8-1. This instruction makes the logic on bit 0 of PORTA toggle between 1 and 0 every time the PIC carried out this instruction.

Line 29 delay(4);

This calls the subroutine delay and sends the value "4" up to it. This will basically create a one-second delay before the PIC carries out the instruction on line 26 again, as long as the value in count is not equal to or greater than 20.

This part of the ISR, which is executed if INT0 created the interrupt, simply gets the PIC to flash the LED on ten times and off ten times with a one-second delay between each change.

Line 31 IFS0bits.INT0IF = 0;

With this instruction, we are simply clearing the INT0 interrupt flag. This is so that the PIC will see the transition from 0 to 1 when this flag is next set to a logic '1'. We could have used the macro instruction as with **mINT0ClearIntFlag();**. I am just trying to make you aware of the different approaches. However, you must clear the interrupt flag so that the PIC can notice it going back to a logic '1' when the INT0 input goes high again.

Line 32 mINT0IntEnable(1);

Here, we are using the macro to reenable the INT0 interrupt. We could have used the following instruction instead, and it would work perfectly well:

```
IEC0bits.INT0IE = 1;.
```

However, it might be simpler to just use the macros within the plib header file.

Line 34 else if (IFS0bits.INT1IF)

This is the instruction the PIC should carry out if the test on line 23 resulted in an untrue result. It is exactly the same instruction except that it is testing to see if it was INT1 that caused the interrupt.

If it was INT1, then the PIC must carry out the instructions between lines 35 and 42. These work in exactly the same way as the previous set of instructions except that it is bit 1 of PORTA that will toggle with one-second intervals.

There are no new instructions in the rest of the program except two that I have added here:

Line 77 _RA7 = (_RA7 ^ 1);
Line 78 delay(4);

These two instructions should simply make the LED connected to bit 7 of PORTA toggle at an interval of one second.

Interrupt Priority

This allows an interrupt of more importance than others to interrupt an interrupt that is already running. The PIC32 has seven main levels of priority, that is, levels 1–7, with 1 being the least important and 7 being the most important. There is also a 0 level of priority.

The PIC also has five levels of subpriority going from 0 to 4. These sublevels are used to allow an interrupt of the same level of priority to interrupt it if it has a higher level of subpriority than the one currently running.

What happens if two or more interrupts have the same main and subpriority levels? Well, the normal queuing of who came first takes over.

So, you see these interrupts are getting very complex.

Multivectored Interrupts with Priority

The next program will look at using multivectors and ISRs. It will use the INT0 interrupt, set at a priority level 1, and the INT1 interrupt, set at a priority level 2. The listing for the program is shown in Listing 8-3.

Listing 8-3. The Listing for Multivectored Interrupts with Priority

```
1   /* Multi Vectored Interrupt test
2   using two external interrupts
3   with different priorities
4   For 32bit PIC
5   Written by H H Ward dated 07/12/2021
6   */
7   #include <xc.h>
8   #include <config72M36MNoWDTNoJTAG.h>
9   #include <peripheral/int.h>
10  int n, count, count2, slowcount;
11  void delay (unsigned int t)
12  {
13  for (n = 0; n < t; n++)
14  {
15  TMR1 = 0;
16  while (TMR1 < 35150);
```

```
17  }
18  }
19  void __ISR(3, ipl1) INTOInterruptHandler(void)
20  {
21  IECObits.INTOIE = 0;
22  for (count = 0; count < 20; count++)
23  {
24  _RAO = (_RAO ^1);
25  delay(4);
26  }
27  IECObits.INTOIE = 1;
28  IFSObits.INTOIF = 0;
29  }
30  void __ISR (7, ipl2) INT1InterruptHandler ()
31  {
32  IECObits.INT1IE = 0;
33  for (count2 = 0; count2 < 20; count2++)
34  {
35  _RA1 = (_RA1 ^1);
36  delay(4);
37  }
38  IECObits.INT1IE = 1;
39  IFSObits.INT1IF = 0;
40  }
41  main()
42  {
43  // set up the timers and PORTS
44  PORTA = 0;
45  PORTB = 0;
46  PORTC = 0;
47  PORTD = 0;
```

```
48   PORTF = 0;
49   TRISA = 0;
50   TRISB = 0x00FF;
51   TRISC = 0x00FF;
52   TRISD = 0x0000;
53   TRISE = 0x0100;
54   TRISF = 0x01F0;
55   AD1PCFG = 0xFFFF;
56   AD1CON1 = 0;
57   DDPCONbits.JTAGEN = 0;
58   count = 0;
59   PR2 = 62000;
60   T2CON = 0x0070;
61   T2CONSET = 0x8000;
62   T1CON = 0x0030;
63   T1CONSET = 0x8000;
64   //set up the interrupts
65   IPC0 = 0x4000000;
66   IPC1 = 0x8000000;
67   IEC0bits.INT0IE = 1;
68   IEC0bits.INT1IE = 1;
69   INTEnableSystemMultiVectoredInt();
70   while (1)
71   {
72   _RA7 = (_RA7 ^1);
73   delay(4);
74   }
75   }
```

Analysis of Listing 8-3

The main aspect of the program is the same as that of Listing 8-2. The obvious difference is that there will be two separate ISRs, and the INT0 interrupt is set at priority 1, whereas the INT1 interrupt is set at priority 2. This means that INT1 can interrupt INT0 even if INT0 has already started. When INT1 finishes, the program will return to the place, in INT0, it was when INT1 interrupted it.

We will look at the more important instructions in this analysis as we have looked at most of the instructions already.

Line 19 void __ISR(3, ipl1) INT0InterruptHandler(void)

This uses the macro to create the ISR for INT0. This is using vector number 3 as indicated by the value "3" in the normal brackets. This is the correct vector for INT0; see Table 8-1.

The instructions for this ISR are between lines 20 and 29. They are virtually the same as those in Listing 8-2, except we don't need to test which interrupt had caused the interrupt. This is because we are using one ISR for each interrupt source used.

Note line 21 IEC0bits.INT0IE = 0; disables the INT0 interrupt as before but doesn't use a macro to do it. This is just to show you that you can use some of the exact instructions to control the interrupts. However, there are still a lot of very complex instructions to control these interrupts, so it is easier to use the macros within the plib.h header file. The macro instruction that performs the same operation would be "mINT0ClearIntFlag()".

Line 30 void __ISR (7, ipl2) INT1InterruptHandler ()

This creates the ISR for INT1 using vector 7 for storing the address of the first instruction of the ISR. Also, the priority is set to level 2, so that this interrupt ISR can interrupt the INT0 ISR. The ISR works in the same way as INT0 ISR except that it controls the LED connected to RA1.

Lines 41–64 are the normal instructions of the main loop that we have looked at before.

Line 65 IPC0 = 0x4000000;

This is loading the control register IPC0, which is the first of the interrupt priority control registers. This will load bits 28, 27, and 26 with 001, while all the rest are set to logic '0' as well. This will set the priority for INT0 to level 1. If we want to keep using the macros inside the plib.h header file, we could have used the following instruction:

mINT0SetIntPriority(1);
Line 66 IPC1 = 0x8000000;

This is loading the control register IPC1, which is the second of the interrupt priority control registers. This will set bits 28, 27, and 26 to 010, while the rest are set to logic '0'. This is setting the interrupt priority for INT1 to level 2.

Note there are 12 such IPC, interrupt priority control, registers that are used to set the priority for the interrupt sources of the PIC. If we want to keep using the macros inside the plib.h header file, we could have used the following instruction:

mINT1SetIntPriority(2);

With these two instructions, on lines 65 and 66, I am trying to show you that you can configure the interrupts by writing directly to the control registers, instead of using the macros inside the plib.h header file. However, there are around 21 different control registers, and how they interact with each other is quite complex. It is for that reason that I am happy to use all the macros available to us within the plib.h header file. However, this does mean that you will have to use a X32C compiler that is earlier than version 1.40. I use version 1.32.

With this program, the main instructions simply get the LED on bit 7 of PORTA to flash on and off at one-second intervals. These instructions can be interrupted by one of the external interrupts INT0 and INT1. However, INT1 can also interrupt INT0, as it has a higher priority. This means that if INT0 had started, and the switch connected to INT1 changed state, then the PIC would interrupt the ISR for INT0 and then go on to carry out the instructions of the ISR for INT1. When the PIC had completed the ISR for INT1, it would then return to where it had left the instructions for the ISR for INT0 and complete them. When it had completed them, the PIC would return to the main program. It should be noted that INT0 cannot interrupt INT1 as it has a lower level of priority. If INT0 was triggered while INT1 was operating, then the PIC would complete the ISR for INT1 and then move to the ISR for INT0 to work through those instructions before going back to the main program.

I hope these three programs and their analysis have shown you how to set up interrupts with the 32-bit PIC. It is unfortunate that I still have to use the macro instructions that are in the plib header file even though it is just the macros to set up the single or multivectored interrupts. This does mean that you will have to use an older compiler program; I am using version 1.32. I am still trying to get around this issue, and if I do that before publishing this book, I will update it. However, as we can still get hold of the earlier versions of the XC32 compilers, we can still make it work.

Figure 8-1 is an attempt to show the multivectored interrupt program working. It is hard to show an action program with a still photo, but I hope you can see that the LED on RA7 is lit, while the LED on RA1, which is controlled by INT1, is starting to flash. The program does work as expected. Also, I have used a nine-pin D-type connector to add some switches to the explorer 16 development board.

Figure 8-1. *The Multivectored Interrupt Program*

Summary

In this chapter, we have learned what interrupts are and how useful they can be within a PIC program. We have looked at how they can be implemented in the PIC32. This has involved studying how the PIC jumps around its memory locations to find the instructions it must carry out.

In the next chapter, we will look at using the timer1 interrupt to make the PIC respond to an external oscillator that can be used to synchronize a Real-Time Clock program.

CHAPTER 9

The Real-Time Clock

In this chapter, we will look at programming the RTC, Real-Time Clock. There are three approaches to programming the Real-Time Clock that we will look at. The first will be when we simply use an external crystal to create a signal that we can count to synchronize the operation of a clock. The second will use the DS3231 RTC module, which is a separate device we can connect to the PIC. This uses the I²C protocol we have looked at in Chapter 7 to communicate with the PIC.

The third approach will use the actual RTC module that comes with the PIC32. This module does make this PIC a more useful device than the 18F4525 PIC I have used in the past.

With the first approach, we will use an LCD to display the time, then move on to use the TM1637 to display the clock, whereas with the other two approaches, we will use the LCD.

As the first approach uses the external crystal oscillator to synchronize the timer1 counter in the PIC, we will be using an interrupt associated with timer1.

After reading this chapter, you will be able to use interrupts and an external crystal to create a digital clock display using the LCD and a group of four seven-segment displays.

© Hubert Ward 2023
H. Ward, *Introductory Programs with the 32-bit PIC Microcontroller*,
Maker Innovations Series, https://doi.org/10.1007/978-1-4842-9051-4_9

The External Crystal 32.768kHz Oscillator

The ability to produce an accurate clock program is very useful. It can be used to synchronize events of time and date and create a calendar. With this program, we will look at using an external crystal oscillator that produces a very accurate 32.768kHz frequency output as the source for timer1. To understand how the process will work, we should appreciate that timer1 will now be used to simply count the clock pulses provided by this crystal oscillator. The current count value will be stored in a 16-bit register, which means the maximum value that timer1 can count up to is 65,535. Knowing that the oscillator runs at 32.768kHz, then it will take exactly one second for timer1 to count from 0 to 32,767. We can use the fact that we can compare the value timer1 has counted up to with a value held in a timer1 preset register, termed PR1. When the two values match, the interrupt flag, or bit, for timer1, TMR1IF, is set to a logic '1'. This means that the PIC will generate an interrupt at the exact moment that timer1 matches the value stored in the PR1 register. If we load the PR1 register with a value of 32,767, then it will take exactly one second to generate the interrupt.

This is exactly what we do. However, to take advantage of the fact that when timer1 matches the value in the PR1 register, we must enable the interrupt for timer1. I have already said that the timer1 interrupt flag will go to a logic '1' when this match happens. However, if we don't enable the interrupt action for timer1, then this setting of the flag won't cause an interrupt to the PIC. We will look at how we do this when we analyze the following program listing.

The 24-Hour LCD Clock Program

Before we look at the program listing, we will consider what we want the program to do and a way in which we can achieve it. This is basically what the algorithm is.

1. We must allow the user to set the clock.

   a. This will require three buttons, which are

   b. An increment button

   c. A decrement button

   d. A set button

2. We will allow the user to set the day of the week and view the day that they are choosing.

3. We must allow the user to see the values displayed on the LCD as we set the day and time.

4. Once the user has set the clock, we will display the current day and time.

5. This display must be updated every minute.

6. We will require three inputs for the three buttons.

7. We will require a port for the LCD. This will be PORTE using all 8 bits. Note we could use the PMP module, but I will use the direct approach for connecting the LCD to PORTE.

8. This means we will require two control outputs for the RS and E pins of the LCD.

9. As we are using the external crystal oscillator, which is used as the secondary oscillator source for the PIC, the secondary oscillator must be enabled in the configuration words for the PIC.

10. Also, we must use timer2 to control the delays for the LCD, as timer1 will be used solely for the interrupt and the external oscillator.

This is the basis of the algorithm. It is really just your initial thoughts about how you are going to write the program. The more accurate you make your algorithm, the easier it will be to create the program.

The listing for this first clock program is shown in Listing 9-1.

Listing 9-1. The 24-Hour Clock on the LCD Display

```
1    /* A program to create a RTC
2     * It uses the external oscillator as the source
3     * It will display the clock on the LCD on PORTE
4    Author: Mr H. H. Ward
5    *Written for the PIC32MX360F512L
6    Created on 01 November 2021, 11:50
7     * The clock can be set by day and time
8     * Using three buttons connected to the PIC
9    */
10   // PIC32MX360F512L Configuration Bit Settings
11   // 'C' source line config statements
12   // DEVCFG3
13   #pragma config USERID = 0xFFFF
14   // DEVCFG2
15   #pragma config FPLLIDIV = DIV_2
16   #pragma config FPLLMUL = MUL_18
17   #pragma config FPLLODIV = DIV_1
18   // DEVCFG1
19   #pragma config FNOSC = PRIPLL
20   #pragma config FSOSCEN = ON
21   #pragma config IESO = OFF
22   #pragma config POSCMOD = XT
23   #pragma config OSCIOFNC = ON
24   #pragma config FPBDIV = DIV_1
25   #pragma config FCKSM = CSDCMD
```

```
26  #pragma config WDTPS = PS1048576
27  #pragma config FWDTEN = OFF
28  // DEVCFG0
29  #pragma config DEBUG = OFF
30  #pragma config ICESEL = ICS_PGx2
31  #pragma config PWP = OFF
32  #pragma config BWP = OFF
33  #pragma config CP = OFF
34  // #pragma config statements should precede project file
    includes.
35  // Use project enums instead of #define for ON and OFF.
36  #include <xc.h>
37  #include <plib.h>
38  // some definitions
39  #define Mon            lcdData = 0x4D; sendData ();
    lcdData = 0x6F; sendData (); lcdData = 0x6E; sendData ();
40  #define Tue            lcdData = 0x54; sendData ();
    lcdData = 0x75; sendData (); lcdData = 0x65; sendData ();
41  #define Wed            lcdData = 0x57; sendData ();
    lcdData = 0x65; sendData (); lcdData = 0x64; sendData ();
42  #define Thur           lcdData = 0x54; sendData ();
    lcdData = 0x68; sendData (); lcdData = 0x72; sendData ();
43  #define Fri            lcdData = 0x46; sendData ();
    lcdData = 0x72; sendData (); lcdData = 0x69; sendData ();
44  #define Sat            lcdData = 0x53; sendData ();
    lcdData = 0x61; sendData (); lcdData = 0x74; sendData ();
45  #define Sun            lcdData = 0x53; sendData ();
    lcdData = 0x75; sendData (); lcdData = 0x6E; sendData ();
46  #define incbutton      _RD0
47  #define decbutton      _RD1
48  #define setbutton      _RD2
```

```
49  #define entryMode       0b00000110
50  #define displayCtl      0b00001110
51  #define functionSet     0b00111000
52  #define clearScreen     0b00000001
53  #define returnHome      0b00000010
54  #define lineTwo         0b11000000
55  #define shiftLeft       0b00010000
56  #define shiftRight      0b00010100
57  #define shDisRight      0b00011100
58  #define lcdPort         PORTE
59  #define RSpin           PORTBbits.RB15
60  #define eBit            PORTDbits.RD4
61  //variables
62  unsigned char count, secunits = 0x30, sectens = 0x30,
    minunits = 0x30, mintens = 0x30, hourunits = 0x30,
    hourtens = 0x30;
63  unsigned char lcdData, n,m, nt, daynumber, secUnits;
64  unsigned char lcdInitialise [5] =
65  {
66  functionSet,
67  entryMode,
68  displayCtl,
69  clearScreen,
70  returnHome,
71  };
72  //some subroutines
73  void debounce ()
74  {
75  TMR2 = 0;
76  while (TMR2 <1900 );
77  }
```

```
78  void delay(unsigned char t)
79  {
80  for(nt = 0; nt < t; nt++)
81  {
82  TMR2 = 0;
83  while (TMR2 <35160);
84  }
85  }
86  void sendData ()
87  {
88  lcdPort = lcdData;
89  eBit = 1;
90  eBit = 0;
91  TMR2 = 0; while (TMR2 < 380);
92  }
93  void setUpTheLCD ()
94  {
95  TMR2 = 0;
96  while( TMR2<6000);
97  RSpin = 0;
98  n = 0;
99  while (n < 5)
100 {
101 lcdData = lcdInitialise [n];
102 sendData ();
103 n ++;
104 }
105 RSpin = 1;
106 }
107 void line2 ()
108 {
```

```
109  RSpin = 0;
110  lcdData = lineTwo;
111  sendData ();
112  RSpin = 1;
113  }
114  void goHome ()
115  {
116  RSpin = 0;
117  lcdData = returnHome;
118  sendData ();
119  RSpin = 1;
120  }
121  void writeString (unsigned char *print)
122  {
123  while (*print)
124  {
125  lcdData = *print;
126  sendData ();
127  *print ++;
128  }
129  }
130  void clearTheScreen ()
131  {
132  RSpin = 0;
133  lcdData = clearScreen;
134  sendData ();
135  RSpin = 1;
136  }
137  void shiftcurleft ( unsigned char l)
138  {
139  RSpin = 0;
```

```
140  for (n = 0; n < 1; n ++)
141  {
142  lcdData = shiftLeft;
143  sendData ();
144  }
145  RSpin = 1;
146  }
147  void shiftcurright (unsigned char r)
148  {
149  RSpin = 0;
150  for (n = 0; n < r; n ++)
151  {
152  lcdData = shiftRight;
153  sendData ();
154  }
155  RSpin = 1;
156  }
157  void shiftdisright (unsigned char r)
158  {
159  RSpin = 0;
160  for (n = 0; n < r; n ++)
161  {
162  lcdData = shDisRight;
163  sendData ();
164  }
165  RSpin = 1;
166  }
167  void cursorPos (unsigned char line, unsigned char pos)
168  {
169  switch (line)
170  {
```

```
171  case 1:
172  {
173  goHome ();
174  shiftcurright (pos);
175  break;
176  }
177  case 2:
178  {
179  line2 ();
180  shiftcurright (pos);
181  break;
182  }
183  case 3:
184  {
185  goHome ();
186  shiftcurright (pos + 20);
187  break;
188  }
189  case 4:
190  {
191  line2 ();
192  shiftcurright (pos + 20);
193  break;
194  }
195  }
196  }
197  void displayday ()
198  {
199  switch (daynumber)
200  {
201  case 1 :
202  {
```

```
203  Mon;
204  line2 ();
205  }
206  break;
207  case 2:
208  {
209  Tue;
210  line2 ();
211  }
212  break;
213  case 3:
214  {
215  Wed;
216  line2 ();
217  }
218  break;
219  case 4:
220  {
221  Thur;
222  line2 ();
223  }
224  break;
225  case 5:
226  {
227  Fri;
228  line2 ();
229  }
230  break;
231  case 6:
232  {
233  Sat;
```

```
234 line2 ();
235 }
236 break;
237 case 7:
238 {
239 Sun;
240 line2 ();
241 }
242 break;
243 }
244 }
245 void setClock ()
246 {
247 writeString ("Set The Day");
248 line2 ();
249 while (!setbutton)
250 {
251 if (incbutton) debounce ();
252 if (incbutton) daynumber ++;
253 while (incbutton);
254 if (decbutton) debounce ();
255 if (decbutton) daynumber --;
256 while (decbutton);
257 if (daynumber == 8) daynumber = 1;
258 if (daynumber == 0) daynumber = 1;
259 displayday();
260 }
261 debounce ();
262 while (setbutton);
263 clearTheScreen ();
264 cursorPos (1,1);
265 writeString ("Set The Clock");
```

```
266  while (!setbutton)
267  {
268  line2 ();
269  writeString ("Hours");
270  lcdData = 0x3A;
271  sendData ();
272  lcdData = hourtens;
273  sendData ();
274  lcdData = hourunits;
275  sendData ();
276  shiftcurleft (1);
277  if (incbutton) debounce ();
278  if (incbutton) hourunits ++;
279  while (incbutton);
280  if(hourunits == 0x3A)
281  {
282  hourunits = 0x30;
283  hourtens ++;
284  }
285  if (hourtens == 0x32 & hourunits == 0x34 )
286  {
287  hourtens = 0x30;
288  hourunits = 0x30;
289  }
290  if (decbutton) debounce ();
291  if (decbutton)
292  {
293  if (hourunits == 0x30)
294  {
295  hourunits = 0x39;
296  hourtens --;
```

```
297  if (hourtens ==0x2F)
298  {
299  hourtens = 0x30;
300  hourunits = 0x30;
301  }
302  }
303  else hourunits --;
304  }
305  while (decbutton);
306  if (setbutton) debounce ();
307  if (setbutton) goto minset;
308  }
309  minset:   line2 ();
310  writeString ("Minutes");
311  lcdData = 0x3A;
312  sendData ();
313  for (n = 0; n < 15; n ++)
314  {
315  TMR2 = 0;
316  while (TMR2 < 4609);
317  }
318  setmins:  lcdData = mintens;
319  sendData ();
320  lcdData = minunits;
321  sendData ();
322  shiftcurleft (2);
323  if (incbutton) debounce ();
324  if (incbutton) minunits ++;
325  while (incbutton);
326  if(minunits == 0X3A)
327  {
```

```
328  minunits = 0X30;
329  mintens ++;
330  }
331  if (decbutton) debounce ();
332  if (decbutton)
333  {
334  if (minunits == 0x30)
335  {
336  minunits = 0x39;
337  mintens --;
338  if (mintens ==0x2F)
339  {
340  mintens = 0x30;
341  minunits = 0x30;
342  }
343  }
344  else minunits --;
345  }
346  while (decbutton);
347  if (!setbutton) goto setmins;
348  }
349  void  __ISR(0, ipl1) T1Interrupt()
350  {
351  mT1ClearIntFlag();
352  mT1IntEnable( 0);
353  secunits ++;
354  PORTA = secunits;
355  mT1IntEnable( 1);
356  }
357  main (void)
358  {
```

```
359   // set up timers
360   T1CON = 0x0002;
361   T1CONSET = 0x8000;
362   T2CON = 0x0070;
363   T2CONSET = 0x8000;
364   ///initalize the ports etc//
365   TRISA = 0x00000000;
366   TRISB = 0x00000000;
367   TRISC = 0x00000000;
368   TRISD = 0x00000007;
369   TRISE = 0x00000000;
370   PORTA = 0;
371   PORTB = 0;
372   PORTC = 0;
373   PORTD = 0;
374   PORTE = 0;
375   AD1PCFG = 0xFFFF;
376   AD1CON1 = 0;
377   OSCCONbits.SOSCEN = 1;
378   PR1 = 32767;
379   __builtin_disable_interrupts();
380   mT1ClearIntFlag();
381   mT1SetIntPriority( 1);
382   INTEnableSystemSingleVectoredInt();
383   mT1IntEnable( 0);
384   __builtin_enable_interrupts();
385   DDPCONbits.JTAGEN = 0;
386   setUpTheLCD ();
387   cursorPos (1,1);
388   setClock ();
389   clearTheScreen ();
```

```
390  while (1)
391  {
392  mT1IntEnable( 1);
393  if (secunits == 0x3A)
394  {
395  secunits = 0x30;
396  sectens ++;
397  if ( sectens == 0x36)
398  {
399  sectens = 0x30;
400  minunits ++;
401  if (minunits == 0x3A)
402  {
403  minunits = 0x30;
404  mintens ++;
405  if (mintens == 0x36)
406  {
407  mintens = 0x30;
408  hourunits ++;
409  if(hourunits == 0x3A)
410  {
411  hourunits = 0x30;
412  hourtens ++;
413  }
414  }
415  }
416  }
417  if (hourtens == 0x32 & hourunits == 0x34 )
418  {
419  hourtens = 0x30;
420  hourunits= 0x30;
```

```
421   daynumber ++;
422   if (daynumber == 8)daynumber = 1;
423   }
424   }
425   cursorPos (1,1);
426   displayday();
427   line2 ();
428   lcdData = hourtens;
429   sendData ();
430   lcdData = hourunits;
431   sendData ();
432   lcdData = 0x3A;
433   sendData ();
434   lcdData = mintens;
435   sendData ();
436   lcdData = minunits;
437   sendData ();
438   }
439   }
```

Analysis of Listing 9-1

Lines 1–9 are the usual comments for the program.

In lines 10–33, I am listing the configuration words, and not using my usual header file, because there is one line that is different from the header file. The line that is different is

Line 20 #pragma config FSOSCEN = ON

This is used to enable the secondary oscillator. This oscillator will be used as the source for timer1. It is the 32.768kHz crystal oscillator that is used for the source of the Real-Time Clock. We couldn't have used our old header file for the configuration words and just added this line afterward, because doing this caused an error saying that we had two configurations for the FSOSCEN. Therefore, we had to use the configuration words as shown in the listing.

Lines 36 and 37 are the usual include directives. Note I am including the complete "plib.h" header file; this is required for the interrupts. This has been covered in Chapter 8.

Line 39 #define Mon   lcdData = 0x4D; sendData ();
lcdData = 0x6F; sendData (); lcdData = 0x6E; sendData ();

This is a macro I have created that is a list of three instructions that load the variable "lcdData" with the ASCII for the three characters stated in the macro definition. It calls the subroutine " sendData ()" to send the characters to the LCD. This line sends the ASCII for the characters "Mon" for Monday.

Lines 40–45 do the same for the other six days of the week. These macros will be used later in the program. For example, wherever the compiler sees the label "Mon," it knows it will have to write the three instructions defined here in line 39.

Lines 46–48 define the inputs used for the three buttons to set the day and time in the program.

Lines 49–60 are the definitions used with respect to the LCD. These are taken from the header file for the 8-bit LCD connected to PORTE. The reason why they are listed here is simply because the header file uses timer1 for the delays. However, with this program, we must use timer2 for the LCD delays, as timer1 is being used solely for the interrupt.

Lines 62 and 63 are setting up the variables used in the program. Note some of them are given initial values. These values are the hexadecimal for the ASCII to display a set number. For example, 0x30 is the ASCII for "0."

Lines 64–71 set up the array for the settings of the LCD. We have looked at these in Chapter 4.

Lines 72–196 are the subroutines for the LCD settings. Note lines 75, 76, 82, and 83 are using timer2 instead of timer1. That is why we could not just simply include the header file for the LCD in 8-bit mode on PORTE, as we have done in previous programs.

In the "cursorPos" subroutine, I am leaving the case statements for "3" and "4" as we could use the LCD2004 connected to PORTE, which has four lines of 20 characters.

Line 197 void displayday ()

This is creating a subroutine that can be used to send the correct characters to display the current choice of what day of the week we are setting the clock to on the LCD. It uses the switch and case directive to decide what day to display, depending upon the current value stored in the global variable "daynumber."

Line 199 switch (daynumber)

This is the switch directive that will be using the value in the variable "daynumber" to determine which "case" function is selected.

Line 201 case 1 :

This is the first of seven possible choices the PIC could make. If the value in the variable "daynumber" was "1," then the PIC would choose this case function. Note the use of the ":" colon at the end of the instruction.

Line 203 Mon;

This is the macro which was defined on line 39. It makes the PIC carry out the three instructions that will send the characters "Mon" to the LCD.

Line 204 line2 ();

This calls the subroutine to send the cursor on the LCD to the beginning of the second line of the LCD.

Line 206 break;

This is the last instruction of the case "1" function. It will make the PIC break away from the list of "case" statements in this switch function. The PIC will exit this subroutine "displayday" and go back to where it called this subroutine from and carry on with the rest of the program.

Lines 207–242 do exactly the same, but for the other six sets of three characters for the remaining days of the week.

Line 245 void setClock ()

This sets up the subroutine that allows the user to set the correct day of the week and time, using the three buttons.

Line 247 writeString ("Set The Day");

This calls the subroutine "writeString" to send the phrase "Set The Day" to the LCD.

Line 248 line2 ();

This sends the cursor to the beginning of the second line on the LCD. We could achieve the same using the "cursorPos" subroutine, that is, using the instruction "cursor (2,0);".

Line 249 while (!setbutton)

This sets up a test that will be true while the logic on the "setButton" was a logic '0'. This test will be true while no one has pressed the "setButton." Pressing the "setButton" means the user wants to confirm the setting of that number and move on to the next one. Therefore, this instruction makes the PIC carry out the instructions between the opening and closing curly brackets on lines 250 and 260 while the "setButton" has not been pressed. I feel I should point out that with this program I am using buttons that are normally at 0V, or logic '0', as long as they have not been pressed. When the user presses these buttons, they will connect to +3.3V, that is, go to a logic '1'.

Line 251   if (incbutton) debounce ();

This is testing to see if the "incbutton" has been pressed. Pressing the "incbutton" will send the logic on the input to a logic '1'. If the "incbutton" has been pressed, the PIC must carry out the instruction "debounce ()". This calls the "debounce" subroutine to create a delay of around 13ms to overcome the problem with switch bounce.

Line 252 if (incbutton) daynumber ++;

This is asking the same type of test, which will be true if the logic on the "incbutton" input had really gone high to a logic '1'. If the test is true, then the PIC will carry out the instruction "daynumber ++". This will simply increment the value stored in the variable "daynumber." The value in this variable will be used to decide which day of the week is displayed on the LCD, in the subroutine "displayday."

Line 253   while (incbutton);

This gets the PIC to do nothing while the logic on the "incbutton" is still high. It is really getting the PIC to wait until the user had released the "incbutton." Note the PIC could have done a lot of things in the time we humans could have pressed and released a simple button.

Lines 254–256 do the same kind of action as that with the increment button, except they test to see if the decrement button had been pressed. If it has, then the PIC should decrement the value in the variable "daynumber."

Line 257 if (daynumber == 8) daynumber = 1;

This is testing to see if the last increment, from line 252, would have incremented the variable "daynumber" to 8, which is above the maximum value we could store in it. If it did, then the PIC must change the value back to 1. This means we can't increase the variable "daynumber" greater than 7. This is because there are only seven days in a week.

Line 258 if (daynumber == 0) daynumber = 1;

This works in the same way as the previous instruction on line 257, except that it prevents us from decrementing the value in "daynumber" lower than 1.

Line 259 displayday();

This calls the subroutine to display the current day characters set by the value stored in the variable "daynumber" on the LCD. This is so that the user can see the day changing as they decrement or increment the variable.

Line 261 debounce ();

The PIC will have come to this instruction because the user has pressed the "setbutton." This means that the logic on that button will no longer be a logic '0', that is, not at (!setbutton). This means that the test on line 249 will be untrue. This would have then caused the PIC to jump to this instruction on line 261.

The PIC will go to the "debounce" subroutine to allow the logic on the "setbutton" to settle down to a logic '1'.

Line 262 while (setbutton);

This gets the PIC to do nothing while the logic on the "setbutton" is at a logic '1', that is, high. This is waiting for the user to release the "setbutton" and allow the logic to go low, that is, to a logic '0.

line 263 clearTheScreen ();

This calls the subroutine to clear the LCD screen of any characters and return the cursor to the beginning of the screen.

Line 264 cursorPos (1,1);

This calls the subroutine "cursorPos" to position the cursor on line 1 and column 1. Note the column 1 is one character in from the first character position on the line.

Line 265 writeString ("Set The Clock");

This sends the phrase "Set The Clock" to the LCD.

Line 266 while (!setbutton)

This gets the PIC to carry out the instructions between the opening and closing curly brackets on lines 267 and 308 while the logic on the "setbutton" is low, that is, at a logic '0'. This would be the situation while no one has pressed the "setbutton."

To try and prevent too much repetition, I will restrict my analysis to the instructions that I think need further analysis, above what we have already done with similar instructions. I hope I don't miss some instructions you would have liked further analysis on.

Line 270 lcdData = 0x3A;

This is loading the variable "lcdData" with 0x3A which is the ASCII for the colon ":". This will then be sent to the LCD with the next instruction.

Line 276 shiftcurleft (1);

This is calling the subroutine "shiftcurleft (1)". This will shift the cursor one place to the left. This will actually move the cursor back one place so that it is under the "hourunits" number we have just sent to the screen. This is because we may want to change the number, and so we want to see it change as we increment or decrement it.

This instruction is included in the listing to show you how we can move the cursor around a screen that is currently displaying values. However, we don't need to do this as we are in a loop while the "setbutton" has not been pressed, and in that loop, we keep refreshing all the characters on the LCD. This means that any changes will be reflected in the next screen refresh.

Line 280 if(hourunits == 0x3A)

Lines 277–279 look at the increment button. This instruction on line 280 asks if the last increment caused the value in the "hourunits" variable to go to 0x3A. This would mean that we would have increased the value to one more than 9. This cannot be allowed. Therefore, if we had incremented the variable to 0x3A, then the PIC must carry out the instructions between the opening and closing curly brackets on lines 281 and 284.

Line 282 hourunits = 0x30;

This is the first instruction we must do if we had tried to increment the value in the variable "hourunits" passed 9, which resets the value in the variable "hourunits" to 0x30, which is the ASCII for 0.

Line 283 hourtens ++;

This is the second instruction, which will increment the value in the "hourtens" variable. However, we must realize that this increment may, or may not, have increased the value in the "hourtens" variable above its maximum, which is "2."

Line 285 if (hourtens == 0x32 & hourunits == 0x34)

This is a test to see if two tests are true, that is, if the variable "hourtens" has become equal to 0x32, and the variable "hourunits" has become equal to 0x34. Note, 0x32 is the ASCII for "2" and 0x34 is the ASCII for "4."

Therefore, we are really testing to see if the hour variables have become equal to 24, as a result of the last increment from the instruction on line 283. If they have, then the hour time should reset to 00.

Lines 286 and 287 are the two instructions that will reset the hour display to 00.

Line 293 if (hourunits == 0x30)

This is testing to see if the decrement instructions on lines 290 and 291 have resulted in the "hourunits" becoming equal to 0. If they have, then the "hourunits" should change to 0x39, that is, 9, and we should decrement the "hourtens" variable.

Line 297 if (hourtens ==0x2F)

This is testing to see if the decrement of the "hourtens" on line 296 has resulted in the "hourtens" variable becoming equal to 0x2F. Note, 0x30 – 1 will result in 0x2F. This is using the hexadecimal number system.

This cannot be allowed, as it would mean the "hourtens" value is less than 0. Therefore, we must set the "hourtens" and "hourunits" variables back to 0. This is done with the instructions on lines 299 and 300.

Line 303 else hourunits --;

This is what the PIC should do if the test on line 293 was not true. The PIC should simply decrement the variable "hourunits."

Line 307 if (setbutton) goto minset;

This is testing to see if the "setbutton" input has gone high, that is, to a logic '1.' It is the second of the "if (setbutton)" test, which is done after the PIC has waited the debounce time, and it is used to make sure the "setbutton" had been pressed. If the test is true and the "setbutton" had been pressed, then it would mean the user has set the time for the hour display and wants to now move on to set the time for the minute display. This is achieved by getting the PIC to carry out the instruction "goto minset." Minset is a label that is on line 309, and it is where the PIC will go to start the process of setting the time for the minutes.

If the test is untrue, that is, the "setbutton" has not been pressed, then the PIC will stay in the while loop, set up on line 249, and carry on changing the hour display.

Line 309 minset: line2 ();

This is the label that the PIC will go to from line 307.

We then display the word Minutes.

Line 318 setmins: lcdData = mintens;

Here, we are creating another label "setmins." The PIC will come here again when it carries out the goto instruction on line 347. The instruction on line 318 is simply loading the variable "lcdData" with a copy of what is in the variable "mintens." This is to get it ready to display the "mintens" on the LCD. This is done with the next instruction.

Lines 320 and 321 send the value of the "minunits" to the LCD.

Line 322 shiftcurleft (2);

This now shifts the cursor two places back to the left. Again, this is just to show you how you can move the cursor around the screen. It is not needed, for the program will refresh the display, as we did with the hour tens and units.

Lines 323–345 have the instructions to set the value for the minute's tens and units in a similar fashion to how we set the hour tens and units.

Line 347 if (!setbutton) goto setmins;

This is how we make the PIC loop back to the label on line 318. If the logic on the "setbutton" is still a logic '0' – note the "!" symbol is C for NOT, which is another way of saying a logic '0' – then it means the setbutton has not been pressed, and we must carry on changing the values of the minute's tens and units.

This completes the subroutine that allows the user to set the current time on the display of the clock. Note, I have split the hours and minutes into tens and units, as we are using four characters to display the time, tens, and units for both hours and minutes.

Line 349 void   __ISR(0, ipl1) T1Interrupt()

This is creating the ISR for the timer1 interrupt. Note there are two underscores before the phrase "ISR". We are using the macro that is with the plib library.

Line 351 mT1ClearIntFlag();

The first thing we do is clear the timer1 interrupt flag. This is so that we can see it change to a logic '1' at the next match of the timer1 value with the PR1 value. If we had left the flag set at a logic '1', then the PIC would not see this change, and it is the change of state that triggers the interrupt.

Line 352 mT1IntEnable(0);

This disables the timer1 interrupt. This is done to stop the PIC from responding to the change of state on the timer1 flag, until we are ready for the PIC to respond.

Line 353 secunits ++;

This simply increments the value in the variable "secunits" as one second in time has now passed. We know this is true because the timer1 interrupt has happened.

Line 354 PORTA = secunits.

This is not needed for the actual program, but it does allow us to see that the PIC has carried out the ISR, and it allows us to keep a count of the number of seconds as they pass.

Line 355 mT1IntEnable(1);

This reenables the timer1 interrupt to allow the PIC to respond to the change of state on the timer1 interrupt flag.

Lines 357–439 are the instructions of the main loop in the program.

Line 360 T1CON = 0x0002;

This turns timer1 off while we set it up, that is, bit 15 = 0, and sets the divide rate to 1, which is no divide. It also sets the secondary oscillator, which is the external 32.768kHz crystal, as the source for timer1, that is, bit 1 is a logic '1'. This means timer1 will simply count at a frequency of 32.768kHz, which means that counting from 0 to 36,767 will take exactly one second.

Line 361 T1CON = 0x8000;

This simply turns timer1 on.

Line 362 T2CON = 0x0070;

This sets timer2 to use the PBCLK as its source with a divide rate of 256. This means it counts at a frequency of 140kHz with a tick of 7.11µs. This is so that it can take over the responsibility of the delays from timer1 used in the delays for the LCD routines.

Lines 365–376 are the usual instructions that set up the PIC.

Line 363 T2CON = 0x8000;

This simply turns timer2 on.

Line 377 OSCCONbits.SOSCEN = 1;

This instruction enables the secondary oscillator. We need to do this, as well as enable the external oscillator, using the configuration words, as we did in line 20.

Line 378 PR1 = 32767;

This loads the PR1 register with the value that timer1 must match. When the match occurs, the timer1 interrupt flag can change from logic '0' to logic '1'. This assumes the flag has previously been set to a logic '0'. We do this in the ISR; see line 351.

Line 379   __builtin_disable_interrupts();

This disables all possible interrupts for the time being. It is good practice to do this while you set up the different interrupts.

Lines 380–383 set up the timer1 interrupt. Note, with line 383, we are disabling the timer1 interrupt as we don't want to use the interrupt until after we have set the current time for the clock.

Line 384 __builtin_enable_interrupts();

This now enables the PIC to respond to interrupts, as we have finished setting up the interrupts. This is using a built-in instruction in the compiler software. Line 379 is also using a built-in instruction.

Lines 385–387 have been looked at in previous listings.

Line 388   setClock ();

This calls the subroutine to allow the user to set the current time for the clock.

Line 392 mT1IntEnable(1);

This is using a macro instruction that is in the plib library that enables the timer1 interrupt. This is so that the program can increment the "secunits" once every second. It is the "secunits" variable that synchronizes the change to the clock display. We have delayed enabling the timer1 interrupt to now, because we didn't want it to interrupt the setting of the clock.

Lines 393–424 control how the "hourtens," "hourunits," "mintens," and "minunits" variables change to display the current time. The instructions work in a similar way to the instructions in the "setClock" subroutine. I hope you can use that analysis to understand how these instructions work.

Line 425 cursorPos (1,1);

This calls the "cursorPos" subroutine to move the cursor to line 1 at column 1. The first number in the normal brackets is the line number, and the second number is the column number. This moves the cursor to the first line on the LCD, but moves it to the second position on that line.

Line 426   displayday();

This calls the subroutine to display the characters that state the current day on the LCD. The actual set of characters that are displayed is controlled by the value in the variable "daynumber."

Line 427   line2 ();

This calls the subroutine to move the cursor to the beginning of the second line on the LCD.

Line 428 lcdData = hourtens;

This loads the variable "lcdData" with a copy of what is in the variable "hourtens." The next line sends the contents of "lcdData" to the LCD.

Lines 430–437 send the remaining values to display the time to the LCD. Note line 432 sends the ASCII 0x3A which is the ASCII for the colon ":" to the LCD.

Lines 438 and 439 are the closing curly brackets for the loops in the program.

I hope there is enough analysis for you to understand how the instructions for the program work and allow the PIC to do what is asked of it. It is always a trade-off between explaining too much and not enough. I hope I have got it right.

Figure 9-1 shows the external RTC program working.

Figure 9-1. *The External RTC Program*

The next program will use an array of four seven-segment displays to show a 24-hour clock, displaying the hours and minutes. The display is the same as those you see on a microwave. It has a semicolon that flashes between the hour and minute display. This is used to show the seconds passing.

The TM1637 and the Four Seven-Segment Displays

To display the time, we will use the TM1637 IC that will allow the PIC to communicate with the four seven-segment displays.

The actual device we will use in this project is shown in Figure 9-2.

Figure 9-2. *The Four Seven-Segment Displays*

This is a very inexpensive display that uses the TM1637 driver IC to communicate with a microcontroller, that is, a PIC micro. This IC allows the display to be controlled by just two outputs from the PIC. It also requires VCC and ground, but that means it uses just four connections. We have looked at using the PIC to drive a seven-segment display in Chapter 2.

We will have to learn how the TM1637 communicates with the PIC. It uses a protocol that is similar to the I²C protocol, but it is **NOT** I²C. It is a protocol that the engineers in Titan have come up with themselves. The following is my explanation of how we can use this protocol with the PIC to communicate with the display using the TM1637.

The TM1637 Driver IC

This is a 20-pin device that can control up to six seven-segment displays. It can also take inputs from a digital keypad. We will use it to control the four seven-segment displays on the module shown in Figure 9-2. We must send a series of command bytes, followed by a series of data bytes, that will turn on and off the LEDs in the seven-segment displays.

Table 9-1 lists the four basic commands we will use.

Table 9-1. *The Table for the Commands for the TM1637*

Bit 7	Bit 6	Bit 5	Bit 4	Bit 3	Bit 2	Bit 1	Bit 0	Usage
0	1	0	0	0	0	0	0	Write data to display registers Normal mode Automatically increase the address pointer
0	1	0	0	0	0	1	0	Read key scan data
0	1	0	0	0	1	0	0	Fixed address
0	1	0	0	1	0	0	0	Test mode

We will be using the normal mode, as it allows us to write data to the display register. The TM1637 uses an address pointer that will start with the address that we initially send to it. After that, the TM1637 will automatically increase the address pointer after we have written data to the current display register.

Table 9-2 lists the six data registers and their addresses that we will use.

Table 9-2. *The Address of the Data Registers for the Seven-Segment Displays*

Bit 7	Bit 6	Bit 5	Bit 4	Bit 3	Bit 2	Bit 1	Bit 0	Usage
1	1	0	0	0	0	0	0	CH0 Display 0
1	1	0	0	0	0	0	1	CH1 Display 1
1	1	0	0	0	0	1	0	CH2 Display 2
1	1	0	0	0	0	1	1	CH3 Display 3
1	1	0	0	0	1	0	0	CH4 Display 4
1	1	0	0	0	1	0	1	CH5 Display 5

The TM1637 gives us the ability to adjust the brightness of the displays. The different command bytes for the brightness settings are shown in Table 9-3.

Table 9-3. *The Command Bytes to Set the Brightness of the Display*

Bit 7	Bit 6	Bit 5	Bit 4	Bit 3	Bit 2	Bit 1	Bit 0	Usage
1	0	0	0	1	0	0	0	1/16 PWM set to 1/16
1	0	0	0	1	0	0	1	2/16 PWM set to 2/16
1	0	0	0	1	0	1	0	4/16 PWM set to 4/16
1	0	0	0	1	0	1	1	10/16 PWM set to 10/16
1	0	0	0	1	1	0	0	11/16 PWM set to 11/16
1	0	0	0	1	1	0	1	12/16 PWM set to 12/16
1	0	0	0	1	1	1	0	13/16 PWM set to 13/16
1	0	0	0	1	1	1	1	14/16 PWM set to 14/16

This brightness variation is achieved by varying the voltage across the LEDs with a pulse-width modulated signal. We will set the LEDs to maximum brightness. Note, if bit 3 of the command was set to a logic '0', then the display would be switched off.

As we are only using four displays, we will use the first four addresses. I will refer to these addresses as

1. **First**: 0b11000000

2. **Second**: 0b11000001

3. **Third**: 0b11000010

4. **Fourth**: 0b11000011

To communicate correctly with the TM1637, we must follow the correct procedure. I believe this procedure is their homemade protocol.

The procedure is as follows.

The Two Communication Lines

There are only two lines required to communicate with the TM1637, and they are

- **CLK**: This is a pseudo clock signal that we must create. This has to change at a frequency of less than 250kHz.

- **DIO**: This is the line that carries the information to the TM1637. The data on this line can only change when the clock signal is high.

These will be outputs from the PIC, and we can use any available output.

The Start Signal for the TM1637

We must create a start signal:

- Starting with the clock line low, we send the CLK to a logic '1'.

- At the same time, we drive the dio line from low to high.

- We then create a 2µs delay.

- After that, we drive the dio line back low.

It is this transition from high to low on the dio line while the clock is high that is interpreted as the start signal by the TM1637.

The First Command Signal to the TM1637

We must now put the TM1637 into normal mode. This is done by sending the command 0b01000000 or 0x40; see Table 9-1.

The Acknowledgment Signal for the TM1637

The TM1637 will now inform us that it has received the command by sending back an acknowledgment signal. The TM1637 must drive the DIO line low, starting at the negative, or falling edge, of the eighth clock signal, as the eighth bit of information has just been sent. This is the acknowledgment signal.

The Stop Signal for the TM1637

The PIC must now send a stop signal to the TM1637 to give it time to set itself into this normal mode of operation. The stop signal is achieved by sending the dio line from low to high while the clock line is high.

Another Start Signal

The PIC must now send another start signal.

The First Address

The PIC now sends the address of the first register it wants to write to. This would be the address of CH0, the first of the four seven-segment displays. The binary value for this is 0b11000000 or 0xC0. The TM1637 would open this register ready for the PIC to send the data to it.

Another Acknowledgment

After the PIC has sent the first address, the TM1637 would respond with an acknowledgment signal.

The First Data

The PIC now sends the data to turn on or off the LEDs on the first seven-segment display.

Another Acknowledgment

The TM1637 would respond with an acknowledgment signal. The TM1637 would also automatically increment the contents of its address pointer and so open the next address register ready for some new data.

The Remaining Data

The PIC now sends the data for the second, third, and fourth seven-segment displays with the TM1637 sending an acknowledgment signal between them.

The Final Stop Signal

After the PIC has received the last acknowledgment signal, the PIC must send a stop signal.

Setting the Brightness of the Display

Now the PIC sends a final start signal which is followed with a command to set the brightness of the display.

After this final command, the PIC should get a final acknowledgment from the TM1637, and the PIC would then send a final stop signal to end all communication.

This process may look similar to the I^2C protocol, but the start and stop signals are not the same, and the information is sent out serially, sending the LSB first. The I^2C sends the MSB first.

The program must conform to the preceding procedure, and the program we will create will have two sections:

- Section one allows the user to set the time of the clock. This will involve the use of three switches, which are

  - Increment on bit 0 of PORTF

  - Decrement on bit 1 of PORTF

  - Set on bit 2 of PORTF

- Then, after we have set the clock, the time will be displayed on the set of four seven-segment displays. The time will be synchronized to the interrupts from the external crystal.

The two outputs for the clock and dio lines are

- CLK on bit 0 of PORTB

- DIO on bit 1 of PORTB

The program listing for the project is shown in Listing 9-2.

Listing 9-2.

```
1  /*
2  * File:    rtcFour7SegProg.c
3  Author: Mr H. H Ward
4  *A set of four 7 segment displays used to
5  display a 24hr clock
6  Created on 18 December 2021, 22:27
7  */
8  // PIC32MX360F512L Configuration Bit Settings
9  // 'C' source line config statements
10 // DEVCFG3
11 #pragma config USERID = 0xFFFF
12 // DEVCFG2
13 #pragma config FPLLIDIV = DIV_2
14 #pragma config FPLLMUL = MUL_18
15 #pragma config FPLLODIV = DIV_1
16 // DEVCFG1
17 #pragma config FNOSC = PRIPLL
18 #pragma config FSOSCEN = ON
19 #pragma config IESO = OFF
20 #pragma config POSCMOD = XT
21 #pragma config OSCIOFNC = ON
22 #pragma config FPBDIV = DIV_1
23 #pragma config FCKSM = CSDCMD
24 #pragma config WDTPS = PS1048576
25 #pragma config FWDTEN = OFF
```

```
26   // DEVCFG0
27   #pragma config DEBUG = OFF
28   #pragma config ICESEL = ICS_PGx2
29   #pragma config PWP = OFF
30   #pragma config BWP = OFF
31   #pragma config CP = OFF
32   // #pragma config statements should precede project file
     includes.
33   // Use project enums instead of #define for ON and OFF.
34   #include <xc.h>
35   #include <peripheral/int.h>
36   //some definitions
37   #define clk        PORTBbits.RB0
38   #define dio        PORTBbits.RB1
39   #define zero       0b00111111
40   #define one        0b00000110
41   #define two        0b01011011
42   #define three      0b01001111
43   #define four       0b01100110
44   #define five       0b01101101
45   #define six        0b01111100
46   #define seven      0b00000111
47   #define eight      0b01111111
48   #define nine       0b01100111
49   #define incButton PORTFbits.RF0
50   #define decButton PORTFbits.RF1
51   #define setButton PORTFbits.RF2
52   // declare any variables
53   unsigned char count, secUnits, minUnits = 3, minTens =
     2, hourUnits = 1, hourTens = 0, first = zero, second =
     one,third = two, fourth = three;
54   unsigned char n,m, nt;
```

```
55   //some subroutines
56   void debounce ()
57   {
58   TMR2 = 0;
59   while (TMR2 <2000 );
60   }
61   void delay(unsigned char t)
62   {
63   for(nt = 0; nt < t; nt++)
64   {
65   TMR2 = 0;
66   while (TMR2 <35160);
67   }
68   }
69   //some arrays
70   unsigned char displaynumber [10] =
71   {
72   zero,
73   one,
74   two,
75   three,
76   four,
77   five,
78   six,
79   seven,
80   eight,
81   nine,
82   };
83   //some more subroutines
84   void delayus (unsigned char t)
```

```
 85  {
 86  TMR3 = 0;
 87  while (TMR3 < t);
 88  }
 89  void tmStart ()
 90  {
 91  clk = 1;
 92  dio = 1;
 93  delayus (2);
 94  dio = 0;
 95  }
 96  void tmAck ()
 97  {
 98  clk = 0;
 99  delayus (5);
100  while (dio);
101  clk = 1;
102  delayus (2);
103  clk = 0;
104  }
105  void tmStop ()
106  {
107  clk = 0;
108  delayus (2);
109  dio = 0;
110  delayus (2);
111  clk = 1;
112  delayus (2);
113  dio = 1;
114  }
115  void tmByteWrite (unsigned char tmByte)
116  {
```

```
117   for (m = 0; m <8; m++)
118   {
119   clk = 0;
120   if (tmByte & 0x01) dio = 1;
121   else dio = 0;
122   delayus (3);
123   tmByte = tmByte >> 1;
124   clk = 1;
125   delayus (3);
126   }
127   }
128   void displaySet()
129   {
130   tmStart();
131   tmByteWrite(0x40);
132   tmAck();
133   tmStop();
134   tmStart();
135   tmByteWrite(0xc0);
136   tmAck();
137   tmByteWrite(first);
138   tmAck();
139   tmByteWrite(second);
140   tmAck();
141   tmByteWrite(third);
142   tmAck();
143   tmByteWrite(fourth);
144   tmAck();
145   tmStop();
146   tmStart();
147   tmByteWrite(0x8f);
```

```
148   tmAck();
149   tmStop();
150   }
151   void displayMsg()
152   {
153   second = second ^(0b10000000);
154   tmStart();
155   tmByteWrite(0x40);
156   tmAck();
157   tmStop();
158   tmStart();
159   tmByteWrite(0xc0);
160   tmAck();
161   tmByteWrite(first);
162   tmAck();
163   tmByteWrite(second);
164   tmAck();
165   tmByteWrite(third);
166   tmAck();
167   tmByteWrite(fourth);
168   tmAck();
169   tmStop();
170   tmStart();
171   tmByteWrite(0x8f);
172   tmAck();
173   tmStop();
174   }
175   void setTime ()
176   {
177   while (!setButton)
178   {
```

```
179  //sethours
180  while (!setButton)
181  {
182  displaySet();
183  first = displaynumber [hourTens];
184  if (incButton)debounce ();
185  if (incButton)
186  {
187  if (hourTens < 2)hourTens ++;
188  else hourTens = 2;
189  first = displaynumber [hourTens];
190  while (incButton);
191  debounce ();
192  while (incButton);
193  }
194  if (decButton)debounce ();
195  if (decButton)
196  {
197  if (hourTens > 0)hourTens --;
198  else hourTens = 0;
199  first = displaynumber [hourTens];
200  while (decButton);
201  debounce ();
202  while (decButton);
203  }
204  }
205  while (setButton);
206  debounce ();
207  while (setButton);
208  while (!setButton)
209  {
210  displaySet();
```

```
211  second = displaynumber [hourUnits];
212  if (incButton)debounce ();
213  if (incButton)
214  {
215  if (hourUnits < 9)hourUnits ++;
216  else hourUnits = 9;
217  second = displaynumber [hourUnits];
218  while (incButton);
219  debounce ();
220  while (incButton);
221  }
222  if (decButton)debounce ();
223  if (decButton)
224  {
225  if (hourUnits > 0)hourUnits --;
226  else hourUnits = 0;
227  second = displaynumber [hourUnits];
228  while (decButton);
229  debounce ();
230  while (decButton);
231  }
232  }
233  while (setButton);
234  debounce ();
235  while (setButton);
236  //set minutes
237  while (!setButton)
238  {
239  displaySet();
240  third = displaynumber [minTens];
241  if (incButton)debounce ();
```

```
242  if (incButton)
243  {
244  if (minTens < 5)minTens ++;
245  else minTens = 5;
246  third = displaynumber [minTens];
247  while (incButton);
248  debounce ();
249  while (incButton);
250  }
251  if (decButton)debounce ();
252  if (decButton)
253  {
254  if (minTens > 0)minTens --;
255  else minTens = 0;
256  third = displaynumber [minTens];
257  while (decButton);
258  debounce ();
259  while (decButton);
260  }
261  }
262  debounce ();
263  while (setButton);
264  debounce ();
265  while (setButton);
266  while (!setButton)
267  {
268  displaySet();
269  fourth = displaynumber [minUnits];
270  if (incButton)debounce ();
271  if (incButton)
272  {
```

```
273  if (minUnits < 9)minUnits ++;
274  else minUnits = 9;
275  fourth = displaynumber [minUnits];
276  while (incButton);
277  debounce ();
278  while (incButton);
279  }
280  if (decButton )debounce ();
281  if (decButton)
282  {
283  if (minUnits > 0) minUnits --;
284  else minUnits = 0;
285  fourth = displaynumber [minUnits];
286  while (decButton);
287  debounce ();
288  while (decButton);
289  }
290  }
291  debounce ();
292  while (setButton);
293  debounce ();
294  while (setButton);
295  return;
296  }
297  }
298  void  __ISR(0, ipl1) T1Interrupt()
299  {
300  mT1ClearIntFlag();
301  mT1IntEnable( 0);
302  secUnits ++;
303  PORTA = secUnits;
```

```
304  displayMsg();
305  mT1IntEnable( 1);
306  }
307  main (void)
308  {
309  // set up timers
310  T1CON = 0x8002;
311  T2CON = 0x8070;
312  T3CON = 0x8070;
313  //initalize the ports etc
314  TRISA = 0x00000080;
315  TRISB = 0x00000000;
316  TRISC = 0x00000000;
317  TRISD = 0x00000007;
318  TRISE = 0x00000000;
319  PORTA = 0;
320  PORTB = 0;
321  PORTC = 0;
322  PORTD = 0;
323  PORTE = 0;
324  AD1PCFG = 0xFFFF;
325  AD1CON1 = 0;
326  OSCCONbits.SOSCEN = 1;
327  DDPCONbits.JTAGEN = 0;
328  PR1 = 32767;
329  __builtin_disable_interrupts();
330  mT1ClearIntFlag();
331  mT1SetIntPriority( 1);
332  INTEnableSystemSingleVectoredInt();
333  mT1IntEnable( 0);
334  __builtin_enable_interrupts();
```

```
335   setTime ();
336   mT1IntEnable( 1);
337   while (1)
338   {
339   if (secUnits == 60)
340   {
341   minUnits ++;
342   secUnits = 0;
343   if (minUnits == 10)
344   {
345   minUnits = 0;
346   minTens ++;
347   if (minTens == 6)
348   {
349   minTens = 0;
350   hourUnits ++;
351   if (hourTens < 2)
352   {
353   if (hourUnits == 10)
354   {
355   hourUnits = 0;
356   hourTens ++;
357   }
358   }
359   else if (hourTens == 2)
360   {
361   if (hourUnits == 4)
362   {
363   hourUnits = 0;
364   hourTens =0;
365   }
```

```
366  }
367  }
368  }
369  fourth = displaynumber [minUnits];
370  third = displaynumber [minTens];
371  second = displaynumber [hourUnits];
372  first = displaynumber [hourTens];
373  }
374  }
375  }
```

Analysis of Listing 9-2

Lines 1–35 are the same as those in Listing 9-1, apart from some of the comments.

Lines 37 and 38 define which outputs the CLK and DIO lines are allocated to.

Lines 39–48 define the phrases for the binary values to be sent to the seven-segment displays to display the appropriate number. The seven-segment displays on this module are of the type common cathode.

Lines 49–51 allocate the three buttons to the inputs of the PIC.

Lines 53 and 54 set out the usual variables, and some of them are given some initial values. This is so that there are some set numbers displayed on the four seven-segment displays when the PIC is turned on. Note we are using decimal values here, instead of hexadecimal. This is because we are not using ASCII codes for the display.

Lines 55–69 are the subroutines for the two delays we use in the program.

Lines 70–82 set up an array to store the binary values for the numbers zero to nine. Note these phrases have been defined in lines 40–48.

Lines 84–88 set up the subroutine "delayus" to create a delay based on a resolution of microseconds. This delay uses timer3.

Line 89 void tmStart ()

This creates a subroutine to create the start signal for the TM1637.

Line 91 clk = 1;

This sends the clock signal high.

Line 92 dio = 1;

This sends the dio signal high.

Line 93 delayµs (2);

This calls the microsecond delay subroutine to create a 2µs delay. This is simply to keep the dio line high for a short period of time.

Line 94 dio = 0;

This sends the DIO line low. It is the transition from high to low on the DIO line while the CLK line is high that is the start signal to the TM1637.

Line 96 void tmAck ()

This creates a subroutine that will set up the PIC to wait for an acknowledgment signal from the TM1637.

Line 98 clk = 0;

This simply sends the clock signal low.

Line 99 delayus (5);

This makes the PIC wait 5µs.

Line 100 while (dio);

This makes the PIC do nothing while the dio line is high.

The TM1637 will send an acknowledgment signal by driving the dio line low. The instruction on line 98 sends the clock signal low to create the negative edge that tells the TM1637 to send the acknowledgment signal back to the PIC. The TM1637 sends the acknowledgment signal by driving the dio line low. The instruction on line 100 makes the PIC wait for this to happen.

Lines 101 and 102 send the clock signal high, then wait 2μs before sending the clock back low on line 103.

Line 105 void tmStop ()

This subroutine creates the stop signal that the PIC must send to the TM1637.

The subroutine sends the clk and dio lines low. It then sends the clk high and then the dio high. It is this transition from low to high on the dio line while the clk is high that creates the stop signal.

Line 115 void tmByteWrite (unsigned char tmByte)

This subroutine allows the PIC to send 8 bits, that is, a byte, of data to the TM1637, one bit at a time. This subroutine expects a value to be sent up to it, which is copied into the local variable "tmByte."

Line 117 for (m = 0; m <8; m++)

This creates a "for do loop" that loops eight times, once for each bit.

Line 119 clk = 0;

This sends the clk line low. This is to ensure the clock signal is low while data is being sent on the dio line.

Line 120 if (tmByte & 0x01) dio = 1;

This is testing to see if the LSB, that is, bit 0, of the "tmByte" is a logic '1.' It is done by performing a logic AND with the 8 bits in the variable "tmByte" and the data 0x01, which is 0b00000001 in binary. This logical

AND test will only be true if the LSB of "tmByte" is a logic '1'. This means we are simply testing to see if the LSB of "tmByte" was a logic '1'. If it was, then we must send the dio line to a logic '1'. This is what is done with the instruction on line 120.

Line 121 else dio = 0;

This is what the PIC must do if the test on line 120 was untrue. If the test was untrue, then it would mean the LSB was a logic '0'. Note if the test on line 120 was true, then the PIC would skip this instruction.

Line 122 delayµs (3);

This creates a 3µs delay.

Line 123 tmByte = tmByte >> 1;

This shifts the 8 bits in the variable "tmByte" one bit to the right. The example in Table 9-4 should help explain what happens.

Table 9-4.

Example Data	MSB Bit 7	Bit 6	Bit 5	Bit 4	Bit 3	Bit 2	Bit 1	LSB Bit 0
Before shift	1	1	0	0	1	0	0	1
After shift	0	1	1	0	0	1	0	0

We can see that what was on the LSB before the shift is lost, and the LSB is replaced by what was in bit 1. Also, the MSB is now replaced by a logic '0', and the data that was in bit 7 has now gone to bit 6, etc.

This instruction is moving the bits to the LSB ready for the next test in line 120 as the PIC loops through the "for do loop."

Line 124 clk = 1;

This now sends the clk signal high.

Line 125 delayµs (3);

This creates a 3µs delay.

The PIC now loops through the "for do loop" another seven times, so that it can send all 8 bits in the variable "tmByte" to the TM1637. Note it does send the LSB bit first.

Line 128 void displaySet()

This is a subroutine to send the commands and data to the TM1637 to initially set up the seven-segment display.

Line 130 tmStart();

This calls the subroutine to send the initial start signal.

Line 131 tmByteWrite(0x40);

This calls the subroutine to send a byte of data to the TM1637. The instruction will send the value 0x40, which will be copied into the local variable "tmByte." This value of 0x40 is the command data to put the TM1637 into normal mode; see Table 9-1.

Line 132 tmAck();

This calls the "tmAck" subroutine that gets the PIC to wait for the acknowledgment signal from the TM1637.

Line 133 tmStop();

This gets the PIC to create the stop signal.

Line 134 tmStart();

This creates another start signal.

Line 135 tmByteWrite(0xC0);

The sends the data 0xC0 to the TM1637. 0xC0 is the address of the first seven-segment display; see Table 9-2.

Line 136 tmAck();

This calls the "tmAck" subroutine that gets the PIC to wait for the acknowledgment signal from the TM1637.

Line 137 tmByteWrite(first);

This sends the data in the variable "first" to the TM1637. This is the data to send the appropriate number to the first of the four seven-segment displays. This will be the data for the hour tens display. The variable "first" has been declared on line 53. It was given the initial value identified by the term "zero." The term "zero" has been defined on line 39 to the binary value that will display the number "0" on the seven-segment display. After this data has been sent, the TM1637 will automatically increment the address pointer, so that it is now pointing to the address of the next seven-segment display. This gets it ready for the next data to be sent to the TM1637.

Line 138 tmAck();

This calls the "tmAck" subroutine, which gets the PIC to wait for the acknowledgment from the TM1637.

Lines 139–146 send the data to display the appropriate value to the remaining seven-segment displays, that is, the data in variables "second, third, and fourth"; see line 53.

Line 147 tmByteWrite(0x8F);

This sends the data 0x8F to the TM1637. This is the value to set the brightness of the display to a maximum.

The PIC now waits for an acknowledgment from the TM1637 and then sends the final stop signal to the TM1637.

Line 151 void displayMsg()

This creates a slightly different subroutine to the "displaySet" subroutine that is created on line 128. The "displaySet" subroutine is called from the subroutine that allows the user to set the time, whereas the "displayMsg" subroutine is called from the ISR.

The only difference between the two subroutines is on line 153.

Line 153 second = second ^(0b10000000);

This performs a logic EXOR with the data in the variable "second" and the data 0b10000000. This will simply make the MSB, bit 7, of the variable "second" toggle on and off, that is, change to a logic '1' or a logic '0', every time the PIC carries out this instruction. It is this MSB bit of the variable "second" that controls whether or not the colon between the hour units and minute tens in the seven-segment display is lit up. A logic '1' on this MSB will light the colon up, whereas a logic '0' will turn the colon off. We should realize that as this subroutine is called from within the ISR, then this toggling action will happen every second. This will make the colon continuously flash on for one second and then flash off for one second.

The rest of the instructions in the "displayMsg" subroutine are exactly the same as the "displaySet" subroutine. However, this one difference means we can't use the one subroutine.

Line 175 void setTime ()

This creates a subroutine that will allow the user to set the display to the correct time. It works in a similar way to the "setTime" subroutine in Listing 9-1. There are only a few slight differences which we will look at here.

Line 182 displaySet();

This simply calls the "displaySet" subroutine to show the changes as we make them.

Line 183 first = displaynumber [hourTens];

461

This loads the variable "first" with the contents of the memory location in the array "displaynumber," as indicated by the value stored in the variable "hourTens." At the moment, as we have not incremented or decremented the variable "hourTens," then it will still have the initial value of "0" as stated on line 53. This means that the PIC will load the variable "first" with the contents of the first memory location in the array "displaynumber." This will be signified by the phrase "zero"; see line 72. This phrase "zero" has been defined on line 39 as the binary value 0b00111111. This is the data required to display the number 0 on the seven-segment display.

Lines 183–192 are the instructions to increment or decrement the variable "hourTens" to set it to what we want.

Lines 193–297 perform similar operations on the variables second, third, and fourth to set the time correctly. Note I am using the "first" seven-segment display to display the "hour tens," with the hour units in the "second," the min tens in the "third," and the min units in the "fourth" seven-segment display.

Lines 298–306 are the ISR instructions. They are similar to the ISR instructions for Listing 9-1. On line 436, we are calling the subroutine "displayMsg();". This takes care of the instruction to turn on and off the colon on the display.

Lines 307–375 are the main instructions for the program. Most of them have been looked at before.

Line 312 T3CON = 0x8070;

This is used to set up timer3 as we are using it for the μs delay. Note, here, as with the other two timers, I am not keeping the timers turned off while I set them up. It does work either way, but it is up to you if you do it this way or use the practice of turning the timers off, and any other control register, while you set them up.

The while loop between lines 338 and 374 allow the interrupt to update the display at one-second intervals.

Lines 369–372 allow the PIC to load the variables fourth, third, second, and first with the appropriately updated data from the memory location in the array "displaynumber."

There are a lot of instructions to look at, but I hope this succinct analysis does, with its reference to the other listing, help you to understand how the instructions work. It is only with a deeper understanding of the instructions we use that we can become better programmers.

Figure 9-3 shows the 24-hour clock working with the four seven-segment displays.

Figure 9-3. *The 24-Hour Clock on the Four Seven-Segment Displays*

Summary

In this chapter, we have looked at how we can use the secondary oscillator to create a very accurate 24-hour clock display. We have learned how to display the clock on the LCD and then on a useful module that houses four seven-segment displays. We have studied how we can get the PIC to communicate with the TM1637 IC and so control the four seven-segment displays.

In the next two chapters, we will look at two fully integrated RTC, Real-Time Clock, systems. The first will use the useful module external to the PIC that is used by the Arduino to provide a real-time clock. This uses the DS1307 IC to communicate with an RTC module.

Then, in Chapter 11, we will look at the internal Real-Time Clock module that the 32-bit PIC has in it. This does make the 32-bit PIC a very useful PIC, as you can create a real-time clock program without buying an expensive module; you only need the external crystal oscillator that runs at 32.768kHz.

CHAPTER 10

The Real-Time Clock and the DS3231

In this chapter, we will continue our investigation into creating a very useful program, that of the Real-Time Clock. In Chapter 9, we looked at simply using the secondary oscillator to drive a 24-hour clock display. We wrote two programs, one for a simple LCD display and the other for a module with four seven-segment displays. In this chapter, we will look at using an external module that can be attached to the PIC32.

After reading this chapter, you will be able to program the DS3231 RTC module using the I²C protocol.

The DS3231 RTC Module

The program will use the DS3231 RTC module, shown in Figure 10-1. This is an external module that can be attached to the 32-bit PIC. It uses the I²C protocol to communicate with the PIC. We will use the LCD2004 display to show the time and date as the clock is running.

© Hubert Ward 2023
H. Ward, *Introductory Programs with the 32-bit PIC Microcontroller*,
Maker Innovations Series, https://doi.org/10.1007/978-1-4842-9051-4_10

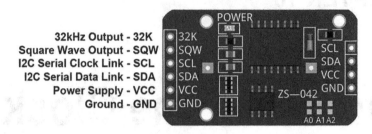

Figure 10-1. *The DS3231 RTC Module*

The DS3231 is an IC that can be used to create an RTC module as shown in Figure 10-1. It is a low-cost, extremely accurate Real-Time Clock (RTC) that uses an integrated temperature-compensated crystal oscillator (TCXO) and crystal. This module comes with a battery that can be used to keep the clock running, even when the PIC is turned off. However, we will not use that functionality. The RTC maintains seconds, minutes, hours, day, date, month, and year information. The date at the end of the month is automatically adjusted for months with fewer than 31 days, including corrections for leap year. It can be set to operate in either the 24-hour or 12-hour format with an am/pm indicator. Unlike the TM1637, the DS3231 has two programmable alarms. When the actual time matches the times set for one of the alarms, then the module can be used to interrupt the main program and run an alarm routine.

To be able to program the DS3231, we need to understand the functions that are available to us and how to set them up. Naturally, we will be able to set the current time and date, which means the program must give us the options to do that. However, the DS3231 can provide us with two separate alarms, that is, alarm 1 and alarm 2. Alarm 1 can be set to hours, minutes, and seconds and has the ability to go off at the intervals shown in Table 10-1.

Table 10-1. *The Data to Set the Frequency of Alarm 1*

Bit 6	Logic in Bit 7 of 4 Addresses				Alarm Repeat Rate
DY = 1	07, 08, 09, and 0A				
DT = 0	A1M4	A1M3	A1M2	A1M1	
X	1	1	1	1	Once a second
X	1	1	1	0	When a match with seconds occurs
X	1	1	0	0	When minutes and seconds match
X	1	0	0	0	When hours, minutes, and seconds match
0	0	0	0	0	When date, hours, minutes, and seconds match
1	0	0	0	0	When day, hours, minutes, and seconds match

Alarm 2 gives us a slightly different set of operations as it does not consider any seconds in the alarm time. Table 10-2 shows the options for alarm 2.

Table 10-2. *Data to Set the Frequency of Alarm 2*

Bit 6	Logic in Bit 7 of 4 Addresses			Alarm Repeat Rate
DY = 1	0B, 0C, and 0D			
DT = 0	A2M4	A2M3	A2M2	
X	1	1	1	Once a minute
X	1	1	0	When a match with minutes occurs
X	1	0	0	When hours and minutes match
0	0	0	0	When date, hours, and minutes match
1	0	0	0	When day, hours, and minutes match

There is one more register in the DS3231 that is used to configure the alarms, and that is the control register. Table 10-3 shows the bits of the control register.

Table 10-3. *The Bits of the Control Register at Address 0x0E*

Bit 7	Bit 6	Bit 5	Bit 4	Bit 3	Bit 2	Bit 1	Bit 0
$\overline{EOSC}$	BBSQW	CONV	RS2	RS1	INTCN	A2IE	A1IE

The bits in the control register have the following usage:

- **Bit 7 $\overline{EOSC}$** : This the Oscillator Enable bit. When the DS3231 is powered from the VCC input, then the oscillator is on regardless of the logic on this bit. However, if this bit is set to a logic '1', then the data in the DS3231 remains static. When the DS3231 is powered from the battery, the oscillator can be stopped by setting this bit to a logic '1'. If it is set to a logic '0', then the oscillator is running while the DS3231 is powered from the battery. This gives us the ability to save some battery power.

- **Bit 6 BBSQW**: The DS3231 has the ability to output a square wave signal. It is outputted on pin 3 of the chip. However, this pin has two uses: one for the square wave output signal and one for an interrupt signal when an alarm is activated. It is the logic on bit 2, the INTCN bit, of this control register that controls what use pin 3 is put to. This is bit 6 of the control register, and it has some control over the output on pin 3. If this bit 6 is a logic '1', then the square wave becomes available at the output of pin 3. However, the INTCN bit must be set to a logic '0' as well. When this bit 6 is set to a logic '0', then the square wave is disabled.

- **Bit 5 CONV bit**: The DS3231 has a temperature transducer on it. This is used to allow temperature compensation for the capacitance used to control the oscillator frequency. This gives the module the ability to maintain accuracy of the time, even when the ambient temperature varies. This CONV bit can be used to force the DS3231 to force the chip to convert the temperature reading to a 10-bit value that can be used by the program of the PIC to display the temperature. The transducer does get a reading every 64 seconds, but you can force the chip to get a reading at any time with this bit. Setting this CONV bit to a logic '1' will force the chip to get a reading from the transducer.

- **Bit 4 RS2:** This is used in conjunction with the logic on bit 3, RS1, to set the frequency of the square wave outputted on pin 3. Table 10-4 shows the available frequencies.

- **Bit 3 RS1:** This works in conjunction with bit 4.

- **Bit 2 INTCN bit:** This is the interrupt control bit, and when it is a logic '0', the output on pin 3 would be a square wave, assuming that bit 6 of this control register is set to a logic '1'. If the INTCN bit is set to a logic '1', then pin 3 of the chip will go low when a match with the current time and one of the two alarms occurs. This is assuming that the alarms have been enabled.

- **Bit 1 A2IE:** This enables alarm 2 to generate an interrupt when the current time matches the time for alarm 2.

- **Bit 0 A1IE:** This enables alarm 1 to generate an interrupt when the current time matches the time for alarm 1.

Table 10-4. *The Frequency Settings for the Square Wave Output on Pin 3*

RS2	RS1	Frequency of the Square Wave on Pin 3
0	0	1Hz
0	1	1.024kHz
1	0	4.096kHz
1	1	8.192kHz

As an example of how we can use this control register, we will set the DS3231 to work as follows:

- There will be no square wave outputted on pin 3.

- We will use the two alarms.

- We will allow the chip to obtain a temperature reading automatically.

This means that we will load the control register with the value 0b00000111. This means that both alarms are enabled and the square wave output on pin 3 is disabled.

We should appreciate that the data to set the time and date is loaded into memory location 0x00 to 0x06 in the DS3231. Then the data to set the alarms must be loaded into registers 0x07 to 0x0D. Next, the data for the control register must be loaded into address 0x0E. The registers of the DS3231 are shown in Table 10-5.

Table 10-5. The Registers on the DS3231

Address	B7	B6	B5	B4	B3	B2	B1	B0	Function
0x00	0		Sec Tens 0–5			Sec Units 0–9			Time seconds
0x01	0		Min Tens 0–5			Min Units 0–9			Time minutes
0x02	0	High 12 Low 24	$\overline{AM}$ / PM / Hr 20s	Hr Tens		Hour Units 0–9			Time hours
0x03	0	0	0	0	0		Day units 1–7		Day number
0x04	0	0	Date Tens 0–3			Date Units 0–9			Date number
0x05	Cent 0–9	0	0	Month Tens 0–1		Month Units 0–9			Month number or century
0x06			Year Tens 0–9			Year Units 0–9			Year number
0x07	A1M1		Sec Tens 0–5			Sec Units 0–9			Alarm 1 seconds
0x08	A1M2		Min Tens 0–5			Min Units 0–9			Alarm 1 minutes
0x09	A1M3	12 / $\overline{24}$	$\overline{AM}$ / PM / Hr 20s	Hour Tens 0–1		Hour Units 0–9			Alarm 1 hours

Register	Bit 7	Bit 6	Bit 5	Bit 4	Bit 3	Bit 2	Bit 1	Bit 0	Function
0x0A	A1M4	Day / Date	Tens 0–3		Units 0–9				Alarm 1 day / Alarm 1 date
0x0B	A2M2	Min Tens 0–5			Min Units 0–9				Alarm 2 minutes
0x0C	A2M3	$12/\overline{24}$	$\overline{AM}/PM$ (Hr 20s)	Hour Tens 0–1	Hour Units 0–9				Alarm 2 hours
0x0D	A2M4	Day / Date	Tens 0–3		Units 0–9				Alarm 2 day / Alarm 2 date
0x0E	$\overline{EOSC}$	BBSQW	CONV	RS2	RS1	INTCN	A2IE	A1IE	Control register
0x0F	OSF	0	0	0	32kHz	Bsy	A2F	A1F	Control status register
0x10	Sign	Data	Data	Data	Data	Data	Data	Data	Aging offset
0x11	Sign	Data	Data	Data	Data	Data	Data	Data	Temp high 8 bits
0x12	Data	Data	0	0	0	0	0	0	Temp low 2 bits

We need to understand this table and how the DS3231 expects the data to be sent to it and in what order. When we do understand this, we can then understand how to ask for data to set the DS3231 and in what order we need to write it to the DS3231.

The DS3231 uses an internal address pointer to control which address any data being sent to it is actually written to. It is simpler to set the address pointer in the DS3231 to address 0 at the start of the write sequence to the DS3231. This is because when we have written to the first location in the memory, the address pointer automatically increments so that it is pointing to the next location in the DS3231, ready for the next data to be sent to the DS3231. If we examine Table 10-5, we can see that this first address, 0x00, is where the DS3231 stores the data for the seconds of the time. This means that when setting the date and time, we should send the data for the seconds to the DS3231 first.

The DS3231 is constantly writing to the registers that it uses to control its format and store the current date and time. These are the registers as listed in Table 10-5. However, we have the ability to write to these same registers when we need to set the time and date. This is just what you expect, so why am I stating what should be obvious now? Well, really, it's only when you want to use the DS3231 in 12-hour format, and not 24-hour format, that you need to understand more fully how to use these registers. Working in 24-hour format is much simpler than using 12-hour format. To appreciate this statement, you need to consider what we, as users, need to tell the DS3231 and how it knows we want to use 12-hour format. These points might help you focus on what we need to do.

We need to get the program to ask if we want to use 12-hour or 24-hour format.

We need to make sure the DS3231 can recognize that we want to use the particular format. It is the register at address 09h that is used for this purpose. Indeed, bit 6 is the 12/24 format control bit. If this bit is a logic '0', then the DS3231 will work in 24-hour format. If this bit is a logic '1', then it will use 12-hour format. This register will also hold the data for the hours, that is, the hour units and the hour tens. To ensure that bit 6 is set to a logic '1', when we want to use 12-hour format, we simply need to add 0x40 to the contents of that register. If we want bit 6 to go to a logic '0', we simply add 0 to it. We will look at this when we analyze the program listing.

If we assume we want to use 12-hour format, we need to tell the DS3231 whether or not the initial time we are setting is for the am or pm. If we look at register 09h, we see that bit 5 is reserved for this purpose. If this bit is a logic '0', then it means the current time is for am, that is, before 12 midday. If bit 5 is a logic '1', then it means the current time is for the pm.

Knowing how we can set the am or pm, for the DS3231, in this way, means we know what data we need to add to the data we want to load into this register. For example:

- If we are using 12-hour format and the current time is 08:00 in the morning, we need to add the value 0x40 as this would load bit 6 with a logic '1' and bit 5 with a logic '0'.

- However, if we are using 12-hour format and the current time is 08:00 in the evening, we need to add the value 0x60 as this would load bit 6 with a logic '1' and bit 5 with a logic '1'.

If we were using 24-hour format, then we would simply need to add 0 to the register. Note in 24-hour format, bit 5 is used to store the value of 0, 1, or 2 for the times of 0, 10, or 20 hours, etc., that is, as the tens value for the hour time. That is why 24-hour format is easier to set and use.

There is one last thing we need to appreciate before we move on to the program. That is, that in 12-hour format, once we have set the am, pm, bit 5 of register 09h, the DS3231 will alter the logic on bit 5 itself as the time moves through am and pm in time. This is so that we can keep track of this change from am to pm in the program and adjust the display accordingly. We will look at this as we analyze the program listing.

The Order the DS3231 Expects the Data

As stated earlier, the DS3231 uses an address pointer to keep track of where it should be writing to or reading from. This means it will access the registers in order, as it will automatically increment the contents of the address pointer, once they have either been written to or read from. However, we, as programmers, can load the address pointer in the DS3231 with a particular address and so make the DS3231 jump to a particular register and progress from there.

This means we need to appreciate that the DS3231 will access its registers in order starting at address 0x00. We can see from Table 10-5 that the DS3231 expects the data for seconds of the current time. This will be the first register in the sequence, as its address is 0x00. This is followed by the data for minutes and hours in address 0x01. The rest of the table will give us the order in which we need to write the data to the DS3231. We can see that the fourth item, in address 0x03, is the number that will be used to represent the day. Note number 1 is used to represent Monday and 7 is for Sunday. It is just bits 0, 1, and 2 that store the day number.

After the day number, we send the data for the date in addresses 0x04, 0x05, and 0x06.

After the date data, we send the time for the seconds of the alarm 1 setting. This is followed by the minutes and then the hours in addresses 0x07, 0x08, and 0x09.

The tenth item to be sent is the day number for the day setting of alarm 1. Alternatively, this could be the date setting for alarm 1. This data will be stored in address 0x0A.

The next three addresses store the data to set the minutes, hours, and day or date for the setting of alarm 2.

Next, at location 0x0E, we must send the data to set the control register as we want to set up the DS3231.

We can read the data in the next register, at address 0X0F, to see the state of some of the control bits to see what the DS3231 is doing.

At address 0x10, we can see how the DS3231 is trying to maintain the accuracy of the clock.

Address 0x11 holds the high byte of the 10-bit value that stores the current temperature reading of the onboard temperature transducer. This data uses a signed number representation and two's complement to handle the reading of negative temperatures. We will see how the PIC deals with this when we analyze the program listing.

Address 0x12 holds the remaining 2 bits of the 10-bit temperature reading that hold the least significant bits of the temperature reading. They are stored in bits 7 and 6 of address 0x12.

Having this appreciation of what the DS3231 expects to be stored in its important registers can help us when we design our program.

The Program Algorithm

Knowing how the DS3231 expects the configuration data to be sent to it, we can now consider writing the algorithm for the program.

- The program will allow the user to configure the DS3231 as follows:
  - The setting for the current year, month, hours, minutes, and seconds: Is it a 24-hour or 12-hour clock? Is it am or pm? If you want an alarm, what will be the settings for the alarm?
- The program will display instructions as to how to enter the required data using a terminal software such as "Tera Term."
- The program will then display a series of screens on the terminal that will allow the user to set the current date in terms of year, month, and day. They will then enter the current time in terms of hours, minutes, and

seconds. All six terms will be split into variables for tens and units. This means we will require six variables of type unsigned char.

- The program will then write these values to the DS3231 and set it to the current time.

- To restrict the amount of data that needs to be inputted, via the terminal software, we will not be setting any alarms.

- We will program the PIC to display the current time, date, month, day, and temperature.

Displaying the Temperature

The DS3231 uses temperature compensation to alter the capacitor value, which is needed to maintain the accuracy of the clock. This means that the module has a temperature transducer to detect the current temperature. This means that the module must store data that represents the current temperature. That being the case, we can program the PIC to make use of this data to display the current temperature on the LCD. To be able to display the temperature, we need to know how the module will store the data that is the result of a temperature reading.

The temperature transducer is a 10-bit transducer. The 10-bit result will be stored in two 8-bit locations in the module. The high 8 bits of the result will be stored in address 0x11, and the remaining low 2 bits will be stored in two bits of the register at address 0x12 on the module. The 8 bits in address 0x11 will hold the integer part of the reading, and the 2 bits in address 0x12 will hold the fractional part of the reading. For example, if the temperature was 22.75°C, then the 22 would be stored using the 8 bits in address 0x11, and the 0.75 would be stored in the 2 bits of address 0x12. Note, the two bits of address 0x12 that are used to hold this fractional bit of the reading will be bits 7 and 8, not bits 0 and 1.

The module uses a signed bit number representation, which means that bit 7 of the 8 bits in address 0x11 is not used as part of the number. Bit 7 is used to indicate if the reading was negative, that is, bit 7 would be a logic '1', or positive, that is, bit 7 would be a logic '0'. This means that the integer part of the reading will go from –127 to +127, as 0b1111111 = 127 in binary. Negative values will use the two's complement format. What this means is that when the temperature goes negative, the transducer creates a two's complement of the magnitude of the reading. It is this two's complement value that is stored in the addresses 0x11 and 0x12. This would mean that bit 7 of the 8 bits in address 0x11 will be set to a logic '1'. Now when the program retrieves the data from the addresses 0x11 and 0x12, the program will recognize that the data is a two's complement of the magnitude of the reading, because bit 7 of the high byte would be a logic '1'. To determine the actual magnitude of the reading, the program must carry out a two's complement of the data it has just retrieved. This is a rather complex process and made more complex as the two's complement is carried out on the full 10-bit number that is stored in two locations. To try and help you understand how the program performs this complex operation, we will look at what binary numbers are and what a two's complement is.

Binary Numbers

Numbers are really a series of digits set out in a series of columns. With our normal number system, the denary number system, we are so used to writing the numbers that we don't show the columns. Consider the number 315.5. If we place the numbers in their columns, we would have what is shown in Table 10-6.

Table 10-6. *The Number 315.5 with Columns*

Hundreds	Tens	Units		Tenths
3	1	5	.	5

The headings for the columns would really be the base number raised to a power. Our base number is 10, as we can only use 10 digits in each column, that is, 0 to 9. The power the base number is raised to relates to the number of the column. This concept is shown in Table 10-7.

Table 10-7. *The Number 315.5 Shown Using the Base Number 10*

Hundreds	Tens	Units		Tenths
10^2	10^1	10^0		10^{-1}
3	1	5	.	5

Table 10-7 shows the title for the columns in the base number 10 for the denary system raised to a power. The power is related to the position of the column. We should be familiar with the idea that $100 = 10^2$. However, we need to appreciate that $10 = 10^1$ and $1 = 10^0$. Indeed, any base number raised to the power of zero will result in "1." Try some values, for example, $20^0 = 1$.

The actual number is made up as follows:

$$3(100) + 1(10) + 5(1) + 5(0.1) = 300 + 10 + 5 + 0.5 = 315.5$$

We are so used to using the denary system that we don't look at numbers in this way. However, all number systems work in the same way.

Now let's look at the binary number system. The base number for the binary system is "2," as there are only 2 digits allowed, 0 and 1. Table 10-8 shows the columns with the base number raised to a power underneath the decimal equivalent value.

Table 10-8. *The Columns of Binary Numbers*

Sixteens	Eights	Fours	Twos	Units	0.5	0.25
2^4	2^3	2^2	2^1	2^0	2^{-1}	2^{-2}

In the binary system, the number can be made up of either 1 in the column or 0 in the column added to the others. Consider the following number shown in Table 10-9.

Table 10-9. *An Example Binary Number*

Sixteens	Eights	Fours	Twos	Units	0.5	0.25
2^4	2^3	2^2	2^1	2^0	2^{-1}	2^{-2}
0	0	1	1	0	1	0

This number has no (16) no (8) 1(4) 1(2) 0(1) 1(0.5) 0(0.25). Therefore, if we add all the values with a logic '1' in the column, we get the number 4+2+0.5 = 6.5.

This shows that 00110.10 is the binary for 6.5.

Consider the next example shown in Table 10-10.

Table 10-10. *Another Binary Example*

Sixteens	Eights	Fours	Twos	Units	0.5	0.25
2^4	2^3	2^2	2^1	2^0	2^{-1}	2^{-2}
1	0	1	0	0	1	1

This number is made up of 1(16) + 1(4) + 1(0.5) + 1 (0.25); therefore, it is 16+4+0.5+0.25 = 20.75.

Adding Binary Numbers

We just need to see what happens when we add binary numbers. There are a few examples shown here:

	Bit 1	Bit 0
	0	0
Add		1
Result	0	1

In this first example, we are simply adding 1 to 0 in binary. It should be obvious that the result is just 1.

	Bit 1	Bit 0
	0	1
Add		1
Result	1	0

In this second example, we see that 1 + 1 does not produce a result of 2 as the digit 2 is not allowed in binary. What happens is the result is 0 and 1 to carry into the next column. Just like we do when we add 1 to 9 in the denary system, we get 0 in the unit's column and 1 in the tens column.

In the second column, Bit 1, we get 0 + 1 = 1. This is how we get the result as shown. I hope you can now see that 0b10 is 2 in binary.

Now consider the following:

	Bit 1	Bit 0
	1	1
Add		1
Result	0	0

Again, the addition in the first column would produce the result of 0 in that column. Also, a 1 would be carried onto column Bit 1, where again the addition of 1 + 1 would produce the result 0. However, as this is a 2-bit number that can only go from 0 to 3, there is no third column to put the carry into. Therefore, it will be simply lost.

I am not going to go any further into looking at number systems. There is a section in the appendix that does all that. However, I hope you can appreciate how we can add binary numbers together and how we can convert binary to decimal.

Reading the Temperature from the TC72

The definition of the temperature transducer is 0.25°C. This means it will be sending data back that consists of the integer and fractional parts of the reading. The integer part of the reading is sent back in the whole 8 bits of the high byte. The fractional part is sent back in just bits 7 and 6 of the low byte. The remaining bits of the low byte are not used at all. An example of the temperature reading is shown in Table 10-11.

Table 10-11. *A Temperature Reading of 13.25*

High Byte								Low Byte		Temperature Reading
0	0	0	0	1	1	0	1	0	1	13.25

I hope you can now understand how the binary number is 13.25 in decimal. Just to make sure, the decimal number is made up of

$$1(8) + 1(4) + 1(1) + 1(0.25)$$

$$= 8 + 4 + 1 + 0.25 = 13.25.$$

Examples of the Two's Complement Process

All computers and microcontrollers use the two's complement to express negative numbers. I hope the following examples will help explain how this whole process works and how we can read negative temperatures from the transducer on the DS3231. First, we will look at the process of creating a two's complement binary number and how it can be used to express a negative value. Let's look at a simple example. Express –56 in 8-bit binary. To create the two's complement, we create the binary number for 56. We then simply invert all the bits and add 1 to the results. This is shown in Table 10-12.

Table 10-12. *–56 Expressed in Two's Complement Format*

Bit 7	Bit 6	Bit 5	Bit 4	Bit 3	Bit 2	Bit 1	Bit 0	
0	0	1	1	1	0	0	0	56 in decimal
1	1	0	0	0	1	1	1	Invert all bits
							1	
1	1	0	0	1	0	0	0	This is the two's complement to describe –56 Note bit 7 is a logic '1'

The micro will receive the two's complement of –56, which is shown in row 4 of Table 10-12. The PIC will recognize that the number should be negative, as bit 7 is a logic '1'. Now the PIC must find out what the value of the negative number is. To do this, the PIC must create a two's complement on the binary number it has just got. This is done on rows 3 and 4 of Table 10-13. The final result is the number 56 shown in row 5. Now the PIC knows the negative number has a value of 56, that is, –56.

Table 10-13. *Another Two's Complement to Determine the*
Magnitude of the Negative Number

Bit 7	Bit 6	Bit 5	Bit 4	Bit 3	Bit 2	Bit 1	Bit 0	
1	1	0	0	1	0	0	0	This is the two's complement to describe −56 Note bit 7 is a logic '1', 56 in decimal
0	0	1	1	0	1	1	1	Invert all bits
							1	
0	0	1	1	1	0	0	0	Back to 56 in decimal

We can see that the PIC, knowing this number is negative, has now determined that the number is −56 in decimal.

However, the requirement for our program is slightly more complicated, because we are using a 10-bit binary number, where the most significant 8 bits represent the integer part of the value and the least significant 2 bits represent the fractional part. However, the two's complement is performed on all 10 bits.

To try and help explain what happens and what we need to get the program to do, we will look at some examples of how the temperature transducer will send the values −1.00, −1.25, −1.50, and −1.75. This is to determine when we need to carry a logic '1' onto the "thigh" variable, which is the variable we will use to store the integer part of the temperature reading. This is because we separate the 10 bits into the two variables "thigh" for the integer part and "tlow" for the fractional part, as the DS3231 only sends 8 bits at a time. Therefore, the carry cannot go onto the "thigh" variable automatically, and the program has to add it when needed.

The first example looks at what happens when the reading is −1.00 as shown in Table 10-14.

Table 10-14. *A Reading of –1.00*

| High Byte | | | | | | | | Low Byte | | |
b7	b6	b5	b4	b3	b2	b1	b0	b7	b6	
0	0	0	0	0	0	0	1	0	0	This is the 10-bit binary for 1.00
1	1	1	1	1	1	1	0	1	1	This is the 10-bit number inverted
									1	Now add 1
1	1	1	1	1	1	1	1	0	0	The result of the transducer performing its own two's complement. Note bit 7 of high byte is a logic '1'. The 10 bits are sent to the PIC and stored in thigh and tlow variables

The program must now perform a two's complement to determine the magnitude of the negative number.

0	0	0	0	0	0	0	0	1	1	Now the PIC will invert both parts
									1	Now add 1. This action does produce a carry to pass onto the high byte. Therefore, in the program, we need to invert the thigh byte and add 1 to it
0	0	0	0	0	0	0	1	0	0	The binary number is back to 1.0

I hope you can see how the process works and that we have to invert the variable "thigh" and add "1" to it at the same time. We will see how this is done when we analyze the program listing.

The next example is for –1.25 shown in Table 10-15.

Table 10-15. *A Reading of –1.25*

High Byte								Low Byte		
0	0	0	0	0	0	0	1	0	1	1.25
1	1	1	1	1	1	1	0	1	0	The transducer will perform its own two's complement by first inverting all the bits. Note bit 7 of high byte is a logic '1'
									1	Now add 1
1	1	1	1	1	1	1	0	1	1	The result of the transducer performing its own two's complement. Note bit 7 of high byte is a logic '1'. The 10 bits are sent to the PIC and stored in thigh and tlow variables

The program must now perform a two's complement to determine the magnitude of the negative number.

0	0	0	0	0	0	0	1	0	0	We now invert the result
									1	Now add 1. This action does not produce a carry to pass onto the high byte. Therefore, in the program, we only need to invert the thigh
0	0	0	0	0	0	0	1	0	1	The binary number is back to 1.25

Now consider the operation on the number –1.50 shown in Table 10-16.

Table 10-16. A Reading of –1.50

High Byte	Low Byte	
0 0 0 0 0 0 0 1	1 0	This is the 10-bit binary for 1.5
1 1 1 1 1 1 1 0	0 1	This is the 10-bit number inverted
	1	Now add 1
1 1 1 1 1 1 1 0	1 0	The result of the transducer performing its own two's complement. Note bit 7 of high byte is a logic '1'. The 10 bits are sent to the PIC and stored in thigh and tlow variables

The program must now perform a two's complement to determine the magnitude of the negative number.

0 0 0 0 0 0 0 1	0 1	We now invert the result
	1	Now add 1. This action does not produce a carry to pass onto the high byte. Therefore, in the program, we only need to invert the thigh
0 0 0 0 0 0 0 1	1 0	The binary number is back to 1.5

Now consider the final possibility: the number –1.75. Note this is the last possible value in the fractional part. The integer part can be any value; really, it will not change the process. This is shown in Table 10-17.

Table 10-17. *A Reading of –1.75*

High Byte								Low Byte		
b7	b6	b5	b4	b3	b2	b1	b0	b7	b6	
0	0	0	0	0	0	0	1	1	1	This is the 10-bit binary 1.75
1	1	1	1	1	1	1	0	0	0	This is the 10-bit number inverted
									1	Now add 1
1	1	1	1	1	1	1	0	0	1	The result of the transducer performing its own two's complement. Note bit 7 of high byte is a logic '1'. The 10 bits are sent to the PIC and stored in thigh and tlow variables

The program must now perform a two's complement to determine the magnitude of the negative number.

0	0	0	0	0	0	0	1	1	0	We now invert the result
									1	Now add 1. This action does not produce a carry to pass onto the high byte. Therefore, in the program, we only need to invert the thigh
0	0	0	0	0	0	0	1	1	1	The binary number is back to 1.75

This covers all four possible fractional numbers. It should be evident that there is only one of the four possible fractional numbers when we would have to invert the high byte and add one to the inversion. With all of the other three possibilities, we only need to invert the high byte. This should make the process of dealing with negative readings easier. We will see how the relevant instructions deal with this as we analyze the program listing.

Using the UART and a Terminal Software

As I started to write this program, it soon became clear that the DS3231 requires a lot of information to be inputted before it can be left to just keep track of time. To create a more user-friendly environment to input the setting of the clock, I decided to use a terminal to input the information. The terminal is actually my laptop using a terminal software program, such as Tera Term or PuTTY, to create a more user-friendly environment. This has meant that we need to connect the PIC to my laptop using a serial port. Now most laptops don't have a serial port on them, but you can buy a USB to serial converter module that will allow you to connect the PIC to your laptop. However, this means that you will have to use one of the two UART modules inside the PIC. We will cover the use of Tera Term and the UART later in the chapter.

Using the Alarms of the DS3231

To restrict the length of the program listing, I have decided not to use the alarms of the DS3231. However, I will be using alarms with the built-in RTCC module of the PIC in the next chapter. If you want to use the DS3231 to set alarms, then I hope I will have explained enough about the module for you to add alarms to your program. The next chapter may give you some idea of how to do that.

The UART

As the program will use one of the two UART modules in the PIC, we should look at what a UART is. UART stands for Universal Asynchronous Receiver/Transmitter. It is a circuit that is used in most microprocessors that communicate with the outside world. This is because the inside world of the micro communicates to itself using a parallel bus system. This makes communication much quicker than serial communications. However, this requires a lot of tracks. The first parallel buses were only 4 bits wide, as micros communicated in nibbles of data. Nowadays, the buses are up to 64 bits wide, which means they communicate 16 times faster, even if they were to use the same clock, which they don't.

With the outside world, we can't afford to have cables that have 64 wires in them. The early printers did use what was called ribbon cables that were 8 or 16 bits wide, but they were restricted in length to around 3m maximum. So, to keep costs down, communication in the outside world has been done serially using only two wires.

This means we needed a device that would change the parallel inside the micro to serial outside. It also needed to change the serial outside the micro to the parallel inside the micro. This is the UART, which has PISO (Parallel In and Serial Out) and SIPO (Serial In and Parallel Out) shift registers.

This means that it is essential, even now, for the would-be embedded programmer to understand how we can use the UART. In this chapter, you will learn that and how to apply it.

Unlike the SPI module, this type of communication is asynchronous, which means it is not synchronized to a clock, and so there is no need for a clock signal. Indeed, with the UART, you only really need two wires which connect to the transmit, TX, and the receive, RX, pins on the PIC. You can, if you so wish, use what is termed "handshaking," whereby you add an RTS (ready to transit) and a CTS (clear to send) signals between each device. However, this will tie up more I/O pins and require more cabling.

There are two UART modules in the PIC32. They are controlled by two control registers: the UxMODE and UxSTA registers. The "x" is either 1 or 2 for the particular UART modules you are using.

The UxMODE Control Register

This is used to control what mode of operation the module can be put into. It is a 32-bit register, but only the lower 16 bits, bits 15 to 0, are used. Table 10-18 describes the primary use of each of the bits.

Table 10-18. *The UxMODE Register*

Bit Number	Name	Usage
15	ON UARTx Enable bit	Logic '1' means UART is turned on Logic '0' means UART is turned off When the UART is turned on, the TX and RX pins' direction is controlled by the UART When the UART is turned off, those pins are controlled by the normal TRIS port
14	FRZ Freeze in Debug Exception Mode bit	Logic '1' means freeze operation when the CPU is in debug exception mode Logic '0' means continue operation when the CPU is in debug exception mode
13	SIDL Stop in Idle Mode bit	Logic '1' means stop operating when the device enters idle mode Logic '0' means continue operating when the device enters idle mode

(continued)

Table 10-18. *(continued)*

Bit Number	Name	Usage
12	IREN IrDA Encoder and Decoder Enable bit	Logic '1' means IrDA is enabled Logic '0' means IrDA is disabled
11	RTSMD Mode Selection for UxRTS Pin bit	Logic '1': UxRTS pin in simplex mode Logic '0': UxRTS pin in flow control mode
10	Not used	
9 and 8	UEN bits	UARTx Enable bits; see Table 10-19
7	WAKE Enable Wake-up on Start bit Detect During Sleep mode bit	Logic '1': Wake-up is enabled Logic '0': Wake-up is disabled
6	LPBACK UARTx Loopback Mode Select bit	Logic '1': Loopback mode enabled Logic '0': Loopback disabled
5	ABAUD Auto-Baud Enable bit	Logic '1': Enable baud rate measurement on the next character Logic '0': Baud rate measurement disabled or completed
4	RXINV Receive Polarity Inversion bit	Logic '1': UxRX idle state is a logic '0' Logic '0': UxRX idle state is a logic '1'

(continued)

Table 10-18. (*continued*)

Bit Number	Name	Usage
3	BRGH High Baud Rate Enable bit	Logic '1': High speed mode – 4x baud clock enabled Logic '0': Standard speed mode – 16x baud clock enabled
2 and 1	PDSEL	Parity and Data Selection bits; see Table 10-21
0	STSEL Stop Selection bit	Logic '1': Use two stop bits Logic '0': Use one stop bit

Table 10-19. *UARTx Enable Bits*

Bit 9	Bit 8	Usage
0	0	UxTX and UxRX pins are enabled and used and controlled by the module. UxCTS and UxRTS/UxBCLK pins are controlled by port latches
0	1	UxTX, UxRX, and UxRTS pins are enabled and controlled by the module. The UxCTS pin is controlled by port latches
1	0	UxTX, UxRX, UxCTS, and UxRTS pins are enabled and controlled by the module
1	1	UxTX, UxRX, and UxBCLK pins are enabled and controlled by the module. UxCTS pin is controlled by port latches

Bits 8 and 9 are really used to determine how you want to control the direction of data through the RX, receive, and TX, transmit, pins for the UART. It should be clear that the RX should be an input and the TX should be an output. You could use the TRIS register, or port latches, to set the direction of the pins. The simplest way, and the method I use, is to allow the module to set the direction of these pins. This is done by setting these two bits to a logic '0'. Note the CTS and RTS/UxBCLK pins are used for handshaking.

The pins of the UART module are allocated to the I/O pins of the 32-bit PIC, as shown in Table 10-20.

Table 10-20. *The UART Allocation Bits*

UART Pin	Allocation
U1RX	Bit 2 PORTF
U1TX	Bit 3 PORTF
U1CTS	Bit 14 PORTD
U1RTS/BCLK	Bit 15 PORTD
U2RX	Bit 4 PORTF
U2TX	Bit 5 PORTF
U2CTS	Bit 12 PORTF
U2RTS/BCLK	Bit 13 PORTF

Table 10-21. *Parity and Data Selection Bits*

Bit 2	Bit 1	Usage
0	0	8-bit data, no parity
0	1	8-bit data, even parity
1	0	8-bit data, odd parity
1	1	9-bit data, no parity

Parity is a simple process to try and confirm that what was received was the data that was transmitted. As all data consist of bits that could be logic '1' or logic '0', then if we just consider the number of logic '1s', there could be an even or an odd number of logic '1s'. With bits 1 and 2, we can select to have no parity, that is, we do not perform parity checking. We could also select checking for an even or odd number of logic '1s'. Also, we could choose 8 or 9 bits of data; I normally used just 8 bits of data with no parity.

The UxSTA Register

This is also a 32-bit register, but 25 bits are used. The register is used to show the status of the module, but the higher bits, 16 to 24, are used for automatic address detection. Table 10-22 shows the bits of the UxSTA register.

Table 10-22. *UxSTA Register*

Bit	Name	Usage
24	ADM_EN Automatic Address Detect Mode Enable bit	Logic '1': The automatic address detection is enabled Logic '0': The automatic address detection is disabled
23–16	ADDR <7:0> Automatic Address Mask	Logic '1' in the bit means that bit is used to mask out that bit and mark it as a don't care
15 and 14	UTXISEL	Tx Interrupt Mode Selection bits; see Table 10-23
13	TXINV	Transmit Polarity Inversion bit; see Table 10-24

(continued)

Table 10-22. *(continued)*

Bit	Name	Usage
12	RXEN Receiver Enable bit	Logic '1': UART RX enabled Logic '0': UART RX disabled
11	TXBRK Transmit Break bit	Logic '1': Send BREAK on the next transmission. Start bit followed by 12 logic '0s' followed by Stop bit; cleared by hardware upon completion Logic '0': BREAK transmission is disabled or completed
10	TXEN Transmit Enable bit	Logic '1': UART TX enabled Logic '0': UART TX disabled
9	UTXBF Transmit Buffer Full Status bit (read-only)	Logic '1': Transmit buffer is full Logic '0': Transmit buffer is not full
8	TRMT Transmit Shift Register is Empty bit (read-only)	Logic '1': Transmit shift register is empty, and transmit buffer is empty (the last transmission has completed) Logic '0': Transmit shift register is not empty, a transmission is in progress or queued in the transmit buffer
7 and 6	URXISEL	Receive Interrupt Mode Selection bit; see Table 10-25
5	ADDEN Address Character Detect (bit 8 of received data = 1)	Logic '1': Address Detect mode enabled. If 9-bit mode is not selected, this control bit has no effect. Logic '0': Address Detect mode disabled

(continued)

Table 10-22. (*continued*)

Bit	Name	Usage
4	RIDLE Receiver Idle bit (read-only)	Logic '1': Receiver is Idle Logic '0': Data is being received
3	PERR Parity Error Status bit	Logic '1': Parity error has been detected for the current character Logic '0': Parity error has not been detected
2	FERR Framing Error Status bit	Logic '1': Framing Error has been detected for the current character Logic '0': Framing Error has not been detected
1	OERR Receive Buffer Overrun	Logic '1': Receive buffer has overflowed Logic '0': Receive buffer has not overflowed
0	RXDA Receive Buffer Data Available bit (read-only)	Logic '1': Receive buffer has data; at least one more character can be read Logic '0': Receive buffer is empty

Table 10-23. *Usage of UTXISEL Tx Interrupt Mode Selection Bits*

Bit 15	Bit 14	Usage
0	0	Interrupt is generated when the Transmit buffer contains at least one empty space
0	1	Interrupt is generated when all characters are transmitted
1	0	Interrupt is generated when the Transmit buffer becomes empty
1	1	Reserved, do not use

Table 10-24. *Usage of TXINV: Transmit Polarity Inversion Bit 13*

IrDA mode is disabled	Usage
0	UxTX idle state is "1"
1	UxTX idle state is "0"
IrDA mode is enabled	
0	IrDA encoded UxTX idle state is "0"
1	IrDA encoded UxTX idle state is "1"

Table 10-25. *Usage of URXISEL Receive Interrupt Mode Selection Bits 7 and 6*

Bit 7	Bit 6	Usage
0	x	Interrupt flag bit is set when a character is received
1	0	Interrupt flag bit is set when the receive buffer is 3/4 full (i.e., has 3 data characters)
1	1	Interrupt flag bit is set when the receive buffer is full (i.e., has 4 data characters)

I hope that the comments around the usage of these bits do help explain their usage. Obviously, we will not use all the functions of these bits, for example, bits 24 to 16, but as we use the bits in the program listings, I will explain how they are used. You should be able to see that bits 5 to 0 are for indicating when some sort of error has occurred or some state has changed. Again, as we use these bits, I will explain further how we use them.

We will not be using the interrupt functions as the terminal will only respond to inquiries from the PIC.

Using Tera Term

As we will need a terminal to receive the instructions from the PIC and input the settings to the PIC, it would be useful to learn how to use the software Tera Term. This is because we will be using this software to make a terminal on our laptop. This is a free software that allows you to use your PC as a terminal that can be used to send and receive data. The version I am using is detailed in Figure 10-2.

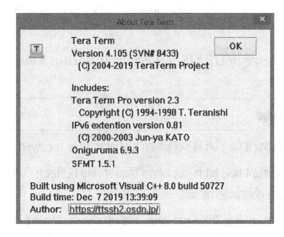

Figure 10-2. *The Version of Tera Term*

When using this software, I used a USB to serial converter to connect the PIC to my laptop. This is because my laptop does not have a serial com port. This is shown in Figure 10-3.

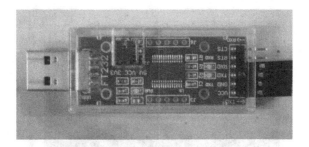

Figure 10-3. *The USB to Serial Converter*

To use the Tera Term software, click the icon for Tera Term. The software will start with the opening screen as shown in Figure 10-4.

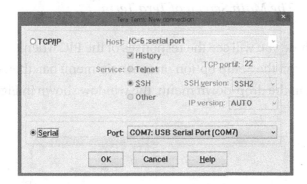

Figure 10-4. *The Opening Screen of Tera Term*

If you click the serial option, as shown in Figure 10-4, the software should automatically find the correct com port that your USB converter is connected to. If it doesn't, or it finds the wrong com port, then you may have to use the device manager to find the correct com port.

Once you have selected the correct serial com port and clicked OK, the main terminal screen should appear as shown in Figure 10-5.

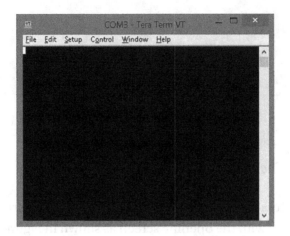

Figure 10-5. *The Main Screen of Tera Term*

This is where you will see the responses of the PIC when the program runs. If you select the Setup option on the main menu bar, then choose the serial port from the drop-down menu, the window shown in Figure 10-6 will appear.

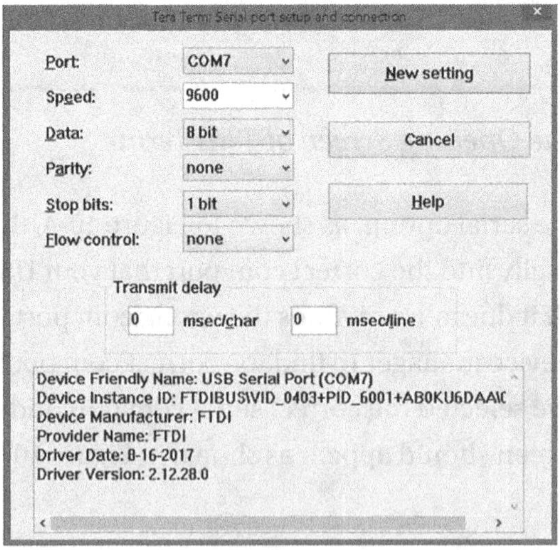

Figure 10-6. *The Serial Port Setup Screen*

This should confirm the correct com port but will also give you the option of setting some other parameters as detailed here:

- **Speed**: This sets the desired baud rate in bits per second. The most common baud rate is 9600, and this is the one we are using in our program. There are quite a few other possible baud rates.

- **Data**: This sets the number of bits used to be sent as data. We will use 8 bits.

- **Parity**: This is a method by which the system can check that what was received is what was sent. At this point, we will use none as we will not be checking what was sent and received. The different types of parity available are

  - None

  - Odd

  - Even

  - Mark

  - Space

- **Stop bits**: This sets how many bits will be used in this way. We will use just 1 bit. The options are

  - 1

  - 1.5

  - 2

- **Flow control**: This is used to ensure it is safe to send data to and from. If you try to send data when the system is not ready, you may cause a collision and the data will not be sent, but you may think it has. This is sometimes referred to as "handshaking." The options available are

- None, which is what we will use for now

- Xon/Xoff software control

- RTS/CTS which are quite popular

- DSR/DTR which is hardware control

The only other aspect of the software you may want to set up is the actual terminal window. If you select the first option of terminal from the drop-down menu that is presented when you click Setup, you will be presented with the window shown in Figure 10-7.

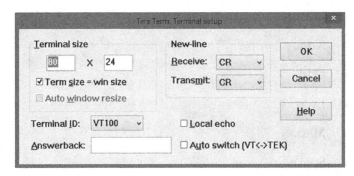

Figure 10-7. *The Setup Terminal Window*

You can leave this with the default setting, but the ones you might want to change are

- **Terminal size**: This is set at 80 characters wide and 24 lines deep at present.

- **New line**: Both for receiving and transmitting.

- The default setting is CR. This means that to move the cursor to the start of a new line, you must send the ASCII for both the LF (line feed) and the CR (carriage return) individually. This is what we will do in our program.

- These can be set up so that sending just the ASCII for LF or CR will produce the same effect.

If you tick the box alongside the local echo, then the terminal will send the character that it is transmitting to its screen automatically. However, we want the PIC to echo the character back to the terminal screen; therefore, we have left this unchecked.

Hopefully, this explanation will help you to set up the Tera Term software, and you can run the program as required. You should appreciate that with the software Tera Term running, whatever you type on your laptop's keyboard will be transmitted to the PIC.

Connecting the Devices to the PIC32

As we will be using the explorer 16 development board, we will use the pinout board, shown in Figure 3 in the "Introduction" section of the book, to connect devices to the PIC. It will simply fit into the PICtail Plus expansion socket. This then enables you to gain access to most of the I/O of the PIC. For this program, we will use the LCD2004 in 8-bit mode. The circuit diagram, shown in Figure 10-8, shows how to connect the LCD. The resistors R1 and R2 are there to provide a voltage divider network to supply the "Vo" terminal, the contrast for the LCD, with a voltage around 250mV. The third resistor, R3, is there to limit the current through the LED that lights up the LCD display.

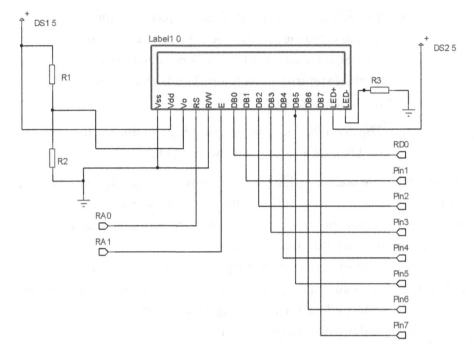

Figure 10-8. *Connecting the LCD to PORTB*

Figure 10-9 shows how to connect the DS3231 to the PIC via the expansion board.

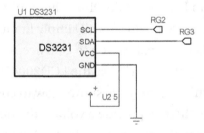

Figure 10-9. *Connecting the RTC DS3231 to the PIC*

Listing 10-1 shows the instructions for the program, and we will analyze most of the instructions.

Figure 10-10 shows the display with the time, date, month, day, and the current temperature. It shows how the LCD2004 can be a more useful display than the 1602 LCD.

Listing 10-1. The DS3231 Program Listing

```
1   /* * File:    RTCCUARTprog.c
2   Author: H. H. Ward
3   *Control RTCC via UART
4   Display on 4 bit LCD on PORTB
5   Created on 1 January 2022, 11:02
6   */
7   #include <xc.h>
8   #include <stdio.h>
9   #include <config72M36MNoWDTNoJTAG.h>
10  #include <8BitLCDPortD.h>
11  #include <32biti2cprotocol.h>
12  //some definitions2
13  #define sdclk1  _RG2
14  #define sdaln1  _RG3
15  #define Mon            lcdData = 0x4D; sendData ();
    lcdData = 0x6F; sendData (); lcdData = 0x6E; sendData ();
16  #define Tue            lcdData = 0x54; sendData ();
    lcdData = 0x75; sendData (); lcdData = 0x65; sendData ();
17  #define Wed            lcdData = 0x57; sendData ();
    lcdData = 0x65; sendData (); lcdData = 0x64; sendData ();
18  #define Thur           lcdData = 0x54; sendData ();
    lcdData = 0x68; sendData (); lcdData = 0x72; sendData ();
19  #define Fri            lcdData = 0x46; sendData ();
    lcdData = 0x72; sendData (); lcdData = 0x69; sendData ();
20  #define Sat            lcdData = 0x53; sendData ();
    lcdData = 0x61; sendData (); lcdData = 0x74; sendData ();
```

```
21  #define Sun              lcdData = 0x53; sendData ();
    lcdData = 0x75; sendData (); lcdData = 0x6E; sendData ();
22  #define Jan              lcdData = 0x4A; sendData ();
    lcdData = 0x61; sendData (); lcdData = 0x6E; sendData ();
23  #define Feb              lcdData = 0x46; sendData ();
    lcdData = 0x65; sendData (); lcdData = 0x62; sendData ();
24  #define Mar              lcdData = 0x4D; sendData ();
    lcdData = 0x61; sendData (); lcdData = 0x72; sendData ();
25  #define Apr              lcdData = 0x41; sendData ();
    lcdData = 0x70; sendData (); lcdData = 0x72; sendData ();
26  #define May              lcdData = 0x4D; sendData ();
    lcdData = 0x61; sendData (); lcdData = 0x79; sendData ();
27  #define Jun              lcdData = 0x4A; sendData ();
    lcdData = 0x75; sendData (); lcdData = 0x6E; sendData ();
28  #define Jul              lcdData = 0x4A; sendData ();
    lcdData = 0x75; sendData (); lcdData = 0x6C; sendData ();
29  #define Aug              lcdData = 0x41; sendData ();
    lcdData = 0x75; sendData (); lcdData = 0x67; sendData ();
30  #define Sep              lcdData = 0x53; sendData ();
    lcdData = 0x65; sendData (); lcdData = 0x70; sendData ();
31  #define Oct              lcdData = 0x4F; sendData ();
    lcdData = 0x63; sendData (); lcdData = 0x74; sendData ();
32  #define Nov              lcdData = 0x4E; sendData ();
    lcdData = 0x6F; sendData (); lcdData = 0x76; sendData ();
33  #define Dec              lcdData = 0x44; sendData ();
    lcdData = 0x65; sendData (); lcdData = 0x63; sendData ();
34  //declare some variables
35  unsigned char sec, min, hour, day, date, month, year,
    daynumber = 1, setbutcounts = 0;
36  unsigned char ms, secunits, sectens, minunits, mintens,
    hourunits, hourtens, day, hourformat, houradd, amformat,
    amdisplay;
```

```
37  unsigned char dayunits, daytens, monthunits, monthtens,
    yearunits, yeartens;
38  unsigned char count, dummy, thigh, tlow, huns, tens,
    units, decten, dechun,thigh, tlow, negbit = 0;
39  unsigned char a1secunits, a1sectens, a1minunits,
    a1mintens, a1hourunits, a1hourtens, a1hour, a1min, a1sec;
40  unsigned char a2secunits, a2sectens, a2minunits,
    a2mintens, a2hourunits, a2hourtens, a2hour, a2min, a2sec;
41  unsigned char alarmnum, alarmfreq, a1daynum, a1freqdaynum;
42  //declare any subroutines
43  void debounce ()
44  {
45      TMR1 = 0;
46      while (TMR1 < 1900);
47  }
48  unsigned char Uart2TX( unsigned char x)
49  {
50      while ( U2STAbits.UTXBF);
51      U2TXREG = x;
52       while ( U2STAbits.UTXBF);
53      U2TXREG = 0x0A; //moves cursor to new line under
    current pos
54       while ( U2STAbits.UTXBF);
55      U2TXREG = 0x0D;                     //move cursor to
    beginning of line
56      return x;
57  }
58  unsigned char Uart2RX( )
59  {
60      while ( !U2STAbits.URXDA);
61      return U2RXREG;
62  }
```

```
63  void sendString (const char *words)
64  {
65      while (*words)
66      {
67          while ( U2STAbits.UTXBF);
68      U2TXREG = *words;
69          *words ++;
70      }
71      Uart2TX( 0x0A);
72  }
73  void convert ()
74  {
75  decten = 0x30;
76  dechun = 0x30;
77  if (tlow == 0b01000000)
78  {
79  decten = (0x32);
80  dechun = (0x35);
81  }
82  if (tlow == 0b10000000)
83  {
84  decten = (0x35);
85  dechun = (0x30);
86  }
87  if (tlow == 0b11000000)
88  {
89  decten = (0x37);
90  dechun = (0x35);
91  }
92  if (thigh & 0b10000000)
```

```
 93  {
 94  negbit = 1;
 95  tlow = ~tlow +1;
 96  decten = 0x30;
 97  dechun = 0x30;
 98  if (tlow == 0b01000000)
 99  {
100  thigh = ~thigh;
101  decten = (0x32);
102  dechun = (0x35);
103  }
104  if (tlow == 0b10000000)
105  {
106  thigh = ~thigh;
107  decten = (0x35);
108  dechun = (0x30);
109  }
110  if (tlow == 0b11000000)
111  {
112  thigh = ~thigh;
113  decten = (0x37);
114  dechun = (0x35);
115  }
116  if (tlow == 0b00000000)
117  {
118  thigh = ~thigh+1;
119  decten = (0x30);
120  dechun = (0x30);
121  }
122  }
```

```
123  if (thigh >= 0 && thigh < 10)
124  {
125  units = (thigh + 48);
126  tens = 48;
127  huns = 48;
128  }
129  if (thigh >= 10 && thigh < 20)
130  {
131  units = (thigh -10 + 48);
132  tens = ( 1 + 48);
133  huns = 48;
134  }
135  if (thigh >= 20 && thigh < 30)
136  {
137  units = (thigh -20 + 48);
138  tens = ( 2 + 48);
139  huns = 48;
140  }
141  if (thigh >= 30 && thigh < 40)
142  {
143  units = (thigh -30 + 48);
144  tens = ( 3 + 48);
145  huns = 48;
146  }
147  if (thigh >= 40 && thigh < 50)
148  {
149  units = (thigh -40 + 48);
150  tens = ( 4 + 48);
151  huns = 48;
152  }
```

```
153  if (thigh >= 50 && thigh < 60)
154  {
155  units = (thigh -50 + 48);
156  tens = ( 5 + 48);
157  huns = 48;
158  }
159  if (thigh >= 60 && thigh < 70)
160  {
161  units = (thigh -60 + 48);
162  tens = ( 6 + 48);
163  huns = 48;
164  }
165  if (thigh >= 70 && thigh < 80)
166  {
167  units = (thigh -70 + 48);
168  tens = ( 7 + 48);
169  huns = 48;
170  }
171  if (thigh >= 80 && thigh < 90)
172  {
173  units = (thigh -80 + 48);
174  tens = ( 8 + 48);
175  huns = 48;
176  }
177  if (thigh >= 90 && thigh < 100)
178  {
179  units = (thigh -90 + 48);
180  tens = ( 9 + 48);
181  huns = 48;
182  }
```

```
183  if (thigh >= 100 && thigh < 110)
184  {
185  units = (thigh -100 + 48);
186  tens = ( 0 + 48);
187  huns = (1+ 48);
188  }
189  if (thigh >= 110 && thigh < 120)
190  {
191  units = (thigh -110 + 48);
192  tens = ( 1 + 48);
193  huns = (1+48);
194  }
195  if (thigh >= 120 && thigh < 130)
196  {
197  units = (thigh -120 + 48);
198  tens = ( 2 + 48);
199  huns = (1+48);
200  }
201  if (negbit == 1) writeString ("Temp is -");
202  else writeString ("Temp is ");
203  if (huns == 48) goto distens;
204  lcdData = huns;
205  sendData ();
206  distens: if (tens == 48 && huns == 48) goto disunits;
207  lcdData = tens;
208  sendData ();
209  disunits: lcdData = units;
210  sendData ();
211  lcdData = 0x2E;
212  sendData ();
213  lcdData = decten;
214  sendData ();
```

```
215  lcdData = dechun;
216  sendData ();
217  lcdData = 0xDF;
218  sendData ();
219  lcdData = 0x43;
220  sendData ();
221  lcdData = 0x20;
222  sendData ();
223  lcdData = 0x20;
224  sendData ();
225  negbit = 0;
226  }
227  void setclock ()
228  {
229  I2Cidle();
230  I2CStart ();
231  I2CWrite (0xD0);
232  I2CWrite (0);
233  I2CWrite (sec);
234  I2CWrite (min);
235  I2CWrite (hour);
236  I2CWrite (daynumber);
237  I2CWrite (date);
238  I2CWrite (month);
239  I2CWrite (year);
240  I2CStop();
241  }
242  void setTheRTC ()
243  {
244      sendString ("Input the tens digits of the year.");
245          sendString ("Note the PIC will echo your
                input");
```

```
246          yeartens = Uart2RX ();
247          Uart2TX (yeartens);
248          lcdData = yeartens;
249          sendData ();
250          yeartens = (yeartens - 0x30);
251           sendString ("Input the units digits of the
              year.");
252          yearunits = Uart2RX ();
253          Uart2TX (yearunits);
254          lcdData = yearunits;
255          sendData ();
256          yearunits = (yearunits - 0x30);
257          lcdData = 0x3A;
258          sendData ();
259          sendString ("Input the tens digits of the
              month.");
260          monthtens = Uart2RX ();
261          Uart2TX (monthtens);
262          lcdData = monthtens;
263          sendData ();
264          monthtens = (monthtens - 0x30);
265          sendString ("Input the units digits of the
              month.");
266          monthunits = Uart2RX ();
267          Uart2TX (monthunits);
268          lcdData = monthunits;
269          sendData ();
270          monthunits = (monthunits - 0x30);
271          lcdData = 0x3A;
272          sendData ();
273          sendString ("Input the tens digits of the day.");
274          daytens = Uart2RX ();
```

```
275         Uart2TX (daytens);
276         lcdData = daytens;
277         sendData ();
278         daytens = (daytens - 0x30);
279         sendString ("Input the units digits of
            the day.");
280         dayunits = Uart2RX ();
281         Uart2TX (dayunits);
282         lcdData = dayunits;
283         sendData ();
284         dayunits = (dayunits - 0x30);
285         lcdData = 0x3A;
286         sendData ();
287         sendString ("Input a number for day of the
            week.");
288         sendString ("i.e. 1 = Mon, 2 = Tues, etc.");
289         daynumber = Uart2RX ();
290         Uart2TX (daynumber);
291         lcdData = daynumber;
292         sendData ();
293         lcdData = 0x3A;
294         sendData ();
295         sendString ("Set the time ");
296         clearTheScreen ();
297         writeString ("Set the time ");
298         line2 ();
299         sendString ("Input the tens digits of the
            hour.");
300         hourtens = Uart2RX ();
301         Uart2TX (hourtens);
302         lcdData = hourtens;
303         sendData ();
```

```
304            hourtens = (hourtens - 0x30);
305            sendString ("Input the units digits of the
               hour.");
306            hourunits = Uart2RX ();
307            Uart2TX (hourunits);
308            lcdData = hourunits;
309            sendData ();
310            hourunits = (hourunits - 0x30);
311            lcdData = 0x3A;
312            sendData ();
313            sendString ("Input the tens digits of the
               minutes.");
314            mintens = Uart2RX ();
315            Uart2TX (mintens);
316            lcdData = mintens;
317            sendData ();
318            mintens = (mintens - 0x30);
319            sendString ("Input the units digits of the
               minutes.");
320            minunits = Uart2RX ();
321            Uart2TX (minunits);
322            lcdData = minunits;
323            sendData ();
324            minunits = (minunits - 0x30);
325            lcdData = 0x3A;
326            sendData ();
327            sendString ("Input the tens digits of the
               seconds.");
328            sectens = Uart2RX ();
329            Uart2TX (sectens);
330            lcdData = sectens;
```

```
331        sendData ();
332        sectens = (sectens - 0x30);
333        sendString ("Input the units digits of the
           seconds.");
334        secunits = Uart2RX ();
335        Uart2TX (secunits);
336        lcdData = secunits;
337        sendData ();
338        secunits = (secunits - 0x30);
339        sendString ("Input a number for 12hrs or 24hr
           display.");
340        sendString ("i.e. 1 = 12hrs, 2 = 24hrs.");
341        hourformat = Uart2RX ();
342        Uart2TX (hourformat);
343        lcdData = hourformat;
344        sendData ();
345        if (hourformat == 0x32) goto alldone;
346        sendString ("Input a number for AM or PM type 1
           for AM or 2 for PM.");
347        amformat = Uart2RX ();
348        Uart2TX (amformat);
349        lcdData = amformat;
350        sendData ();
351        alldone: hour = ((hourtens << 4)+ (hourunits
           & 0x0F));
352        min = ((mintens << 4)+(minunits & 0x0f));
353        sec = ((sectens << 4)+ (secunits & 0x0F));
354        year = ((yeartens << 4)+ (yearunits & 0x0F));
355        month = ((monthtens << 4)+(monthunits & 0X0f));
356        date = ((daytens << 4)+(dayunits & 0x0f));
357        if (hourformat == 0x31)
```

```
358              {
359                  if (amformat == 0x31)
360                  {
361                      amdisplay = 1;
362                      hour = (hour+0x40);
363                  }
364                  else
365                  {
366                      amdisplay = 0;
367                      hour = (hour+0x60);
368                  }
369              }
370              display:  sendString ("Time set");
371  }
372  main (void)
373  {
374  PORTA = 0;
375  PORTB = 0;
376  PORTC = 0;
377  PORTD = 0;
378  PORTE = 0;
379  TRISA = 0;
380  TRISB = 0;
381  TRISC = 0;
382  TRISD = 0x0;
383  TRISE = 0;
384  AD1PCFG = 0xFFFF;
385  AD1CON1 = 0;
386  T1CON = 0x8030;
387  DDPCONbits.JTAGEN = 0;
388      setUpTheLCD ();
```

```
389        writeString ("Setting the RTC ");
390        cursorPos (2,0);
391            writeString ("Date ");
392        I2CInit();
393        U2MODE = 0x8808;
394        U2STA = 0x1400;
395        U2BRG = (36000000/4/9600)-1;
396        setTheRTC ();
397        setclock ();
398        I2Cidle ();
399        I2CStart ();
400        I2CWrite (0xD0);       // another write operation to load
           the DS1307 address pointer with the correct start address
401        I2CWrite (0);
402        I2CStop();
403        clearTheScreen ();
404          while (1)
405          {
406      writeString ("Time ");
407      I2Cidle ();
408      I2CStart ();
409      I2CWrite (0xD1);
410      sec = I2Cread();
411      min = I2Cread();
412      hour = I2Cread();
413      daynumber = I2Cread();
414      date = I2Cread();
415      month = I2Cread();
416      year = I2CreadNAck();
417  I2CStop();
418            if (hourformat == 0x31)
```

```
419                {
420                    if (hour & 0b00100000)
421                    {
422                        amdisplay = 0;
423                        hour = (hour-0x60);
424                    }
425                    else
426                    {
427                        amdisplay = 1;
428                        hour = (hour - 0x40);
429                    }
430            }
431  //get ready to read temperature
432  I2Cidle ();
433  I2CStart ();
434  I2CWrite (0xD0);       // another write operation to load
     the DS1307 address pointer with the correct start address
435  I2CWrite (0x11);
436  I2CStop();
437  //read the temperature
438  I2Cidle ();
439  I2CStart ();
440  I2CWrite (0xD1);
441  thigh = I2Cread();
442  tlow = I2CreadNAck();
443  I2CStop();
444  I2Cidle ();
445  I2CStart ();
446  I2CWrite (0xD0);       // another write operation to load
     the DS1307 address pointer with the correct start address
447  I2CWrite (0);
```

```
448  I2CStop();
449   lcdData = ((hour>>4)+0x30);
450  sendData ();
451  lcdData = ((hour & 0x0F)+0x30);
452  sendData ();
453  lcdData = 0x3A;
454  sendData ();
455  lcdData = ((min>>4)+0x30);
456  sendData ();
457  lcdData = ((min & 0x0F)+0x30);
458  sendData ();
459  lcdData = 0x3A;
460  sendData ();
461  lcdData = ((sec>>4)+0x30);
462  sendData ();
463  lcdData = ((sec & 0x0F)+0x30);
464  sendData ();
465  if (hourformat == 0x31)
466  {
467     if (amdisplay == 1) writeString (" AM");
468  else writeString  (" PM");
469  }
470  line2();
471  writeString ("Date ");
472  lcdData = ((date >>4)+0x30);
473  sendData ();
474  lcdData = ((date  & 0x0F)+0x30);
475  sendData ();
476  lcdData = 0x3A;
477  sendData ();
478  lcdData = ((month >>4)+0x30);
479  sendData ();
```

```
480   lcdData = ((month  & 0x0F)+0x30);
481   sendData ();
482   lcdData = 0x3A;
483   sendData ();
484   lcdData = ((year >>4)+0x30);
485   sendData ();
486   lcdData = ((year  & 0x0F)+0x30);
487   sendData ();
488   cursorPos (3,0);
489   switch (month)
490      {
491         case 1:
492         {
493             Jan;
494         break;
495         }
496         case 2:
497         {
498             Feb;
499         break;
500         }
501         case 3:
502         {
503             Mar;
504         break;
505         }
506         case 4:
507         {
508             Apr;
509         break;
510         }
511         case 5:
```

```
512          {
513              May;
514          break;
515          }
516          case 6:
517          {
518              Jun;
519          break;
520          }
521          case 7:
522          {
523              Jul;
524          break;
525          }
526          case 8:
527          {
528              Aug;
529          break;
530          }
531          case 9:
532          {
533              Sep;
534          break;
535          }
536          case 0X10:
537          {
538              Oct;
539          break;
540          }
541          case 0X11:
542          {
```

```
543              Nov;
544         break;
545         }
546         case 0x12:
547         {
548             Dec;
549         break;
550         }
551  }
552  cursorPos (3,6);
553  switch (daynumber)
554     {
555         case 1:
556         {
557             Mon;
558         break;
559         }
560         case 2:
561         {
562             Tue;
563         break;
564         }
565         case 3:
566         {
567             Wed;
568         break;
569         }
570         case 4:
571         {
572             Thur;
573         break;
574         }
```

```
575         case 5:
576         {
577               Fri;
578         break;
579         }
580         case 6:
581         {
582               Sat;
583         break;
584         }
585         case 7:
586         {
587               Sun;
588         break;
589         }
590   }
591   cursorPos (4,0);
592   convert ();
593   cursorPos (1,0);
594   }
595   }
```

Figure 10-10. *The Display from the DS3231 Program*

Analysis of Listing 10-1

Lines 1–6 are the normal comments we have for our programs.

Lines 7–11 are the normal include files. Lines 13 and 14 allocate the two communication lines for the DS3231 to the I/O of the PIC. Lines 15–33 create the macros for the days of the week and the months of the year. This type of macros has been looked at in Chapter 9.

Lines 35–41 declare the variables we will be using within the program. Note some of them have been given initial values that will be loaded into them, for example, "secunits = 0x30." This will create a location in the memory that has the label "secunits," which is loaded with the value 0x30. This is the ASCII value for the character "0." Note most of these variables will be used to send data to the LCD, and so they will store the relevant ASCII for the characters to be displayed.

All the variables are of type "unsigned char" which use 8 bits, and all 8 bits are used for the value, that is, 0 to 255.

Line 43 void debounce ()

This creates a subroutine "debounce" which is a delay we will use to overcome the problem with switch bounce. The instructions for the subroutine are listed between lines 44 and 47.

Line 48 unsigned char Uart2TX(unsigned char x)

This creates a subroutine that is used to transmit a single character to the terminal. It expects a byte of data, which will contain the ASCII for the character we want to send, to be sent up to the subroutine. This will be copied into the local variable "x."

The subroutine will also be sending back, to the main program or where it was called from, data of the type unsigned char. This is indicated with the phrase "unsigned char" before the name of the subroutine.

Line 50 while (U2STAbits.UTXBF);

There could be data in the buffer register of the UART module still being transmitted. This instruction makes the PIC wait until the transmit buffer is empty. This is a "while (test is true) do what I say" instruction. The test will be true while the logic on the U2STAbits.UTXBF, the transmit buffer flag, is a logic '1'. When the last bit of data has been transmitted, the PIC will automatically reset this bit to a logic '0'. At this point, the test will become untrue, and the PIC can move on to the next instruction. While the test is true, the PIC will do nothing.

Line 51U2TXREG = x;

This loads the transmit register of the UART with the data that was sent up to the subroutine. This would be the ASCII of the character we want to transmit. This action will automatically start the process of transmitting the data.

Line 52 while (U2STAbits.UTXBF);

We now know there is data in the transmit buffer. This instruction makes the PIC wait until all 8 bits have been transmitted.

Line 53 U2TXREG = 0x0A;

This loads the transmit buffer with the ASCII for a new line. This will move the cursor, on the terminal, to the next line, but place it directly under the character that has just been transmitted.

Line 54 while (U2STAbits.UTXBF);

This makes sure the last character has finished being transmitted.

Line 55 U2TXREG = 0x0D;

This sends the ASCII for CR, that is, carriage return. This will send the cursor to the beginning of the current line. In this way, these two ASCII characters place the cursor at the beginning of the next new line on the terminal.

We could follow this instruction with another while (U2STAbits. UTXBF); do nothing, but there is one at the beginning of this subroutine.

Line 56 return x;

This closes the subroutine and returns back to the main loop with the data in the variable "x." This could be used to get the LCD to echo what character we are sending to the terminal on the LCD display; that is what we will do.

Line 58 unsigned char Uart2RX( )

This creates a subroutine that allows the PIC to receive a character from the terminal.

Line 60 while (!U2STAbits.URXDA);

This makes the PIC wait until the receive buffer of the UART has been filled by what is being transmitted to the PIC.

Line 61 return U2RXREG;

This ends the subroutine and returns to the main program with the contents of the receive register. This should be holding the data that has just been sent to the PIC.

Line 63 void sendString (const char *words)

This creates a subroutine that will send a string of characters to the terminal. We have looked at this instruction in Chapter 4.

Line 65 while (*words)

This is a complex instruction that, while the test is true, makes the PIC carry out the instructions between the opening and closing curly brackets on lines 66 and 70. We have looked at this instruction in Chapter 4.

Line 67 while (U2STAbits.UTXBF);

This is to make sure there is no data in the transmit buffer waiting to be transmitted.

Line 68 U2TXREG = *words;

This will load the, now empty, transmit buffer, with the contents of the array that the pointer "*words" is pointing to. In this instance, it will be the first character in the array that the call to the subroutine is transmitting.

Line 69 *words ++;

This simply increments the contents of the pointer "words." Therefore, the pointer will now be pointing to the next character in the array.

The PIC now goes back to line 65, and if the pointer is still NOT pointing to the null character, the PIC will carry out the instructions on lines 67, 68, and 69.

Line 71 Uart2TX(0x0A);

This instruction will be carried out after all the characters, in the string, have been sent to the terminal. It makes the PIC transmit the ASCII to send the cursor on the terminal to the next line, but stay in the same column, that is, the cursor will not go to the beginning of the new line.

Line 73 void convert ()

This is a subroutine, which takes a binary number that represents the numbers 0–9 and converts it into the ASCII to be displayed on the LCD. This particular version of the subroutine is to display the temperature data from the transducer on the LCD. This means it will cope with a temperature range of +127 to –127, with a definition of 0.25°C. We could have used the "sprint" function, but this would take up more memory. Really, if you think about what you want to do, you might find that you can come up with instructions that do it for you. You will have to do more of this type of programming as you expand your experience. Therefore, why not start with something that should be fairly straightforward, such as this convert subroutine?

Before we go too far with this analysis, I think I should explain how I have split the possible temperature readings up into characters to be displayed. The numbers could range from 127.75 to –127.75. Therefore, they will be made up of hundreds, tens, units, tenths, and hundredths. I have used variables for each part of the numbers, and they are

- "huns" for the hundreds part

- "tens" for the tens part

- "units" for the units part

- "decten" for the tenths part

- "dechun" for the hundredths part

Each of these variables will be used to store a single character that together makes up the whole value.

The overall number has an integer part that will be stored in the variable "thigh" and a fractional part that will be stored in the variable "tlow."

We start by considering the fractional part of the temperature reading.

Line 75 decten = 0x30;

As any number can start from 0, we need to load each digit that will be displayed with the ASCII for 0. The hexadecimal 0x30 is the ASCII for 0. This will load the variable "decten," which is for the tenths digit of the temperature reading, with the ASCII for "0."

Line 76 dechun = 0x30;

This does the same for the hundredths of the fractional part of the reading.

Line 77 if (tlow == 0b01000000)

This instruction is of the type "if (the test described here is true) do what I tell you to do next." The test for this "if" is, has the value in the variable "tlow" become equal to "0b0100000." The variable "tlow" will have been loaded with the contents of the fractional part of the temperature reading earlier in the program. It is the most significant two bits, that is, bits 7 and 6, that hold the two bits that make up the fractional part of the reading. These two bits will give four possible values which are shown in Table 10-26.

Table 10-26. *The Possible Fractional Readings*

Bit 7	Bit 6	Decten	dechun
0	0	0	0
0	1	2	5
1	0	5	0
1	1	7	5

With this test, on line 77, we are really testing to see if the fractional part of the temperature reading was 0.25. If the test is true, then the PIC must carry out the instructions written between the opening and closing curly brackets on lines 78 and 81.

Line 79 decten = (0x32);

This loads the variable "decten" with the ASCII for the character "2."

Line 80 dechun = (0x35);

This loads the variable "dechun" with the ASCII for the character "5."

Lines 82–91 perform the same type of test for the other two possible readings of the fractional part of the temperature reading.

Line 92 if (thigh & 0b10000000)

This "if" test performs a logical bit AND operation with the contents of the variable "thigh" and the binary number 0b10000000. As bits 6 to 0 of the binary number are all logic '0', then the result of the test will only be true if bit 7 of the variable "thigh" is also a logic '1'. We should appreciate that the integer part of the temperature reading, which will have been loaded into the variable "thigh" earlier in the program, uses a "signed number representation." This is where bit 7 of the variable is used to indicate whether the reading is positive, that is, bit 7 is a logic '0', or it is negative, that is, bit 7 is a logic '1'. This means that this instruction is testing to see if the temperature reading is negative. If it is, the result of the test will be true, and the PIC must carry out the instructions between the curly brackets on lines 93–122.

Line 94 negbit = 1;

This simply loads the variable "negbit" with a logic '1'. This is used later in the program to control the LCD display.

Line 95 tlow = ~tlow +1;

This performs a two's complement operation on the variable "tlow." The "~" part of the instruction is the C for invert. This will invert all the bits in the variable "tlow." The last part, the "+ 1", simply adds 1 to the contents of the now inverted variable "tlow." This means we now have the two's complement of the negative fractional part of the reading.

Line 96 decten = 0x30;

This ensures the variable "decten" has the ASCII for "0."

Line 97 dechun = 0x30;

This does the same for the "dechun" variable. These two instructions are needed to take care of the first possibility of the logic in bits 7 and 6 of the fractional reading as shown in Table 10-26.

Line 98 if (tlow == 0b01000000)

This test is to see if the fractional part of the reading is the second possibility, that is, the fractional part is 0.25, as shown in Table 10-15. If the test is true, the PIC must carry out the instructions between the curly brackets on lines 99 and 103.

Line 100 thigh = ~thigh;

This simply inverts all the bits in the variable thigh. Note we don't need to add "1" to "thigh" as no carry is produced.

Line 101 decten = (0x32);

This loads the variable "decten" with the ASCII for the character 2.

Line 102 dechun = (0x35);

This loads the variable "dechun" with the ASCII for the character 5.

Lines 104–122 are the test to take care of the other possible negative readings of the fractional part. Note in line 125, thigh = ~thigh+1; we do have to add 1 to the inverted variable "thigh." The explanation of why we need this has been gone through with Tables 10-14 to 10-17.

Line 123 if (thigh >= 0 && thigh < 10)

This is testing to see if the reading in "thigh" is between 0 and 9, that is, greater than or equal to 0 and less than 10. This would mean that the tens and hundreds of the reading would be 0, and the units would be the value stored in the variable "thigh."

Line 125 units = (thigh + 48);

This adds the decimal value of 48. This is the same as adding 0x30 as 30 in hexadecimal is 3x16, that is, 48 in decimal. Therefore, this converts the number in "thigh" into the ASCII to display the character for the units on the LCD display. Note, the ASCII for the numbers 0–9 are all represented, in ASCII, with 0x3?. The "?" question mark is replaced by the particular number from 0 to 9.

Lines 126 and 127 load the tens and the huns part of the reading with the ASCII for the character "0." We are using the decimal number, 48, for the ASCII for "0."

Line 129 if (thigh >= 10 && thigh < 20)

This tests to see if the value in the variable "thigh" is between 10 and 20. If the test is true, the PIC must carry out the instructions between lines 130 and 134.

Line 131 units = (thigh -10 + 48);

This loads the variable units with the contents of the variable "thigh." However, before it does that, it subtracts 10 from the variable "thigh" to ensure the units part of the reading is from 0 to 9. It then adds 48 to ensure the variable units are loaded with the ASCII for the character from "0 to 9."

Line 132 tens = (1 + 48);

This loads the variable "tens" with the ASCII to display "1."

Line 133 huns = 48;

This loads the variable "huns" with the ASCII for the character "0."

Lines 135–200 do the same for the other ranges of temperature readings. You might say that we could simply use the "sprintf" function that is in the "stdio" header file. Well, yes, you can, and it may be simpler, but you will miss out in understanding your programs. Also, I have used both approaches, and this approach actually uses less memory than using the "sprint" function. Really, the instructions are not too difficult to understand, and the more you use different instructions, the more you actually learn how to use C programming.

Line 201 if (negbit == 1) writeString ("Temp is -");

This is testing to see if the negbit has the value "1" in it. Note we may or may not have loaded this variable with a "1" earlier in the program; see line 92.

If the test is true, then the PIC must carry out the instruction writeString ("Temp is -"). This will call the subroutine "writeString," which is in the header file 8BitLCDPortD.h. It gets the PIC to display the characters written between the quotation marks. Note as this is a single-line instruction that the PIC must do if the test is true, there is no need to enclose it between curly brackets.

Line 202 else writeString ("Temp is ");

This is what the PIC must do if the result of the test on line 201 was untrue. It will call the subroutine "writeString" and send the characters "Temp is," that is, no negative sign, as the temperature is positive. If the test on line 201 was true, the PIC would skip this instruction on line 202.

Line 203 if (huns == 48) goto distens;

This is testing to see if the value in the variable "huns" is the ASCII for "0." If the test is true, then we would not want to display a 0 in the reading, as you don't want to show a temperature of 025.25 ^{0}C; it would be better to display 25.25^{0}C. If the test is true, then the PIC must skip the following instructions and jump to the label "distens," which is on line 206. If the test is untrue, then the PIC simply moves on to the next instruction on line 204.

Line 204 lcdData = huns;

This loads the variable "lcdData" with the ASCII data that is in the variable "huns."

Line 205 lcdOut ();

This calls the subroutine "lcdOut" that is in the header file 8BitLCDPortD.h. This simply sends the data in the variable "lcdData" to the LCD.

Line 206 distens: if (tens == 48 && huns == 48) goto disunits;

This is where the label "distens" is. The instruction here is a test to see if the variables "tens" and "huns" both have the ASCII for the characters "0." If they do, then the PIC must skip the following instructions and jump to the label "disunits" at line 209.

Lines 207 and 208 send the value for the "tens" reading to the LCD.

Lines 211 and 212 send the value for the decimal point, "," to the LCD.

Lines 213 and 214 send the value for the "decten" reading to the LCD.

Lines 215 and 216 send the value for the "dechun" reading to the LCD.

Lines 217–224 send the ASCII of ^{0}C and two spaces to the LCD.

Line 225 negbit = 0;

This ensures that the variable "negbit" has the value of "0" in it.

Line 227 void setclock ()

This creates the subroutine that writes the correct time and date to the DS3231.

Line 229 I2Cidle();

This calls the subroutine to check that the I^{2}C module is doing nothing.

Line 230 I2CStart ();

This calls the subroutine to send the start signal on the I^{2}C bus.

Line 231 I2CWrite (0xD0);

This calls the subroutine to write the address of the DS3231 to the I^{2}C bus. Bit 0 of the data is a logic '0', which tells the DS3231 we want to write to it. Note the hex value 0xD0 in binary is 0b11010001, where bits 1 to 7 contain the actual address of the DS3231. Bit 0 of the data is a control bit that is used to tell the device if we want to write to it or read from it. If this bit is a logic '1', then we want to read from the device; if it is a logic '0', then we want to write to the device. As bit 0 is a logic '0', then this instruction tells the DS3231 we will be writing to it.

Line 232 I2CWrite (0);

This sends the value "0" to the DS3231, which is then loaded into the address pointer of the DS3231. This is done to ensure we will write to the first address in the DS3231. This register holds the value for the seconds of the current time.

Line 233 I2CWrite (sec);

This calls the "I2CWrite" subroutine to send the value in the "sec" variable to the DS3231.

Lines 234–239 write the remaining settings for the current time and date to the DS3231.

Line 240 I2CStop();

This calls the "I2CStop" subroutine to put the stop signal on the I²C bus. This is because we have finished writing to the DS3231.

Line 242 void setTheRTC ()

This creates a subroutine that will allow the user to set the clock using the terminal software "Tera Term."

Line 244 sendString ("Input the tens digits of the year.");

This calls the subroutine "sendString" on line 63. This will get the PIC to send the characters written between the two quotation marks to the terminal.

Line 245 sendString ("Note the PIC will echo your input");

This sends another message to the terminal.

Line 246 yeartens = Uart2RX ();

The PIC will then call the subroutine "Uart2RX," which gets the PIC to wait until data is sent back from the terminal. When data is sent back, the PIC will load that data into the variable "yeartens."

Lines 247 Uart2TX (yeartens);

This loads the TX register of the UART module with the character for the "yeartens" inputted from the terminal, ready to transmit it to the terminal. In this way, it is the PIC that echoes the characters back to the terminal.

Lines 248 and 249 send the same character to the LCD. This is so that we can see what value we are setting for the tens of the current year.

Line 250 yeartens = (yeartens - 0x30);

This is removing the "0x30" value from the data in the variable "yeartens." This is because the data would be the ASCII for the number. However, later we would only need the number. For example, if the "yeartens" value was supposed to be 2 for 20, the actual value, returned from the terminal, would be 0x32, the ASCII for the number "2." However, when we send this value to the DS3231, we would only need the number 2. Therefore, we need to remove the 0x30 from the variable. This is what this instruction does.

Line 251 sendString ("Input the units digits of the year.");

This sends a new string of characters to the terminal.

Lines 252–286 allow the user to set the remaining data for the current date.

Line 287 sendString ("Input a number for day of the week.");

This sends the characters to ask the user to set the current day of the week.

Line 288 sendString ("i.e. 1 = Mon, 2 = Tues, etc.");

This sends the instructions of how the PIC expects the days of the week to be identified.

Line 289 daynumber = Uart2RX ();

This loads the variable "daynumber" with the value sent from the terminal to identify the current day of the week.

Lines 290–292 echo the value to the terminal and the LCD.

Lines 293 and 294 send the ASCII for the colon ":" to the LCD.

Line 295 sendString ("Set the time ");

This sends the message "Set the time" to the terminal.

Lines 296 and 297 clear the LCD screen and send the same message to the LCD.

Line 298 sends the cursor to the beginning of the second line on the LCD.

Line 299 sendString ("Input the tens digits of the hour.");

This sends the next message to the terminal.

Lines 300–338 allow the user to set the current time, echoing the settings to the terminal and the LCD. They also get the respective variables ready to be written to the DS3231.

Lines 339 and 340 send messages to the terminal telling the user how to tell the PIC the format, 12hrs or 24hrs, of the time.

Line 341 hourformat = Uart2RX ();

This loads the variable "hourformat" with the response from the user.

Lines 342–344 echo that data to the terminal and the LCD.

Line 345 if (hourformat == 0x32) goto alldone;

This is testing to see if the data in the variable "hourformat" is the ASCII for the number "2." If it is, then this would mean the format is 24hrs. If the test is true, then the PIC must carry out the instruction "goto alldone." This will make the PIC jump to the label "alldone" which is on line 351. If the test is not true, as the value in the variable "hourformat" is "1," then the PIC would move on to the next instruction on line 346.

Line 346 sendString ("Input a number for AM or PM type 1 for AM or 2 for PM.");

This sends the message, explaining how the user can identify which time of day format they want to use, to the terminal.

Lines 347–349 load the variable "amformat" with the value inputted by the user. This value is then echoed to the terminal and the LCD.

Line 351 hour = alldone: ((hourtens << 4)+ (hourunits & 0x0F));

This is the label "alldone" that the PIC would go to if we are using 24-hour format. However, the PIC would also come here naturally if the time format is 12hrs. The "hour" variable will contain the data to be sent to the DS3231, to be loaded into register 0x02, and so set the hours to the current time. Note the "hourtens" value must be placed in the high nibble of the variable "hour." That is why the bits in the variable "hourtens" are shifted four places to the left before being loaded into the variable "hour." Then the instruction will add the value of the contents of the variable "hourunits," but only the low nibble. That is why the data in the "hourunits" variable is being bit ANDed with 0x0F to mask out the high nibble of the "hourunits" variable.

Lines 352–356 do the same for the other variables for the time and date setting for the display.

Line 357 if (hourformat == 0x31)

This is a test to see what hour format the user has set, that is, 12hrs or 24hrs. This is testing to see if the user has chosen the 12-hour format, which would have loaded the "hourformat" variable with the value 0x31. If the test is true, then the PIC would carry out the instructions between the curly brackets on lines 358 and 369. If the test is untrue, the PIC would simply jump to line 370.

Line 359 if (amformat == 0x31)

This is testing to see if the user has inputted the value "1," that is, to the question is it am now, when they are setting the time. If the test is true, the PIC would carry out the instructions between lines 360 and 363. It would also skip the instructions between lines 364 and 368.

Line 361 amdisplay = 1;

If the user has selected the time period "am," then the PIC would carry out this instruction that loads the variable "amdisplay" with a logic '1.'

Line 362 hour = (hour+0x40);

This is the other instruction the PIC must carry out if the time period is "am." This adds the hex value of 0x40 to the variable "hour." This will ensure that bit 6 of the register 0x02 is a logic '1,' which sets the time format to 12hrs, and bit 5 is a logic '0,' which sets the time period to "am." See Table 10-5.

Line 366 amdisplay = 0;

If the user has selected "2," that is, pm, for the time period, then the PIC would carry out the following two instructions. This instruction loads the variable "amdisplay" with the value "0." Note this variable "amdisplay" is used on line 467 to determine what time period is displayed on the LCD. This and the next instruction on line 367 are within the "else" statement that the PIC would carry out if the "if" test, on line 359, was untrue.

Line 367 hour = (hour+0x60);

This adds the value of 0x60 to the variable "hour." This will set both bits 6 and 5 of the register at address 0x02 to tell the DS3231 that we are setting the time format to 12hrs and the time period to pm. See Table 10-5.

Line 370 display: sendString ("Time set");

This will call the subroutine "sendString" which will send the characters "Time set" to the terminal.

Lines 372–388 are the normal instructions we have looked at in previous programs.

Line 389 writeString ("Setting the RTC ");

This calls the subroutine "writeString" to display the message "Setting the RTC" on the LCD.

Line 390 cursorPos (2,0);

This calls the subroutine "cursorPos" and moves the cursor on the LCD to line 2 column 0, that is, the beginning of line 2.

Line 391 writeString ("Date ");

This displays the characters "Date" on the LCD, as the first thing we set is the current date.

Line 392 I2CInit();

This calls the subroutine "I2CInit" which is in the 32biti2cprotocol.h header file. This and all the subroutines that use the I2C protocol have been analyzed in Chapter 7.

Line 393 U2MODE = 0x8808;

This writes to the U2MODE register and loads the value 0x8808 into it. This register controls the mode you want to use for the second of the two UART modules the PIC32 has. The data written to the register does the following:

- It turns the module 2 on by setting bit 15 to a logic '1.'

- It sets the UART into simplex mode by setting bit 11 to a logic '1.'

- As bits 9 and 8 are both set to a logic '0,' then the U2TX and U2RX are set to simplex mode, and their direction is controlled by the module. The directions of handshaking pins U2CTS, U2RTS, and U2BCLK are set by the normal TRIS settings.

- The baud rate is set to high speed as bit 3 is a logic '1.'

We could have loaded the control register, U2MODE, with 0x0808, which would have done the same, except turned the UART off while we configured it. It may be good practice to do this, but we would then have to add another instruction to turn the UART on, using U2MODESET = 0x8000;. It does seem to work well using both methods. It is up to you which method you use.

Line 394 U2STA = 0x1400;

This loads the status register for the U2 module with 0x1400. This has the following actions:

- Bits 24 to 13 are set to 0, as we are not using those aspects of the UART module.

- Bit 12 is set to a logic '1' which enables the U2 receiver.

- Bit 10 is also set to a logic '1' which enables the U2 transmitter.

These are the major settings for this register.

Line 395 U2BRG = (36000000/4/9600)-1;

This instruction carries out the correct expression to load the U2BRG register with the correct value to set the baud rate for the UART to 9600. The 36000000 is the frequency of the PBCLK. To ensure correct communication with the terminal, you must ensure the baud rate for the terminal is also set to 9600. You could have used a different baud rate, but 9600 is one of the common baud rates.

Line 396 setTheRTC ();

Now that we have set up the UART module, ready for communicating with the terminal, we can set the current time and date, etc., for the RTC. This instruction calls the subroutine we have set up to do this.

Line 397 setclock ();

This calls the subroutine to load the DS3231 with the setting for the current time and date.

Lines 398–402 are used to write to the DS3231 and load the address pointer with the value 0. This is to ensure that the address pointer is pointing to the first register, at address 0x00, ready for the program to read the current data, for the seconds, when we start to read the time data from the DS3231. We have looked at these instructions in the "setclock" subroutine.

Line 403 clearTheScreen ();

This calls the subroutine "clearTheScreen" to clear the LCD and send the cursor to the beginning of line 1.

Line 404 while (1)

This is a forever loop that is used to prevent the PIC from trying to carry out the instructions between lines 372 and 403, as they only need be carried out once, at the start of the program.

Line 406 writeString ("Time ");

This just sends the characters "Time" to the LCD, as we will be displaying the current time, etc., on the LCD. Note there is an empty space between the letter "e" and the quotation marks. This is to ensure a space is between the word "Time" and the value of the data on the LCD screen.

Line 407 I2Cidle ();

The program now needs to communicate with the DS3231 to get the current time, etc., from it. As we are using the I²C protocol to communicate with the DS3231, we need to go through the normal protocol to ensure good communication. This instruction calls the subroutine to check that the I²C module is not currently doing anything.

Line 408 I2CStart ();

This instruction calls the subroutine to send the start signal.

Line 409 I2CWrite (0xD1);

This calls the subroutine to write to the DS3231. Note the hex value 0xD1 in binary is 0b11010001, where bits 1 to 7 contain the actual address of the DS3231. Bit 0 of the data is a control bit that is used to tell the device if we want to write to it or read from it. If this bit is a logic '1', then we want to read from the device; if it is a logic '0', then we want to write to the device. This instruction tells the DS3231 we will be reading from it.

Line 410 sec = I2Cread();

This calls the subroutine to read from the address that the address pointer in the DS3231 is currently pointing to. This will actually be the first address, that is, address 0x00, of the registers in the DS3231. This will contain the value of the information of the seconds of the current time. When the subroutine finishes, it will send back that information in the RX register of the PIC that will be loaded into the variable "sec," as detailed in the instruction.

Lines 411–415 do the same for the other variables, of the program, for the time and date. Note, after each read, the address pointer of the DS3231 will increment so that it is pointing at the address of the next register the program wants to read from. You must ensure that you know what the contents of the next address are and ensure they are loaded into the correct variable.

Line 416 year = I2CreadNAck();

This is reading the last item we want from the DS3231. That being the case, the PIC will not need to send an acknowledgment signal to the DS3231, it will send the NACK or not acknowledged signal. This is why we are using a different subroutine, as with the I2CreadNAck subroutine.

Line 417 I2CStop();

Now we have got all the time and data information we want from the DS3231, we can put a stop signal on the I²C bus.

Line 418 if (hourformat == 0x31)

Here, we are testing to see if the data in the variable "hourformat" has become equal to 0x31. You should appreciate that I interpret the use of the double equal sign, "==", as meaning the data has "become equal to" what I indicate here. The single equal sign, "=", forces the variable to become the value indicated here. You should remember that with line 339, we asked the user to indicate what format we would use, that is, 12hrs or 24hrs. A logic '1' means we are using 12-hour format. Therefore, this is asking if we are using 12-hour format. If we are, then the PIC must carry out the instructions between lines 419 and 430.

Line 420 if (hour & 0b00100000)

This performs a logical bit AND between the bits in the variable "hour" and the binary value 0b00100000. As only bit 5 of the binary number is a logic '1', then really this is testing to see if bit 5 of the variable "hour" has been set to a logic '1'. This would happen if bit 5 of the register 0x02 has been set to a logic '1', by the DS3231. This would mean that the current time is now in "pm" format. This then means that this instruction is now asking whether it is now pm or not. Note, this test is only required if we are using 12-hour format for the time, hence why we only need to carry it out if the test on line 418 was true. If this test on line 420 is true, that is, it is now pm, the PIC must carry out the instructions between lines 421 and 424.

Line 422 amdisplay = 0;

This loads the variable "amdisplay" with the value 0. We will use this variable later to determine what time period we should display; see line 465.

Line 422 hour = (hour-0x60);

This will subtract the hex value 0x60 from the current contents of the variable "hour." Note on line 412 we loaded the variable "hour" with what date was in register 0x02 in the DS3231. Bits 6 and 5 of address 0x02 are used to state what time format we are using and whether the time period is am or pm. If we are at this instruction of the program, both bits 6 and 5 would be a logic '1', as we are using 12-hour format and the current time must be in the pm time period. These two bits do not make up the value of the data for the current hour part of the time. This instruction will ensure that both bits 6 and 5 in the "hour" variable will be changed to a logic '0'. Note no other bits in the variable "hour" are affected. Therefore, the contents of the variable "hour" will simply hold the value of the hour time.

Line 425 else

If the test on line 420 is untrue, then the PIC must carry out the instructions set out here between lines 426 and 429. Note there is no semicolon at the end of this line as this instruction does not end until line 430. Also, if the test on line 420 was true, the PIC would simply skip lines 425–429.

Line 427 amdisplay = 1;

This sets the value in the variable "amdisplay" to 1. This is used later in the program; see line 465.

Line 431 hour = (hour - 0x40);

If the test in line 420 is untrue, then the time period is now am, and bit 5 of the register 0x02 is a logic '0'. This means we only need to subtract 0x40 from the variable "hour" as only bit 6 of the variable "hour" would be a logic '1'.

Line 431 //get ready to read temperature

This is just a comment to try and split the listing up into logical sections.

Line 432 I2Cidle ();

We have to start the I²C process again, and so we start by making sure the I²C bus is idle.

Line 433 I2CStart ();

This subroutine puts a start signal on the I²C bus.

Line 434 I2CWrite (0xD0);

We now call the subroutine to write to the DS3231, but the control bit, bit 0 of the data sent, is a logic '0'. This is because we will be writing to the DS3231.

Line 435 I2CWrite (0x11);

This is writing the number 0x11 to the DS3231. This value will be loaded into the DS3231 address pointer to ensure it is pointing to that address. You should appreciate that after the instruction on line 416, where we read the data for the year of the current date, the address pointer would have been increased to the value 0x0E; see Table 10-5. This is the register for the control data for the DS3211. The temperature reading is at address 0x11. Therefore, we must load the address pointer with that address. That is what this instruction does. We should appreciate that, with a new write procedure to the DS3231, the DS3231 will be expecting that the data sent after the initial write to it will be the value of the address that it must load into its address pointer. That is why we are sending the address "0x11" now, as we know the DS3231 will load this value into its address pointer.

Line 436 I2CStop();

We have finished writing to the DS3231, and we need to get ready to read from it. Therefore, we must put a stop signal on the I²C bus.

Line 437 //read the temperature

Just some more comments to make it clear what each section of the listing is doing. These are optional.

Line 438 I2Cidle ();

Check that the I²C bus is idle.

Line 439 I2CStart ();

Put another start signal on the I²C bus.

Line 440 I2CWrite (0xD1);

Now write to the DS3231 to inform it that we want to read from it; hence, bit 0 is a logic '1'.

Line 441 thigh = I2Cread();

Now read the integer part of the temperature reading and load it into the variable "thigh."

Line 442 tlow = I2CreadNAck();

Now read the fractional part of the temperature reading and load it into the variable "tlow." This is the last register we need to read from; therefore, we use the "I2CreadNAck" subroutine.

Line 443 I2CStop();

We have now finished reading from the DS3231, so put a stop signal on the I²C bus.

We now need to reload the address pointer in the DS3231 with the value 0. This is to ensure the pointer is pointing to the first register, ready for repeating the whole read sequence. This is done with lines 444–448.

Line 449 lcdData = ((hour>>4)+0x30);

We are now ready to display all the data for the current time, date, and temperature on the LCD. However, we need to ensure the data is in the correct position in the variables to be sent to the LCD. We will start by displaying the "hourtens" character on the LCD. We should also appreciate that the LCD will currently be displaying the word Time, as stated on line 406.

The "hour" variable will contain the value of the tens at bits 5 and 4 of the register 0x02 that was copied into the variable "hour" with line 412. This now needs to be placed into the low nibble of the variable "lcdData," ready to be sent to the LCD. This instruction does that in two parts. The complete instruction will load the variable "lcdData" with the result of firstly shifting the bits in the variable "hour" four places to the right. This simply moves the high nibble of the data in the variable "hour" to the low nibble and replaces the high nibble with four logic '0s'. The next part simply adds the value 0x30 into the result. This means the result will have 0x3 in the high nibble and the value of the tens in the low nibble. This result will be loaded into the variable "lcdData" ready to be sent to the LCD. In this way, the value in the variable "lcdData" will be the correct ASCII for the number in the tens part of the hour value. You should appreciate that after this instruction the original value in the variable "hour" will not have changed.

Line 450 lcdOut ();

This calls the subroutine "lcdOut" which will send the data in the variable "lcdData" to the LCD.

Line 451 lcdData = ((hour & 0x0F)+0x30);

This performs a similar operation on the variable "hour," but we just use the low nibble of the variable "hour." This is done by bit ANDing the data in the variable "hour" with the hex value 0x0F. As the high nibbles of 0x0F are all logic '0,' then this part of the instruction masks out the high nibble, which is what we want. The second part of the instruction adds the hex value 0x30 to ensure the high nibble of the result now has the hex value 0x3. This is required for the ASCII for all numbers from 0 to 9.

Line 452 sends the data in "lcdData" to the LCD.

Lines 453 and 454 send the ASCII for the colon ":" to the LCD, which is used to separate the characters of time and date.

Lines 455–464 perform the same action for the remaining value of the current time and date.

Line 465 if (hourformat == 0x31)

Here, we are again testing to see if the time used is 12-hour or 24-hour format. If it is using 12-hour format, then we need to know if the display should be showing am or pm. If the test is true, the PIC will carry out the instruction between lines 466 and 469. If the test was untrue, then the PIC would skip over these lines.

Line 467 if (amdisplay == 1) writeString (" AM");

Here, we are testing to see if we have loaded the variable "amdisplay" with the value 1. This would have been done with line 427. If the value in "amdisplay" has become equal to 1, then we should call the subroutine "writeString" to send the characters AM to the LCD. This is a one-line instruction for the result of the test, and so we don't need the curly brackets.

If the test is true, then the PIC will skip the instruction on the next line.

Line 468 else writeString (" PM");

This is the "else" statement that states what the PIC must do if the test, on line 467, was untrue. Again, this is a one-line instruction which will simply send the characters PM to the LCD.

Line 470 line2();

We have finished displaying the current time, so we can move the cursor to the beginning of line 2 on the LCD. This is done by calling the subroutine to do that.

Line 471 writeString ("Date ");

This sends the characters "Date" to the LCD. Note there is an empty space between the letter "e" and the quotation marks. This is to ensure a space is between the word Date and the value of the data on the LCD screen.

Lines 472–487 send the values for the current date to the LCD in the correct position. This is done in a similar process as to the values for the time.

Line 488 cursorPos (3,0);

This calls the subroutine "cursorPos" to send the cursor to line 3 at column 0 on the LCD.

Line 489 switch (month)

This instruction uses the switch and case directive to choose which month of the year to display on the LCD. It is the contents of the variable "month" that will determine which of the 12 case directives the PIC carries out. The choices use the macro statements for the months as declared between lines 22 and 33.

Lines 491–548 list the 12 choices that the PIC can choose from. The choices send the correct characters to display the current month on the LCD at the start of line 3.

Line 552 cursorPos (3,6);

This moves the cursor to column 6 on the LCD. Note this is the seventh position on line 3. This is where we want the cursor to be to display the day of the month.

Lines 553–590 set out a second switch and case directive, with the variable "daynumber" being used to choose which characters are used to display the current day of the month on the LCD. The choices use the macro statements for the days as declared between lines 15 and 21.

Line 591 cursorPos (4,0);

This moves the cursor to the beginning of line 4 on the LCD.

Line 592 convert ();

This calls the subroutine that converts the data for the current temperature into the ASCII to display it on the LCD. It sends the characters, in the correct position, to the LCD.

Line 593 cursorPos (1,0);

This sends the cursor to the beginning of the first line on the LCD.

The PIC now goes back to line 404, with the while (1) loop, and starts the process all over again.

Figure 10-11 shows an example of the Tera Term display while setting the current time.

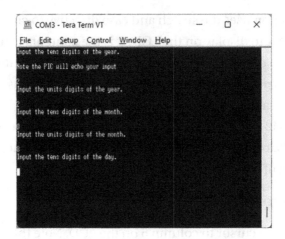

Figure 10-11. *The Tera Term Display While Setting the Time and Date*

I hope this analysis has gone some way to helping you understand how the instructions work and carry out the requirements of the program. It is always a difficult choice of writing too much or too little.

Summary

In this chapter, we have looked at how we can use the DS3231 module to provide a Real-Time Clock for the PIC. We have studied how we can apply the two's complement on a 10-bit binary number that has an integer and a fractional part. The analysis has, I hope, shown you that you need to understand how the devices you want to use actually work. We have studied the registers of the DS3231 and how the internal address pointer controls what registers we are writing to or reading from. We have studied how we can use the temperature sensor on the DS3231 to display the current temperature on the LCD. We have studied how we can manipulate the bits of the data to ensure they are ready to be displayed correctly on the LCD and a terminal. I hope you have found this chapter useful and informative.

In the next chapter, we will look at using the internal Real-Time Clock module that comes with the 32-bit PIC.

CHAPTER 11

The RTCC Module

This is the final chapter that deals with a Real-Time Clock and Calendar, that is, the RTCC program. This time, we are going to look at the module that comes with the PIC32. This PIC has an internal module that provides you with all the aspects you would want from an RTCC system. It can be used to provide you with everything you need to create a complete calendar and alarm system. It only requires an external crystal oscillator that provides the 32.768kHz signal that synchronizes the RTCC.

After reading this chapter, you will know how to configure the RTCC and use many of its features.

The RTCC Module of the 32-Bit PIC

This module can be used to provide a Real-Time Clock and Calendar function over long periods of time with very good accuracy. It can provide a 100-year calendar with automatic leap year adjustment. The following is a list of some of its features:

- Time: Hours, minutes, and seconds
- 24-hour format (military time)
- Visibility of one-half second period
- Provides calendar: Weekday, date, month, and year

H. Ward, *Introductory Programs with the 32-bit PIC Microcontroller*,
Maker Innovations Series, https://doi.org/10.1007/978-1-4842-9051-4_11

- Alarm configurable for half a second, one second, ten seconds, one minute, ten minutes, one hour, one day, one week, one month, and one year

- Alarm repeats with decrementing counter

- Alarm with indefinite repeat: Chime

- Year range: 2000 to 2099

- Leap year correction

- BCD format for smaller firmware overhead

- Optimized for long-term battery operation

- Fractional second synchronization

- User calibration of the clock crystal frequency with auto-adjust

- Calibration range: ±0.66 seconds error per month

- Calibrates up to 260 ppm of crystal error

- Requirements: External 32.768kHz clock crystal

- Alarm pulse or seconds clock output on the RTCC pin

The RTCC uses two main 32-bit registers that hold the time and date of the RTCC. These registers will be continually updated on each increment of the clock signal. However, the user must be able to write to these registers so that they can set the correct time and date for the RTCC.

The PIC uses BCD, binary-coded decimal, format to store the information in these registers. Therefore, it is essential that you understand how the PIC uses BCD to format these two registers. The format is best explained with an example; we will create two 32-bit memory locations in which we will store the new time and date we want to set the RTCC to. As an example, the time and date we will write to these two locations are

newTime = 0x01020300

newDate = 0x21012601

The values written here are in hexadecimal format, which means each digit represents four binary bits. We will now look at what each bit of the two variables relates to.

With the data in "newTime," the first 8 bits, that is, "00," set the half second value to 0.

The next 8 bits, "03," set the seconds value to 03.

The next 8 bits, "02," set the minutes value to 02.

The final 8 bits, "01," set the hours value to 01.

This means that we would be setting the current time to 01 hrs 02 mins 03 seconds exact, that is, 01:02:03.

With the data in "newDate," the first 8 bits, 01, would be setting the day of the week to Monday; see Table 11-1.

The next 8 bits set the date of the month to 26.

The next 8 bits set the month of the year to 01, that is, January.

The final 8 bits set the year to 21 in the century 20.

This means we would be setting the current date to Monday 26th January 2021, that is, 26:01:21.

The data sheet for the PIC32, under the section for the RTCC, provides us with tables we must use to set the format of the date and time. These are shown in (Tables 11-1 to 11-3).

Table 11-1. *The Format to Represent the Days of the Week*

Day of the Week	Number to Represent the Day
Sunday	0
Monday	1
Tuesday	2
Wednesday	3
Thursday	4
Friday	5
Saturday	6

Table 11-2. *The Format to Represent the Months of the Year*

Month of Year	Number to Represent the Months	Maximum Number of Days
January	01	31
February	02	28/29
March	03	31
April	04	30
May	05	31
June	06	30
July	07	31
August	08	31
September	09	30
October	10	31
November	11	30
December	12	31

Table 11-3. *The Meaning of the Bits in the RTCTIME and RTCDATE 32-Bit Registers*

Year		Month		Date		Day of Week	
0–9	0–9	0–1	0–9	0–3	0–9	0	0–6
Hour		**Minutes**		**Seconds**		**Half Second**	
0–2	0–9	0–5	0–9	0–5	0–9	0	0–1

The following shows the basic principles of how we can set the current time and date of the RTCC:

1. unsigned long newTime, newDate; //declare the required variables of type unsigned long, that is, 32 bits.

2. newTime = 0x01020300; //load the "newTime" variable with the correct time.

3. newDate = 0x21012601; //load the "newDate" variable with the correct date.

4. Now disable all interrupts.

5. Unlock the RTCC by sending the two unlock codes to the SYSKEY. The two unlock codes will be examined later.

6. Next, turn off the RTCC.

7. RTCCONCLR 0x8000; // use the CLR declaration to clear, that is, force to logic '0', bit 15 of the RTCCON register. This turns the RTCC off.

8. Wait for the RTCC to turn off.

9. RTCTIME = newTime; // The register "RTCTIME" is used to hold the data for the current time. This instruction loads the register with the time we set the clock to.

10. RTCDATE = newDate; // The register "RTCDATE" is used to hold the data for the current date. This instruction loads the register with the data to set the date of the RTC to what we want.

11. RTCCONSET 0x8000; // use the SET declaration to set, that is, force to logic '1', bit 15 of the RTCCON register. This turns the RTCC on.

12. while (!RTCCKLON); wait for the RTCC to come back on.

This is the basic approach to loading the RTCC module with the correct time and date. To unlock the RTCC module, we must write the first unlock code to the SYSKEY, 0xaa996655. Write the second unlock code to the SYSKEY, 0x556699aa. This is to ensure you don't accidentally overwrite the current time and date. We will look at how we do this when we analyze the first program listing that uses the RTCC module of the PIC32.

Of course, we are just setting a random time and date by loading the "newTime" and "newDate" variables with a value as shown with "newTime = 0x01020300" and "newDate = 0x21012601". Really, the program must allow the user to set the RTCC to the current time and date. Also, we must get the program to display the time and date that is recorded by the RTCC as we set it.

We have looked at a program that allows the user to set the current time using three buttons to increment, decrement, and set in Chapter 9. We also allowed the program to display the current time and date in Chapters 9 and 10. So really, we could say we have covered it. That would be true except that the programs of Chapters 9 and 10 were using unsigned chars as we used 8 bits of data. However, the RTCC stores the current time and date in 32-bit registers. We can still allow the user to input the current time and date using unsigned chars, that is, 8 bits. We could also send the data to the LCD in 8 bits, but we must change the 8 bits, inputted by the user and sent to the LCD, into 32 bits for the specific 32-bit data registers. It is also slightly more complicated in that the data in the time and date are entered into the 32-bit register by the RTCC using BCD (binary-coded decimal). Therefore, before we move on, we should take a look at what BCD is.

BCD (Binary-Coded Decimal)

The following analysis is quite involved, and it may take some repeated reading before you fully appreciate what I am trying to put across. I feel that I should explain why I am putting so much effort into analyzing the process. Well, in writing this book, I am not only trying to explain how the instructions in C work, I am trying to show you what you need to do to write challenging programs. There is no real blueprint that will fit all programs you write. However, there are some essential processes that I use, which are as follows:

1. Study how the devices you are using work.

   a. This entails studying their data sheet to fully understand how the registers control the actions of the device.

2. Once you have studied the requirements of the devices you will be using, and what you are trying to do with your program, you should break every action down to steps that have just one or two responses.

     a. Break every response to a series of questions that have only two possible answers.

     b. Now look for the instructions in your chosen programming language that can fulfill those two possible answers.

This is only a brief attempt to try and help you appreciate what you must do to write good programs. I hope it will help you appreciate why I have devoted so much of my book into explaining how the devices we use work. This following section of the book is aimed at explaining how we manipulate numbers and how we get them ready to be displayed on some useful devices, the LCD being a common device. I hope you find it useful.

So, what is BCD? Well, it is really a way of making sure that an 8-bit binary number can be used to represent numbers in tens and units. Really, the idea is that the 8 bits can be split into two 4 binary bits, or two nibbles, which can only store values from 0 to 9. The high nibble would store the tens data, and the low nibble would store the unit's data. Really, they can only store values from 0 to their respective maximum. Normally, with our denary system, this would be from 0 to 9, but with the time and date, some of the high nibbles will have a lower maximum. For example, the seconds can only go from 00 to 59, that is, the tens nibble, the high nibble, has a maximum of 5.

This idea works in that when the low nibble has reached 9, and the high nibble is showing 0. Then, at the next increment, we actually add 7 and not 1 to the binary value. This would mean that, in decimal, the value would go to 16, but in binary it would go to 00010000, that is, 1 in the high nibble and 0 in the low nibble. This is "1" in the tens nibble and "0" in the units nibble. Then, when the low nibble next reaches 9, we again add 7 to the binary number. The result of this is shown in Table 11-4.

Table 11-4. *Adding in BCD*

Hex	B7	B6	B5	B4	B3	B2	B1	B0
0x19	0	0	0	1	1	0	0	1
+ 0x07	0	0	0	0	0	1	1	1
0x20	0	0	1	0	0	0	0	0

In this example, which I will use to try and explain the process, we will use the variable "result." The variable "result" is the 8-bit variable that is holding the number we want to display as two characters, "tens" and "units," on the LCD. This means that the 8-bit number would look correct, as shown in Table 11-4, if we looked at the value written in hex, that is, it would be 0x20. This is "2" in the tens nibble and "0" in the low nibble. However, the real value would be 32 in decimal, not 20 as we would want. Also, if we wanted to display the result on the LCD, we would want the first character to be the 2 in hex, or 0010 in the high nibble, that is, show the "tens" first. We also need to remember that we would have to send these values to the LCD in ASCII. We have seen that the ASCII for any number from 0 to 9 needs to be 0x30 to 0x39, using the hexadecimal format. This means we would have to add the value 0x30 in hex, or 48 in decimal. We will work in hex. The next character on the LCD would be 0, that is, the "units." It is quite easy to get the 0 in the second character to be 0x30, ready for the LCD, as we could mask out the high nibble of the variable "result" and then add the 0x30. This could be done using the following instructions:

- **lcdData = ((result & 0x0F) + 0x30);**: This would simply load "lcdData," which is the variable we send the LCD, as with our previous program, with a copy of what's in the low nibble of the result, ignoring the high nibble, as this is masked out. This is done with the (result & 0x0F) instruction, which performs a logical bit AND with the 8 bits in the variable "result" and the 8 bits 0x0F, that is, 0b00001111. The last part of the instruction adds 0x30 to the result of the bit AND operation. This ensures the high nibble, loaded into the variable "lcdData," would be 0011. Once this instruction has been completed, the binary value in the variable "lcdData" would be 0b00110000, which is what we want to send the "units" part of the number, that is, the ASCII for "0." This would be the second character we would send to the LCD.

- **sendData ();:** This just sends the contents of the variable "lcdData" to the LCD using the subroutine "sendData."

However, the instruction to load the variable "lcdData" with the contents of the high nibble of the result, ready for the first character to be displayed, is slightly more difficult. This instruction would be

```
lcdData = ((result>>4 & 0x0F) + 0x30);
```

This would firstly shift the data in the variable "result" four places to the right. Then we would mask out the high nibble in the same way as the previous instruction. Then, finally, we would add the value 0x30, as we need the whole 8 binary values to equal the ASCII for the character we want to display. To help you understand this process, Table 11-5 shows how the process works.

Table 11-5. *Manipulating the High Nibble Ready to Send to the LCD*

	B7	B6	B5	B4	B3	B2	B1	B0
Data in result	0	0	1	0	0	0	0	0
Data shifted four places right	0	0	0	0	0	0	1	0
Logical bit AND	0	0	0	0	1	1	1	1
Result of AND	0	0	0	0	0	0	1	0
Add 0x30	0	0	1	1	0	0	1	0
Data to be sent to LCD	**0**	**0**	**1**	**1**	**0**	**0**	**1**	**0**

Row 1 in Table 11-5 is the data in result after we have added the 7, that is, 0b111, to the binary value 0b00011001.

Row 2 is the data after it has been shifted 4 bits to the right. This moves the data that was in the high nibble into the low nibble. The data that was in the low nibble, before the shift, is just lost.

Row 3 is the 8 bits that will be used to perform the logical bit AND operation with the data in row 2.

Row 4 is the result of the logical bit AND. You can see that only bit 2 is a logic '1.' This is because only with bit 2 of both sets of 8-bit data is there a logic '1' in both bits.

Row 5 is the data after the final part of the instruction has been carried out, that is, the adding of the data 0x30.

Row 6 is the data that will be loaded into the variable "lcdData" ready to be sent to the LCD.

I hope you can see that the process would work, and the LCD would display what we would expect to see using BCD. It is not a difficult process to achieve in C programming, but I have used a slightly different approach. The approach I use reserves a memory location, or variable, for the tens character, that is, tens column, and another memory location, or variable, for the units character, or units column. This concept can easily be extended for hundreds and thousands columns, as needed, and even tenths and hundredths, etc.

The process by which I have achieved this, in my programs, is to split the 8 bits in the number as follows:

- Split seconds into "sectens" and "secunits."

- Split minutes into "mintens" and "minunits."

- Split hours into "hourtens" and "hourunits."

- Etc.

This can be easily implemented by using hexadecimal notation. For example, the hexadecimal value 0x38, which would normally be 0b00111000 or 56 in decimal, can actually represent 3 in the "sectens" variable and 8 in the "secunits" variable to represent the value of 38 seconds. This is because the low nibbles, the first 4 bits, are stored in their own separate 8-bit variable called "secunits," and in this case, they would store the value 8. Then the high nibbles, that is, last 4 bits, are stored in their separate variable called "sectens," and in this case, they would store the value 3. Using this approach, we can ensure that when the value in the variable "secunits" reaches 9, that is, 0b00001001, then the next time we try to increment the value in "secunits," instead of it going to A, that is, 00001010, "secunits" goes to 0 and we increment the value in "sectens" by one. In this way, the program actually implements BCD. The same approach is used for the minutes, hours, and any other values we want to store in 8 bits of data.

Well, that's OK, but how do we get the 8 bits to be stored correctly in the 32-bit registers the RTCC uses? To do this, we need to know exactly how the relevant data is stored in the 32-bit registers and how it relates to the data we are using. I will use Table 11-6 to try and explain how this can be achieved.

Table 11-6. *What the Bits in the 32-Bit Registers RTCTIME and RTCDATE Relate to*

Year		Month		Date		Day of Week	
31–28	27–24	23–20	19–6	15–12	11–8	7–4	3–0
0–9	0–9	0–1	0–9	0–3	0–9	0	0–6
yeartens	yearunits	monthtens	monthunist	daytens	dayunits		daynumber
Hour		**Minutes**		**Seconds**		**Half Second**	
31–28	27–24	23–20	19–6	15–12	11–8	7–4	3–0
0–2	0–9	0–5	0–9	0–5	0–9	0	0–1
hourtens	hourunits	mintens	Minunits	sectens	secunits	Not used	Not used

Table 11-6 is an attempt to show you how each nibble of the two 32-bit registers relates to the variables, used in the program, to store the settings inputted by the user. If we just consider the time register, we can see that the low nibble, or 4 bits, of the 8 bits that we are using to store the "sectens" value needs to be stored in bits 15–12 of the 32-bit register for the time. As it is only the low nibble, or the first 4 bits, of the variable "sectens" that goes from 0–9, we can mask out the high nibble of the "sectens" variable by performing a bit AND with the data in "sectens" and 0b00001111 or 0x0F. However, we also need to shift those 4 bits that are in bits 0, 1, 2, and 3 of the "sectens" variable to bits 12, 13, 14, and 15 of the 32-bit register for the time. This means shifting them 12 places to the left once we have masked out the high nibble. This is achieved with the instruction **newTime = newTime + ((sectens & 0x0F)<<12);**. We will look at how this is achieved more closely when we analyze the program listing. The instructions that deal with these issues are on lines 480–485 in the listing. The instructions between lines 486 and 492 deal with this issue of changing the 32-bit data to the date to be displayed on the LCD.

Displaying the 32-Bit Value on the LCD

This is another problem we have to overcome in the program listing. This is because all data sent to the LCD is in 8-bit format, not 32-bit. Also, it would be just the 4 bits of the 8 bits in question that are of importance. Consider the situation that the "sectens" should be showing 3 for the seconds value of 0x38, that is, 3 tens and 8 units. This value of 3 would be in the 32-bit register in bits 15–12. As we use the variable "lcdData" to store the 8 bits we want to send to the LCD, then we need to get these 4 bits in bits 15, 14, 13, and 12 of the RTCTIME register into bits 3, 2, 1, and 0 of the variable "lcdData." This again requires us to mask off the high nibble but also shift the bits 12 places to the right. This is achieved with the instruction **lcdData = (((RTCTIME>>12) & 0x0F)+0x30);**. Again, we will see how this is achieved when we look at the program listing.

I hope this analysis does show you that I could not have programmed the PIC to run this RTCC program without first understanding how we use the registers of the RTCC module.

RTCC Module Program

The program is using three switches to increment, decrement, and set the values used. The full listing for the program is shown in Listing 11-1.

Listing 11-1. The Listing for the First Program with the RTCC Module of the PIC

```
1   /* A program just to set up the LCD on PORT Using
    8bit control
2   * File:    justLCDPortb4bit.c
3   Author: Mr H. H. Ward
4   *Written for the PIC32MX360F512L
5   Created on 01 November 2021, 11:50
```

```
 6  */
 7  // PIC32MX360F512L Configuration Bit Settings
 8  // 'C' source line config statements
 9  // DEVCFG3
10  #pragma config USERID = 0xFFFF
11  // DEVCFG2
12  #pragma config FPLLIDIV = DIV_2
13  #pragma config FPLLMUL = MUL_18
14  #pragma config FPLLODIV = DIV_1
15  // DEVCFG1
16  #pragma config FNOSC = PRIPLL
17  #pragma config FSOSCEN = ON
18  #pragma config IESO = OFF
19  #pragma config POSCMOD = XT
20  #pragma config OSCIOFNC = ON
21  #pragma config FPBDIV = DIV_1
22  #pragma config FCKSM = CSDCMD
23  #pragma config WDTPS = PS1048576
24  #pragma config FWDTEN = OFF
25  // DEVCFG0
26  #pragma config DEBUG = OFF
27  #pragma config ICESEL = ICS_PGx2
28  #pragma config PWP = OFF
29  #pragma config BWP = OFF
30  #pragma config CP = OFF
31  // #pragma config statements should precede project file
    includes.
32  // Use project enums instead of #define for ON and OFF.
33  #include <xc.h>
34  #include <plib.h>
35  //#include <lcdPORTEGood.h>
```

```
36  // some definitions
37  #define Mon              lcdData = 0x4D; sendData ();
    lcdData = 0x6F; sendData (); lcdData = 0x6E; sendData ();
38  #define Tue              lcdData = 0x54; sendData ();
    lcdData = 0x75; sendData (); lcdData = 0x65; sendData ();
39  #define Wed              lcdData = 0x57; sendData ();
    lcdData = 0x65; sendData (); lcdData = 0x64; sendData ();
40  #define Thur             lcdData = 0x54; sendData ();
    lcdData = 0x68; sendData (); lcdData = 0x72; sendData ();
41  #define Fri              lcdData = 0x46; sendData ();
    lcdData = 0x72; sendData (); lcdData = 0x69; sendData ();
42  #define Sat              lcdData = 0x53; sendData ();
    lcdData = 0x61; sendData (); lcdData = 0x74; sendData ();
43  #define Sun              lcdData = 0x53; sendData ();
    lcdData = 0x75; sendData (); lcdData = 0x6E; sendData ();
44  #define incbutton        _RA7
45  #define decbutton        _RD6
46  #define setbutton        _RD7
47  #define entryMode        0b00000110
48  #define displayCtl       0b00001110
49  #define functionSet      0b00111000
50  #define clearScreen      0b00000001
51  #define returnHome       0b00000010
52  #define lineTwo          0b11000000
53  #define shiftLeft        0b00010000
54  #define shiftRight       0b00010100
55  #define shDisRight       0b00011100
56  #define lcdPort          PORTE
57  #define RSpin            PORTBbits.RB15
58  #define eBit             PORTDbits.RD4
59  #define endAlarm         _RD7
```

```
60  //variables
61  unsigned char count, secunits = 0x30, sectens = 0x30,
    minunits = 0x30, mintens = 0x30, hourunits = 0x30,
    hourtens = 0x30;
62  unsigned char lcdData, n,m, nt, daynumber, secUnits;
63  unsigned char dayunits = 0x30, daytens = 0x30,
    monthunits = 0x30, monthtens = 0x30, yearunits = 0x30,
    yeartens = 0x30;
64  unsigned long time, atime;
65  unsigned long newTime = 0, newYear = 0, distens, disunits;
66  unsigned char ahourtens,ahourunits, amintens, aminunits,
    asectens, asecunits, alarmOn = 0, alarmCount = 0,
    alarmRepeat = 0;
67  unsigned char lcdInitialise [5] =
68  {
69  functionSet,
70  entryMode,
71  displayCtl,
72  clearScreen,
73  returnHome,
74  };
75  //some subroutines
76  void debounce ()
77  {
78  TMR2 = 0;
79  while (TMR2 <1900 );
80  }
81  void delay(unsigned char t)
82  {
83  for(nt = 0; nt < t; nt++)
84  {
```

```
85   TMR2 = 0;
86   while (TMR2 <35160);
87   }
88   }
89   void sendData ()
90   {
91   lcdPort = lcdData;
92   eBit = 1;
93   eBit = 0;
94   TMR2 = 0; while (TMR2 < 380);
95   }
96   void setUpTheLCD ()
97   {
98   TMR2 = 0;
99   while( TMR2<6000);
100  RSpin = 0;
101  n = 0;
102  while (n < 5)
103  {
104  lcdData = lcdInitialise [n];
105  sendData ();
106  n ++;
107  }
108  RSpin = 1;
109  }
110  void line2 ()
111  {
112  RSpin = 0;
113  lcdData = lineTwo;
114  sendData ();
115  RSpin = 1;
116  }
```

```
117  void goHome ()
118  {
119  RSpin = 0;
120  lcdData = returnHome;
121  sendData ();
122  RSpin = 1;
123  }
124  void writeString (unsigned char *print)
125  {
126  while (*print)
127  {
128  lcdData = *print;
129  sendData ();
130  *print ++;
131  }
132  }
133  void clearTheScreen ()
134  {
135  RSpin = 0;
136  lcdData = clearScreen;
137  sendData ();
138  RSpin = 1;
139  }
140  void shiftcurleft ( unsigned char l)
141  {
142  RSpin = 0;
143  for (n = 0; n < l; n ++)
144  {
145  lcdData = shiftLeft;
146  sendData ();
147  }
```

```
148  RSpin = 1;
149  }
150  void shiftcurright (unsigned char r)
151  {
152  RSpin = 0;
153  for (n = 0; n < r; n ++)
154  {
155  lcdData = shiftRight;
156  sendData ();
157  }
158  RSpin = 1;
159  }
160  void shiftdisright (unsigned char r)
161  {
162  RSpin = 0;
163  for (n = 0; n < r; n ++)
164  {
165  lcdData = shDisRight;
166  sendData ();
167  }
168  RSpin = 1;
169  }
170  void cursorPos (unsigned char line, unsigned char pos)
171  {
172  switch (line)
173  {
174  case 1:
175  {
176  goHome ();
177  shiftcurright (pos);
178  break;
179  }
```

```
180  case 2:
181  {
182  line2 ();
183  shiftcurright (pos);
184  break;
185  }
186  case 3:
187  {
188  goHome ();
189  shiftcurright (pos + 20);
190  break;
191  }
192  case 4:
193  {
194  line2 ();
195  shiftcurright (pos + 20);
196  break;
197  }
198  }
199  }
200  void displayday ()
201  {
202  switch (daynumber)
203  {
204  case 0:
205  {
206  Sun;
207  line2 ();
208  }
209  break;
210  case 1 :
```

```
211  {
212  Mon;
213  line2 ();
214  }
215  break;
216  case 2:
217  {
218  Tue;
219  line2 ();
220  }
221  break;
222  case 3:
223  {
224  Wed;
225  line2 ();
226  }
227  break;
228  case 4:
229  {
230  Thur;
231  line2 ();
232  }
233  break;
234  case 5:
235  {
236  Fri;
237  line2 ();
238  }
239  break;
240  case 6:
241  {
```

```
242  Sat;
243  line2 ();
244  }
245  break;
246  }
247  }
248  void changeItem ()
249  {
250  while (setbutton)
251  {
252  cursorPos (2,2);
253  lcdData = distens;
254  sendData ();
255  lcdData = disunits;
256  sendData ();
257  shiftcurleft (1);
258  if (!incbutton) debounce ();
259  while (!incbutton)
260  {
261  disunits ++;
262  cursorPos (2,2);
263  lcdData = distens;
264  sendData ();
265  lcdData = disunits;
266  sendData ();
267  shiftcurleft (1);
268  if(disunits == 0x3A)
269  {
270  disunits = 0x30;
271  distens ++;
272  }
```

```
273  if (distens == 0x39 & disunits == 0x39 )
274  {
275  distens = 0x30;
276  disunits = 0x30;
277  }
278  delay (2);
279  }
280  if (!decbutton) debounce ();
281  while  (!decbutton)
282  {
283  cursorPos (2,2);
284  lcdData = distens;
285  sendData ();
286  lcdData = disunits;
287  sendData ();
288  shiftcurleft (1);
289  if (disunits == 0x30)
290  {
291  disunits = 0x39;
292  distens --;
293  }
294  else disunits --;
295  if (distens < 0x30)
296  {
297  distens = 0x30;
298  disunits = 0x30;
299  }
300  delay (2);
301  }
302  }
303  while (!setbutton);
304  }
```

```
305  void setDay ()
306  {
307  while (!setbutton);
308  clearTheScreen ();
309  cursorPos (1,0);
310  writeString ("Set The Day");
311  line2 ();
312  while (setbutton)
313  {
314  if (!incbutton) debounce ();
315  if (!incbutton) daynumber ++;
316  while (!incbutton);
317  if (!decbutton) debounce ();
318  if (!decbutton) daynumber --;
319  while (!decbutton);
320  if (daynumber == 0)
321  {
322  Sun;
323  line2 ();
324  }
325  if (daynumber == 1)
326  {
327  Mon;
328  line2 ();
329  }
330  if (daynumber == 2)
331  {
332  Tue;
333  line2 ();
334  }
```

```
335  if (daynumber == 3)
336  {
337  Wed;
338  line2 ();
339  }
340  if (daynumber == 4)
341  {
342  Thur;
343  line2 ();
344  }
345  if (daynumber == 5)
346  {
347  Fri;
348  line2 ();
349  }
350  if (daynumber == 6)
351  {
352  Sat;
353  line2 ();
354  }
355  if (daynumber == 7) daynumber = 0;
356  if (daynumber == 0xFF) daynumber = 0;
357  if (!setbutton) debounce ();
358  }
359  while (!setbutton);
360  }
361  void  __ISR(0, ipl1) RTCCInterruptHandler()
362  {
363  mRTCCClearIntFlag();
364  mRTCCIntEnable( 0);
365  alarmOn = 1;
```

```
366   mRTCCIntEnable( 1);
367   }
368   void main (void)
369   {
370   // set up timers
371   T1CON = 0x8002;
372   T2CON = 0x8070;
373   ///initalize the ports etc//
374   TRISA = 0x00000080;
375   TRISB = 0x00000000;
376   TRISC = 0X00000000;
377   TRISD = 0X000000C0;
378   TRISE = 0x00008000;
379   TRISF = 0;
380   PORTA = 0;
381   PORTB = 0;
382   PORTC = 0;
383   PORTD = 0;
384   PORTE = 0;
385   AD1PCFG = 0xFFFF;
386   AD1CON1 = 0;
387   OSCCONbits.SOSCEN = 1;
388   SYSKEY = 0xaa996655;
389   SYSKEY = 0x556699aa;
390   RTCCONbits.RTCWREN = 1;
391   RTCCONbits.ON = 1;
392   RTCCONbits.RTCOE = 1;
393   while (!RTCCONbits.RTCCLKON);
394   PR1 = 32767;
395   __builtin_disable_interrupts();
396   mRTCCClearIntFlag();
```

```
397  mRTCCIntEnable( 1);
398  mRTCCSetIntPriority( 1);
399  INTEnableSystemSingleVectoredInt();
400  __builtin_enable_interrupts();
401  DDPCONbits.JTAGEN = 0;
402  setUpTheLCD ();
403  clearTheScreen ();
404  cursorPos (1,0);
405  writeString ("Set The Year 'nn'");
406  changeItem ();
407  yeartens = distens;
408  yearunits = disunits;
409  distens = 0x30;
410  disunits = 0x30;
411  clearTheScreen ();
412  cursorPos (1,0);
413  writeString ("Set The Month 'nn'");
414  changeItem ();
415  monthtens = distens;
416  monthunits = disunits;
417  distens = 0x30;
418  disunits = 0x30;
419  clearTheScreen ();
420  cursorPos (1,0);
421  writeString ("Set The Date 'nn'");
422  changeItem ();
423  daytens = distens;
424  dayunits = disunits;
425  distens = 0x30;
426  disunits = 0x30;
427  setDay ();
428  clearTheScreen ();
```

```
429   cursorPos (1,0);
430   writeString ("Set Time in 24hr");
431   delay (32);
432   clearTheScreen ();
433   cursorPos (1,0);
434   writeString ("Set The Hour'nn'");
435   changeItem ();
436   hourtens = distens;
437   hourunits = disunits;
438   distens = 0x30;
439   disunits = 0x30;
440   clearTheScreen ();
441   cursorPos (1,0);
442   writeString ("Set The Min'nn'");
443   changeItem ();
444   mintens = distens;
445   minunits = disunits;
446   distens = 0x30;
447   disunits = 0x30;
448   clearTheScreen ();
449   cursorPos (1,0);
450   writeString ("Set The Sec'nn'");
451   changeItem ();
452   sectens = distens;
453   secunits = disunits;
454   distens = 0x30;
455   disunits = 0x30;
456   clearTheScreen ();
457   cursorPos (1,0);
458   writeString ("Set Alarm Hr 'nn'");
459   changeItem ();
460   ahourtens = distens;
```

```
461  ahourunits = disunits;
462  distens = 0x30;
463  disunits = 0x30;
464  clearTheScreen ();
465  cursorPos (1,0);
466  writeString ("Set Alarm Min 'nn'");
467  changeItem ();
468  amintens = distens;
469  aminunits = disunits;
470  distens = 0x30;
471  disunits = 0x30;
472  clearTheScreen ();
473  cursorPos (1,0);
474  writeString ("Set Alarm Sec 'nn'");
475  changeItem ();
476  asectens = distens;
477  asecunits = disunits;
478  distens = 0x30;
479  disunits = 0x30;
480  newTime = (hourtens <<28);
481  newTime = newTime + ((hourunits & 0x0F)<<24);
482  newTime = newTime +  ((mintens & 0x0F)<<20);
483  newTime = newTime +  ((minunits & 0x0F)<<16);
484  newTime = newTime +  ((sectens & 0x0F)<<12);
485  newTime = newTime +  ((secunits & 0x0F)<<8);
486  newYear = (yeartens <<28);
487  newYear = newYear + ((yearunits & 0x0F)<<24);
488  newYear = newYear +  ((monthtens & 0x0F)<<20);
489  newYear = newYear +  ((monthunits & 0x0F)<<16);
490  newYear = newYear +  ((daytens & 0x0F)<<12);
491  newYear = newYear +  ((dayunits & 0x0F)<<8);
492  newYear = newYear +  (daynumber & 0x0F);
```

```
493   RTCDATE = newYear;
494   RTCTIME = newTime;
495   atime = (ahourtens <<28);
496   atime = atime + ((ahourunits & 0x0F)<<24);
497   atime = atime +  ((amintens & 0x0F)<<20);
498   atime = atime +  ((aminunits & 0x0F)<<16);
499   atime = atime +  ((asectens & 0x0F)<<12);
500   atime = atime +  ((secunits & 0x0F)<<8);
501   while (RTCALRM & 0x1000);
502   RTCALRMCLR = 0xCFFF;
503   ALRMTIME = atime;
504   RTCALRM = 0x8403;
505   SYSKEY = 0xFFFFFFFF;
506   clearTheScreen ();
507   while (1)
508   {
509   alarmCount = (RTCALRM & 0xFF);
510   if(alarmOn == 1)
511   {
512   PORTA = alarmCount;
513   clearTheScreen ();
514   while (endAlarm)
515   {
516   cursorPos(1,5);
517   writeString ("Wake Up");
518   }
519   alarmOn = 0;
520   clearTheScreen ();
521   }
522   cursorPos (1,1);
523   lcdData = (((RTCTIME>>28) & 0x0F)+0x30);
524   sendData ();
```

```
525  lcdData = (((RTCTIME>>24) & 0x0F)+0x30);
526  sendData ();
527  lcdData = 0x3A;
528  sendData ();
529  lcdData = (((RTCTIME>>20) & 0x0F)+0x30);
530  sendData ();
531  lcdData = (((RTCTIME>>16) & 0x0F)+0x30);
532  sendData ();
533  lcdData = 0x3A;
534  sendData ();
535  lcdData = (((RTCTIME>>12) & 0x0F)+0x30);
536  sendData ();
537  lcdData = (((RTCTIME>>8) & 0x0F)+0x30);
538  sendData ();
539  PORTF = ((RTCTIME>>8) & 0xFF);
540  line2 ();
541  daynumber = (((RTCDATE) & 0x0F));
542  displayday();
543  cursorPos (2,5);
544  lcdData = (((RTCDATE>>12) & 0x0F)+0x30);
545  sendData ();
546  lcdData = (((RTCDATE>>8) & 0x0F)+0x30);
547  sendData ();
548  lcdData = 0x3A;
549  sendData ();
550  lcdData = (((RTCDATE>>20) & 0x0F)+0x30);
551  sendData ();
552  lcdData = (((RTCDATE>>16) & 0x0F)+0x30);
553  sendData ();
554  lcdData = 0x3A;
555  sendData ();
```

```
556  lcdData = (((RTCDATE>>28) & 0x0F)+0x30);
557  sendData ();
558  lcdData = (((RTCDATE>>24) & 0x0F)+0x30);
559  sendData ();
560  }
561  }
```

Analysis of Listing 11-1

We will look at the important and new instructions in this listing.

Lines 1-6 are the usual comments, and lines 7-32 are the configuration words we are using instead of the header file we have used before. Line 17 is #pragma config FSOSCEN = ON, which is the command to enable the use of the external crystal. Lines 33 and 34 are the normal include files.

Line 34 #include <plib.h>

We are including the plib.h header file as we are using the firmware instructions to set up the interrupt; see lines 361–367 for the ISR, created to deal with the interrupt, and lines 395–400, which set up the interrupt. This also means we must be using the XC32 compiler software version 1.32, as the newer versions don't have the plib.h header file included in them. Also, when you compile the program, you will see a lot of warnings. They are not a problem, and it will compile correctly.

Lines 37–43 are the definitions for the macros to display the days of the weeks. We have looked at these in Chapter 9. Lines 44–46 define which buttons we are using. Lines 47–58 define the command words and control outputs for the LCD.

Line 59 # define endAlarm _RD7

This is adding another definition for the input switch on bit 7 of PORTD. This will not cause any issue for the PIC, as it is just a switch that is being used as an input to the PIC. I am just giving the input an alternative name, as I am using the switch for a different purpose in the program. The new name just means I can differentiate the use of the switch easier. Note, I have already defined the same switch, _RD7, as the "setbutton"; see line 46. This will not cause a problem in this program, but you must be careful doing this. I am only doing this because I only have four switches on the explorer 16 development board.

Lines 60–66 set up the variables we are going to use in the program. Line 64 is setting up two variables of the type unsigned long, which are newTime = 0, newYear = 0. This is used to set up the two 32-bit memory locations, that is, data type unsigned long, which are used to store the settings of the time and date. We are also giving them both an initial value of "0."

Lines 67–199 are where I set up the array and subroutines that are used to set up and control the LCD. We are not using the normal header file because we are using timer2, not timer1, to control the delays for the LCD.

Line 200 void displayday ()

This creates a subroutine that allows the user to set the current day of the week. The program will display the day name, as we change the settings, on the LCD. It uses the switch and case directives that we have looked at before. The variable "daynumber" is being used to determine which case statement is chosen. We have looked at these instructions in Chapter 10.

Line 248 void changeItem ()

This creates a subroutine that will allow the user to change the value, for a range of settings, for the current date and time. It will display the settings, as the user changes them, on the LCD. The one subroutine can be used for the whole series of items that need setting.

Line 250 while (setbutton)

This is a "while the test is true, do what I say" type of instruction. The test is testing to see if the logic on the set button, which has been defined as bit 7 of PORTD (see line 46), is at a logic '1'. We could have used the following instruction as an alternative:

```
while (setbutton == 1)
```

which would work in the same way. It is just down to personal preference.

Note, with the buttons on the explorer 16 development board, the switches are connected such that if they are not pressed, the logic will be a logic '1'. When they are pressed, the logic goes to a logic '0'. Therefore, this means that the instruction is saying that, while no one has pressed the "setbutton," the PIC must carry out the instructions between the opening and closing curly brackets on lines 251 and 302.

Line 252 cursorPos (2,2);

This calls the subroutine "cursorPos" to move the cursor to line 2 at column 2. This is because we would have written the name of the item we want to change on line 1 above on the LCD.

Line 253 lcdData = distens;

This loads the variable "lcdData" with the contents of the variable "distens" ready to send to the LCD.

Line 254 sendData ();

This calls the subroutine "sendData" to send the contents of the variable "lcdData" to the LCD.

Lines 255 and 256 do the same with the variable "disunits."

This will display the two digits, that is, the tens and units of the item we are currently changing, on the LCD ready for the user to change their values.

Line 257 shiftcurleft (1);

This calls the subroutine "shiftcurleft" and sends the value "1" to it. This will shift the cursor back one place to the left to ensure it is under the units column of the display.

Line 258 if (!incbutton) debounce ();

This is testing to see if the logic on the "incbutton" input has gone to a logic '0'. Note the use of the NOT symbol "!". The logic would only go to a logic '0' if the user has pressed the "incbutton" to try and increment the value on the display. If the test is true, the PIC will carry out the one-line instruction that is written on the same line here. This would call the subroutine "debounce" which starts the 13ms delay to compensate for switch bounce.

Line 259 while (!incbutton)

This is testing the logic on the "incbutton" to see it has really been pressed. If the logic on the "incbutton" is still a logic '0', which, after the 13ms delay in the "debounce" subroutine, it would be if someone had pressed the "incbutton," the PIC must carry out the instructions between the curly brackets on lines 260 and 279. These instructions call the subroutine "cursorPos (2,2)" again; see line 262. This really means we don't need to use the shiftcurleft(1) instruction on line 257. However, I wanted to show you a situation where we might use the instruction.

Line 261 disunits ++;

This gets the PIC to increment the value in the variable "disunits."

Lines 262–267 get the PIC to display the values again in the same place on the LCD, thus overwriting the units value displayed with the new value.

Line 268 if(disunits == 0x3A)

This is testing to see if the value in the variable "disunits" has been incremented so much that it would have gone from 9 to 10; note "A" is 10 in hexadecimal. Obviously, the units cannot go to 10, they can only be 0 to 9.

Therefore, if it has gone from 9 to 10, we must increment the tens and return the units to 0. This is done between lines 269 and 272. This is how I implement my idea of BCD, as described earlier.

Line 270 disunits = 0x30;

This returns the units to 0.

Line 271 distens ++;

This increments the tens.

Line 273 if (distens == 0x39 & disunits == 0x39)

This is testing to see if both the "distens" and "disunits" have reached the value 9. If they have, then they should both go back to 0, as we can't have a value of 100, as we don't have a hundred column. You could say that the "distens" should not go above "5" as we can only go up to 59 seconds or minutes. However, this subroutine must accommodate the tens and units of all the items we need to change. That being the case, in any century we could have a year of 99 years. This approach is different, in this aspect, from the program in Chapter 10.

Lines 275 and 276 reset both variables to 0.

Line 278 delay (2);

This calls the subroutine "delay" and passes up the value "2" to it. This would create a half second delay. This is required to allow the user to see the result of them pressing the increment button and give them time to release the increment button. If we didn't have this delay, the display would not show us the result of any changes until we let go of the button, and we would not know the result until then.

Lines 280–302 perform the same function but for the decrement of the values displayed.

Line 303 while (!setbutton);

The PIC would return to line 250 while the user did not press the "setbutton." If the user did press the "setbutton," then the PIC would break out of the "while (setbutton)" loop on line 250 and carry out this instruction on line 303. All this instruction does is make the PIC wait for the user to let go of the "setbutton." Really, we should call the debounce routine again here, as the logic on the switch would still bounce. However, it is only really crucial in more sensitive applications where we might need to do that.

Line 305 void setDay ()

This creates a subroutine that allows the user to change the day setting while displaying the current selected day.

Line 307 while (!setbutton);

This is just making sure the PIC does nothing until the user has let go of the "setbutton."

Line 308 clearTheScreen ();

This calls the subroutine to clear the LCD screen of all characters.

Line 309 cursorPos (1,0);

This calls the subroutine "cursorPos" to ensure the cursor goes to the first column on line 1 of the LCD. I have found that this instruction is necessary because the "clearScreen" instruction, while clearing the characters off the LCD, does not always take the cursor to the first column, on line 1, of the LCD. This instruction, on line 309, ensures that the cursor does go to the first column on line 1. There is always something for anyone to learn, and I am one of them, and perhaps some of you, reading this, can identify what causes this slight snag.

Line 310 writeString ("Set The Day");

This sends the message "Set The Day" to the LCD.

Line 311 Line2 ();

This calls the subroutine to send the cursor to the beginning of the second line on the LCD. We could have used the instruction "cursorPos(2,0)" which would have done the same operation.

Line 312 while (setbutton)

This sets up a while loop that keeps the PIC carrying out the instructions between the curly brackets on lines 313 and 358. The while test is true as long as the user does not press the "setbutton." The following instruction gets the PIC to set the current parameter being changed.

Lines 314–319 are checking which button has been pressed and changing the variable "daynumber" accordingly. Note, we call the "debounce" subroutine, on seeing the logic, on the particular button, go to a logic '0', and then ask the question, has the button really gone low, as with the test on line 315. This process does help prevent the PIC from responding to noise on the switch, that is, the switch going low without being pressed, which can happen.

Lines 320–354 are testing to see if the value in the variable "daynumber" has been changed by one of the actions in lines 314–319. If it has, the PIC will display the appropriate characters for the day set. This method uses a series of "if" tests. An alternative approach would be to use the "switch" and "case" directives we have used before.

Line 355 if (daynumber == 7) daynumber = 0;

This is testing to see if the value in the variable "daynumber" has been increased to 7, which is not allowed. If it has, the test will be true, and the PIC will carry out the one-line instruction, written here, that loads the variable "daynumber" with the value 0.

Line 356 if (daynumber == 0xFF) daynumber = 0;

This is testing to see if the variable "daynumber" has been decremented past 0. You should appreciate that in binary, if you decrement an 8-bit value of 0 by 1, it will roll over to 0xFF, that is, all 8 bits will be logic '1'. The variable "daynumber" cannot be allowed to take on this value, and so if the test is true, the PIC will load the variable "daynumber" with 0.

Line 357 if (!setbutton) debounce ();

This is testing to see if the logic on the input "setbutton" has gone to a logic '0'. Note the use of the "!", which is the symbol for NOT in C. This would happen if the user has pressed the "setbutton" to set the parameter to the current setting. If the test is true, the PIC will call the "debounce" subroutine. This is done to accommodate the physical bouncing of the switch. Note this routine can also be used to eliminate the problem of intermittent voltage spikes on the switch. This is because the voltage spike would make the PIC call the "debounce" subroutine. However, after coming back from the subroutine, we could get the PIC to check that the button is still at logic '0'. This would not be the case if the going low was just a voltage spike or "noise" on the switch. That's why most programs do use a "debounce" routine for their switches.

Line 359 while (!setbutton);

This while test is there just to make sure the user has let go of the "setbutton" before the program carries on. If we don't have this instruction here, there is the possibility that the PIC will think we have set the next parameter before we have made any changes to it.

Line 361 void   __ISR(0, ipl1) RTCCInterruptHandler()

This creates the interrupt service routine for the alarm interrupt. As we are using a single vectored interrupt, the vector should be set to 0, as shown in the normal brackets of the instruction. Also, we will set the priority of the interrupt to level 1. This must be stated in the ISR instruction inside the normal brackets, which is done with the "ipl1." This instruction is using the macros of the interrupts which require the compiler version 1.32.

Line 363 mRTCCClearIntFlag();

This is another macro that is being used to clear the RTCC interrupt flag. This is to ensure we are ready to see the flag go to a logic '1' on the next interrupt.

Line 364 mRTCCIntEnable(0);

This uses another macro to disable the RTCC interrupt. This makes sure the RTCC cannot initiate an interrupt until we are ready.

Line 365 alarmOn = 1;

This is the only thing that the ISR gets the PIC to do. It will load the variable "alarmOn" with the value 1. This variable will be used later in the program to determine if the alarm has gone off or not.

We could add more instructions in the ISR, even those that call subroutines. However, I have found it better to not allow the ISR to call too many subroutines or nested subroutines, as this could cause a problem with the stack. Therefore, I try to keep my instructions in the ISR to a minimum. Also, with this program, the fact that timer1 kept initiating an interrupt, every second, compounded this effect.

Line 366 mRTCCIntEnable(1);

This uses the macro to reenable the RTCC interrupt.

Line 368 void main (void)

This sets up the main loop between the curly brackets on lines 369 and 560.

Lines 371 T1CON = 0x8002;

This turns timer1 on and sets it to use the external crystal as its source; that is, bit 15 is a logic '1' to turn it on, and bit 2 is a logic '1' to select the external oscillator. Note bits 5 and 4 are both logic '0' to select a divide rate of 1:1. This means timer1 counts at a rate of 32.768kHz, which is the frequency of the external crystal oscillator.

Line 372 T2CON = 0x8070;

This turns timer2 on and makes it count at a rate of the PBCLK divided by 256, that is, 140.625kHz. We will use timer2 for all the main delays in the program.

Lines 373–386 are the normal settings for the PIC.

Line 387 OSCCONbits.SOSCEN = 1;

This allows the external oscillator to be used. This is used in conjunction with the #pragma config FSOSCEN = ON; see line 17. Both of these instructions are required so that the PIC can use the external oscillator.

Line 388 SYSKEY = 0xaa996655;
Line 389 SYSKEY = 0x556699aa;

These are the two unlock codes we must write to the SYSKEY register to unlock the RTCC. We must unlock the RTCC before we try to write anything to it. If we try to write instructions, or data, to the RTCC before we have unlocked it, the RTCC will simply ignore what we are trying to do.

Line 390 RTCCONbits.RTCWREN = 1;

Now we can write commands to the RTCC. This will set the RTCWREN bit of the RTCCON register, which is the RTCC write enable bit, to a logic '1'. This enables the registers of the RTCC to be written to.

Line 391 RTCCONbits.ON = 1;

This simply turns the RTCC on.

Line 392 RTCCONbits.RTCOE = 1;

This enables the RTCC output, which is on bit 8 of PORTD. This can be used to output a clock signal or an alarm signal. This is not required if you only want to run the RTCC.

Line 393 while (!RTCCONbits.RTCCLKON);

This simply makes the PIC wait until this bit goes to a logic '1'. This will happen when the RTCC clock does actually turn on. For these very important, yet complex, modules, you can't just say, well I have turned it on, as we did with line 390. Note also it does take a finite time for the module to turn on. Therefore, we should wait until we are sure it has turned on properly.

Line 394 PR1 = 32767;

This loads the period register for timer1 with the value 32767. When the count in timer1 matches this value, timer1 will initiate the interrupt.

Line 395 __builtin_disable_interrupts();

This is a built-in compiler directive that we can use to disable all interrupts. This is something you should do before setting up any interrupts.

Line 396 mRTCCClearIntFlag();

This uses the macro in the plib header file to clear the interrupt flag for the specified interrupt source, which, as stated in the instruction, is RTCC.

Line 397 mRTCCIntEnable(1);

This uses the macro to enable the RTCC interrupt.

Line 398 mRTCCSetIntPriority(1);

This sets the priority for the RTCC interrupt. Note interrupts with higher priorities can interrupt any interrupt with lower priority.

Line 399 INTEnableSystemSingleVectoredInt();

This enables the PIC to use single vectored interrupts. This aspect has been looked at in Chapter 8.

Line 400 __builtin_enable_interrupts();

This uses the built-in compiler directive to enable all interrupts. Without these two built-in directives, you would have had to use assembler instructions.

Lines 401–404 have been looked at before.

Line 405 writeString ("Set Year 'nn'");

We are now ready to allow the user to set up the clock in terms of the data, time, and alarm. This instruction writes the message to the LCD to tell the user what parameter we are setting. In this instance, it is the "Year," and we will use two digits, that is, the "nn."

Line 406 changeItem ();

This calls the subroutine "changeItem" to allow the user to change the settings.

Line 407 yeartens = distens;

Now the "distens" variable has been set within the subroutine "changeItem," we get the PIC to load the variable "yeartens" with the setting. This is the first parameter we wanted to set.

Line 408 yearunits = disunits;

This does the same with the variable "disunits" but loads a copy into the variable "yearunits."

These two instructions set the date for the current year into the variables ready to display on the LCD.

Line 409   distens = 0x30;

This loads the variable "distens" with the ASCII for 0 ready for the next call to the subroutine "changeItem."

Line 410 disunits = 0x30;

This does the same for the variable "disunits."

Line 411 clearTheScreen ();

This calls the subroutine "clearTheScreen" to clear the LCD ready for the next call to "changeItem."

Line 412 cursorPos (1,0);

This calls the subroutine "cursorPos" to move the cursor to line 1 column 0.

These instructions get the LCD ready for the next call to the subroutine "changeItem" again.

Lines 413–479 are used to allow the user to set the remaining parameters. The idea by calling the same subroutine, some nine times, is that the subroutine changes just the two variables, "distens" and "disunits," but then we save them to different variables in the main program. You should appreciate that any item – month, day, mins, hours, etc. – has a tens value and a unit's value.

Line 480 newTime = (hourtens <<28);

The 4 bits in the variable "newTime" that hold the data for the hour tens value are bits 28, 29, 30, and 31 of the 32-bit variable "newTime" that will be loaded into the RTCC register "RTCCTIME"; see Table 11-6. However, the 4 bits that we want to store in those bits of the variable "newTime" are currently bits 0, 1, 2, and 3 of the variable "hourtens." This means that we can't just copy them into the variable "newTime." We must copy them in and then shift them 28 places to the left. That is what this instruction does.

Line 481 newTime = newTime + ((hourunits & 0X0F)<<24);

We now need to place the value for the "hourunits" in bits 24, 25, 26, and 27 of the variable "newTime." We must do this while keeping the data in bits 28, 29, 30, and 31 of the 32-bit variable "newTime," the same as when we loaded them with the instruction on line 476. That is why we are now adding data to the variable "newTime" instead of making it equal to the new data. The instruction will add the contents of our variable "hourunits," but with the high nibble masked out. The masking out is done with the part "hourunits & 0x0F." We have looked at this type of instruction earlier in the chapter. The next part of the instruction, the <<24, will shift the data, added to the variable "newTime," 24 places to the left and so places the "hourunits" value in the correct place in the variable "newTime." To help explain this instruction, we can refer to Table 11-7.

Table 11-7. *Manipulating the Data in the Variable "newTime," "hourtens," and "hourunits"*

	31	30	29	28	27	26	25	24	23	22	21	20	19	18	17	16	15	14	13	12	11	10	9	8	7	6	5	4	3	2	1	0
R1	0	0	0	0	0	0	0	0	0	0	0	0	0	0	0	0	0	0	0	0	0	0	0	0	0	0	0	0	0	0	0	0
R2	0	0	0	0	0	0	0	0	0	0	0	0	0	0	0	0	0	0	0	0	0	0	0	0	0	0	0	1	0	0	0	1
R3	0	0	0	0	0	0	0	0	0	0	0	0	0	0	0	0	0	0	0	0	0	0	0	0	0	0	0	0	0	0	0	0
R4	0	0	0	1	1	0	0	0	0	0	0	0	0	0	0	0	0	0	0	0	0	0	0	0	0	0	0	0	0	0	0	0
R5	0	0	0	0	0	0	0	0	0	0	0	0	0	0	0	0	0	0	0	0	0	0	0	0	0	0	1	1	0	0	1	1
R6	0	0	0	0	0	0	0	0	0	0	0	0	0	0	0	0	0	0	0	0	0	0	0	0	0	0	0	0	0	1	1	1
R7	0	0	0	0	0	0	1	1	0	0	0	0	0	0	0	0	0	0	0	0	0	0	0	0	0	0	0	0	0	0	0	0
R8	0	0	0	1	0	0	1	1	0	0	0	0	0	0	0	0	0	0	0	0	0	0	0	0	0	0	0	0	0	0	0	0

Before we look at the table, we will set the initial value in the variables as follows:

- "newTime" to 0.

- "hourtens" is 0x31 or 0b00110001.

- "hourunits" is 0x33 or 0b00110011.

1. Row 1, R1, shows the full 32 bits of the variable "newTime." All set to logic '0'.

2. Row 2, R2, shows the 8 bits, that is, bits 7 to 0, of the data in the variable "hourtens," which are 0b00110001.

3. Row 3, R3, shows the effect of shifting the bits in "hourtens" 28 bits to the left, instruction on line 476.

4. Row 4, R4, shows the full 32 bits of the variable "newTime" after we have loaded it with contents of R3, instruction on line 476.

5. Row 5, R5, shows the 8 bits, that is, bits 7 to 0, of the data in the variable "hourtens," which are 0b00110011.

6. Row 6, R6, shows the effect of performing the logical bit AND with the data 0x0F or 0b00001111, instruction on line 477.

7. Row 7, R7, shows the effect of shifting the bits in "hourunits" 24 bits to the left after the logical AND.

8. Row 8, R8, shows the full 32 bits of the variable "newTime" after we have added it to the contents of R7, the final part of the instruction on line 477.

The two instructions are quite complex, but I hope this table, and the description, does help explain how they work. One thing that does raise some concern is that the variables "hourtens" and "hourunits" are declared as unsigned char, which are just 8 bits. However, the instructions suggest that they should be declared as unsigned long, which are 32 bits. I have tried the instructions with both types, and there is no difference. Therefore, I have left them as unsigned chars, as this should use less memory space. However, it may be that all variables default to 32 bits in this 32-bit PIC, and we can specify how much of the 32 bits we want to use. Well, I am not a microchip design engineer, so I will leave it to those who are to answer that query. I am perfectly happy that the instructions work in the way I expect them to.

Lines 482–485 place the remaining correct values into their correct places in the variable "newTime."

Lines 486–492 do the same but place the correct data for the date settings into their correct places in the variable "newYear."

Line 493 RTCDATE = newYear;

This overwrites the data in the RTCDATE register with the new date values the user has inputted in the program.

Line 494 RTCTIME = newTime;

This does the same but with the data for the new time. The RTCC should now have the correct time and date, and it will continue to update the time and date as the seconds are incremented via the interrupt.

Lines 495–500 load the 32-bit variable "atime" with the setting of the alarm time.

Line 501 while (RTCALRM & 0x1000);

This while test is testing to see if bit 12 of the RTCALRM control register is a logic '1'. Note, while the test is true, the PIC must do nothing. The instruction is testing if bit 12 is a logic '1' because the logical bit AND operation will only be true if bit 12 of the control register, RTCALRM, is also a logic '1'. This is just making sure the ALRMSYNC bit has gone to a logic '0' before the PIC can carry out the next instruction.

Line 502 RTCALRMCLR = 0xCFFF;

This loads the RTCALRMCLR register with the value 0xCFFF. This will clear the bits in the RTCALRM control register that map onto the logic '1s' in this instruction. This means that all bits except bits 13 and 12 in the RTCALRM control register are cleared, that is, set to a logic '0.' This basically disables the alarm function of the RTCC. We need to do this while we set up the alarm function of the RTCC.

Line 503 ALRMTIME = atime;

This loads the ALRMTIME register with the time we have set for the alarm to go off.

Line 504 RTCALRM = 0x8403;

This loads the RTCALRM control register with the value 0x8403. This instruction is analyzed further with Table 11-8.

Line 505 SYSKEY = 0xFFFFFFFF;

This instruction simply loads the SYSKEY register with the value 0xFFFFFFFF. This is done to simply lock the RTC registers so that you can't accidently write to them. You would have to send the two unlock values as we did in lines 388 and 389 if you wanted to write to them again.

Line 506 clearTheScreen ();

This just clears the LCD screen of characters.

Line 507 while (1)

This sets up the forever while loop, getting the PIC to carry out the instructions between the curly brackets on lines 508 and 560 forever.

Line 509 alarmCount = (RTCALRM & 0xFF);

This loads the 8-bit variable "alarmcount" with the low 8 bits from the RTCALRM control register. This will load the variable with the value of the ARPT number. It is the ARPT number that controls how many times the alarm will repeat before it stops going off in its attempt to wake you. Every time the alarm goes off, the contents of the ARPT register are decremented. When the value reaches 0, after the last repeat, then the alarm is disabled.

Line 510 if (alarmOn == 1)

This tests to see if the value in the variable "alarmOn" has been set to 1. This would happen if the ISR had been called; see line 364.

If the test is true, then the PIC would carry out the instructions between the curly brackets on lines 511 and 521.

Line 512 PORTA = alarmCount;

This copies the value in the variable "alarmCount" onto PORTA. This is just a debug instruction so that I can confirm how the PIC decrements the contents of the ARPT data. That is why I loaded the variable "alarmCount" on line 509.

Line 513 clearTheScreen ();

This just clears the LCD screen.

Line 514 while (endAlarm)

This while test is testing to see if the logic on the "endAlarm" switch, which is bit 7 of PORTD, is still a logic '1'. This would mean that the user has not pressed this button to stop the alarm. The PIC would carry out the instructions between the curly brackets on lines 515 and 518.

Line 516 cursorPos(1,5);

This would move the cursor to column 5 on line 1 of the LCD.

Line 517 writeString ("Wake Up");

This sends the string of characters Wake Up to the LCD.

Line 519 alarmOn = 0;

This resets the value in the variable "alarmOn" to 0. This is so that the line 514 becomes untrue.

Line 520 clearTheScreen ();

This clears the LCD again.

Line 522 cursorPos (1,1);

This moves the cursor to column 1 on line 1.

Line 523 lcdData = (((RTCTIME>>28) & 0x0F)+0x30);

We know the time, and eventually the date, will change as the seconds increase. That being the case, we need to display this change on the LCD. This instruction is to get the PIC to display the new time on the LCD. The instruction loads a copy of the data that is in bits 28, 29, 30, and 31 of the 32-bit register "RTCTIME," but shifts them 28 bits to the right, to place them into bits 0, 1, 2, and 3 of the variable "lcdData" ready to be sent to the LCD display. Note we are masking out the high nibble, as we need to make sure the high nibble of the variable "lcdData" is 0000. Finally, we add the value 0x30, which ensures the high nibble of the variable "lcdData" now becomes 0011. This is to make sure that the final data in the variable "lcdData" is actually the ASCII for the number of the hour tens, ready to be displayed on the LCD. You should be aware that all the numbers 0 to 9 in ASCII have a high nibble of 0011. For example, 2 in ASCII is 00110010, and 9 in ASCII is 00111001.

Line 524   sendData ();

This now calls the subroutine "sendData" that sends the data in the variable "lcdData" to the LCD.

Lines 525–538 send the data for the current time in the same way as the previous instruction to be displayed in their correct places on the LCD.

Line 539 PORTF = ((RTCTIME>>8) & 0xFF);

This is another example of using a set of LEDs, connected to a PORT, to try and debug a program. This instruction was used to check that the program was loading the variable seconds value with the expected value. If the display then showed the wrong value, then I would know there is a problem somewhere in the program. I did find the error and corrected it.

Line 540 line2 ();

This just calls the subroutine to move the cursor to the beginning of line 2 on the LCD.

Line 541 daynumber = (((RTCDATE) & 0x0F));

This will load the variable "daynumber" with the appropriate low byte from the RTCDATE register, ready to display the appropriate characters, for the current day, on the LCD. This instruction just looks at the lower 8 bits of the RTCDATE register and masks out the high nibble. This is because it is the low nibble that contains the number for the current day setting.

Line 542 displayday();

This calls the subroutine "displayday" to display the correct characters for the day setting, according to the value in the variable "daynumber."

Line 543 cursorPos (2,5);

This moves the cursor to column 5 on line 2. This is an alternative to using the "shiftcurright (n)" subroutine call, where "n" would be the required number we want to shift the cursor to the right. This is to give some space between the characters for the day and the next display.

Lines 544–559 now ensure that the correct data for the day and date are displayed in the correct places on the LCD.

Understanding Instruction on Line 504 RTCALRM = 0x8403;

To appreciate what this is doing, we need to look at the usage of the bits in that register. This is shown in Table 11-8.

Table 11-8. *The Bit Usage for the RTCALRM Control Register*

Bit	Name	Usage
15	ALRMEN Alarm enable bit	Logic '1' turns the alarm function on Logic '0' turns the alarm function off
14	CHIME Chime enable bit	Logic '1' chime is enabled. This means that the value in the ARPT can roll over to 0XFF when it is decremented from 0 Logic '0' chime is disabled. The ARPT stops when it reaches 0
13	PIV Alarm Pulse Initial Value bit	When the ALRMEN is a logic '0', this bit can be used to set the starting logic outputted on the RCC pin. If the PIV is set to a logic '1', then the start level of the RCC output is high. If the PIV is a logic '0', then the start level is low. Note this needs the output of the RCC pin to be enabled When the ALRMEN is a logic '1', this bit can be used to read the logic level on the RCC pin
12	ALRMSYNC Alarm Sync Bit	A read-only bit
11–8	AMSK Alarm mask configuration bits	These bits set the repeat frequency of the alarm. See Table 11-9

(continued)

Table 11-8. (*continued*)

Bit	Name	Usage
7–0	ARPT Alarm Repeat Counter	These bits set the number of repeats you want for the alarm. This count is decremented every time an alarm event occurs
		If the CHIME bit is a logic '1', then this counter can roll over when it reaches 0
		If the CHIME bit is a logic '0', then the counter stops when it gets to 0

The data 0x8403 (see line 504) is 0b1000,0100,0000,0011, in 16-bit binary. If we extend it to 32-bit binary, the high 16 bits are all logic '0'. However, as they are not used in the RTCALRM control register, they are not relevant. This means that bit 15 is a logic '1', which turns the alarm function on. It also means bit 14 is a logic '0', which disables the chime function. This means that when the ARPT value reaches 0, the decrement stops, and the number in the ARPT register does not roll over to 0xFF. Bits 11 to 8 are set to 0100, which means the alarm will repeat every ten minutes. Table 11-9 shows how the logic on bits 11, 10, 9, and 8 control when the alarm repeats.

Bits 7 to 0 are set to 0000,0011, which loads the ARPT counter with 3 in decimal. This means that the alarm will repeat four times, 3, 2, 1, and 0, before it rolls over. Note, if you want the alarm to repeat forever, then you need to set the CHIME bit, bit 14, to a logic '1'. This will enable the ARPT counter to roll over when it gets to 0. I have done this with the second example later in this chapter.

I have set the alarm to repeat every ten minutes in my program, as I didn't want to wait four days for the ARPT to stop repeating. Remember, I am loading PORTA with the value in the ARPT register, so that I can monitor how the value in the ARPT register alters when the alarm repeats.

Configuring the Alarm: Another Example

The alarm can be configured to operate in a wide variety of modes. In this example, we will simply set it to go off once every day at the same time. The alarm feature is enabled by setting bit 15 of the RTCALRM control register to a logic '1'.

The 4 bits of the AMSK (see Table 11-9) allow the user to select how often the alarm repeats. As we will be setting the alarm to repeat at the same time once every day, we will set these bits to 0110.

We need to set the time when the alarm will go off. This is done by loading the ALRMTIME register. The bits of that register set the following aspects of the alarm time. This is shown in Table 11-10.

Table 11-9. *The Alarm Repeat Options As Set by the AMSK Bits*

Bit 11	Bit 10	Bit 9	Bit 8	Alarm Repeat Frequency
0	0	0	0	Every half second
0	0	0	1	Every second
0	0	1	0	Every ten seconds
0	0	1	1	Every minute
0	1	0	0	Every ten minutes
0	1	0	1	Every hour
0	1	1	0	Once a day
0	1	1	1	Once a week
1	0	0	0	Once a month
1	0	0	1	Once a year except if set for Feb 29th
1	0	1	0	Reserved, do not use
1	0	1	1	Reserved, do not use
1	1	X	X	Reserved, do not use

Table 11-10. *What the Bits of the ALRMTIME Represent*

Bit Range	Representation
31–28	Hour tens, a value of 0–2
27–24	Hour units, a value of 0–9
24–20	Minute tens, a value of 0–5
19–16	Minute units, a value of 0–9
15–12	Second tens, a value of 0–5
11–8	Second units, a value of 0–9
7–0	Not used, read as 0

This actually fits the principle by which I use variables to represent the BCD value. I will use the variables shown in Table 11-11 to set the alarm time.

Table 11-11. *The Variables to Fill the 32-Bit Register ALRMTIME*

Variable	Bit Range in Register ALRMTIME
ahourtens	31–28
ahourunits	27–24
amintens	23–20
aminunts	19–16
asectens	15–12
asecunits	11–8
Not used	7–0

These will be used in a similar way in which we have set up and used the time variables. These variables are loaded with the alarm time using the instructions on lines 458–479; see Listing 11-1. They will be loaded into the ALRMTIME register in the same way using the instructions on lines 495–500 and line 503 in Listing 11-1.

If you were going to set an alarm to go off at the same date every month or year, then you would use the ALRMDATE register. It works in the same way as the ALRMTIME register, but as we will not be using it in my program, I have left the detail out.

The following series of instructions will set the alarm to go off once a day at a time of 07:35:30. To set a time of 07:35:30 for the alarm, we would simply write the following 32-bit number to the ALRMTIME register using the variable "atime":

0x07353000 or 0b0000,0111,0011,0101,0011,0000,0000,0000

```
1   ahourtens = 0;
2   ahourunits = 7;
3   amintens = 3;
4   aminunits = 0;
5   asectens = 3;
6   asecunits = 0;
7   atime = (ahourtens <<28);
8   atime = atime + ((ahourunits & 0x0F)<<24);
9   atime = atime +  ((amintens & 0x0F)<<20);
10  atime = atime +  ((aminunits & 0x0F)<<16);
11  atime = atime +  ((asectens & 0x0F)<<12);
12  atime = atime +  ((asecunits & 0x0F)<<8);
13  while (RTCALRM & 0x1000);
14  RTCALRMCLR = 0xCFFF;
15  ALRMTIME = atime;
16  RTCALRM = 0xC600;
```

Instructions on lines 7–12 load the 32-bit variable "atime" with the desired alarm time. Instruction on line 15 copies that into the register ALRMTIME.

Note, line 16 RTCALRM = 0xC600 turns the alarm on and sets the CHIME bit, bit 14, to a logic '1' to ensure the alarm repeats forever, as the ARPT value does roll over when it reaches '0'. This instruction also loads the AMSK bits with 0110, which sets the alarm to repeat once a day; see Table 11-9.

I did modify the program, in Listing 11-1, to set the chime bit to a logic '1'. I did this so that I could monitor the ARPT value, using the LEDs on PORTA, to see that it did roll over to 0xFF on the next decrement when it had reached a value of "0." This was to see that the alarm did repeat every ten seconds forever.

The RTCC module, in this 32-bit PIC, is quite a complex module. However, I hope this analysis has helped you to understand how it works and how you can program it. It should show you that to program anything properly, you must have a thorough understanding of how it works. It also shows you that you need to appreciate binary numbers, and how they are formatted, as well as hexadecimal numbers. As you deepen your understanding, you will become a better programmer.

Figure 11-1 shows the time, day, and date display from the program. Figure 11-2 shows the display when the PIC runs the ISR that runs when the alarm goes off.

This is a basic program for using the RTCC module of the PIC32, but I hope it has given you a good grounding to attempt a more detailed use of the module in your programs.

Figure 11-1. *The Time, Day, and Date Display*

Figure 11-2. *The Alarm Display*

Summary

In this chapter, we have learned how to set up and use the RTCC module inside the PIC32. There is a lot more you can do with this module, but I hope I have given you the confidence to try using the module.

In the next chapter, we will start our investigation into using analog signals and learn how to set the PIC up to receive analog inputs and use them.

CHAPTER 12

The Real Analog World

In this chapter, we will move into the analog world. We will study the difference between analog and digital signals. We will learn how microcontrollers, which exist in the digital world, can make use of analog signals. This will involve using the ADC, which stands for analog-to-digital converter, within the PIC.

After reading this chapter, you will be able to use one or more analog inputs that the 32-bit PIC can use. You will be able to control the ADC module of the PIC. You will then be able to use real-world signals and get the PIC to respond to them.

The Real-World Signals

While the PIC micro, like all microprocessor-based systems, lives in a digital world, we humans live in an analog world. To appreciate what this means, and why I call the analog signal a real-world signal, we must understand the difference between analog and digital signals.

© Hubert Ward 2023
H. Ward, *Introductory Programs with the 32-bit PIC Microcontroller*,
Maker Innovations Series, https://doi.org/10.1007/978-1-4842-9051-4_12

An Analog Signal

This is a signal, usually a voltage, that can take up any value between the two extremes. Let's assume, for example, we have a potentiometer, that is, a variable resistor, that could supply a voltage, as an input to our PIC, from 0V to 3.3V. The variable resistor would produce an analog voltage, as it could be any voltage, from 0V to 3.3V; that is, it could be 0.0000125V, 0.125V, 1.25V, 3.125V, or, indeed, any voltage imaginable between 0 and 3.3V.

However, we humans would not be able to see any value imaginable, because we are not really analog. We would find it hard to see the difference between 0.25V, which we would say is a quarter of a volt, and 0.251V, 0.253V, or 0.255V. It would depend upon the definition of the scale on the voltmeter. Also, we don't need that sort of accuracy, for example, how many times we have said it was quarter past three when it was really 14 mins past or 16 mins past.

The Digital World

In the digital world, we use a digital signal to try and represent a real-world analog signal. The difference with a digital signal, from the analog signal, is that the digital signal can only change in discrete steps. The size of the steps, that is, the resolution of the steps, depends upon the number of bits the digital system uses. To appreciate this, we will consider how the 32-bit PIC will use the ADC to represent a variable voltage applied to it as an analog input. The resolution of the ADC can be determined using Equation 12-1.

$$resolution = \frac{range}{2^n}$$

Equation 12-1. The Resolution of an ADC

With the 32-bit PIC, the range is 0 to 3.3V. If the ADC is an 8-bit ADC, then n = 8. Putting these values into Equation 12-1 gives

$$resolution = \frac{3.3}{2^8} = 0.012890625 = 12.9mv$$

Equation 12-2. An 8-Bit ADC

Note, I am rounding the resolution up to 12.9mV, that is, we are not truly analog.

This means that the lowest voltage the ADC could recognize would ideally be 0V. Then the next would be 12.9mV, then the next would be 25.8mV. Note the PIC could not see 10mV or 21mV, that is, any voltage between the discrete steps. This means that the digital world cannot truly represent the real analog world. The error of the digital system, which is sometimes called "quantization noise," is equal to half the resolution, that is, 6.45mV in this case.

The actual ADC, in the 32-bit PIC, is a 10-bit ADC and that would produce a resolution of

$$resolution = \frac{3.3}{2^{10}} = 0.00322265625 = 3.223mv$$

Equation 12-3. A 10-Bit ADC

This shows that the ADC in the PIC has a pretty good resolution, much better than the 8-bit example before.

A Simple Voltmeter Program

OK, so I hope we know what an analog signal is and that all PICs use an ADC to convert the analog signal to a digital value. Now let's see how we can make use of the ADC, in the PIC, to measure a simple analog input.

The PIC has lots of bits, at its PORTS, that can be set as inputs. In all PICs, some of those inputs can be used for analog inputs, as they can be connected to the ADC that is within the PIC. With the 32-bit PICs, it is PORTB that has inputs that can be used as analog. There are 16 analog inputs, which are AN0, on bit 0 of PORTB, to AN15, on bit 15 of PORTB. This does not mean there are 16 ADC circuits within the PIC. Indeed, there is only one ADC, and the PIC uses multiplexing to connect one of the 16 inputs to the ADC in the PIC. Due to the number of analog inputs, there are indeed two multiplexers. AN0 to AN7 use multiplexer A, and AN8 to AN15 use multiplexer B.

You must also appreciate that these 16 analog inputs on PORTB could be used as a digital input, and it is up to you to tell the PIC how you want to use the inputs, that is, as analog or digital. To see how this is done, we will look at a simple voltmeter program.

The Algorithm of the Voltmeter Program

Here is a list of the most important aspects of the program:

- This will use the output from a variable resistor as the analog input. With the explorer 16 development board, there is a variable resistor connected to AN5, that is, bit 5 of PORTB of the PIC. We must ensure that bit 5 of PORTB is set as analog input, and the rest are set as digital. This will use the control register **AD1PCFG: ADC PORT CONFIGURATION REGISTER.**

- We must ensure that AN5 is connected to the ADC. This will use the control register **AD1CHS: ADC INPUT SELECT REGISTER.**

- We must turn on the ADC within the PIC and configure its operation correctly. This will involve the use of a variety of control registers, which we will look at in the analysis of the program listing.

- We will use a simple LCD that is on PORTE, which is the LCD on the explorer 16 development board, to display the voltage reading. This will use the appropriate header file.

The program listing is shown in Listing 12-1.

Listing 12-1. The Simple Voltmeter Program

```
1   /*A Program That Uses The ADC
2   It uses the variable resistor connected to ch5 of ADC
3   Written for PIC32MX360F512L by Mr H.H. Ward
4   Dated 07/08/2012
5   Displays the voltage at the pot on channel 5 on the LCD
6   This program uses the sprintf function to display floating
    point numbers
7   */
8   #include <xc.h>
9   #include <config72M36MNoWDTNoJTAG.h>
10  #include <LCDPORTE.h>
11  #define startButton     _RA7
12  //variables
13  float sysVoltage;
14  char str[80];
15  //some subroutines
16  unsigned int readADC( unsigned char ch)
17  {
18  AD1CHSbits.CH0SA = ch;
```

```
19   AD1CON1bits.SAMP = 1;
20   while (!AD1CON1bits.DONE);
21   return ADC1BUF0;
22   }
23   void displayVoltage(float reading)
24   {
25   sprintf(str, "%.2f", reading);
26   writeString(str);
27   writeString(" Volts");
28   }
29   void main()
30   {
31   // set up the timers and PORTS
32   T1CON = 0x8030;
33   TRISA = 0x0080;
34   TRISB = 0x00FF;
35   TRISC = 0X00FF;
36   TRISD = 0X0000;
37   TRISE = 0x0000;
38   PORTA = 0;
39   PORTB = 0;
40   PORTC = 0;
41   PORTD = 0;
42   PORTE = 0;
43   AD1PCFG = 0xFFCF;
44   AD1CON1 = 0x80E0;
45   AD1CON2 = 0;
46   AD1CON3 = 0x1F3F;
47   DDPCONbits.JTAGEN = 0;
48   setUpTheLCD ();
49   //the main part of the program
50   while (startButton);
```

```
51  writeString ("The voltage is");
52  line2 ();
53  while (1)
54  {
55  sysVoltage = readADC (5)*0.003223;
56  displayVoltage (sysVoltage);
57  line2 ();
58  }
59  }
```

Analysis of Listing 12-1

I will restrict the analysis to the important instructions, as most of the instructions have been looked at before.

Line 43 AD1PCGF = 0xFFCF;

This uses the AD1PCGF register to set which bits will be analog or digital. The bits that are set to logic '1' mean those corresponding inputs will be digital. Those that are set to logic '0' mean the corresponding bit will be analog. The hexadecimal data 0xFFCF means that only bits 4 and 5 of the AD1PCGF register will be logic '0', and so only inputs AN4 and AN5 will be analog, and the rest will be digital. The AN4 is connected to a temperature transducer on the explorer 16 development board. The AN5 is connected to the variable resistor.

Line 44 AD1CON1 = 0x80E0;

This will load the AD1CON1 control register with the data 0x80E0. To appreciate what this will do, we need to look at the bits of this control register. This is looked at in Table 12-1.

Table 12-1. *The Bits of the AD1CON1 Control Register*

Bit	Name	Usage
15	ON	Logic '1': Turn on the ADC
		Logic '0': Turn the ADC off
14	FRZ	Logic '1': Freeze the CPU during debug mode
	Freeze	Logic '0': Do not freeze the CPU during debug mode
13	SIDL	Logic '1': Stop operations when the CPU is put in idle mode
	Stop	Logic '0': Don't stop operations when in idle mode
12–11		Not used
10–8	Form	See Table 12-2
7–5	SSRC	See Table 12-3
4	CLARSAM	Logic '1': Stop conversion when first ADC interrupt is generated
		Logic '0': ADC continues normal operation
3		Not used
2	ASAM	Logic '1': Sampling begins immediately after last conversion completes
		Logic '0': Sampling begins when SAMP bit is set to a logic '1'
1	SAMP	Logic '1': This will start the ADC procedure if the ASAM bit is a logic '0'
		Logic '0': This indicates the sample and hold circuit has a sample of the input ready to be read
0		Logic '1': This starts the ADC conversion
		Logic '0': The ADC conversion has completed

Table 12-2. *The Form Control Bits*

Bit 10	Bit 9	Bit 8	Data Output Format
0	0	0	16-bit integer
0	0	1	Signed 16-bit integer
0	1	0	16-bit fractional
0	1	1	Signed 16-bit fractional
1	0	0	32-bit integer
1	0	1	Signed 32-bit integer
1	1	0	32-bit fractional
1	1	1	Signed 32-bit fractional

Table 12-3. *The Conversion Trigger Source*

Bit 7	Bit 6	Bit 5	Conversion Trigger Source
0	0	0	Clearing SAMP bit ends the sampling and starts the conversion
0	0	1	Active transition on INT0 pin ends the sampling and starts the conversion
0	1	0	Timer3 period match ends the sampling and starts the conversion
0	1	1	Reserved
1	0	0	Reserved
1	0	1	Reserved
1	1	0	Reserved
1	1	1	Internal counter ends the sampling and starts the conversion

The ADC Process

To help interpret the bits of the AD1CON1 control register, it might be useful to look at the process of capturing an analog input and converting it to a digital value.

The first thing that has to happen is that the analog input is connected to the sample and hold circuit, within the ADC module, in the 32-bit PIC. This would involve selecting which input is switched, via the multiplexer, A or B. Although this action does not take long, it does take a finite time and so must be accounted for.

The next thing that happens is the capacitor, which is part of the sample and hold circuit, is allowed to charge up to the voltage at the input. This will take some time, and the switching of the input to the sample and hold circuit, and the time taken for the capacitor to charge up, is termed the "acquisition time."

Once the capacitor has fully charged up to the input voltage, the analog input is disconnected from the sample and hold circuit, and the voltage is held in the capacitor, so that the ADC can convert the voltage into a binary value, ready for the PIC to use. This binary value will then be stored in one of the 16 buffer registers of the ADC.

The Acquisition Time

The programmer must ensure that they create an acquisition time that is long enough for the capacitor, in the sample and hold circuit, to fully charge up to the input voltage. There are basically two ways we can do that. One is by manually starting the acquisition process by setting the SAMP bit, bit 1 of the AD1CON1 register, to a logic '1'. Then, after allowing a sufficient period of time for the capacitor to charge up, complete the acquisition by clearing the SAMP bit, that is, forcing it to a logic '0', after which the conversion can commence. To select this manual method, you must ensure the SSRC bits, bits 7, 6, and 5 of the AD1CON1 register, are all set to a logic '0'; see Table 12-3.

This method is fine, but you must get the timing correct. If you stop the acquisition too early, then you might not get a true reading of the input voltage. If you take too long, then you may be wasting too much time.

The other method is to let the ADC module cater for the acquisition time automatically. This option is chosen by ensuring the ASAM bit, bit 2 of the AD1CON1 control register, is set to a logic '0' and starting the ADC process by setting the SAMP bit to a logic '1'. This will start the sample and hold process to capture the input voltage. Then, to ensure the conversion process starts automatically when the acquisition has completed, we must ensure the SSRC bits, bits 7, 6, and 5 of the AD1CON1 register, are all set to a logic '1'; see Table 12-3.

I normally choose the automatic option.

We can now look at the instruction on line 44 and see what it is doing. It loads the AD1CON1 register with the data 0x80E0.

- Bit 15 is set to a logic '1' which simply turns the ADC module on.

- Bit 14 is a logic '0' which means we don't freeze the CPU in debug mode.

- Bit 13 is also a logic '0' which means the CPU does not stop while in idle mode.

- Bits 12 and 11 are not used.

- Bits 10 to 8 are all set to a logic '0' which means we are formatting the data as a 16-bit long integer.

- Bits 7 to 5 are all set to a logic '1' as we want to start the conversion automatically after the acquisition process has completed.

- Bit 4 is a logic '0' which means the buffer will be overwritten after the next conversion.

- Bit 3 is not used.

- Bit 2 is a logic '0' which means the acquisition process will start when we set the ASAM bit, bit 1, to a logic '1'.

- Bit 1 has been left at a logic '0', because we will set this bit to a logic '1' to start the whole ADC process, starting with the acquisition process.

- Bit 0 is left as a logic '0', as we monitor this bit to see when it goes to a logic '1'. This will happen automatically when the conversion process has completed.

I hope this analysis helps you to understand how we are controlling the major aspects of the ADC module. We will now carry on with the analysis of the program.

Line 45 AD1CON2 = 0;

This loads the AD1CON2 control register with all logic '0s'. To see what this does, we will look at the individual bits of the AD1CON2 register. Bits 15 to 13 will set the reference supply for the ADC according to Table 12-4.

Table 12-4. *The Reference Supply Selection Options*

Bits 15, 14, 13	ADC Positive Supply	ADC Negative Supply
000	AVDD	AVSS
001	External VREF+ Pin	AVSS
010	AVDD	External VREF− Pin
011	External VREF+ Pin	External VREF− Pin
1xx	AVDD	AVSS

The effect of loading the AD1CON2 control register with all logic '0s'

- Bits 15 to 13 are all logic '0', ensuring we select the VDD and VSS supply to the PIC as the reference supply voltages for the ADC module, as shown in Table 12-4.

- Bit 12 is a logic '0' which means we disable the offset calibration mode.

- Bit 11 is not used.

- Bit 10 is a logic '0' which means we don't allow the ADC to scan the inputs.

- Bits 9 and 8 are not used.

- Bit 7 is set to a logic '0' which means we should use the buffers 0x8 to 0xF to retrieve the ADC result.

- Bit 6 is not used.

- Bits 5 to 2 are set to a logic '0' which means interrupts are generated at the end of each conversion process.

- Bit 1 is set to a logic '0' which means the buffer is configured as a single 16-bit register.

- Bit 0 is set to a logic '0' which means we will always use the multiplexer A.

Line 46 AD1CON3 = 0x1F3F;

The AD1CON3 is the control register that is used to set the timing of the ADC module to ensure there is enough acquisition time for the ADC to work correctly. The bits are used as follows:

- Bits 31 to 16 are not used.

- Bit 15, the ADRC, sets which clock the conversion process will use. A logic '1' means it will use the internal RC clock, and a logic '0' means it will use the peripheral bus clock, PBCLK. This is the option we will use, as we set this bit to a logic '0'.

- Bits 14 and 13 are not used.

- Bits 12 to 8, the SAMC, set the auto sample time bits; see Table 12-5.

- Bits 7 to 0, the ADCS, set the conversion clock; see Table 12-6.

Table 12-5. *Selection of the Number of TADs Used*

Bit 12	Bit 11	Bit 10	Bit 9	Bit 8	Number of TADs
1	1	1	1	1	31 TADs
1	1	1	1	0	31 TADs
–	–	–	–	–	–
0	0	0	0	1	1 TAD
0	0	0	0	0	0 TAD not allowed

Table 12-6. *Time Selection for One TAD*

B7	B6	B5	B4	B3	B2	B1	B0	Time for 1 TAD
1	1	1	1	1	1	1	1	$= \dfrac{512}{PBCLK}$
0	1	1	1	1	1	1	1	$= \dfrac{256}{PBCLK}$
0	0	1	1	1	1	1	1	$= \dfrac{128}{PBCLK}$
–	–	–	–	–	–	–	–	
0	0	0	0	0	0	0	1	$= \dfrac{4}{PBCLK}$
0	0	0	0	0	0	0	0	$= \dfrac{2}{PBCLK}$

This shows that in general $1TAD = \dfrac{number}{PBCLK}$ assuming we are using the PBCLK as the frequency for the ADC.

The instruction, on line 46, loads the AD1CON3 register with the following data 0x1F3F, that is, 0b0001,1111,0011,1111 in binary.

This has the following action.

Bits 12 to 8 are all set to logic '1.' This means we will use the maximum number of TADs, that is, 31 TADs.

Bits 7 to 0 are set as 0011,1111, which means the time for one TAD is

$$\frac{128}{PBCLK} = \frac{128}{36,000,000} = 3.56\mu S$$

TADS and What They Are

The operations of the ADC, which are basically to acquire the input voltage, that is, acquisition time, and then convert that voltage into a 10-bit binary number, the conversion time, are synchronized to a clock. The units that are used to describe the time period for these operations are termed "TAD." The two main operations require a number of TAD periods to allow sufficient time for the operations to complete. The conversion of the voltage to a binary number requires 12 TAD periods. The minimum number of TAD periods for the acquisition of the voltage is 1 TAD period.

So how do we set the period for 1 TAD and how long should it be? These are two important aspects of how we use the ADC. It is really the acquisition time that sets the period of the TAD. The acquisition time is a function of the sample and hold circuit, as shown in Figure 12-1.

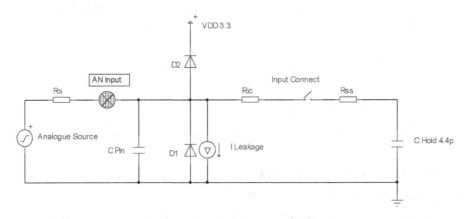

Figure 12-1. *The Typical Sample and Hold Circuit*

If we assume the following typical values:

- Rs at 5kΩ

- Rss at 3kΩ

- Ric at 250Ω

- The capacitor set at 4.4pF

then the time constant for the sample and hold circuit would be

$$8250 \times 4.4E^{-12} = 36.3\text{ns}.$$

As it takes approximately five time constants for the capacitor to fully charge up to the input voltage, then the minimum acquisition time would be 181.5ns. If the value of the Rs resistor was less than 5kΩ, then the acquisition time would reduce. However, we have to settle on a reasonable acquisition time, so we will use the value of 181.5ns. If we allow a reasonable leeway, then a value of 200ns would be OK. Therefore, that is the acquisition time we will use for our programs that use the ADC.

This means that the time period for our TAD is approximately 200ns. If it turns out to be too short, then we will change it, if need be. We now need to see how we derive this time period for the TAD. It is bits 7 to 0 that give us a variety of options for deriving this time period. The concept is to use an expression like that shown in Equation 12-4.

$$1TAD = \frac{(number + 1) \times 2}{ADCFrequency}$$

Equation 12-4. Time for 1 TAD Period

The "number" is set by the data in bits 7 to 0 of the AD1CON3 register. We have already determined what the time for the TAD period should be, that is, 200ns. Therefore, we need to rearrange this equation to give us the "number," that is, the value we need to load into bits 7 to 0 of the AD1CON3 register. This is done in Equation 12-5.

$$number = \frac{1TAD \times ADCFrequency}{2} - 1$$

Equation 12-5. The Number for the TAD

This means we need to set the ADC frequency before we can determine this number. The ADC frequency is set using bit 15 of the AD1CON3 control register. If this bit is a logic '1', then we will use the internal RC clock. If this bit is a logic '0', then we will use the PBCLK. In our programs, we will set this bit to a logic '0'. This means that the ADC frequency will be the same as the PBCLK, that is, 36MHz in this case.

This means we can calculate the number for the TAD as follows:

$$number = \frac{200E^{-9} \times 36E^{6}}{2} - 1 = 2.6$$

If we round this up to 3, we can set bits 7 to 0 to 0000,0011, that is, 3 in binary.

Putting this into Equation 12-4 gives a TAD time of

$$1TAD = \frac{(3+1) \times 2}{36E^{6}} = 222.22ns$$

This TAD period should meet the requirements for the acquisition time, assuming we used just 1 TAD period for the acquisition time. We could, if we wanted, use more than 1 TAD time. We could use up to 31 TAD periods for this acquisition time. The number of TAD periods used, to accommodate the acquisition time, is controlled by bits 12, 11, 10, 9, and 8 of the AD1CON3 control register; see Table 12-5. Using the preceding calculations, we can try just 1 TAD time for the acquisition period. This means we can try setting these bits to 00001.

Therefore, using the preceding values of 00001 for bits 12 to 8 and 0000,0011 for bits 7 to 0, we can write the following data to the AD1CON3 control register:

AD1CON3 = 0b0000,0001,0000,0011 or 0x0103

This gets the ADC to use the PBCLK as the frequency source and uses just 1 TAD for the acquisition time, with a TAD value of 222.22ns.

To test these settings for the TAD and the acquisition time, we should run the program and see how the voltmeter performs. On running the program, I found that the display would show 3.3V, as the maximum voltage, and 0V as the minimum. This is what was expected. A second test could be done to check the accuracy of the reading. As I have said earlier, if the acquisition time was too short, then we could get inaccurate readings. This would be because we had not allowed enough time for the capacitor, in the sample and hold circuit, to charge up to the full analog voltage applied. The simplest way to increase the acquisition time would be to increase the number of TADs used for this time. The higher the number of TADs used, the longer the acquisition time. The highest number of TADs we could use is 31; see Table 12-6. I therefore changed the value I loaded into the AD1CON3 control register to 0x1F03; this would set all five bits 12 to 8 to a logic '1', setting the TAD count to 31. The time for 1 TAD was still kept to 222.22ns. When I now ran the program, there was no difference in the voltage displayed. This assured me that the calculations I have done for the time period of the TAD and the number of TADS used for the acquisition time were acceptable.

With the assumption that we can use just 1 TAD for the acquisition time, and knowing that we will need 12 TAD periods for the conversion time, then knowing we should use 1 TAD period for a delay between the acquisition time and the conversion time, this would make a total of 14 TAD periods for the complete ADC process. Knowing that the TAD time is 222.22ns, then the total time for the ADC process would be around 3.1µs. If we wanted to continuously repeat the ADC process, then this would give us a rate of 321k sps, that is, samples per second. This is assuming the Rs resistance was at 5kΩ. If we required a higher rate of samples per second, then we would have to reduce this resistance.

I hope this analysis of the ADC process and the TAD time has helped you understand how the ADC works and what we need to do to program the module correctly. I will now carry on with the analysis of Listing 12-1.

Lines 47–54 have been looked at in previous listings.

Line 55 sysVoltage = readADC (5)*0.003223;

This calls the subroutine "readADC " and sends up the number 5 to it. This is the ADC channel we want to connect to the sample and hold circuit, when we acquire the analog input from the variable resistor, on the explorer 16 development board. The subroutine will return the result from reading the ADC back to the main program where, with this instruction, it is multiplied by the value 0.003223 and then loaded into the variable "sysVoltage." The value of 0.003223 is the resolution of the 10-bit ADC. The resolution is simply the maximum voltage of 3.3V divided by 2^{10}, that is, by 1024, which gives the value of 3.223mV or 0.003223 volts.

We will now look at the instructions of the subroutine "readADC," which are between lines 16 and 22.

Line 16 unsigned int readADC(unsigned char ch)

This creates the subroutine "readADC." The term "unsigned int," at the beginning, means that this subroutine will be returning a value of type unsigned int, that is, a 16-bit variable, to the main program, when the subroutine finishes. The term unsigned char ch, inside the normal brackets, sets up a local variable, one that is only used in this subroutine, called "ch" of type unsigned char, that is, an 8-bit variable. When the subroutine is called, a value must be passed up to it, and that value will be copied into the variable "ch." In this case, it will be the value "5," as the analog input we will be looking at is connected to channel 5.

Line 18 AD1CHSbits.CH0SA = ch;

This will load the bits 19 to 16 of the AD1CHS control register with the value 5. This will connect the multiplexer A to channel 5 of the ADC inputs.

Line 19 AD1CON1bits.SAMP = 1;

This starts the sampling process to acquire the voltage at the input. Once the acquisition has completed, the conversion process will start automatically.

Line 20 while (!AD1CON1bits.DONE);

This makes the PIC do nothing while the DONE bit, that is, bit 0, on the AD1CON1 control register is at a logic '0'. The logic will change to a logic '1' when the conversion process has completed and the result of the ADC has been stored in the ADC buffer.

Line 21 return ADC1BUF0;

This calls an end to the subroutine and returns the PIC to where the subroutine was called from. It will also present the contents of the ADC1BUF0 register, in which the PIC has already stored the result of the ADC process, to be copied into a variable associated with the call instruction. In this way, then, when the PIC returns to the call instruction, it will place a copy of the contents of the buffer register into the variable "sysVoltage" as per that call instruction.

This completes the analysis of the "readADC" subroutine.

Line 56 displayVoltage (sysVoltage);

This calls the subroutine "displayVoltage" and passes up to it the contents of the variable "sysVoltage" to the subroutine. We will look at the instructions of the subroutine "displayVoltage" to see what it does. The instructions for that subroutine are between lines 23 and 28.

Line 23 void displayVoltage(float reading)

This creates the subroutine "displayVoltage" and sets up a local variable, of the type float, called "reading." It is into this variable that the PIC will place a copy of the contents of the variable "sysVoltage" that was sent up with the subroutine call. Note the variable "sysVoltage" was declared as type float on line 13.

Line 25 sprintf(str, "%.2f", reading);

This calls the function "sprintf." This then fills the array "str" which was declared on line 14 with the contents of the variable "reading." The "%.2f" is used to format the display to show just two decimal places.

Line 26 writeString(str);

This calls the subroutine "writeString" and sends the contents of the array "str" to be displayed on the LCD.

Line 27 writeString(" Volts");

This calls the same subroutine, but it sends the characters " Volts" to be displayed on the LCD. Note the intentional space between the opening quotation marks and the letter "V". This is to leave a space between the reading and the word Volts on the LCD.

This completes the analysis of the subroutine "displayVoltage."

Line 57 line2 ();

This simply calls the subroutine to move the cursor to the start of line 2 on the LCD. This is because the display on line 1 of the LCD will display the message "The Voltage is"; see line 51.

I hope this analysis has given you some understanding of how to use the ADC. We can, as we can with most of the peripherals within the PIC32, use the ADC to generate interrupts, but at this point in the book, we will not look at that aspect of the ADC.

The 4–20mA Transducer

In many industrial applications of analog inputs to the PIC, a transducer is used to convert the physical quantity being measured into either a voltage or a current. A typical transducer could be

- Speed

- Temperature

- Pressure, etc.

Some people call them sensors, but I prefer to call them transducers, as a sensor is used to sense when something occurs, but no matter. I am trying to make you aware of an issue, if you are using a current transducer. Current transducers avoid the problem of loading, which can occur with a voltage transducer. However, there is a problem with current transducers. The normal application is to pass the current through a resistor, at the input, to change the current to an appropriate voltage – usually, a 250Ω resistor for a 5V system or a 165Ω for a 3.3V system. The problem is that when passing the current through the resistor, some of that current would flow into the holding capacitor once the input is connected to the sample and hold circuit. This would actually reduce the expected input voltage, as not all the current from the transducer would flow through the resistor. One possible solution to this problem that I have used successfully is to place an op amp, arranged as a unity gain buffer, between the resistor and the analog input of the PIC. This would ensure that all the current from the transducer would pass through the resistor, and none would go into the holding capacitor.

Controlling Two Analog Inputs

This next program is just to show you how you can use the PIC to monitor two, or more if you wanted to, analog inputs. The explorer 16 development board has two analog inputs: the variable resistor, which is on channel 5, and the TC107A, a temperature transducer, which is on channel 4. The program shown in Listing 12-2 uses the LCD on PORTE to display the voltage obtained from the potentiometer and then the temperature reading from the TC107A, temperature transducer. There is a three-second delay before the display switches from the voltmeter to the temperature reading, and vice versa.

Listing 12-2. The Voltmeter and Temperature Readings

```
1   /* File:    voltmeterTemperatureADC.c
2   Author: Mr H. H. Ward
3   A program to use the ADC
4   to measure a voltage and the temperature
5   Written for the 32bit PIC
6   Created on 13 May 2022, 13:19
7   */
```

```
 8  #include <xc.h>
 9  #include <stdio.h>
10  #include <con72Meg36Meg32Bit.h>
11  #include <lcdPORTEGood.h>
12  #define startButton    _RA7
13  //variables
14  unsigned char nt;
15  float sysVoltage, sysTemp;
16  char str[80];
17  //some subroutines
18  void delay250 (unsigned char dt)
19  {
20  for (nt = 0; nt < dt; nt ++)
21  {
22  TMR1 = 0;
23  while (TMR1 < 35150);
24  }
25  }
26  unsigned int readADC( unsigned char ch)
27  {
28  AD1CHSbits.CH0SA = ch;
29  AD1CON1bits.SAMP = 1;
30  while (!AD1CON1bits.DONE);
31  return ADC1BUF0;
32  }
33  void displayReading(float reading)
34  {
35  sprintf(str, "%.2f", reading);
36  writeString(str);
37  }
38  void main()
```

```
39  {
40  // set up the timers and PORTS
41  T1CON = 0x8030;
42  TRISA = 0x0080;
43  TRISB = 0x00FF;
44  TRISC = 0x00FF;
45  TRISD = 0x0000;
46  TRISE = 0x0000;
47  PORTA = 0;
48  PORTB = 0;
49  PORTC = 0;
50  PORTD = 0;
51  PORTE = 0;
52  AD1PCFG = 0xFFCF;
53  AD1CON1 = 0x80E0;
54  AD1CON2 = 0;
55  AD1CON3 = 0x1F3F;
56  DDPCONbits.JTAGEN = 0;
57  setUpTheLCD ();
58  //the main part of the program
59  while (startButton);
60  while (1)
61  {
62  clearTheScreen ();
63  writeString ("The voltage is");
64  line2 ();
65  sysVoltage = readADC (5)*0.003223;
66  displayReading (sysVoltage);
67  writeString(" Volts");
68  delay250 (18);
69  clearTheScreen ();
```

```
70  writeString ("Temperature is");
71  line2 ();
72  sysVoltage = readADC (4)*0.003223;
73  sysTemp = ((sysVoltage - 0.5))*100;
74  displayReading (sysTemp);
75  writeString(" C ");
76  displayReading (sysVoltage);
77  delay250 (16);
78  }
79  }
```

Analysis of Listing 12-2

The program is very much the same as Listing 12-1, so we will look at some of the changes.

Line 9 #include <stdio.h>

I have included this header file with this program, even though I removed it from the previous program, in Listing 12-1. It is required for the "sprintf" instruction on line 35. The "sprint" function works without this include file, but you do get a warning message when you compile the listing. If, as we do with Listing 12-2, we include the stdio.h header file, that warning is removed when we compile the listing.

Line 14 unsigned char nt;

As we have a three-second delay between displays, we will need a global variable. I have named it "nt" here, and it is of type "unsigned char," that is, an 8-bit variable that can hold a value between 0 and 255. I am trying to make it a unique variable for just this delay.

Line 15 float sysVoltage, sysTemp;

We will need two variables of type "float," and this instruction creates them both.

Lines 18–25 create the usual "delay250" subroutine which we have used in our previous programs.

Line 31 void displayReading(float reading)

This creates a subroutine to display the reading from the potentiometer or temperature transducer. It is basically the same as the "displayVoltage" subroutine in Listing 12-1, except we don't write a string to the display. This is done, instead, on line 67 for the voltage and line 75 for the temperature.

Line 65 sysVoltage = readADC (5)*0.003223;

This calls the "readADC" subroutine and sends the number 5 to it. This value will be copied into the local variable "ch." This gets the PIC to connect channel 5 to the ADC. This is where the variable resistor is connected to the PIC. The result of the ADC is multiplied by 0.003223. This converts the digital value to a voltage reading from the variable resistor. The converted value is copied into the variable "sysVoltage," as stated in the instruction.

Line 66 displayReading (sysVoltage);

This calls the subroutine "displayReading" and sends the data in the variable "sysVoltage" up to it. This then gets the PIC to display the voltage on the LCD.

Line 68 delay250 (16);

This calls the "delay250" subroutine and sends the value 16, in decimal, to it. This will create a four-second delay. This is to give the user time to see the reading of the voltmeter on the display. We call the "delay250" subroutine again on line 77. We again send the value 16 up to the subroutine to create another four-second delay. This is to give the user time to read the temperature on the display.

Line 72 sysVoltage = readADC (4)*0.003223;

This calls the subroutine to read the ADC result and store it in the variable "sysVoltage." However, the difference between this instruction and the one in line 65 is that we are sending the value "4" up to the subroutine. This will be copied into the local variable "ch" (see line 26), which tells the PIC to connect the ADC to channel 4. This is where the temperature transducer is connected to the PIC. I have kept the same variable and expression for the analog input because the input will be a voltage.

This is basically all you have to do to get the PIC to accommodate more than one analog input. We should use a small delay between attempting to change the channel the ADC is connected to. However, on line 68, there is a four-second delay, so we will use that for the delay between changing the ADC input.

Line 73 sysTemp = ((sysVoltage - 0.5))*100;

This is the expression that will change the voltage, obtained from the TC107A temperature transducer, into a reading for the temperature. If you study the data sheet for the TC107A, you will find a graph that depicts the voltage output of the TC107A against changes in temperature. It does give you an expression for the output voltage, which is

$$vout = 10mV \times {}^\circ C + 500mv \qquad \text{(Equation 12-6)}$$

This can be transposed for $^\circ C$ as follows:

$$^\circ C = \frac{vout - 500mv}{10mv} \qquad \text{(Equation 12-7)}$$

or

$$°C = (vout - 500mv) \times 100 \qquad \text{(Equation 12-8)}$$

I have used Equation 12-8 in the program; see line 73.

One thing I feel I must say is that I didn't find the TC107A a very accurate transducer. When I compared it to two others, the DT11 being one of them, I found the TC107A did not agree with the other two transducers. However, the program is really to show you how you can multiplex the single ADC, within the PIC, to more than one analog input.

There are two figures which show the displays of the program. Figure 12-2 shows the display of the voltage reading from the potentiometer. Figure 12-3 shows the temperature reading. Note the second figure on line 2, that is, the 0.74, is the actual voltage output of the TC107A transducer. I have included it in the display to show you that it is a true voltage and also that Equation 12-8 works to produce a temperature reading. The 0.74 – 0.5 = 0.24 and when multiplied by 100 gives 24.0. The slight difference is because the resolution of the "sprintf" function is set to two decimal places; see line 35.

Figure 12-2. *The Voltage Display*

Figure 12-3. *The Temperature Display*

Summary

In this chapter, we have studied how the PIC32 accommodates analog inputs and the difference between analog and digital signals. We have learned how to set up the ADC inside the PIC and how to multiplex more than one analog input. As always, I hope you have found this useful, and you will go on to write applications that use analog inputs.

In the next chapter, we will learn how to use the DHT11. This is a transducer that can monitor humidity and temperature.

CHAPTER 13

The DHT11 Transducer

In this chapter, we will write a program for the DHT11, a humidity and temperature transducer.

After reading this chapter, you will learn how to communicate with the DHT11, a humidity and temperature transducer, and display the readings on the LCD connected to PORTE of the PIC32.

The DHT11 Humidity and Temperature Sensor

This is a device that can be used to monitor the humidity and temperature in a room.

The actual transducer we will use is shown in Figure 13-1.

© Hubert Ward 2023
H. Ward, *Introductory Programs with the 32-bit PIC Microcontroller*,
Maker Innovations Series, https://doi.org/10.1007/978-1-4842-9051-4_13

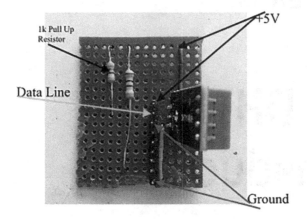

Figure 13-1. *The DHT11 Transducer on My Veroboard with a Pull-Up Resistor on the Data Line*

I call it a transducer, although many people call it a sensor. I am possibly being a bit pedantic, but this is a device which changes the physical quantities of humidity and temperature into a voltage. That is what a transducer does, whereas a sensor simply senses when a particular event has occurred, that is, a metal object has come within the range of a position sensor. It is really up to you what you call it, but I call any device which changes a physical quantity into a different quantity a transducer.

Communicating with the DHT11

The DHT11 has three pins; some may have four, but the fourth is normally left unconnected, as shown in Figure 13-1.

Communication with the device uses just one pin, the data pin. We can connect this pin to any bit of any of the ports on the PIC. We will use bit 0 of PORTD. The process by which the PIC communicates with the HCT11 is as follows:

1. We must first wait at least one second, after power-up, before attempting to communicate with the DHT11. This is to let all the internal circuitry of the transducer to settle down.

2. The PIC can then send a start signal to the DHT11. This is done by loading the data bit with a logic '0' and keeping it at a logic '0' for 18ms. Note at this point, the data bit must be set as an output.

3. After the 18ms has passed, the PIC must load a logic '1' on the data bit and keep it a logic '1' for 20μs to 40μs. We will keep it high for 25μs. This is termed the wait time, to allow the DHT11 to get ready to respond.

4. We should now change the bit to an input as the DHT11 will now be inputting data to the PIC.

5. The DHT11 will now send a response signal to the PIC to inform the PIC it has received its start signal. This response signal sends the data line low for 54μs and then high for 80μs.

6. This means we must set the data bit to an input, then, after a short delay, check to see if the data bit has gone low. We will wait 40μs before checking the data bit. We should be in the 54μs period in which the DHT11 has sent the data line low.

7. We must then wait another time period and check to see if the data bit has been sent high. We will wait 75μs, then check the logic on the data bit. We should be in the 80μs period in which the DHT11 has sent the data line high.

651

8. If the data bit had been sent high, it would mean that the DHT11 has responded correctly to our start signal and that it is ready to send the readings.

9. The DHT11 will now send 40 bits of data in five sets of 8 bits. The five sets are in the following order:

   a. Set one is the integer part of the humidity reading.

   b. Set two is the fractional part of the humidity reading.

   c. Set three is the integer part of the temperature reading.

   d. Set four is the fractional part of the temperature reading.

   e. Set five, the final part, is a "checksum" byte which is simply the binary sum of the first four parts. This checksum is used to validate the reception of the data being sent.

10. The data consists of binary logic '0' and logic '1', and these are represented as voltage states on the data line as follows:

    a. A logic '0' is represented by the data line being held at 0V for 54μs and then at logic high, 5V or 3.3V, for a further 24μs.

    b. A logic '1' is represented by the data line being held at 0V for 54μs and then at logic high, 5V or 3.3V, for a further 70μs.

11. After sending the five sets of data, the DHT11 will drive the data line low for 54μs and then send it high. This is an end-of-frame signal.

12. Having received the data from the DHT11, the PIC, having saved each of the five sets or bytes of data, must sum the first four bytes of data to create its own "checksum."

13. Having created its own checksum, the PIC must compare it with the fifth byte, which is the checksum from the DHT11, to confirm they are the same.

   a. If they are the same, the PIC can use the data. However, if they are not the same, the PIC cannot use the data.

This description helps create an algorithm for the program. The basis of the algorithm is as follows:

- The PIC sends the start signal.

- The PIC then looks for the response signal, which is a low period for 54µs, followed by a high period on the data line for 80µs. This can be achieved by waiting for a period of around 40µs and then checking to see if the data line is low. It should be. Then wait a further 80µs and check to see if the data line is high. It would still be high only if the DHT11 is sending a response signal; see the respective timing diagram. Note, it is unlikely to be an end-of-frame signal as no data has been sent from the DHT11.

- Now that the PIC has confirmed the DHT11 has received the start signal, the PIC can now wait for the first 8-bit set of data. This can be achieved as follows:

   - After the correct response from the DHT11, the data line would go low. Therefore, we should wait for the logic on the data line to go high, which should take around 54us. This is because any data, be it logic '0' or logic '1', starts with a 54µs period of 0V on the data line, after which the data line goes high to a logic '1'.

- Now wait around 30µs and check the logic level on the data line again.

  - If it has now gone back to a logic low, that is, to 0V, it means the data must have been a logic '0' as the line is held high for only 24µs when the DHT11 is sending a logic '0'; see Figure 13-2.

  - If the data line is still high, then it means the data was a logic '1'. The PIC should now wait for the data line to go low.

- Either way, if the data is a "0" or a "1," this first bit must be saved as the MSB in a memory location to be used later. We will use an array to save all 40 bits of data in five separate memory locations.

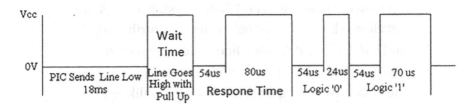

Figure 13-2. *The Timing Wave Form for Communicating with the DHT11*

Figure 13-2 shows that the only difference between the logic '0' and the logic '1', transmitted by the DHT11, is that the high time period for the logic '0' is 24µs, whereas for the logic '1', it is 54µs. Therefore, we simply have to get the PIC to wait until the line goes high, as the data line goes low for both a logic '0' and a logic '1'; see Figure 13-2. Then, after say 30µs, check the logic on the data line. If the data line is still high, the DHT11 must be transmitting a logic '1'. If it has already gone low, then it must be transmitting a logic '0'. This is what we do in the program.

The Use of a Pull-Up Resistor

One thing you must do is connect the data output of the DHT11 to VCC via a pull-up resistor. This is to ensure that when the DHT11 is not switching the output low, the output does go high. The pull-up resistor is there to limit the current, through the device, when the DHT11 does switch the output to 0V.

The DHT11 Program Listing

This is shown in Listing 13-1.

Listing 13-1. The Listing for the DHT11 Program

```
1  /*
2  * File:   humidityTemp32Prog.c
3  Author: H. H. Ward
4  *A program to use the DHT11 humidity and temperature
   transducer
5  Written for the PIC42MX360F512L
6  Created on 17 March 2022, 14:47
7  */
8  //configuration bit settings, Fcy=72MHz, Fpb=36MHz
9  #pragma config POSCMOD=XT, FNOSC=PRIPLL
10 #pragma config FPLLIDIV=DIV_2, FPLLMUL=MUL_18,
   FPLLODIV=DIV_1
11 #pragma config FPBDIV=DIV_2, FWDTEN=OFF, CP=OFF, BWP=OFF
```

```c
12   #include <xc.h>
13   #include <LCDPORTE.h>
14   //some general definitions
15   #define datapin PORTDbits.RD0
16   unsigned char mess[30], *messpointer, n, m,
     DHTresponse = 0, mychecksum, valid = 0;
17   char str[80];
18   void delay250 (char x)
19   {
20   while (x>0)
21   {
22   TMR4 = 0;
23   while (TMR4<35211);
24   x--;
25   }
26   }
27   void displayreading(float dp)
28   {
29   sprintf(str, "%.1f", dp);
30   writeString(str);
31   }
32   void main()
33   {
34   T1CON = 0x8030;
35   T3CON = 0x8020;
36   T4CON = 0x8070;
37   TRISA = 0x0080;
38   TRISB = 0x00FF;
39   TRISC = 0x00FF;
40   TRISD = 0x0000;
41   TRISE = 0x0000;
```

```
42  PORTA = 0;
43  PORTB = 0;
44  PORTC = 0;
45  PORTD = 0;
46  PORTE = 0;
47  AD1PCFG = 0xFFCF;
48  AD1CON1 = 0x80E0;
49  AD1CON2 = 0;
50  AD1CON3 = 0x0103;
51  DDPCONbits.JTAGEN = 0;
52  setUpTheLCD ();
53  writeString ("DHT11 Humid Temp");
54  line2 ();
55  delay250 (4);
56  getreading:  TRISDCLR = 0x0001;
57  datapin = 0;
58  for (n = 0; n < 4; n++)
59  {
60  TMR3 = 0;
61  while (TMR3 < 42000);
62  }
63  datapin = 1;
64  TMR3 = 0;
65  while (TMR3 < 225);
66  TRISDSET = 0x0001;
67  TMR3 = 0;
68  while (TMR3 < 360);
69  if (datapin == 0)
70  {
71  TMR3 = 0;
72  while (TMR3 < 675);
```

```
73   if (datapin == 1) DHTresponse = 1;
74   TMR3 = 0;
75   while (TMR3 < 405);
76   }
77   else DHTresponse = 0;
78   if (DHTresponse == 1)
79   {
80   for (m = 0; m < 5; m++)
81   {
82   for (n= 0; n < 8; n++)
83   {
84   while (!datapin);
85   TMR3 = 0;
86   while (TMR3 < 225);
87   if (datapin == 0)
88   {
89       shifter = 0b00000001;
90       shifter = (shifter << (7-n));
91       shifter = ~shifter;
92       mess[m] &= shifter;
93   }
94   else
95   {
96       shifter = 0b00000001;
97       shifter = (shifter << (7-n));
98       mess[m] |= shifter;
99   while (datapin);
100  }
101  }
102  }
103  mychecksum =(mess[0]+mess[1]+mess[2]+mess[3]);
```

```
104  if (mychecksum - mess[4] == 0) valid = 1;
105  else valid = 0;
106  if (valid == 1)
107  {
108  clearTheScreen ();
109  writeString ("Humidity = ");
110  displayreading(mess[0]);
111  lcdData = 0x25;
112  sendData();
113  line2 ();
114  writeString ("Temp = ");
115  displayreading (mess[2]);
116  writeString(" 0C");
117  }
118  }
119  else writeString ("no response");
120  delay250(20);
121  goto getreading;
122  }
```

Analysis of Listing 13-1

Lines 1–7 are the usual comments.

Lines 8–11 are using pragma statements to set the configuration words. This is a different approach to that of setting the configuration bits using the "Target Memory Views" from the "Window" option on the main menu bar. This approach allows you to change the particular configuration bits that you want to change while leaving the others with their default settings.

We want to increase the 8MHz crystal oscillator output to provide the 72MHz system clock and the 36MHz peripheral clock. This is achieved using the following instructions:

Line 9 #pragma config POSCMOD=XT, FNOSC=PRIPLL

This sets the primary oscillator to the XT mode which is required for an oscillator of up to 10MHz. It also directs the oscillator to pass through the phase lock loop circuit, the PLL, as this is required to multiply the oscillator frequency.

Line 10 #pragma config FPLLIDIV=DIV_2, FPLLMUL=MUL_18, FPLLODIV=DIV_1

This initially divides the 8MHz by 2 to make it 4MHz, as the input to the PLL must be 4MHz. It then multiplies the 4MHz by 18, making it 72MHz. Finally, the output of the PLL is divided by 1 so as not to keep it at 72MHz.

Line 11 #pragma config FPBDIV=DIV_2, FWDTEN=OFF, CP=OFF, BWP=OFF

This then divides the 72MHz by 2 to provide a frequency of 36MHz for the peripheral clock. It also turns off the watchdog timer, WDT, as we don't use it. The CP=OFF turns the code protection off. This is something you do if you are not worried about other programmers uploading your code from the PIC. If you don't want other programmers to be able to do this, then you should turn the CP on. The final statement, BWP = OFF, is disabling the write protection for the "Boot Flash" area of memory.

I am just trying to show you an alternative method of setting the configuration bits.

Line 15 #define datapin PORTDbits.RD0

This is just allocating data pin to bit 0 of PORTD.

Line 16 unsigned char mess[30], *messpointer, n, m, DHTresponse = 0, mychecksum, valid = 0;

This is creating the array to store the bytes sent from the DHT11 to the PIC. It also creates the pointer for the array and some more variables.

Line 17 char str[80];

This creates the array for storing the characters used in the subroutine "displayreadings." This is required by the sprint function on line 29.

Line 18 void delay250 (char x)

This creates the subroutine that runs the instructions to make a variable delay with the resolution of 250ms delay. It expects a value to be passed up to the subroutine that will be loaded into the local variable "x." This will set how many times the 250ms delay runs. For example, if x = 4, then the 250ms delay runs four times creating an overall delay of around 1 second. The instructions for the subroutine are listed between the opening and closing curly brackets of line 19 and 26.

Line 20 while (x>0)

This creates a "while x is greater than 0" test. If the result of the test is true, the PIC must carry out the instructions between the opening and closing curly brackets on lines 21 and 24.

Line 22 TMR4 = 0;

We are using timer4 as the timer for this delay. With this instruction, we are ensuring the timer starts counting from 0.

Line 23 while (TMR4<35211);

This test will be true while the value in timer4 is less than 35,211. While the test is true, the PIC will do nothing. Timer4 is set to count one every 7.11µs. Therefore, to get to a value of 35,211, it will take 35,211 x 7.11µs = 250ms.

Line 24 x--;

This simply decrements the variable "x" by 1. This is so that the value will eventually become equal to 0. This would then mean the while (test) on line 20 would become untrue. The PIC would then move on to the instruction on line 27.

Line 27 void displayreading(float dp)

This creates the subroutine "displayreading." It will expect a variable of type "float," that is, floating-point number, which is a value with decimals, to be sent up to it. This will be loaded into the local variable "dp" to be used in the subroutine.

Line 28 sprintf(str, "%.1f", dp);

This calls the function "sprintf" which is within the compiler version 1.32. If you use another version of the x32 compiler, then you may need to include the stdio library. It will retrieve the characters that have been saved into the array "str" until it comes up to the special "null" character upon which it will stop. The "%.1f" sets the display to show just one number after the decimal point. The "dp" is the local variable that will be used to load the array "str" ready for being sent to the LCD.

Line 29 writeString(str);

This calls the subroutine "writeString" and sends all the characters stored in the array "str" to the LCD until it reaches the special "null" character.

Line 35 T3CON = 0x8020;

This turns timer3 on, that is, bit 15 is a logic '1.' It sets the PBCLK as the source for timer3, that is, bit 1 is a logic '0.' It also sets the divide rate to "4," that is, bits 6, 5, and 4 are 010. This means that timer3 will count at a frequency of 9MHz, making it increment every 111.111ns. We will use timer3 to control the timing of the data to and from the DHT11.

Line 36 T4CON = 0x8070;

This turns timer4 on, using the PBCLK as its source, which it divides by 256, making it increment every 7.11µs, that is, count at a frequency of 140.625kHz. Timer4 is used in the "delay250" subroutine.

The other timer, timer1, is used in the delays for the LCD, that is, within the LCDPORTE.h header file.

Lines 37–51 are the normal instructions to set up the PIC as we want.

Line 52 setUpTheLCD ();

This calls the subroutine to set up the LCD. This subroutine, along with all the other subroutines for the LCD, is written within the header file LCDPORTE.h.

Line 53 writeString ("DHT11 Humid Temp");

This calls the subroutine "writeString" to send the opening message to the LCD.

Line 54 line2 ();

This calls the subroutine to move the cursor to the beginning of line 2 on the LCD.

Line 55 delay250 (4);

This calls the subroutine "delay250" and passes the value 4 to it. This creates the initial one-second delay to give the DHT11 time to settle down.

Line 56 getreading: TRISDCLR = 0x0001;

This creates a label "getreading" that the PIC will go to later in the program. The instruction TRISDCLR = 0x0001; simply clears bit 0 on the TRISD register. This sets bit 0 to output and does not affect the other bits. We are using bit 0 of PORTD as the "datapin"; see line 15, to communicate with the DHT11.

Line 57 datapin = 0;

This sets the logic on the datapin, that is, bit 0 of PORTD, to a logic '0'. This is the beginning of the start signal for the DHT11.

Line 58 for (n = 0; n < 4; n++)

This sets up a "for do loop" that makes the PIC run the instructions within the curly brackets, on lines 59 and 62, four times.

Line 61 TMR3 = 0;

We are using timer3 for this delay, so we need to set it to 0 so it starts timing from 0.

Line 61 while (TMR3 < 42000);

This gets the PIC to do nothing while the value in timer3 is less than 42,000. As timer3 is set to count at a frequency of 9MHz (see line 35), then 1 count = 111.111ns. Therefore, a count of 42,000 will take approximately 4.67ms. If, as we do, we run this delay four times, we will achieve a delay of around 18.67ms. This is the delay we must wait until we ask the DHT11 to respond to our start signal.

Line 63 datapin = 1;

This sends the logic on the datapin to a logic '1'. This asks the DHT11 to respond.

Lines 64 and 65 create a 25µs delay. This is the delay we wait before we change the direction of the datapin, so that we can check to see the response from the DHT11.

Line 66 TRISDSET = 0x0001;

This sets just bit 0 of the TRISD register to a logic '1.' This will make bit 0 of PORTD an input ready to receive the response signal from the DHT11.

Lines 67 and 68 create the 40µs delay before we check the logic on the "datapin" to see if it has been sent low by the DHT11.

Line 69 if (datapin == 0)

This instruction tests to see if the logic on the "datapin" has been sent low. If the result of the test is true, the PIC will carry out the instructions between the curly brackets on lines 70 and 76. If the test is untrue, then the PIC will carry out the instruction on line 77.

Lines 71 and 72 create a 75µs delay which is required before we test to see if the logic on the "datapin" has gone high, that is, to a logic '1.' This caters for the "Response Time"; see Figure 13-2.

Line 73 if (datapin == 1) DHTresponse = 1;

This tests to see if the "datapin" has gone high, and if the test is true, the PIC will carry out the one-line instruction DHTresponse = 1; which just sets the data in the variable "DHTresponse" to a value of 1. This is used to show that the response from the DHT11 is true and the DHT11 is ready to send the readings from it to the PIC.

Lines 74 and 75 create a 45µs delay.

Line 77 else DHTresponse = 0;

This is the instruction the PIC must carry out if the result of the test on line 69 was untrue. If the result of the test was true, then the PIC would simply skip this instruction. This instruction simply loads the variable

"DHTresponse" with the value "0." This is used to indicate the response from the DHT11 was not true and the PIC should start again, as no data will be sent from the DHT11.

Line 78 if (DHTresponse == 1)

This instruction tests to see if the value in the variable "DHTresponse" is equal to 1. If it is true, then this would mean the DHT11 has responded correctly to the start signal from the PIC, and it will be sending the 8 bytes of data to the PIC. If the value in the variable "DHTresponse" is not 1, then the PIC must jump to the instruction on line 119. If the value in the variable "DHTresponse" is equal to 1, then the PIC must carry out the instructions between lines 79 and 118.

We now know the DHT11 will send five blocks of 8 bits of data. Therefore, we will load the array "mess" that we created in line 16 with the data that follows.

We start by creating an outer "for do loop," on line 80, with the variable "m" that makes the PIC loop five times, that is, m = 0, m = 1, m = 2, m = 3, and m = 4. This is used to store the next 8 bits that arrive on the data pin into the first, m = 0, of five locations in the array "mess." The 8 bits to be stored in this first location in the array will start to arrive on the data pin.

We now create an inner "for do loop," on line 82, which loops eight times to look at the data coming into the PIC from the DHT11. It will store these 8 bits of data into the location in the array, controlled by the variable "m," which at present is 0, that is, the first run through the outer "for do loop."

By now, we should be well inside the 54μs time period when the DHT11 has sent the data line into a low state; see Figure 13-2. Therefore, on line 84, we wait for this logic low state to finish. Note, we know this low state will only last 54μs; see Figure 13-2. Then we create a 25μs delay, with lines 85 and 86. If you refer to Figure 13-2, you should see that if the data being sent is a logic '0', then the data line should stay high for 24μs. Then, on line 87, we ask whether the data line has gone back to low from the DHT11. If it has, then it means the data the DHT11 has just sent was the code for a logic '0'; see the timing diagram in Figure 13-2. This is because we would now be inside the 54µs low period of a new bit of data. If the test on line 87 was true, and the DHT11 had just sent a logic '0', then the PIC will carry out the instructions between lines 88 and 93. We will look at how this instruction works later.

If the test on line 87 was not true, this would mean the data line is still high, at a logic '1', then the PIC would carry out the instructions between lines 94 and 99. Also, it would mean the DHT11 is sending the code for a logic '1'. Note if the test on line 87 was true, then the PIC would ignore all the instructions on lines 94–99 inclusive. It would then go back to line 82, where we created the inner loop, and, as "n" would still be less than 8, it would carry out the instructions between lines 83 and 101 again.

This inner loop would repeat eight times and so receive the first of the 5 bytes that the DHT11 would be sending. The PIC would then go through the outer loop, created on line 80, to store the second byte of data in the second location in the array mess.

This whole process carries out a total of 40 times, in which the PIC will store the 40 bits of data in the five memory locations in the array – each memory location storing one byte of data.

In line 103, the PIC creates its own checksum by adding the bits of the data in the first four memory locations in the array. The result is stored in the variable "mychecksum."

In line 104, we subtract this result from the 8 bits in the last memory location used in the array, mess[m]. This is how the PIC will compare the two checksums. This is done to check the validity of the data received. If the result of the subtraction is zero, then the data is valid.

Line 104 if (mychecksum - mess[4] == 0) valid = 1;

With this instruction, we are setting up a test to see if the subtraction produces a zero result. If the test is true, then we load the variable "valid" with 1. The PIC would then skip the instruction on line 105.

Line 105 else valid = 0;

If the test on line 99 was untrue, then the PIC would carry out this instruction which loads the variable valid with the value 0.

Line 106 if (valid == 1)

This tests to see if the variable "valid" has the value 1 in it. If it does, then this means that the checksum validated the data sent, and we can use it.

Line 108 clears the LCD screen of any characters and sends the cursor back to the beginning of the first line.

Line 109 simply displays the words "Humidity =" on the LCD.

Line 110 displayreading(mess[0]);

This instruction calls the subroutine "displayreading" and sends the ASCII that is stored in the first location in the array "mess." The location is identified by the phrase "mess[0]", and [0] indicates the first location in the array. This would be the integer part of the humidity reading.

Next, with lines 111 and 112, the PIC sends the value 0x25, which is the ASCII for the "%" sign, to be displayed on the LCD.

Next, lines 114–117 send the temperature reading that is stored in the third location, that is, mess[2], in the array "mess" to the LCD.

Line 119 else writeString ("no response");

This is the "else" part of the "if (test is true) then do this, else do that" set up on line 78. If the test on line 78 was untrue, then the PIC will ignore all the instructions between lines 79 and 118 and carry out the instruction on line 119. This instruction simply sends the message "no response" to the LCD.

Line 120 delay250(20);

This calls the subroutine delay and sends the value of 20 up to it. This will create a delay of around five seconds.

Line 121 goto getreading;

This makes the PIC go to line 56 where it starts the whole process again.

I hope this description does explain how the instructions achieve the desired result. It is a rather complex process, and you may need to read through it and examine Figure 13-2 a few times. However, I hope it shows that once you fully understand what it is you are trying to achieve, with the PIC, then it is simply a matter of finding the instructions you need and learning how to implement them. This only comes with understanding and experience. I hope this book will give you some of that.

The Logical OR and AND Truth Tables

The program uses two logic operations, the logical OR and the logical AND. Therefore, before we go too far with the analysis, I thought we should look at the truth tables for these two operations.

Table 13-1. *The Logical OR Operation*

B	A	Result
0	0	0
0	1	1
1	0	1
1	1	1

Table 13-1 shows the logical OR response to two inputs, A and B. It shows that the result of this operation will always end up with a logic '1', except when both inputs are at a logic '0'. You might think that the logical OR operation should only result in a logic '1' if input "A" OR "B" was a logic '1', not when both are at a logic '1', as the truth table shows. However, it does, and that is why this operation is more correctly called the "Inclusive OR" as it includes the logical AND operation; see Table 13-2. The EXOR, or "Exclusive OR," is what I call the true OR as it excludes the AND function.

Table 13-2. *The Logical AND Operation*

B	A	Result
0	0	0
0	1	0
1	0	0
1	1	1

Table 13-2 shows the logical AND operation with two inputs, A and B. It shows that the result will only be a logic '1' when both inputs are at a logic '1'.

A Design Procedure

This section of this chapter is an attempt to show you a possible procedure that you can use to create a program to fulfill a specific task. The purpose of writing this book, while mostly concerned with explaining how instructions in "C" work, is also aimed at helping you develop into an embedded programmer. So, I thought that this program presents us with a problem that gives me an opportunity to describe a methodology in creating a series of instructions for the program. You can skip this section, if you so wish, and move on to the next chapter. However, it may be useful to look at how I came up with some of the program instructions. Also, there is a useful, well I think it is useful, example of how to use the simulation facility of MPLAB X to examine how the instructions work.

The problem we will look at is how to receive 8 bits of unknown data, one bit at a time, and store a record of them in a memory location. Also, we need to do this five times, so that we can store 5 bytes of data in total that we will receive from the DHT11. An added problem is that normally when data is sent to the PIC, the 8 bits are stored in a register that we can read from later. However, with the DHT11, the data is sent one bit at a time, but it is not stored in a register. The program needs to recognize the logic of the bits, as they become available at the input, and store the logic of the bit in a memory location as it is presented at the input. Quite an interesting challenge. I hope this analysis will show you how I came up with the instructions to solve this problem.

Know the Events You Want to Control

It may seem obvious that you need to understand what it is you are trying to do, but you do need to be very precise in your description of what you are trying to do. With this small program, I am trying to emulate the part of the program inside the "for do loop" on line 80 of Listing 13-1. There is one major difference in that we will not be connecting the PIC to the DHT11. Also, we will run a simulation to test how the instructions work.

The following is a description of what we will try to do:

- We will use 8 bits in a variable "data" to represent the unknown 8 bits we would have received from the DHT11. In setting these 8 bits up, we will have to pretend we don't know the logic of the 8 bits, as in reality we would not know the logic of the bits sent from the DHT11.

- We need to create five memory locations that we can easily access to store the 5 bytes of data being sent, making a total of 40 bits. We will create an array of ten locations for this, which means we will have five spare memory locations. We will also create a pointer to access the locations easily. We will create the pointer, as it is always good practice to have a pointer associated with an array. However, in this particular program, we will not use the pointer.

- We will create a "for do loop" that will allow us to access the locations in the array, both when we want to write to them and when we want to read from them. We need to write to the array when we receive the bits from the DHT11, that is, when we determine the logic of the 8 bits in the variable "data." We need to read from the array when we want to display the readings on the LCD.

- We will check to see what the logic of each bit in the variable "data" is, starting with the MSB, as that is how the DHT11 would send the 8 bits. Then record the response in the variable "datapin," that is, load "datapin" with a value of 1 if the bit is a logic '1' or a value of '0' if the bit is a logic '0.'

- This check will have to be done eight times, once for each bit, for each of the 5 bytes being sent. This means we will need to create a second "for do loop "within the first "for do loop" to keep track of the number of bits tested. It should stop when the number gets to 8.

- Once we have determined the correct logic of the bits, one at a time, we will force the logic of the appropriate bits in the current location of the array to be the same logic, starting with the MSB, of the bits in "data." Note, locations in the array will start with a value of "0," but this could be anything.

- The process by which the program will force the respective bits of the location in the array to change is to use either a logical OR operation, if we are trying to force the bit to a logic '1', or a logical AND operation, to force the bit to a logic '0.' Note, a logical OR operation will result in a logic '1' if either one or both bits, being tested, are a logic '1.' Therefore, as we will force one of the bits to a logic '1', the result must be a logic '1.'

- As the program will be performing a bit logical operation on one bit at a time, starting at the MSB, and then moving down the 8 bits one at a time, we will use an extra variable, which I will call "shifter," to change the actual bit we will be testing each time after each test. This is because we will be shifting the bit we are testing with, and we will need a variable, within which we can shift it the logic '1.' You can't shift nothing.

- With the DHT11, the logic of the current bit is determined by the timing of the change from logic '0' to logic '1'. However, we can't do that with this short program, as we are not connecting the PIC to the DHT11. Therefore, to test the logic of each bit, one at a time, we will use the logical bit AND operation between the bits of the variable "data" and a checking variable. We will call this checking variable "datacheck." Also, as we will start by checking the MSB, bit 7, of the variable "data," we must start off by loading "datacheck" with 0b10000000. This means the first logical bit AND operation will only test bit 7 of the variable "data," that is, the MSB.

The next step in the design process would be to create a flowchart. This flowchart should show how the program would carry out its actions. Each action should be described within the symbol of the flowchart, and each symbol should link up with the instructions in the program listing. The flowchart for this design program is shown in Figure 13-3.

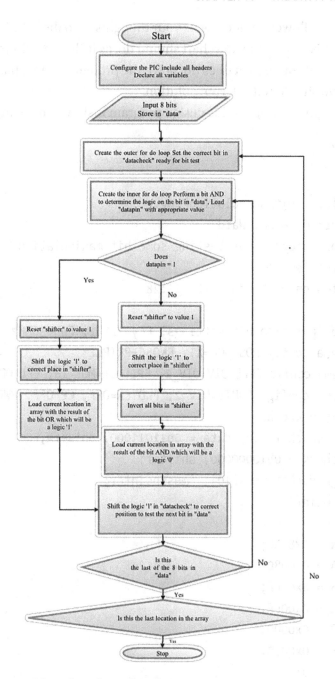

Figure 13-3. *The Flowchart for the Design Program*

I hope the flowchart does focus your thoughts onto the solution to the problem. This is what the flowchart should do, as it should help you solve the problem. If you think it does not solve the problem, then it has done its job, and you should rethink your solution.

The program listing for this design program is shown in Listing 13-2.

Listing 13-2.

```
1  /*
2  * File:    bitManipulationProg.c
3  Author: Mr H. H. Ward
4  A short program for testing some bit manipulation
   instructions.
5  Created on 20 March 2022, 15:28
6  */
7  //configuration bit settings, Fcy=72MHz, Fpb=36MHz
8  #pragma config POSCMOD=XT, FNOSC=PRIPLL
9  #pragma config FPLLIDIV=DIV_2, FPLLMUL=MUL_18, FPLLODIV=DIV_1
10 #pragma config FPBDIV=DIV_2, FWDTEN=OFF, CP=OFF, BWP=OFF
11 #include <xc.h>
12 unsigned char m,n, data = 0b11011000, datapin,
   datacheck = 0b10000000, shifter;
13 unsigned char mess[10], *messpointer;
14 void main()
15 {
16 T1CON = 0x8030;
17 TRISA = 0x0080;
18 TRISB = 0x00FF;
19 TRISC = 0x00FF;
20 TRISD = 0x0000;
21 TRISE = 0x0000;
22 PORTA = 0;
23 PORTB = 0;
```

```
24   PORTC = 0;
25   PORTD = 0;
26   PORTE = 0;
27   AD1PCFG = 0xFFFF;
28   AD1CON1 = 0x00E0;
29   DDPCONbits.JTAGEN = 0;
30   for (m =0; m < 5; m++)
31   {
32   datacheck = 0b10000000;
33   for (n = 0; n < 8; n++)
34   {
35   if (data & datacheck)datapin = 1;
36   else datapin = 0;
37   if (datapin == 0)
38   {
39   shifter = 0b00000001;
40   shifter = (shifter << (7-n));
41   shifter = ~shifter;
42   mess[m] &= shifter;
43   datacheck = datacheck >>1;
44   }
45   else
46   {
47   shifter = 0b00000001;
48   shifter = (shifter << (7-n));
49   mess[m] |= shifter;
50   datacheck = datacheck >>1;
51   }
52   }
53   }
54   while (1);
55   }
```

Analysis of Listing 13-2

To try and remove the need to repeat the term "variable" every time I refer to a variable in this analysis, I will just write the variable within quotation marks, for example, "data." I hope this is OK with you.

Lines 7–13 deal with the first block of the flowchart. Note, the start block is not the first block of the flowchart.

You should see that in line 12, we load the value in "data" with the binary value 0b11011000. This is to represent the data that would have been sent from the DHT11. Remember, we should pretend we don't know the logic of the individual bits. This deals with the second block of the flowchart.

We will use the variable "m" to keep track of how many bytes we have tested. We set "m" to 0 in the "for do loop" in line 30.

Line 30 for (m =0; m < 5; m++)

This creates the outer, or first, "for do loop." It is used to set which location in the array mess[m] we will be storing the 8 bits, that is, one complete byte, we detect from the DHT11. The instructions associated with this "for do loop" are between lines 31 and 53. This deals with the third block of the flowchart.

Line 32 datacheck = 0b10000000;

This will load "datacheck" with 0b10000000, as this gets it ready to test the logic of the MSB, bit 7, of "data." This has to be done at the start of checking the 8 bits of data sent to the PIC. However, as this is not the full program, it is the start of checking the 8 bits in the variable "data."

Line 33 for (n = 0; n < 8; n++)

This sets up the inner "for do loop," or second "for do loop," that gets the PIC to check the logic of the 8 bits in "data." It also gets the PIC to force the logic of the bits in the "result" and the current location in the array. The logic will depend upon the logic of the current bit being tested in "data." This is the fourth block of the flowchart.

Line 35 if (data & datacheck)datapin = 1;

This performs an "if" test that will be true if the logical AND operation between the bits in "data" and "datacheck" results in a logic '1'. As, in this first run through the inner loop, only bit 7 of "datacheck" is a logic '1', then we are only testing to see if bit 7 of "data" is a logic '1'. If the bit of "data" is a logic '1', then the test will be true and the PIC will load the variable "datapin" with a value of '1'.

Line 36 else datapin = 0;

If the test on line 35 is untrue, that is, the bit being tested in "data" is not a logic '1', then the PIC will carry out this "else" instruction and load "datapin" with the value "0." If the test on line 35 is true, then the PIC will skip this instruction.

Line 37 if (datapin == 0)

This will test to see if the value in "datapin" is "0." If the value in "datapin" is "0," then the test is true, and the PIC must carry out the instructions between lines 38 and 44. Note, the PIC will also skip the instructions between lines 45 and 51. This creates the NO path of the first decision box in the flowchart.

Line 39 shifter = 0b00000001;

This sets all bits in "shifter" to a logic '0' except bit 0, which is set to a logic '1'. This is to get the logic '1' in place so that we can shift it left the required number of places to test the logic of the particular bit in "data." This is the first block in the NO path. We had to create this extra variable "shifter" as we need to store the logic '1' in a variable so that we can shift it.

Line 40 shifter = (shifter << (7-n));

This will shift the logic '1' that is currently in bit 0 the required number of places. If this was the first run through the inner "for do loop," then n will equal "0." Therefore, this instruction will shift the logic '1' seven places to the left. This will put it in the MSB of "shifter." This will make bit 7 a logic '1' and all the other bits in "shifter" a logic '0'. This carries out the second block in the NO path of the flowchart.

Line 41 shifter = ~shifter;

This will invert all the bits in "shifter." This means that the bits in "shifter" will be

0b01111111

This gets the data in "shifter" ready for the bit logical AND operation next. Note we are trying to force the current bit in the location in the array to a logic '0'. This carries out the third block in the NO path.

Line 42 mess[m] &= shifter;

This will perform a bit logical AND operation between the contents of the location in the array mess[m] and "shifter." It will then load the location in the array mess[m] with the response of the bit AND operation. As bit 7 of "shifter" is a logic '0', then as one of the bits in the logical AND operation is a logic '0', the result will be a logic '0'. This means bit 7 of the location in the array will be forced to a logic '0'. All the other bits in the location will be unchanged. See Table 13-2, the truth table for the logical AND operation. The actual location in the array is controlled by the value in "m." As this would be the first run through the outer "for do loop," then m would equal 0, and so we would be using the first location in the array and forcing the current bit, in this case the MSB, to a logic '0'. This carries out the fourth block in the NO path of the flowchart.

Line 43 datacheck = datacheck >>1;

This shifts all the bits in "datacheck" one bit to the left. As this is the first run through the inner "for do loop," then, before this instruction, the bits in "datacheck" would be

0b10000000

After the instruction, they would be

0b01000000

The logic '1' in bit 7 has been shifted to bit 6, and bit 7 was replaced with a logic '0'. The old bit 0 that was a logic '0' before has just been lost off the end of the variable.

This gets the bits in "datacheck" ready to test the logic of the next bit in "data." This is carrying out the block that is the end of both the NO and YES paths in the flowcharts.

Line 45 else

This sets out the instructions between lines 46 and 51 that the PIC would carry out if the test on line 37 was untrue. This creates the YES path of the flowchart.

Line 47 shifter = 0b00000001;

This does the same as line 39. This is the first block of the YES path.

Line 48 shifter = (shifter << (7-n));

This does the same as line 40. This is the second block of the YES path.

Line 49 mess[m] |= shifter;

This will perform a bitwise logical OR operation between the contents of the location in the array mess[m] and "shifter." It will then load the location in the array mess[m] with the response of the bit OR operation. As bit 7 of "shifter" is a logic '1', then bit 7 in the location in the array will be forced to a logic '1'. See Table 13-1, the truth table for the logical OR operation. Also, as all the other bits are a logic '0', then all these bits will be the same as what they were already in the location in the array. The important aspect of this is that if the current bit being tested in "data" was a logic '1', then the respective bit in the location in the array mess[m] would be forced to a logic '1' regardless of what it was before. The actual location in the array is controlled by the value in "m." As this would be the first run through the outer "for do loop," then m would equal 0, and so we would be using the first location in the array. This is the third block in the YES path.

Line 50 datacheck = datacheck >>1;

This will do the same as line 43.

The second decision box of the flowchart is executed within the inner "for do loop" on line 33, with "n" controlling the number of times the PIC runs through the loop.

The third decision box in the flowchart is executed on line 30, with "m" controlling the number of times the PIC runs through the loop.

Line 54 while (1);

This will get the PIC to halt, or stop, at this instruction. This is because it is a "forever loop" that will constantly get the PIC to do nothing.

I hope you have found this design exercise and the analysis useful. Designing the instructions for a program is not an exact science, and it will take time and experience to get better and better at it. However, I hope this example will help you develop your design process.

Simulating the Program in MPLAB X

Now that we have a good idea of what should happen with this design program, well at least I hope you have, let's see how we can use the simulator in MPLAB X to confirm what happens.

Firstly, when you create the project in MPLAB X, you should select the simulator tool and not the ICD can. This allows MPLAB X to use its own simulated PIC to run the program.

When you are ready to run the program, you should click the mouse on the "Debug Main Program" icon from the main menu bar, as shown in Figure 13-4.

Figure 13-4. *The Debug Main Program Icon*

The program should compile as normal, and then the "Debugger Console" window should show

Launching

Initializing simulator

User program running

Also, the debug control menu bar will appear, as shown in Figure 13-5.

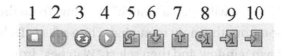

Figure 13-5. *The Control Buttons of the Debug Menu*

You may not see all the buttons, as there may not be room on the menu, so you may have to expand the debug menu to see all the buttons.

There are ten buttons that have the following functions:

1. Finish Debug Session.

2. Pause Debug Session. This is grayed out as the session is paused.

3. Reset Debug Session.

4. Continue Debug Session.

5. Step Over.

6. Step Into.

7. Step Out.

8. Run to Cursor.

9. Set PC at Cursor where PC stands for Program Counter.

10. Focus Cursor at PC.

There are some keys, such as the last three, that I have not used in my debug sessions.

Before we will use the other debug buttons, we will select the variables we want to look at, that is, watch. Therefore, you should click the pause the session button, button 2, followed by the reset button, button 3, to reset the simulation. Now we will open a "watch" window. To do this, select the window option from the main menu bar. Then select "Debugging" from the drop-down window and then select "Watches" from the fly-out window as shown in Figure 13-6.

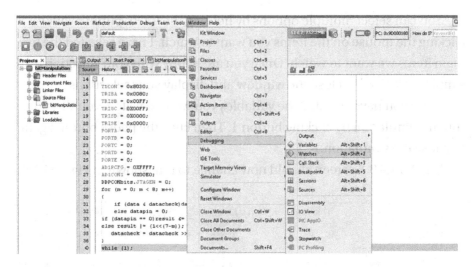

Figure 13-6. *Selecting the Watches Window*

A window should open within which you can add the items you want to watch. This is shown in Figure 13-7. You may have to right-click the mouse on the phrase <Enter new watch> to open the window.

Figure 13-7. *The New Watch Window*

You can select multiple options by holding the CTRL button while clicking the mouse on the items you want to watch. I have selected the five main items we want to watch. Once you are happy with your selections, simply click "OK" to close the window and display your selections.

Once you have selected the variables you want to watch, you should run the simulation by clicking button 4. Then click the pause button again to pause the simulation.

The MPLAB X screen should now change to that shown in Figure 13-8.

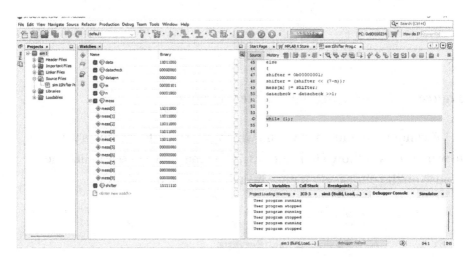

Figure 13-8. *The Simulation Paused with the Watches Displayed*

You should see that the bits in the first five locations in the array "mess[m]" have the same logic state as those in the variable "data." This is because the program has gone through a complete cycle of the instructions, and it is now stuck at the while (1); instruction on line 54.

We now want to reset the PIC to the beginning of the program, so that we can single-step through the instructions. To reset the program, simply click the mouse on the reset button, button 3 of the control buttons. The green highlight will now move to the first instruction on line 15 of the listing. We could now single-step through every instruction to see what each of them does. However, we are not interested in the first 15 instructions. Therefore, you should click the mouse at the beginning of line 30, just before the "f" of the "for" keyword. Now click the "Run to Cursor" button, button 8 on the control menu. The program will start to run, but it will then pause at the place you have placed the cursor, that is, at the beginning of line 30. This is the instruction that sets up the outer "for do loop." The variable "m" controls how many times the PIC runs through the loop.

Now we are ready to single-step through some instructions of interest. To do this, click the mouse on the "Step Into" button, button 6 on the control menu. Alternatively, you could press the "F7" button on your keypad.

The cursor will now jump to line 32. None of the watches will change at this moment. We are now ready to carry out the instruction datacheck = 0b10000000;. This places a logic '1' in bit 7 of "datacheck" ready to test the MSB of "data" in the next instruction.

Pressing the "Step Into" button again carries out the instruction and moves the cursor to line 33 "for (n = 0; n < 8; n++)". This sets up the inner loop. The variable "n" controls how many times the PIC runs through the loop.

Pressing the "Step Into" button again executes this instruction and moves the cursor to line 35, ready to carry out the "if (data & datacheck) datapin = 1;". You should appreciate that bit 7 of the "datacheck" is a logic '1' and bit 7 of the "data" is also a logic '1'. This means that the logical AND operation between these two bits will be true and result in a logic '1'. Also, as all the other bits in the "datacheck" are logic '0', then none of the remaining logical ANDs will produce a true result. Really, as only bit 7 of "datacheck" is a logic '1', then this instruction is simply testing if bit 7 of the "data" is a logic '1'. If it is, then the result of the "if" test will be true and the PIC must carry out the instruction that follows the test, that is, datapin = 1;.

As bit 7 of "data" is a logic '1', then the PIC will load the "datapin" with the value "1."

When we press the "Step Into" button again, you will see the green cursor jump to line 37. Also, if we look at the watch window, we will see that the variable "datapin" has changed to a "1." You should also realize that the PIC has skipped the instruction on line 36, which is "else datapin = 0;". The PIC would only carry out that instruction if the result of the "if" test, on line 35, was untrue.

When we press the "Step Into" button again, the PIC carries out the instruction on line 37, if (datapin == 0). This will be untrue, and so the cursor will jump to line 47 as it carries out the "else" instruction on line 45.

Pressing the "Step Into" button again gets the PIC to carry out the instruction on line 47 which resets the value in "shifter" to 0b00000001. You should see this happen in the watch window.

When we get the PIC to carry out the instruction on line 48, you should see "shifter" change to 0b1000000, that is, shift the bits (7-n) places to the left, in the watch window. Remember, at this point, the control variable "n" will equal 0. Therefore, the instruction shifts the bits 7-0 = 7 places to the left.

After carrying out that instruction, the cursor will now be on line 49 waiting to carry out the instruction mess[m] |= shifter;, which will load the current location in the array with the result of the logical OR operation.

Once we have carried out that instruction, the cursor will now be on line 50, datacheck = datacheck >>1;. This will shift the bits in "datacheck" one bit to the right. This is to get it ready for the next logical AND operation on line 35, after checking that the PIC should still be in the inner "for do loop" on line 33.

If you now keep pressing the "Step Into" button until the PIC has carried out the "for do loop" a total of eight times, you should see that the contents of the array will become the same as the contents of "data." This should help confirm that the instructions do allow us to fill an 8-bit variable with unknown data being sent to the PIC.

I do apologize for the wordy description of this simulation process, but I do hope it helps you to understand how the instructions actually work.

However, I know you may have to read through the description and repeat the simulation a few times until it starts to make sense. Also, I hope it gives you some insight into how to use some of the debugging tools of the MPLAB X software to help confirm how the instructions work.

Summary

In this chapter, we have learned how to use the DHT11 humidity and temperature transducer and how to interface it to the PIC32. We have also looked at how to use the simulation tool of the MPLAB X software to help confirm the operation of some of the instructions and confirm that they work as we expect.

In the next chapter, we are going to look into creating and using square waves. We will also look at using an RGB LED.

CHAPTER 14

Creating a Square Wave

In this chapter, we will look at creating a square wave. This might seem a simple exercise, but it can be a very useful aspect of electronics and microcontrollers. There are many instances when a square wave can be useful, such as producing sound or signals of different frequencies or controlling the speed of a DC motor. In this chapter, we will look at creating a square wave of different frequencies and controlling the speed of a DC motor.

After reading this chapter, you will be able to use the CCP module of the PIC to produce a square wave and control the speed of a DC motor. We will also look at the CCP module and how we can use all three modes.

Creating a Simple Square Wave

To appreciate what we mean by a simple square wave, we should look at what a square wave looks like. This is shown in Figure 14-1.

© Hubert Ward 2023
H. Ward, *Introductory Programs with the 32-bit PIC Microcontroller*,
Maker Innovations Series, https://doi.org/10.1007/978-1-4842-9051-4_14

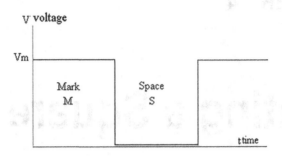

Figure 14-1. *A Simple Square Wave*

The simple square wave has two periods in it. One is called the mark time, which can be referred to as the "on time." This is when the voltage goes to its maximum value. This could be a positive voltage as shown in Figure 14-1, but it could also be a negative. The other period is called the "space time," which could be referred to as the "off time." This is normally the time period when the voltage is at 0V, as shown in Figure 14-1. All square waves have a mark-to-space ratio, which refers to the amount of time the square wave is high and low. The ratio of the mark to space time is normally referred to as the "duty cycle." The simplest of square waves has a mark-to-space ratio of 50/50. This means that the mark time is 50% of the total periodic time for the square wave, and the space time has the other 50% of the periodic time. Note the periodic time, normally given the symbol "T," is the time the waveform takes to go through all its possible values, that is, the time the wave uses to go through one cycle. The first square wave we will look at is this simplest square wave with a duty cycle of 50/50.

Using the Output Compare Module (OCMP) of the PIC32

To create this simple square wave, we will use the compare action of the OCMP module of the PIC32. Using the compare module is possibly the easiest approach to create a square wave with the PIC. The only issue is that the square wave can only have a duty cycle of 50/50. We will see later in this chapter why this may be a drawback in creating a square wave.

The principle on which this program works is that the waveform, as shown in Figure 14-1, has just two states; the output stays high for a period of time, the mark time, then it switches low for the same period of time, the space time. This is exactly what we do with the compare function of the OCMP module. OCMP stands for Output CoMPare, and there are two such modules in the PIC. We get the PIC to wait for a set period of time and then get an output to change its state from high to low or from low to high. This is referred to as toggling an output. To do this, with the compare function, we simply get a counter to count from zero until it reaches a number that is stored in a particular register. We will use a timer to work as the counter. It is termed as a compare operation as we are continually comparing the value in the timer with the value stored in the register. When the two values are the same, then we can manipulate the output in a variety of ways:

1. Initialize the output with a low state, and when there is a match, we can send the output high. This is using the module to work as a monostable where its stable state is a logic high.

2. Initialize the output with a high state, and when there is a match, we can send the output low. This is using the module to work as a monostable where its stable state is a logic low.

3. Force the output to toggle when there is a match.

693

4. Initialize the output with a low state, and when there is a match, we can generate a single pulse on the output.

5. Initialize the output with a low state, and when there is a match, we can generate continuous pulses on the output.

It is bits 0, 1, and 2 that allow the user to select which mode of operation we set the module to. The options are set as shown in Table 14-1.

Table 14-1. *The Usage of Bits 0, 1, and 2*

Bit 2	Bit 1	Bit 0	Mode of Operation
0	0	0	Output compare peripheral is disabled
0	0	1	Initialize OCx pin low, compare event forces OCx pin high
0	1	0	Initialize OCx pin high, compare event forces OCx pin low
0	1	1	Compare event toggles OCx pin
1	0	0	Initialize OCx pin low, generate single output pulse on OCx pin
1	0	1	Initialize OCx pin low, generate continuous output pulses on OCx pin
1	1	0	PWM mode on OCx, fault pin disabled
1	1	1	PWM mode on OCx, fault pin enabled

It is bit 3 that sets which timer the module will use as shown in Table 14-2.

Table 14-2. *The Usage of Bit 3*

Bit 3 logic '0'	Timer2 used
Bit 3 logic '1'	Timer3 used

The program listing is shown in Listing 14-1.

Listing 14-1. The Simple Square Wave

```
1  /*
2  * File:   squarewave1.c
3  Author: Mr H. H. Ward
4  Create a simple square wave at 5kHz
5  Created on 01 February 2022, 16:22
6  */
7  #include <xc.h>
8  #include <con72Meg36Meg32Bit.h>
9  void main()
10 {
11 PORTA = 0;
12 PORTB = 0;
13 PORTC = 0;
14 PORTD = 0;
15 PORTE = 0;
16 TRISA = 0;
17 TRISB = 0;
18 TRISC = 0;
19 TRISD = 0x0000;
20 TRISE = 0;
21 AD1PCFG = 0xFFFF;
22 AD1CON1 = 0;
23 T1CON = 0x8030;
24 DDPCONbits.JTAGEN = 0;
25 OC1CON = 0x0000;
26 OC1CON = 0x0003;
27 PR2 = 3599;
28 T2CON = 0x8000;
29 OC1CONbits.ON = 1;
30 while (1);
31 }
```

The program will use the compare function of the first OCMP module in the PIC to create a square wave, with a 50/50 duty cycle, at a frequency of 5kHz on the OC1 output of the PIC. It will use timer2 to create the square wave. The important instructions for this program are analyzed as follows:

Line 25 OC1CON = 0x0000;

This turns the OCMP module off. It is good practice to turn a module off while you are setting it up. Note we are using the module 1 of the two OCMP modules.

Line 26 OC1CON = 0x0003;

This now sets up the OCMP module up as we want. It is bit 3 that is used to select which timer we are going to use for the compare module of the PIC. The data 0x0003 in binary is 0b0000000000000011. This means bits 0 and 1 are both logic '1s' while bit 2 is a logic '0'. This sets the OCMP to toggle its output on a match of the timer count to the PR register value. Also, bit 3 is a logic '0' which means we will be using timer2 to make the comparison with its PR2 register.

Line 27 PR2 = 3599;

As we are using timer2, we need to load the PR2 register with the value that we want timer2 to reach before the module can toggle the output. We can calculate the value to be loaded into the PR2 register using the following equation:

$$PR2 = \frac{PBCLK}{2 \times Freq \times T2Prescale} - 1$$

$$PR2 = \frac{36000000}{2 \times 5000 \times 1} - 1 = 3599$$

The minus one is there to account that the counter counts from 0 to 3599, and this will take 3600 cycles of the timer2 counter. You will see that we will set the divide rate, that is, the T2Prescale, for timer2 to 1. This means timer2 will count at the same rate as the PBCLK which is 36MHz. Therefore, 1 count takes 27.77ns, and so 3600 counts take 100µs. This is just half of the periodic time for a 5kHz square wave. However, this is the time for both the mark time and space time of the square wave output. This means that as the square wave will have a 50/50 duty cycle, the total periodic time will be 200µs which gives a frequency of 5kHz.

Therefore, line 27 loads the PR2 register with the required value to create a 5kHz square wave at the OC1 output pin. The data sheet shows us that the OC1 output is on RD0, that is, bit 0 of PORTD.

Line 28 T2CON = 0x8000;

This is simply turning timer2 on, that is, bit 15 is a logic '1'. It also sets the prescaler to 1:1 bits 6, 5, and 4 are all logic '0'. Bit 3 either sets timer2 into a single 32-bit register, that is, bit 3 is a logic '1', or it uses two 16-bit registers, that is, bit 3 is a logic '0'. We are using timer2 as two bit 3 registers as bit 3 is a logic '0'.

Line 29 OC1CONbits.ON = 1;

This simply turns the OCMP 1 module on. It sets bit 15 of the OC1CON register to a logic '1'.

Line 30 while (1);

As there is nothing else we need to do with the PIC, we simply get the PIC to constantly do nothing. This is using the forever loop of while (1).

Now we should be able to see a square wave, with a frequency of 5kHz, appear on the OC1 pin. We could use an oscilloscope to display the square wave, and this is shown in Figure 14-2.

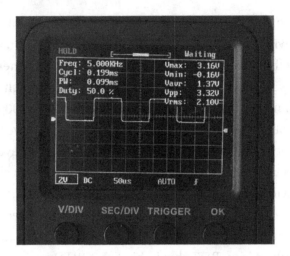

Figure 14-2. *The 5kHz Square Wave with 50/50 Duty Cycle*

However, if you haven't got an oscilloscope, you could use the logic analyzer within the MPLAB software to display the output on RD0, the OC1 pin. The following describes the process you need to go through to do this.

Using the Logic Analyzer Within MPLAB X

If you have already created the project and set a tool to download the project, then you will need to change the tool to simulator. If you have already set the tool to simulator, then you can miss this first step.

To change the tool to simulator, you need to right-click the mouse on the project name in the project tree. You will then be able to select the configuration, as shown in Figure 14-3.

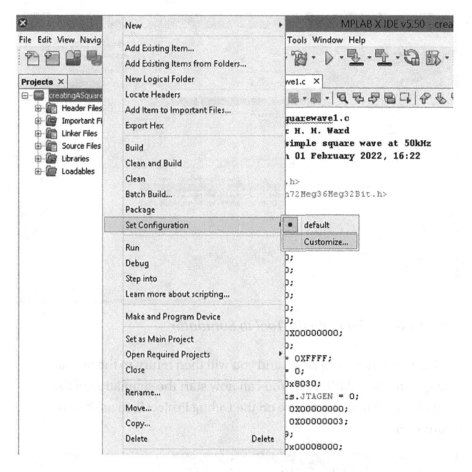

Figure 14-3. *Customizing the Project Configuration*

You need to select Customize, as shown in Figure 14-3. You will then be presented with the Project Properties window, as shown in Figure 14-4. You should open the Connected Hardware Tool window and select the Simulator, as shown in Figure 14-4. You should then click Apply and then OK.

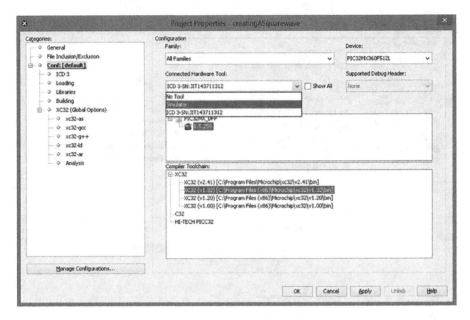

Figure 14-4. *Changing the Tool to Simulator*

The window should close, and you will then return to the normal editing window of MPLAB X. You can now start the simulation of the program by clicking the mouse on the Debug Project icon as shown in Figure 14-5.

Figure 14-5. *Selecting the Debug Tool*

The project will compile, and the output window should indicate that the program is running. You can now click the mouse on the "Window" option on the main menu bar. A fly-out window will appear from which you should select "Simulator" and then "Logic Analyzer" from the options that appear. This is shown in Figure 14-6.

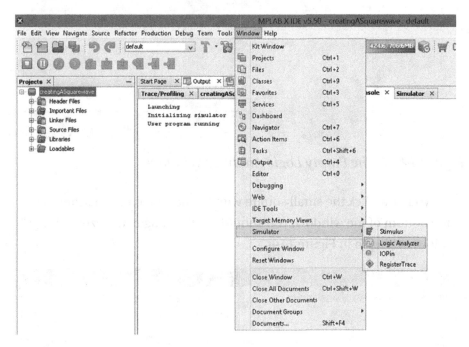

Figure 14-6. *Selecting the Logic Analyzer Option*

An empty Logic Analyzer window should appear in the display as shown in Figure 14-7. You may have to move some of the windows around to get it as shown in Figure 14-7.

Figure 14-7. *The Empty Logic Analyzer Window*

If you now click the small square with the hammer and spanner in it, at the bottom of the window, you should see the "Logic Analyzer Settings" window, as shown in Figure 14-8.

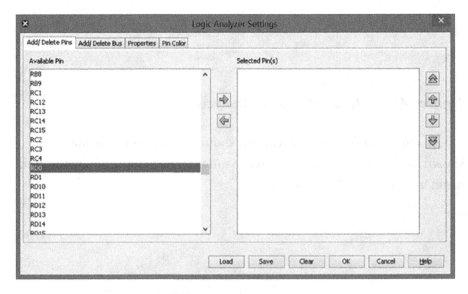

Figure 14-8. *The Logic Analyzer Option*

You should now scroll down and find the pin RD0, as shown in Figure 14-8. Now simply move it across to the selected Pin(s) window by clicking the orange right-facing arrow in the middle column of the window. The selected pin will move into the right-hand pane. Now click OK and the window will close, and the Logic Analyzer will show a grayed display. To display the output on pin RD0, you must click the mouse on the pause button from the simulation control buttons. The Logic Analyzer window should now display the square wave output from the OC1 pin on RD0 as shown in Figure 14-9. You may have to click the continue arrow and then click the pause button again to get the display to show in the window.

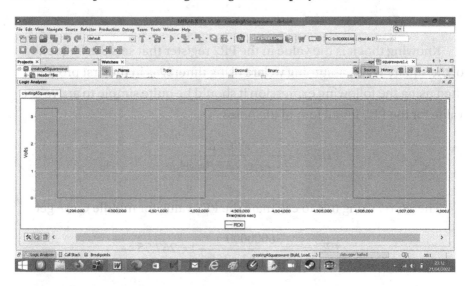

Figure 14-9. *The 50/50 Square Wave Output on Pin RD0*

The output does confirm that a square wave is present on the pin and that it has a duty cycle of 50/50. However, I am not confident in explaining how you can confirm it has a frequency of 5kHz, but you can see that we do have a square wave on the pin.

Creating Some Musical Notes

We can distinguish every sound, no matter what it is, because every sound has its own frequency, either a unique frequency as in the pure musical note or a compound of different frequencies. We will look at creating just a few musical notes such as middle C, E, F, and G. The frequencies of these four notes are

- Middle C is 261.63Hz.

- E is 329.62Hz.

- F is 349.23Hz.

- G is 392Hz.

Knowing that it is the value in the PR2 register that sets the frequency of the square wave, assuming we are using timer2, as in the first program, then using the following expression it should be quite simple to arrive at a value for the PR2 for all four of the notes:

$$PR2 = \frac{PBCLK}{2 \times Freq \times T2Prescale} - 1$$

Therefore, using this to calculate the PR2 value for middle C, we get

$$PR2 = \frac{36000000}{2 \times 261.63 \times 256} - 1 = 267.75$$

The T2Prescale value has been increased to 256, as a value of 1 would have resulted in a PR2 value of 68,798, which is too high. Therefore, using a T2Preset value of 256 divides the timer2 frequency to 140.625kHz. The value of 267.75 needs to be rounded up to 268.

Using the same expression, the PR2 values for the remaining notes were calculated as follows:

- Middle C is 261.63Hz with a PR2 of 268.

- E is 329.62Hz with a PR2 of 212.

- F is 349.23Hz with a PR2 of 200.

- G is 392Hz with a PR2 of 178.

Listing 14-1 was changed to accommodate the creation of these four notes. The listing is shown in Listing 14-2.

Listing 14-2. The Program for Four Musical Notes

```
1  /*
2  * File:    musicNotesProg.c
3  Author: Mr H. H. Ward
4  Create three music notes
5  Created on 01 February 2022, 16:22
6  */
7  #include <xc.h>
8  #include <con72Meg36Meg32Bit.h>
9  #define midC    268
10 #define noteE    212
11 #define noteF    200
12 #define noteG    178
13 unsigned char n, nt;
14 delay250 (unsigned char t)
15 {
16 for (nt = 0; nt < t; nt ++)
17 {
18 TMR1 = 0;
19 while (TMR1 < 35150);
20 }
21 }
22 void main()
23 {
24 PORTA = 0;
25 PORTB = 0;
```

```
26  PORTC = 0;
27  PORTD = 0;
28  PORTE = 0;
29  TRISA = 0;
30  TRISB = 0;
31  TRISC = 0;
32  TRISD = 0x0000;
33  TRISE = 0;
34  AD1PCFG = 0xFFFF;
35  AD1CON1 = 0;
36  T1CON = 0x8030;
37  DDPCONbits.JTAGEN = 0;
38  OC1CON = 0x0000;
39  OC1CON = 0x0003;
40  PR2 = midC;
41  T2CON = 0x8070;
42  OC1CONbits.ON = 1;
43  while (1)
44  {
45  delay250(20);
46  PR2 = noteE;
47  delay250(20);
48  PR2 = noteF;
49  delay250 (20);
50  PR2 = noteG;
51  delay250 (20);
52  PR2 = midC;
53  }
54  }
```

This is just to show you how you could get the PIC to output four different preset frequencies. If these were outputted to a speaker, then you would hear the four notes as prescribed earlier. I have just monitored the output on my small oscilloscope to show that the frequencies are what they were supposed to be. I hope there are no new instructions that need any analysis.

The principle of the program is that there are four phrases, as defined in lines 9–12, to represent each of the numbers to be loaded into the PR2 register to create the required frequencies. Then, in the main part of the program, there is a continuous loop that changes the value in the PR2 register every five seconds to produce one of the four notes starting with middle C.

Figure 14-10 shows the oscilloscope display for note E.

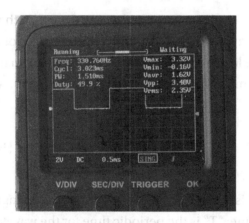

Figure 14-10. *The Display for Middle E*

Creating a PWM Square Wave with the OC1MP Module

We will now look at creating a square wave with which we can vary the time period of the mark time while keeping the periodic time of the square constant. This means if we increase the mark time, we must decrease the space time, and vice versa. This is termed pulse-width modulation, that is, PWM. The reason why we do this is so that we can vary the output voltage that would appear on the chosen OCMP output. In this case, we will use the OC1 output on bit 0 of PORTD.

The Average of a Square Wave

When a square wave voltage is applied to any device, such as a DC motor or an LED, then that device will respond to the average voltage of the square wave. If we look at the square wave voltage shown in Figure 14-1, then we can determine the average voltage, which I term "Vavge," as follows:

$$Vavge = \frac{VmM}{T} \, or = \frac{VmM}{M + S} \qquad \text{(Equation 14.1)}$$

Note: "Vavge" is the average voltage; "Vm" is the voltage maximum; "M" is the mark time; "T" is the periodic time for the waveform, that is, the time to complete one full cycle; and finally, "S" is the space time.

Note $\dfrac{M}{M + S}$ is termed the duty cycle. When the M time is equal to the space time, then the duty cycle is termed 50/50, and the average voltage is $\dfrac{Vm}{2}$.

If we now vary the mark time, it should be clear that we would vary the average voltage. Indeed, if the mark time, "M," was the same as the periodic time, "T," this would mean the space time "S" would be zero, and the average voltage would be a maximum of Vm. Conversely, if the space time was equal to the periodic time, then the average voltage would be 0V. The next program will use the PWM aspect of the OCMP module to create a DC voltage that we can vary the average output from close to the maximum to almost 0V. Although it does not really matter what frequency we use for the square wave, we will set it using the same value of 3599 for the PR2 register. However, as we will be setting the OCMP module to operate in PWM mode, this value in the PR2 register will correspond to the complete periodic time "T." This means that the frequency of the square wave will be 10kHz, not 5kHz as with the previous program. The listing for the program is shown in Listing 14-3. We will also use the logic analyzer in MPLAB X to display the output voltage.

Listing 14-3. The Program for the 5kHz Square Wave with PWM

```
1  /*
2  * File:    squarewavePWMProg.c
3  Author: Mr H. H. Ward
4  Create a simple square wave at 5kHz
5  Created on 01 February 2022, 16:22
6  */
7  #include <xc.h>
8  #include <con72Meg36Meg32Bit.h>
9  void main()
10 {
11 PORTA = 0;
12 PORTB = 0;
13 PORTC = 0;
14 PORTD = 0;
15 PORTE = 0;
16 TRISA = 0x0000;
17 TRISB = 0x0000;
```

```
18   TRISC = 0;
19   TRISD = 0x0000;
20   TRISE = 0;
21   AD1PCFG = 0xFFFF;
22   T1CON = 0x8030;
23   DDPCONbits.JTAGEN = 0;
24   OC1CON = 0x0000;
25   OC1R = 1599;
26   OC1RS = 2000;
27   OC1CON = 0x0006;
28   PR2 = 3599;
29   T2CON = 0x8000;
30   OC1CONbits.ON = 1;
31   while (1);
32   }
```

This is virtually the same as Listing 14-1. The main difference is the inclusion of two new instructions, which are

Line 25 OC1R = 1599;
Line 26 OC1RS = 2000;

These are two very important registers. OC1RS holds the value that specifies the setting for the mark time, and OC1R specifies the setting for the space time. You should appreciate that if we add the two values together, we get the total value of 3599, which is the value stored in the PR2 register. The value in the PR2 is used to specify the periodic time of the square wave. This is the PR2 value to achieve a square wave that will run at a frequency of 5kHz.

This means we can control both the mark time "M" and space time "S" simply by varying the values in the OC1RS and OC1R. Note though we must keep the total of M+S the same as the period "T."

For example, with the OC1R = 1599 and OC1RS = 2000, we should get a square wave with a mark time that is slightly longer than the space time. Figure 14-11 shows the output of OC1 in the Logic Analyzer window in MPLAB X. On it you can see that the M is longer than the S time.

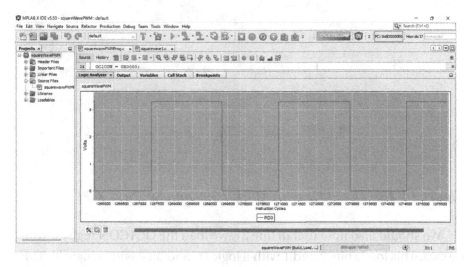

Figure 14-11. *The PWM Square Wave Output*

If we now increase the OC1R to 3000 and decrease the OC1RS to 599, note the M+S total is still = 3599, we should see that the "M" is decreased and the "S" is increased. This is shown in Figure 14-12.

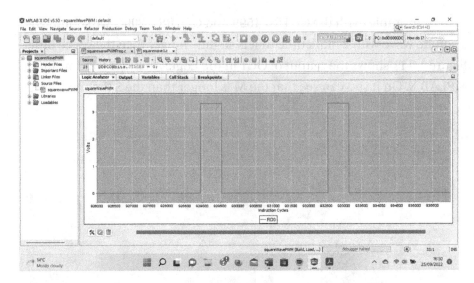

Figure 14-12. *The 5kHz with Mark = 599 and Space = 3000*

We should also note that in line 27, we load the OC1CON register with
0x0006. This loads bits 2 and 1 with a logic '1' and bit 0 with a logic '0'. This
sets the OCMP module into PWM mode. Table 14-1 shows the settings for
bits 2, 1, and 0 of the OC1CON register.

This ability of being able to vary the average voltage output from the
PIC can easily be developed into a basic circuit for varying the brightness
of an LED connected to the PIC.

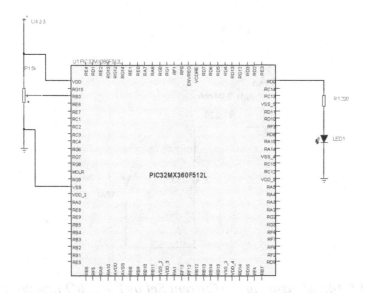

Figure 14-13. *The Basic Circuit for Varying the Brightness of an LED*

Figure 14-13 shows a 220Ω resistor R1 in series with the LED. It is there to limit the current flowing through the LED. With a maximum voltage of 3.3V and assuming that the LED drops around 1.5V, this would limit the current to around 8.2mA. This is confirmed in Figure 14-14.

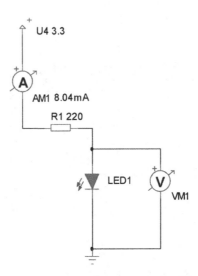

Figure 14-14. *Measuring the Current Set by the 220Ω Resistor in Series with the LED*

In Figure 14-13, a variable resistor is applied to bit 0 of PORTB. The purpose of this is that the variable resistor can control the average output voltage of the PWM. This is done by allowing the variation of the voltage from the variable resistor to vary the settings for the OCR1 and OCR1S. This would mean that the PIC would have to use the ADC, analog-to-digital converter, to change the varying analog voltage into a digital value that would vary the settings of the two registers. The program listing to achieve this is shown in Listing 14-4.

Listing 14-4. The Program for the PWM with a Potentiometer on Bit 0 of PORTB

```
1  /*
2  * File:    squarewavePWMADCProg.c
3  Variable using a potentiometer on channel 5
4  Author: Mr H. H. Ward
5  Create a simple square wave at 137.5Hz
```

```
 6  Created on 01 February 2022, 16:22
 7  */
 8  #include <xc.h>
 9  #include <con72Meg36Meg32Bit.h>
10  #define startButton    _RA7
11  //variables
12  unsigned int sysInput;
13  //some subroutines
14  unsigned int readADC( unsigned char ch)
15  {
16  AD1CHSbits.CH0SA = ch;
17  AD1CON1bits.SAMP = 1;
18  while (!AD1CON1bits.DONE);
19  return ADC1BUF0;
20  }
21  void main()
22  {
23  T1CON = 0x8030;
24  TRISA = 0x0080;
25  TRISB = 0x00FF;
26  TRISC = 0x00FF;
27  TRISD = 0x0000;
28  TRISE = 0x0000;
29  PORTA = 0;
30  PORTB = 0;
31  PORTC = 0;
32  PORTD = 0;
33  PORTE = 0;
34  AD1PCFG = 0xFFCF;
35  AD1CON1 = 0x80E0;
36  AD1CON2 = 0;
37  AD1CON3 = 0x0103;
```

```
38  DDPCONbits.JTAGEN = 0;
39  OC1CON = 0x0000;
40  OC1R = 511;
41  OC1RS = 511;
42  OC1CON = 0x0006;
43  PR2 = 1023;
44  T2CON = 0x8070;
45  OC1CONbits.ON = 1;
46  //the main part of the program
47  while (startButton);
48  while (1)
49  {
50  sysInput = readADC(5) ;
51  OC1RS = sysInput;
52  OC1R = (1023 - sysInput);
53  }
54  }
```

The program will produce a square wave that starts off with a 50/50 duty cycle. This output will be applied to a circuit that supplies an LED. The LED will be switched on with supply being at 50% of its maximum.

Then, after a start switch connected to bit 7 of PORTA has been momentarily pressed, the output of the square wave being fed to the LED will be subjected to some PWM. The pulse width can be made to vary by varying the voltage applied to the PIC from a potentiometer connected to channel 5 of the ADC inputs. In this way, the brightness of the LED can be varied as the variable resistor is varied through its full range.

The ADC on the PIC is a 10-bit ADC, which means it has 1024 values, that is, 2^{10}. To get the brightness of the LED to respond to all 1024, that is, 0 to 1023, values, we must make the maximum value of the PR2 equal to this 1023 value. This is done in line 43 PR2 = 1023. As it is the average voltage we are varying, then the actual frequency of the square wave has no bearing on the output. Therefore, we can choose any frequency we like. As the value in the PR2 register sets the value the timer2 should count up to before a new cycle of the square wave begins, then it is the time for one count that will set the frequency of the square wave. I have decided to slow the frequency at which timer2 counts by its maximum divide rate of 256. This means as timer2 uses the peripheral clock as its source, then the frequency of timer2 will be 36,000,000 divided by 256 = 140625. This means that one count takes 7.111µs. This in turn means timer2 will take 1024, that is, 0 to 1023, counts, which takes 7.282ms for one cycle of the square wave. This gives the square wave a frequency of 137.33Hz. This can be confirmed using an oscilloscope as shown in Figure 14-15.

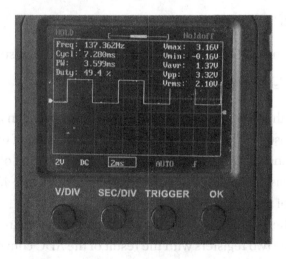

Figure 14-15.   *The Square Wave with 50/50 Duty Cycle at 137.4Hz*

Analysis of Listing 14-4

The main difference now is that we are using the result of the ADC to change the values in the OC1R and OC1RS registers. I have created a variable of type unsigned int called "sysInput"; see line 12. This creates a 16-bit memory location that we will use to store the 10-bit result of the

ADC. We will use the value in this variable to alter the values in the two registers. This is done as follows:

Line 48 while (1)

This creates the forever loop that keeps the PIC carrying out the instructions between the opening and closing curly brackets on lines 49 and 53.

Line 50 sysInput = readADC(5);

This calls the subroutine "readADC(5)" which gets the PIC to read the ADC input on channel 5. We have looked at this subroutine in Chapter 10. It then loads the variable "sysInput" with the result of the ADC.

Line 51 OC1RS = sysInput;

This loads the OC1RS register with a copy of the ADC result.

Line 52 OC1R = (1023 - sysInput);

This loads the OC1R register with the difference between the value of 1023 and the result of the ADC. This ensures that the sum of the two values in the OC1RS and OC1R registers will always equal the total of 1023. This value of 1023 has been loaded into the PR2 register (see line 43) to set the periodic time of the square wave.

With just these three instructions, we are constantly changing the values in the two registers with the result of the ADC conversion. In this way then, when we vary the input to channel 5 by altering the potentiometer, we will vary the mark-to-space ratio of the square wave and so the average voltage at the output on bit 0 of PORTD. This will in turn vary the brightness of the LED. This is because the LED will respond to the average voltage at the output on the OC1 pin, bit 0 of PORTD, on the PIC.

Note in line 40 OC1R = 511;, we are loading the OC1R register with 511. In line 41, we do the same with the OC1RS register. This sets up the square wave for a 50/50 duty cycle, which is maintained until the user presses the start button.

Line 47 while (startButton);

This makes the PIC do nothing while the logic on the "startButton" is at a logic '1'. It will stay at a logic '1' until the user momentarily presses the switch and drives the logic to a logic '0'. In this way, we keep the duty cycle at 50/50 until the user presses the start button.

Figure 14-16. *The Mark Time Is Reduced and the Space Time Is Increased*

Figure 14-16 shows the display after the potentiometer has been turned almost to 0. The mark time is reduced, and you can see the average voltage is now showing as 0.08V. In Figure 14-15, it was 1.37V, which is about 50% of its maximum. This shows that the average voltage does respond as we expected it to.

Varying the Brightness of a Lamp

We could use the PWM output from the PIC to control the brightness of a lamp. However, I want to make the PIC vary the brightness automatically. This means we can't simply use a potentiometer, like we did in the previous program, as this would require an operator to vary the potentiometer. Also, I will use a different LED. There are LEDs that have red, green, and blue elements in them, that is, an RGB-type LED. Figure 14-17 depicts one of these LEDs.

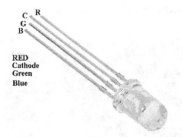

Figure 14-17. *The RGB LED*

The program will start off with the RED LED permanently turned on, with a 50/50 duty cycle for the square wave used to supply the voltage to the LED. Then, after the start switch has been pressed and released, the RED LED will increase in brightness. Then it will decrease in brightness and finally turn off. Then the blue LED will increase and decrease in brightness until it also turns off. Then the green LED will go through the same sequence. After the green LED has turned off, all three LEDs will increase and decrease in brightness together. Then, when the three LEDs have dimmed completely, they will all turn off, and the sequence will repeat until the PIC is turned off. This is an attempt to create a mode light effect with the LED.

When all three LEDs come on together, the LED should create a white light effect, but it does depend on how you view the LED. It is an interesting use of the PWM facility of the OCPM module of the PIC. The module allows the programmer to create four PWM outputs on OC1, OC2, OC3, and OC4, which are on bits 0, 1, 2, and 3 of PORTD.

The program listing for this project is shown in Listing 14-5.

Listing 14-5. The Program Listing for the Mode Lamp Using an RGB LED

```
1   /*
2   * File:    dimmingRGBThreeLEDsProg.c
3   Varying the brightness of the RGB LEDS
4   Author: Mr H. H. Ward
5   Create a simple square wave at 137.5Hz
6   Created on 01 February 2022, 16:22
7   */
8   #include <xc.h>
9   #include <con72Meg36Meg32Bit.h>
10  #define startButton      _RA7
11  //variables
12  unsigned char nt, change = 0, turn = 1;
13  unsigned int sysInput, mark = 50;
14  //some subroutines#
15  void delay250 (unsigned char t)
16  {
17  for (nt = 0; nt < t; nt ++)
18  {
19  TMR1 = 0;
20  while (TMR1 < 35150);
21  }
22  }
23  void main()
```

```
24  {
25  T1CON = 0x8030;
26  TRISA = 0x0080;
27  TRISB = 0x00FF;
28  TRISC = 0x00FF;
29  TRISD = 0x0000;
30  TRISE = 0x0000;
31  PORTA = 0;
32  PORTB = 0;
33  PORTC = 0;
34  PORTD = 0;
35  PORTE = 0;
36  AD1PCFG = 0xFFFF;
37  AD1CON1 = 0;
38  DDPCONbits.JTAGEN = 0;
39  OC1CON = 0x0000;
40  OC1R = 511;
41  OC1RS = 511;
42  OC1CON = 0x0006;
43  OC2CON = 0x0000;
44  OC2R = 511;
45  OC2RS = 511;
46  OC2CON = 0x0006;
47  OC3CON = 0x0000;
48  OC3R = 511;
49  OC3RS = 511;
50  OC3CON = 0x0006;
51  PR2 = 1023;
52  T2CON = 0x8010;
53  //the main part of the program
54  OC1CONbits.ON = 1;
55  while (startButton);
```

```
56  while (1)
57  {
58  OC1RS = mark;
59  OC1R = (1023 - mark);
60  OC2RS = mark;
61  OC2R = (1023 - mark);
62  OC3RS = mark;
63  OC3R = (1023 - mark);
64  switch (turn)
65  {
66  case 1:
67  OC1CONbits.ON = 1;
68  OC2CONbits.ON = 0;
69  OC3CONbits.ON = 0;
70  break;
71  case 2:
72  OC1CONbits.ON = 0;
73  OC2CONbits.ON = 1;
74  OC3CONbits.ON = 0;
75  break;
76  case 3:
77  OC1CONbits.ON = 0;
78  OC2CONbits.ON = 0;
79  OC3CONbits.ON = 1;
80  break;
81  case 4:
82  OC1CONbits.ON = 1;
83  OC2CONbits.ON = 1;
84  OC3CONbits.ON = 1;
85  break;
86  }
87  if (change == 0)
```

```
88  {
89  mark = mark + 10;
90  delay250(4);
91  if (mark == 450)
92  {
93  change = 1;
94  delay250(4);
95  }
96  }
97  if (change == 1)
98  {
99  mark = mark - 10;
100  delay250(4);
101  if (mark == 40)
102  {
103  change = 0;
104  delay250(4);
105  turn ++;
106  if (turn == 5) turn = 1;
107  }
108  }
109  }
110  }
```

Analysis of Listing 14-5

There is no need for the ADC, so the subroutine has been removed, and in line 36 AD1PCFG = 0xFFFF;, we make all the inputs that could be analog inputs to be used as digital inputs. In line 37 AD1CON1 = 0;, we ensure the ADC module is turned off.

There are no new instructions to analyze, but there are some interesting aspects of the program. The output compare outputs, OC1, OC2, and OC3, can be turned on and off by setting or clearing, that is, logic '1' or logic '0', their respective "on" bits. Initially, all outputs are disabled; see lines 39, 43, and 47. In line 54 OC1CONbits.ON = 1;, OC1 is enabled. This is so that the RGB starts with the red LED lit with a 50/50 duty cycle. Then after the start switch has been pressed and released, to start the sequence, the different LEDs are enabled depending on the value in the variable "turn."

Line 105 turn ++;

This increments the value in the variable "turn" from its initial setting of '1'; see line 12.

Line 106   if (turn == 5) turn = 1;

This "if test" tests to see if, by incrementing the variable "turn," it has reached the value of 5. This value is not allowed, as we will see later. Therefore, if the test is true, and the variable "turn" has got to a value of 5, then this instruction will set it back to 1. This is so that the cycle of the LEDs will start again.

Lines 64–86 set up a switch and a case statement that is used to determine which LED is enabled and which are disabled. This uses the value in the variable "turn" to turn on and off the appropriate LEDs. For example, if the value in "turn" was 2, then "case 2:" would be chosen as follows:

Line 72 OC1CONbits.ON = 0;

This turns OC1 off.

Line 73 OC2CONbits.ON = 1;

This turns OC2 on.

Line 74 OC3CONbits.ON = 0;

This turns OC3 off.

Line 75 break;

This forces the PIC to break away from the switch and case statements to carry on with the rest of the program.

To enable the LEDs to brighten and then dim, the program must change from incrementing the value in the OCxRS registers to decrementing them. To facilitate this action, I have used the variable "change" to determine if we should be incrementing or decrementing the value. If the value in change is 0, then the program will increment the registers, whereas if the value in change was 1, then it would decrement the registers.

Line if (change == 0)

This tests to see if the value in "change" is 0. If it is, then the result of the test will be true, and the PIC must carry out the instructions between lines 88 and 96.

Line 89 mark = mark + 10;

This increases the value in the variable "mark" by 10. The variable "mark" is copied into the OCxRS registers, where "x" is 1, 2, or 3. See lines 58, 60, and 62.

Note in lines 59, 61, and 63, the OCxR registers are loaded with the value (1023 – mark).

Line 90 delay250(4);

This calls the 250ms delay to run four times and so creates a one-second delay.

Line 91 if (mark == 450)

This tests to see if the variable "mark" has reached the value of 450. I have set this as the maximum value which will produce a suitable level of brightness for the LEDs. If the test is true, then the PIC must carry out the instructions between lines 92 and 95. If the test is untrue, then the PIC will move to line 97.

Line 93 change = 1;

This loads the variable "change" with the value "1." This is because we have finished incrementing the variable "mark," and we should start decreasing it.

Line 94 delay250(4);

This creates another one-second delay.

Line 97 if (change == 1)

If the test is true, then the PIC must carry out the instructions between lines 98 and 108.

Line 99 mark = mark - 10;

This simply takes 10 off the value in "mark." Line 100 creates a one-second delay.

Line 101 if (mark == 40)

If mark has reached the value "40," then the PIC must carry out the instructions between lines 102 and 107.

Line 103 change = 0;

This now reloads the variable "change" with "0" as we have finished dimming the LEDs.

Lime 104 delay250(4);

This creates a one-second delay.

Lines 105 and 106 have been looked at.

This completes the analysis of Listing 14-5. I hope it is enough for you to understand how the program works.

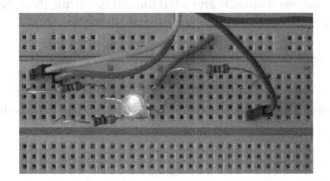

Figure 14-18. *The RGB LED Illuminated*

Figure 14-18 shows the RGB program working with the simple circuit built up temporarily on a board. The LED is showing green at the moment. The three resistors are all 220Ω with two red bands followed by a single brown band indicating 220 as the value.

Summary

In this chapter, we have learned how we can use the output compare module to create a simple square wave at any frequency, but with a fixed 50/50 duty cycle. We used this capability to create four musical notes to show you the principle behind creating a simple musical keypad.

Then we went on to learn how we can use the module to create a PWM square wave. Finally, we learned how to use this PWM square wave to vary the brightness of a single LED and then a three-element RGB LED.

Correction to: Introductory Programs with the 32-bit PIC Microcontroller

Correction to:

Hubert Ward, *Introductory Programs with the 32-bit PIC Microcontroller*

https://doi.org/10.1007/978-1-4842-9051-4

This book was published without Series ID, Print ISSN number & Electronic ISSN Number. This has now been updated in the book with the Series ID - 17311, Print ISSN: 2948-2542 & Electronic ISSN: 2948-2550.

The updated version of this book can be found at
https://doi.org/10.1007/978-1-4842-9051-4

© Hubert Ward 2023
H. Ward, *Introductory Programs with the 32-bit PIC Microcontroller*,
Maker Innovations Series, https://doi.org/10.1007/978-1-4842-9051-4_15

Appendix

In this appendix, I will analyze some of the more common aspects of C programming and how they apply to PIC microcontrollers. I will also cover some useful concepts that will help in the understanding of how microcontrollers work, such as operators, number systems, and keywords.

Data Types and Memory

To help understand the different data types used in C, it would be helpful to appreciate their relationship to the micro's memory. PIC micros have three areas of memory, which are

- Program memory area
- Data RAM
- Data EEPROM

The Program Memory Area

This is where all the instructions of your programs are stored.

This memory is nonvolatile, which means that when the power is removed, the information in the memory is not lost.

© Hubert Ward 2023
H. Ward, *Introductory Programs with the 32-bit PIC Microcontroller*,
Maker Innovations Series, https://doi.org/10.1007/978-1-4842-9051-4

The Data RAM

This is where the program can store any temporary information. Therefore, any variables that you declare in your program use this area of memory.

This memory is volatile, which means when the power is removed, all the information is lost.

The Data EEPROM

This is used for storing any information that the program does not want to lose if the power to the PIC is removed. This means it is nonvolatile memory.

Variables

When we create a variable in the program listing, we are actually getting the compiler to reserve one or more memory locations in the PIC's data memory area. The number of memory locations required by the label depends upon the number of bits required by what you want to store using the variable. In this way, the term variable is linked with the different data types used in C programming. You should appreciate that all data, no matter what it represents, is just a collection of binary bits. As such, they are simply binary numbers. We simply give these binary numbers some meaningful names which all go under the heading variables.

This then gives rise to the term "data types," as the variables will have different numbers of binary bits, such as

- 8 bits termed a byte

- 16 bits termed a word

- 32 bits termed a double word

The more common data types are listed in Appendix 1.

Appendix 1: Data Types

Type	Size	Minimum Value	Maximum Value
char	8 bits	−128	127
unsigned char	8 bits	0	255
int	16 bits	−32,768	32,767
unsigned int	16 bits	0	65,535
short	16 bits	−32,768	32,767
unsigned short	16 bits	0	65,535
short long	24 bits	−8,388,608	8,388,607
unsigned short long	24 bits	0	16,777,215
long	32 bits	−2,147,483,648	2,147,483,647
unsigned long	32 bits	0	4,294,967,295
Float	32 bits		

Floating-Point Numbers

Type	Size	Min Exponent	Max Exponent	Min Normalized	Max Normalized
float	32	−126	128	2^{-126}	2^{128}
Double	32	−126	128	2^{-126}	2^{128}

All C programs use operators that perform logical operations on data within programs. The more common operators are listed in Appendix 2.

© Hubert Ward 2023
H. Ward, *Introductory Programs with the 32-bit PIC Microcontroller*,
Maker Innovations Series, https://doi.org/10.1007/978-1-4842-9051-4

Appendix 2: Some Useful Definitions

Bit Operators

Operator	Description
&	AND each bit
|	OR each bit (Inclusive OR)
^	EXOR each bit (Exclusive OR)
<<n	Shift left n places
>>n	Shift right n places
~	One's complement (invert each bit)

Example: If "x" = 1111 1111, Then

Operation	Result
x & 0x0F	0000 1111
x | 0x0F	1111 1111
x^0x0F	1111 0000
x = x<<2	1111 1100
x = x>>4	0000 1111
x = ~x	0000 0000

© Hubert Ward 2023
H. Ward, *Introductory Programs with the 32-bit PIC Microcontroller*,
Maker Innovations Series, https://doi.org/10.1007/978-1-4842-9051-4

Appendix 3: Mathematical and Logic Operators

Operator	Description
+	Leaves the variable as it was
-	Creates the negative of the variable
++	Increments the variable by 1
--	Decrements the variable by 1
*	Multiplies the two variables y = a*b
/	Divides y = a/b
%	Used to get the remainder of a division of two variables m = a%b
<	Less than; if (y < a) means y is less than a
<=	Less than or equal to; if (y < =a) means y is less than or equal to a
>	Greater than; if (y > a) means y is greater than a
>=	Greater than or equal to; if (y > =a) means y is greater than or equal to a
=	Makes the variable equal to y = 3 After this, y takes on the value of 3
!	Not If (!PORTBbits.RB0) if not bit 0 of PORTB which means if bit 0 of PORTB is logic 0

(continued)

© Hubert Ward 2023
H. Ward, *Introductory Programs with the 32-bit PIC Microcontroller,*
Maker Innovations Series, https://doi.org/10.1007/978-1-4842-9051-4

Operator	Description
&&	Whole register AND
||	Whole register OR
?	This is a test operator y=(a>0) ? a : -1;
	This tests to see if "a" is greater than 0. If it is, then y becomes equal to "a"; if it's not, then y = -1

Appendix 4: Keywords

Keyword	What It Does
typedef	Allows the programmer to define any phrase to represent an existing type
#ifndef	This checks to see if a label you want to use has not been defined in any include files you want to use
	If it has, it does not allow you to define it now. If it hasn't, you are allowed to define it now
#define	You can define what your label means here
#endif	This denotes the end of your definition after the #ifndef code
sizeof	Returns the size in number of bytes of a variable

Global variables are variables that once declared can be read from or written to anywhere from within the program.

© Hubert Ward 2023
H. Ward, *Introductory Programs with the 32-bit PIC Microcontroller*,
Maker Innovations Series, https://doi.org/10.1007/978-1-4842-9051-4

Appendix 5: Numbering Systems Within Microprocessor-Based Systems

Introduction

As will become evident in the study to come, microprocessor-based systems use the binary number system. This is because the binary number system can only have one of two digits, either a "0" or a "1." These states have been called logic '0' or logic '1' as in electronic devices. Note, also, all the logic operations, such as AND, OR, NAND, NOR, NOT, and EXOR, work using binary format. The binary format can be used to mimic the logic states of "TRUE" or "FALSE" precisely, and best of all, they can be represented by voltage, that is, 0V for logic '0' and +5V for logic '1.'

Therefore, it is essential that the modern engineer gains a full understanding of the binary number system. This appendix is aimed at teaching the reader all they need to know about binary numbers.

Binary Numbers

These are a series of "0s" and "1s" that represent numbers. With respect to microprocessor-based systems, the numbers they are representing are themselves representing codes for instructions and data used within microprocessor-based programs. We, as humans, cannot easily interpret

© Hubert Ward 2023
H. Ward, *Introductory Programs with the 32-bit PIC Microcontroller*,
Maker Innovations Series, https://doi.org/10.1007/978-1-4842-9051-4

binary numbers as we use the denary number system. The denary number system uses the base number 10, which means all the columns we put our digits in to form numbers are based on powers of 10. For example, the thousand column is based on 10^3 and the hundreds column is based on 10^2. The tens column is 10^1 and the unit's column is 10^0. Try putting 10^0 in on your calculator using the x^y button, and you will find it equals 1; in fact, any number raised to the power 0 will equal 1.

Converting Decimal to Binary

Probably the first step to understanding binary numbers is in creating them, that is, converting decimal to binary. There are numerous ways of doing this, but I feel the most straightforward is to repeatedly divide the decimal number by 2, the base number of binary. This is shown as follows.

Example 1

Convert 66 to binary.

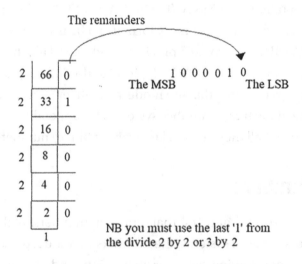

Simply keep on dividing the number by 2, putting the answer underneath as shown, with the remainder to the side. You should note that all the remainders are either **0** or **1**. These digits actually make up the binary number. Note also the last division always results in an answer "**1**"; we stop there, no more dividing.

To create the binary number, we take the top of the remainders, as shown, and put it into the least significant bit, or column, for the binary number. The other remainder digits follow on, thus making up the complete seven-digit number.

Converting from Binary to Decimal

It would be useful to determine if the binary number shown does actually relate to 66 in decimal. This is done by converting back into decimal the binary number 1 0 0 0 0 1 0. To do this, we must realize that numbers are displayed in columns. The columns are based on the base number of the system used. With binary numbers, the base number is 2. Therefore, the columns are based on powers of 2. This is shown in the following table:

Base No	2^7	2^6	2^5	2^4	2^3	2^2	2^1	2^0
Decimal equivalent	128	64	32	16	8	4	2	1
Binary number		1	0	0	0	0	1	0

To complete the conversion, we simply sum all the decimal equivalents where there is a 1 in the binary column.

In this case, the sum is 64+2 = 6.

Example 2

Convert 127 to binary and check the result.

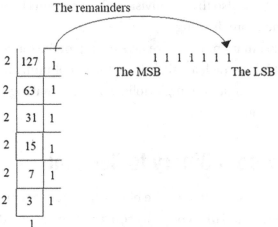

Base No	2^7	2^6	2^5	2^4	2^3	2^2	2^1	2^0
Decimal equivalent	128	64	32	16	8	4	2	1
Binary number	0	1	1	1	1	1	1	1

To complete the conversion, we simply sum all the decimal equivalents where there is a 1 in the binary column.

In this case, the sum is 64+32+16+8+4+2+1 = 127, which is what we expect.

Exercise 1

Convert the following numbers to binary and check your results by converting back to decimal. **Show all workings out.**

99

255

137

Adding and Subtracting Binary Numbers

Adding and subtracting numbers are perhaps the most basic operations we can carry out on numbers. Binary numbers follow the same rules as decimal, but there are only two allowable digits. Also, computers don't actually subtract numbers as the following will show.

Exercise 2

Add the following decimal numbers in 8-bit binary notation. Check your answers:

23+21, 35+123, 125+75

Worked Example

Remember binary numbers have only two digits: "0" or "1."

Add 23 to 21 in 8-bit binary.

Method:

Convert to 8-bit binary and add; remember the following four rules:

0+0 = 0

0+1 = 1

1+0 = 1

1+1 = 0 with 1 to carry

23 in 8-bit binary is

0 0 0 1 0 1 1 1

Note we must state all 8 bits as it is an 8-bit binary.

By the same process, 21 in binary is

0 0 0 1 0 1 0 1

Therefore, the sum is 00010111
$+00010101$

00101100

To check your answer, put the result into the lookup table, then add the decimal equivalent.

Power	2^7	2^6	2^5	2^4	2^3	2^2	2^1	2^0
Decimal equivalent	128	64	32	16	8	4	2	1
Binary number	0	0	1	0	1	1	0	0

The sum is 32+8+4 = 44.

Subtracting Binary Numbers

Exercise 3

Microprocessor-based systems actually subtract numbers using a method which is addition. This involves using the two's complement of a number, and it is best explained by the following example.

Subtract the following decimal numbers using 8-bit binary two's complement; check your answers:

128 – 28, 79 – 78, 55 – 5, 251 – 151

Worked Example

Convert the two numbers to binary using the method shown previously.

128 in 8-bit binary is 10000000. **Note we MUST use ALL 8 bits.**

28 in 8-bit binary is 00011100.

Take the two's complement of 00011100 as this is the number that we are subtracting from 128.

Only create the two's complement of the number we are subtracting with.

Note we must use a full 8-bit number, putting extra 0 in where needed.

To take the two's complement, firstly take the complement and then add binary 1 to the complement. The complement of the binary number is found by simply flipping all the bits, that is, a "0" becomes a "1" and a "1" becomes a "0."

Complement of 00011100 is	1 1 1 0 0 0 1 1
Add binary 1	+ 0 0 0 0 0 0 0 1
	1 1 1 0 0 1 0 0

Now add the two's complement to the first binary number as shown:

$$
\begin{array}{r}
1\,0\,0\,0\,0\,0\,0\,0 \\
+\,1\,1\,1\,0\,0\,1\,0\,0 \\
\hline
\end{array}
$$

Result is	0 1 1 0 0 1 0 0

NOTE THE LAST CARRY INTO THE NINTH DIGIT IS DISCARDED AS THERE CAN ONLY BE A SPECIFIED NUMBER OF DIGITS, 8 IN THIS CASE. Don't forget we added 1 so we should give it back.

The binary result converts to 100 in decimal. This is the correct result.

Check your answers in the usual way.

Note computers subtract in this method because we can only create an adder circuit in logic.

The Hexadecimal Number System

A microprocessor-based system can only recognize data that is in binary format. In its most basic form, this means that all data inputted at the keyboard should be in binary format. This is quite a formidable concept.

Just think every letter of every word must be inputted as a binary number. It takes at least four binary digits to represent a letter, and so typing words into a computer would be very difficult indeed. Thankfully, word processing programs take ASCII characters to represent the letters you press at the keyboard.

With the type of programs we will be writing into microcomputers, we will actually be typing in two characters to represent the codes for the instructions or data of the programs we will write. If we were to type these in as binary numbers, it would take 8 binary bits to make each code. This would be very time consuming and difficult to make sure we get it right. To make things easier, we will use the hexadecimal numbering system. This system has 16 unique digits, which are

0 1 2 3 4 5 6 7 8 9

After this, we cannot use 10 in the hexadecimal system, as this uses two digits, a 1 and a 0. Therefore, we must use six more unique digits. To do this, we use the first six letters of the alphabet. Therefore, the full 16 digits are

0 1 2 3 5 6 7 8 9 A B C D E F

Remember we are going to use the hexadecimal number to represent binary digits, and this revolves around the idea that one hexadecimal digit represents four binary digits as the 4 binary bits in decimal go from 0 to 15 that is, 16 numbers. Therefore, every 8-bit binary number can be represented by two hexadecimal digits. This makes typing in the code for programs much quicker and more secure than using the full binary numbers that computers use. Note to accommodate typing inputs as hexadecimal digits, there is a program in the micro's ROM to convert the hexadecimal to binary for us. However, we will look at converting binary to hexadecimal.

Exercise 4

Convert the following 8-bit binary numbers to hexadecimal:
10011110, 10101010, 11111111, 11110000, 00001111, and 11001101

Worked example

Method: Split the 8 bits into two 4-bit numbers. Convert each 4-bit number into the decimal equivalent, then look up the hexadecimal for the decimal equivalent in the lookup table. **Note treat each 4 binary bits as a separate binary number.**

Convert	1 0 0 1	1 1 1 0
Dec	9	14
Hex	9	E

Answer 10011110 in hex is 9E

In this way, 8-bit binary numbers can be converted into two hexadecimal digits.

Appendix 6: The ASCII Character Set

This is just an extract of the ASCII character set, but it does show the main ones we use.

High Nibble	0000 CGRAM Location		0010	0011	0100	0101	0110	0111
Low Nibble								
XXXX 0000	1			0	@	P	\	p
XXXX 0001	2		!	1	A	Q	a	q
XXXX 0010	3		"	2	B	R	b	r
XXXX 0011	4		#	3	C	S	c	s
XXXX 0100	5		$	4	D	T	d	t
XXXX 0101	6		%	5	E	U	e	u
XXXX 0110	7		&	6	F	V	f	v

(continued)

© Hubert Ward 2023
H. Ward, *Introductory Programs with the 32-bit PIC Microcontroller*,
Maker Innovations Series, https://doi.org/10.1007/978-1-4842-9051-4

xxxx 0111	8	'	7	G	W	g	w
xxxx 1000	1	<	8	H	X	h	x
xxxx 1001	2	>	9	I	Y	i	y
xxxx 1010	3	*	:	J	Z	j	z
xxxx 1011	4	+	;	K	[	k	{
xxxx 1100	5	'	<	L		l	|
xxxx 1101	6	-	=	M	]	m	}
xxxx 1110	7	.	>	N	^	n	
xxxx 1111	8	/	?	O	_	o	

Appendix 7: The LCD Instruction Set

Function	B7	B6	B5	B4	B3	B2	B1	B0	Execution Time
Clear Screen	0	0	0	0	0	0	0	1	1.53ms
Description	Clear all display data. It also sends the cursor back to the start of the display. Sets the DDRAM address to 0								
Return Home	0	0	0	0	0	0	1	x	1.53ms
Description	This sends the cursor back to the start of the display. Sets the DDRAM address to 0. The "x" means it does not care what logic is in that bit								
Entry Mode	0	0	0	0	0	1	I/D	SH	39μs
Description	This sets the cursor movement after entry (I/D); logic '0' in this bit means cursor is decremented; logic '1' means cursor is incremented In the SH bit, logic '0' means don't shift the cursor; logic '1' means shift the cursor							39μs	
Display Control	0	0	0	0	1	D	C	B	39μs

(continued)

© Hubert Ward 2023
H. Ward, *Introductory Programs with the 32-bit PIC Microcontroller,*
Maker Innovations Series, https://doi.org/10.1007/978-1-4842-9051-4

Function	B7	B6	B5	B4	B3	B2	B1	B0	Execution Time
Description	D bit logic '0' means the display is off; logic '1' means the display is on C bit logic '0' means the cursor is off Logic '1' means the cursor is on B bit logic '0' means the cursor blink is off Logic '1' means the cursor blink is on								
Cursor/ Display Shift	0	0	0	1	S/C	R/L	X	x	39µs
Description	S/C bit logic '0' means the cursor is shifted Logic '1' means the display is shifted R/L bit logic '0' means shift left; logic '1' means shift right								
Function Set	0	0	0	1	1	0	X	x	39µs
Description	Configuration data to set up the LCD (send first)								
Set CGRAM address	0	1	A5	A4	A3	A2	A1	A0	
Set DDRAM address	1	A6	A5	A4	A3	A2	A1	A0	
Write data CGRAM or DDRAM RS pin is a logic '1'	D7	D6	D5	D4	D3	D2	D1	D0	43µs

Index

© Hubert Ward 2023
H. Ward, *Introductory Programs with the 32-bit PIC Microcontroller*,
Maker Innovations Series, https://doi.org/10.1007/978-1-4842-9051-4

I, J, K

L

Printed in the United States
by Baker & Taylor Publisher Services